2 vols
$ 10 —

D0642582

ECONOMIC DEVELOPMENT
IN
CENTRAL AMERICA

V

Date Due

C

Intern

Harvard Studies in International Development

---

*published jointly by the International Center for Economic Growth

Harvard Studies in International Development

Companion volumes in this Central America Project include:

Economic Development in Central America:
Volume II—Structural Reforms
Edited by Felipe Larraín B., 2001

Environment for Growth: Environmental Management
for Sustainability and Competitiveness
in Central America
Edited by Theodore Panayotou, 2001

Legal Reform in Central America:
Dispute Resolution and Property Systems
by Martha A. Field and William W. Fisher III, 2001

To my father, Vincente,

for a lifetime of love and support

Harvard Studies in International Development

ECONOMIC DEVELOPMENT
IN
CENTRAL AMERICA

VOLUME I

Growth and Internationalization

Edited by

Felipe Larraín B.

John F. Kennedy School of Government
Harvard University
Cambridge, Massachusetts

DISTRIBUTED BY HARVARD UNIVERSITY PRESS

Published by the John F. Kennedy School of Government

Distributed by Harvard University Press

Copyright ©2001, by the President and Fellows of Harvard College
All rights reserved.

Editorial Management: Tara Mantel, Gillian Charters
Editorial Assistance: Joan Campbell
Design and Production: Northeastern Graphic Services, Inc.

CIP data available from the Library of Congress

ISBN 0-674-00352-7 (cloth)   ISBN 0-674-00353-5 (paper)

Printed in the United States of America

Contents

Preface

In a lucid and far-sighted decision, the Presidents of Central America formed the Alliance for Sustainable Development in August 1994. Responding to the opportunity that the advent of peace offered, the governments of the region launched this initiative to join efforts in achieving higher and sustainable levels of human development. The objective was to pursue economic development in tandem with social welfare, political democracy, and environmental balance.

It was in this context that the Harvard Institute for International Development at Harvard University was commissioned to help design the policies that would lead Central American countries toward these objectives. This project has been a joint effort with the Instituto Centroamericano de Administración de Empresas (INCAE), a regional business school. It has also counted on the active participation of government and private sector representatives from the region and the important support of the Banco Centroamericano de Integración Económica (BCIE). The initial assessment determined the need to direct research and advisory efforts into five main areas: business competitiveness, environment, governance, legal reform, and macroeconomics. Because economic and social development is a multifaceted process, isolated progress in a particular area cannot produce successful development. Only a coherent effort on several fronts can succeed.

This set of four volumes represents the outcome of three years of research and practical work conducted in Central America and in Cambridge. The first two volumes analyze the macroeconomic situation of the region, with particular stress on economic growth, the process of internationalization, and structural reforms. The next volume deals with several aspects of the environment, including deforestation, sustainable agriculture, eco-tourism and carbon markets. The fourth volume is devoted to legal reform, with particular regard to the judicial system, alternative dispute resolution methods, and property rights.

We hope that these volumes will serve to further the cause of social and economic development in Central America, and that they may be useful to policy makers, scholars, and future generations.

Jose Alejandro Arévalo
President,
   Banco Centroamericano
   de Integración Economica
   (BCIE)

Roberto Artavia
Rector,
   Instituto Centroamericano
   de Administración de
   Empresas (INCAE)

Felipe Larraín B.
Professor of Economics
Universidad Católica de Chile
   Robert F. Kennedy
   Visiting Professor of
   Latin American Studies,
John F. Kennedy School of
   Government, Harvard University
   (1997–1999)

Jeffrey D. Sachs
Professor of Economics
Director, Center for
   International Development
   Harvard University

Contributors

Benjamín Alvarez has conducted research on education and human development in several countries in the Americas and Europe. He is a consultant for the World Bank, USAID, and the Program for Educational Reform in Latin America and the Caribbean.

Gerardo Esquivel is an assistant professor of economics at El Colegio de México. He received his Ph.D. in economics from Harvard University in 1997, his M.A. in economics from El Colegio de México in 1991, and his B.A. from the National University Autonomous of Mexico. He has previously served as a development associate and macroeconomics researcher at the Harvard Institute for International Development and as a consultant for the World Bank.

Cristina García López was formerly an associate at the Harvard Institute for International Developmen. Her work has focused on optimal currency areas in Central America, currency crises, natural resources and growth in Chile, urban concentration and economic volatility, and income inequality and growth in the US. She has research interests in trade diversification and growth, income inequality, and unemployment and social networks. She was a consultant at the Research Department of the Inter-American Development Bank in 1994–95.

Mauricio Jenkins is currently a doctoral candidate in international economics and finance at Brandeis University, where he also received his M.Sc. in the same field. He also holds a MBA degree from INCAE, where he currently serves as a faculty member in the areas of finance and economics.

Felipe B. Larraín, a Chilean citizen, is a professor of economics at the Universidad Católica de Chile. Between 1997 and 1999 he was the Robert F. Kennedy Visiting Professor of Latin American Studies and director of the Central America Project at Harvard. Since 1985 he has served as economic advisor to the governments of Bolivia, Canada, Costa Rica, Ecuador, El Salvador, Guatemala, Honduras, Jamaica, Mexico, Nicaragua, Paraguay, Peru and Venezuela. Professor Larraín is the editor and author of eight books and over 80 articles in books and specialized journals in Latin America, the U.S. and Europe.

Luis F. López-Calva holds a master's degree in economics from Boston University and a Ph.D. in economics from Cornell University. He has collaborated with the Harvard Institute for International Development since 1996. López-Calva is currently a faculty member at the Centro de Estudios Económicos, El Colegio de México, and also teaches at the Universidad de las Américas-Puebla, in Cholula, México.

Andres Rodriguez-Clare received his Ph.D. in economics from Stanford University in 1993 with emphasis on economic development and international trade. He has published papers in major journals on those topics. He was an assistant and then associate professor at the Graduate School of Business at the University of Chicago from 1994 to 1997 and has served as the coordinator of the Council of Presidential Advisors in Costa Rica since 1998.

Jeffrey D. Sachs is director of the Center for International Development at Harvard, and the Galen L. Stone Professor of International Trade in the Department of Economics. He serves as economic advisor to governments in Latin America, Eastern Europe and the former Soviet Union, Asia, and Africa. He is the author of more than one hundred scholarly articles and books. He received his B.A., M.A. and Ph.D. degrees from Harvard University and joined the Harvard faculty in 1980.

José Tavares is an assistant professor of economics at the Universidade Nova (New University) in Lisbon, Portugal, and a visiting assistant professor of economics at the University of California, Los Angeles. He holds a Ph.D. from Harvard University, where he taught and conducted research in the field of macroeconomics, focusing on the political economy of fiscal policy and economic growth. Tavares has conducted research at the Harvard Institute for International Development and the Banco de Portugal (Portuguese Central Bank). His work has been published in academic journals in the United States and Europe, including the *European Economic Review*, the *Brookings Papers on Economic Activity* and the *European Review of Economic History*.

1

Central America at the Crossroads

FELIPE LARRAÍN B.

After decades of armed conflict and political instability, Central America[1] is entering a period of peace and democracy that opens promising perspectives of economic and social progress. The signing of the Guatemalan Peace Treaties in December 1996 marked the end of four decades of violent confrontation in that country. For Central America as a whole, 1997 was a particularly meaningful date: for the first time in a century the region had a year without any internal or external armed struggle.

At the end of this long period of internal conflicts, the countries of Central America are facing the immense challenge of improving the living conditions of their people and taking advantage of the rich base of resources they possess. Although the situation varies from country to country, more than 50 percent of Central Americans still live below the poverty line. This provides a moral imperative for countries in the region to make a deliberate effort to implement policies that would result in better living conditions for the people of Central America.

The Economic Volumes

The two economic volumes that we present here include some of the most significant studies in the area of macroeconomics conducted as part of

---

1. Hereafter, the term Central America refers to Costa Rica, El Salvador, Guatemala, Honduras and Nicaragua. Although Belize and Panama also belong to this geographical region, they do not share many of the characteristics of the other countries, and do not belong to the Alliance for Sustainable Development. In consequence, the latter countries are usually excluded from the definition of the region. Throughout the book, we will follow this convention.

1

the joint effort between Harvard University and the Instituto Centro-americano de Administración de Empresas (INCAE). The first volume focuses on two crucial aspects of Central America's development process: its long-term macroeconomic performance and the growing internationalization of the region. The second volume analyzes various aspects of the structural reforms that have been (or need to be) implemented in Central America in order to establish the basis for sustained economic growth in the near future.

Each chapter in these volumes is intended to be self-contained. For that reason, some commonality of the material is inevitable, although we have attempted to reduce repetition to a minimum. Many aspects lie within the scope of two or more different chapters. In these cases, we have tried to emphasize the specific aspects that are relevant for each particular chapter. On a few occasions, we have offered alternative approaches to the same issue in different chapters. In most cases, however, we have opted simply for cross-referencing between the chapters.

The studies in these two volumes are intended for a wide array of people, including policymakers, analysts, scholars, and—in general—those interested in the problems of Central America. Broadly speaking, there are three types of chapters. First, there are those that provide a broad analysis of some of the most important issues for the region. This is the case of chapters that analyze economic (2), trade (5), fiscal (11), infrastructure (12), and social (16) problems in the region.

A second group of chapters provides a more specific and in-depth discussion of some narrowly defined issues. They offer a detailed analysis, focusing on Central America, for people with some general knowledge of the topic. This applies to the chapters that deal with recent macroeconomic performance (3), export processing zones (7), currency crises (10), fostering private sector participation through privatization (13), telecommunications (14), electricity (15), education (17), and financial development (20). Finally, a third group of chapters discusses, in detail, specific aspects that are especially relevant in the region today. Among the chapters that lie within this group are long- run economic performance (4), Intel as a successful case of foreign direct investment (6), external debt (8), alternative exchange rate regimes (9), policies to confront natural disasters (18), and pension reform (19). Finally, it is important to mention that some chapters are directed towards a more specialized audience and require knowledge of the relevant literature. This is the case of chapters 4, 9, and 10. Even these chapters, however, include a nontechnical discussion of the main topics.

Volume I: Growth and Internationalization

In addition to this introduction, the first Macroeconomics volume has another nine chapters, broadly divided into two parts. The first three chapters review, in detail, the long-run macroeconomic performance of Central America; the remaining chapters deal with various topics related to the growing internationalization of the Central American economies.

Part One: Long-Term Macroeconomic Performance

The first part of this volume is heavily influenced by a single, yet tragic, economic fact: in the early 1960s, Central America had an average per capita income comparable to that of other Latin American countries and higher than East Asia's; yet, three decades, later, per capita income in East Asia and Latin America as a whole was, respectively, five times higher and twice as high as in Central America.

What happened to Central America over these 30 years? Why, in spite of its privileged geographical location close to the largest world market, did the region stagnate? The answer must be found in the mix of political instability, violence and failed economic policies that was so pervasive in Central America throughout this period. Chapters 2 through 4 analyze some of the main elements that help explain the relatively poor macroeconomic performance of Central America over the last decades. Each chapter, however, emphasizes different aspects of this process.

Background and Recent Developments

Chapter 2 provides an initial description of the region's main characteristics and discusses important historical, geographical, and economic aspects in detail. The objective of this chapter is twofold: first, to present a broad yet succinct picture of Central America; second, to introduce the main economic themes that recur throughout the two Macroeconomics volumes. This chapter emphasizes three aspects that are crucial to understanding Central America's economies: the geography of the region, the export-led model of economic growth, and the continuous and almost incessant search for regional integration. As the chapter makes clear, these aspects are, in fact, intertwined. For example, the geographical aspects of the region (country size and location) help to explain, among other factors affecting Central America's economic history, the geopolitical relevance of the region, the rationale for a primary exports-based economic model, and the necessity of a continuous search for regional integration.

Chapter 3, on the other hand, studies a specific period in the macroeconomic history of Central America: the 1980s and 1990s. The decade of the 1980s was particularly hard for the region, which saw its income per capita decline at an average rate of 1.5 percent per year. In contrast, the decade of the 1990s was characterized by the resumption in the region of economic growth, increases in real wages, and the resolution of major political conflicts and armed struggles. Chapter 3 examines three dimensions of the Central American crisis of the 1980s: the interruption of international capital flows which resulted in the debt crisis; the terms-of-trade shocks that afflicted the region; and the role of political instability, which had a negative economic impact throughout the region. The analysis of the 1990s underscores the liberalization of trade flows and the implementation of macroeconomic stabilization programs to explain the improvement in economic conditions during the decade. This chapter highlights the need for export diversification as insurance against external shocks, and the relevance of peace and stability as prerequisites to better macroeconomic performance.

The Long-Term Growth Perspective

Chapter 4 examines the long-run performance of the economies of Central America in terms of both per capita GDP growth and productivity. It presents an international comparison of economic progress in Central America, which illustrates the true magnitude of the region's economic tragedy. This chapter also includes a determinants-of-growth analysis, which estimates the effect of institutional, political, and economic variables on the pattern of economic growth in Central America since 1960. This exercise shows that there is no single explanatory factor behind the disappointing growth rate of the region. Instead, the explanation consists of a number of economic elements (low investment rates), institutional elements (lack of rule of law), policy elements (lack of trade openness), and structural elements (high primary-exports intensity). Finally, this chapter shows that most of the growth gains achieved since 1960 were due to the rapid accumulation of inputs rather than to productivity increases. Clearly, faster productivity growth is essential for the economic development of Central America.

Part Two: The Internationalization of Central America

The characteristics of the region in terms of location, size, cost of the labor force, and climate, make export-led growth the only viable economic development strategy. Central America is privileged by its proximity to the U.S. market, but so far this advantage has not been exploited adequately. For example, despite the fact that the distance between Central America and the United States is a third of that between Asia and the United States, the cost of shipping goods to North America from Asia is lower.

The chapters in this part discuss various topics related to the growing internationalization of the region. Chapters 5, 6 and 7 analyze international trade and foreign direct investment. Chapters 8, 9 and 10 focus on international finance issues such as foreign indebtedness and exchange rate policy.

Export Diversification, Trade Access, and the Role of NAFTA

So far, Central America's exports have been concentrated on a few natural resources. The share of natural resource exports within total exports ranged between 40 percent and 60 percent for every country in the region in 1999. Even though these are large numbers, they show an improvement with respect to 1985, when the same ratio ranged between 70 percent and 90 percent of total exports. Efforts are currently focused on diversification, moving towards a composition of exports with a larger base of manufactures and higher value added products. Over the last decade, Honduras, Nicaragua and, more recently, Costa Rica, have experienced a remarkable change in this respect.

Chapter 5 evaluates the status of Central America in the areas of international trade and foreign direct investment. This chapter presents an overview of the trade liberalization policies implemented in the region recently, and reviews the various trade agreements that exist between Central America and other trade areas. It discusses the significance and main characteristics of trade flows, and evaluates the determinants of Central American exports to the rest of the world. It also surveys the trends and policies regarding foreign direct investment. Finally, the chapter discusses guidelines for a successful trade and investment strategy for the region.

Chapter 5 also sheds light on the relevance for Central America of getting on an equal footing with Mexico in access to the U.S. market. Perhaps paradoxically, Central America has become a casualty of the North American Free Trade Agreement (NAFTA). Although NAFTA was, of course, never intended to hurt this region, as a consequence of this agreement Mexico now enjoys preferential accessing the U.S. market on better terms than Central America. Mexican goods now face lower tariffs in the United States through NAFTA than do Central America imports through the Caribbean Basin Initiative (CBI). This is especially important for apparel, as the garment industry is vital for Central America. Moreover, NAFTA is a treaty, whereas the CBI is a unilateral concession. For foreign investors with an eye on the U.S. market, Mexico thus appears as a safer bet. In the dynamic and competitive global economy, NAFTA hurts both exports from Central America and foreign investment in the region.

The Intel Case and Export Processing Zones

Chapter 6 evaluates a specific case of foreign direct investment within the region: the successful investment of Intel in Costa Rica. Remarkably, the arrival of Intel in Costa Rica has given a big boost to the diversification of manufactures and exports there. By itself, Intel is already generating over $2 billion of exports, or more than 20 percent of Costa Rica's national output. Using the results of a survey among firms associated with Intel in Costa Rica, this chapter illustrates the importance of attracting this type of foreign direct investment. The results of the survey underscore the importance of attracting investments that not only promote exports, create jobs, or transfer technology, but also contribute to the development of a strong industrial sector based on effective linkages of domestic firms with a highly competitive foreign firm. Several policy recommendations are drawn, based on the Intel experience.

As Chapter 5 suggests, export diversification should have a beneficial effect on the economies of Central America by reducing the vulnerability of the region to external shocks. Chapter 7 explores one way to support this goal: the development of Export Processing Zones (EPZs) throughout the region. The current expansion of EPZs has already served to broaden the export base. The analysis of this chapter shows that during the 1990s, the economic significance of EPZs and other export-oriented regimes increased rapidly, although not uniformly, throughout Central America. Chapter 7 also presents a series of considerations and policy proposals for the development of EPZs within the region. Among other policies, it focuses on the promotion of industry diversification of export-oriented activities, on the development of stronger backward linkages, and on the upgrading of the export-oriented legislation in Central America.

The Foreign Debt Problem

Chapters 8 through 10 discuss international finance issues that are relevant for Central America. In particular, Chapter 8 tackles an issue that may have played a significant role in constraining development in some countries of the region: the burden of the external debt, which severely affects Honduras and Nicaragua. Their low level of income makes it even more urgent for them to obtain relief from their debt obligations from the international community. The Highly Indebted Poor Countries Initiative (HIPC)—including its recent flexibilization—appears as a possible alternative, although current conditions may still delay relief quite substantially and/or provide insufficient relief. As this chapter makes clear, the international financial community should provide a fast and deep response to this problem by canceling an important share of the foreign debt of these two countries.

Exchange Rate Options

Chapter 9 reviews the evolution of the exchange rate regimes in Central America and explores two possible monetary arrangements for the region: a regional currency area and the adoption of the American dollar as a legal medium of exchange. Regarding the first alternative, this chapter provides an assessment of how close the region is to an optimum currency area as compared with other possible integration areas such as Europe, Latin America, and East Asia. The second option is evaluated by assessing the degree of economic integration between Central America and the United States. The exercises carried out in this chapter show that the similarity of export structures and the symmetry of output shocks make a regional monetary arrangement both feasible and advisable over the medium term. In contrast, several factors militate against dollarization.

Chapter 10 analyzes the main characteristics of currency crises in Central America since 1975. Among other results, this paper shows that a small set of macroeconomics indicators is useful to explain the occurrence of exchange rate crises in the region. Also, out-of-sample forecasts show that the probabilities of a currency crisis in the region have been relatively low and declining for the 1997-99 period. This trend may be the result of the sounder macroeconomic policies that have been implemented recently in the region. Chapter 10 concludes by suggesting that a careful look at a small set of macroeconomic variables may serve as a policy guide to reduce the risks of a currency crisis in all countries in the region.

VOLUME II: STRUCTURAL REFORMS

The second volume is devoted to the study of structural reforms in Central America. In some cases, these reforms have already begun to be implemented; in most cases, however, they still remain to be addressed. The chapters in this volume present initial evaluations of what already has been done and suggest avenues for further deepening the reforms. In those cases where structural reforms are still pending, the alternative options are discussed.

The various structural reforms considered in this volume are fiscal policies (11), infrastructure provision (12), privatization (13), deregulation of telecommunications (14), fostering of regional electricity markets (15), social policies (16), education (17), policies to reduce vulnerability to natural disasters (18), social security reform (19), and the development of financial markets (20).

Fiscal Reform and the State of Public Finance

Chapter 11 evaluates the current state of public finances in Central America and identifies the main challenges that the countries face in this regard. This chapter argues that changes in fiscal policy can make a substantial contribution to the region's development. For example, public sector expenditures to fulfill the necessary role of the government as provider of goods and services are probably too low in Guatemala and El Salvador and too high in Nicaragua. Furthermore, there is a problem with the composition of public expenditures in almost every country in the region: with the notable exception of Costa Rica, public spending in education and health is notoriously low. In most countries, resources are clearly insufficient to meet the most basic needs and to promote an equitable development process. In this connection, it is important to emphasize that the Guatemala Peace Treaties of 1996 included an important commitment to improve social expenditure.

Chapter 11 also argues that region-wide tax reform is needed to achieve two objectives: an increase in total tax collection in the countries where the public sector is too small, and a reduction of distortions caused by overly complex tax systems (as in Costa Rica, for example). A simplified tax system will rebuild public trust and will help combat tax evasion. Tax policy also must contemplate specific corrective levies designed to align private incentives with environmental considerations.

Infrastructure and Privatization

The next two chapters in this volume (Chapters 12 and 13) address two important and intertwined aspects of structural reform that are still pending in Central America: the provision of quality infrastructure and the fostering of private sector participation through privatization. The establishment of an appropriate infrastructure network is fundamental in any economy because it may influence the intricate interactions that exist between geography and economic development. The analysis of this chapter suggests that the establishment of an adequate infrastructure network can help to overcome the obstacles and to exploit the opportunities that a given geographical location poses to an economy. This chapter shows that the provision of energy, telecommunications, and transport services throughout the region has fallen behind the levels required to promote and sustain even moderate economic growth rates. New investment and higher maintenance expenditures in infrastructure are much needed in almost every country in the region.

The latter aspect is strongly linked to the theme of Chapter 14, which highlights the relevance of promoting higher levels of participation of the private sector through privatization. This chapter emphasizes some of the advantages of promoting more active private sector participation, in particular, higher efficiency gains and the strengthening of the public sector accounts. It also stresses that the larger the extent to which an economy is privatized, the more important the role of the government as an efficient regulator. Privatization imposes a new role on the government in terms of providing skilled and up-to-date regulation techniques. This may seem costly, but countries can lower the costs by avoiding duplication through the integration of regulatory efforts across the region. Such a move would save resources and would constitute a significant step towards economic integration. Moving towards regional institutions that regulate and supervise different activities will be a strong force towards homogenization of rules and standards. This, in turn, will facilitate the operation of firms across borders.

The Telecommunications and Energy Sectors

Chapters 14 and 15 deepen our understanding of two specific but crucial economic sectors in Central America: telecommunications and energy. Chapter 14 describes the situation of the telecommunications sector in Central America in 1995, that is, right before the first steps of reform in this sector had begun. It then analyzes the reforms proposed in Nicaragua and Honduras, and discusses the aggressive liberalization strategies that had taken place in El Salvador and Guatemala. Finally, this chapter evaluates the alternative policies that have been followed in the different countries of the region.

Chapter 15 analyzes the recent evolution of the electricity sector in Central America. Comparing the electricity sector across Central American countries in terms of infrastructure, contracts, tariffs, and structure, the chapter highlights the challenges that each country faces in order to adjust its electricity sector to the worldwide transformation that has occurred in recent years. It also underscores the relevance of three aspects that have been developed elsewhere in this volume: private sector participation, infrastructure building, and public sector regulation.

Social Policies, Poverty, and Education

The ultimate goal of economic policy is human development. Macroeconomic stability and economic growth are necessary but not sufficient conditions to that end. In other words, the topics described in previous chapters are insufficient to provide an overview of the well being of the Central American people. The next four chapters in this volume (16-19) tackle several social aspects that have a direct effect on the economic prospects of Central America. Chapter 16 assesses the current status of poverty and social policies in the region. Chapter 17 analyzes the current situation on the provision of education in Central America. Then, Chapter 18 discusses the devastating effects of the hurricane that hit the region severely in 1999 and suggests alternative policy measures that can be implemented to confront similar unfortunate events in the future. Finally, Chapter 19 evaluates the status of social security reform throughout the region.

Chapter 16 assesses the status of poverty in the region and analyzes the causes of the low income-generation capabilities of poor households. It focuses on labor market conditions, educational attainment, and health status of the population. The analysis in this chapter shows that Central America as a whole faces an important social development challenge. Another result underscored in this chapter is that labor market informality is a major problem in the region: a large fraction of the population earns low wages and lacks social security benefits. Chapter 16 also discusses the need to reallocate fiscal resources to this end. Two key possibilities are targeting subsidies and eliminating generalized transfers (which typically end up being wasteful and ineffective); and pushing decentralization of social policies to the limits imposed by the management capacities of local governments.

Chapter 17 focuses on the provision of education in Central America. The chapter shows that the region has achieved substantial gains in access to primary and secondary education. Educational quality, however, remains low and sharp inequalities in educational supply and output persist, both within countries and between Central America and other regions. This chapter underscores the fact that education reform is a potent channel for promoting income growth and reducing economic inequality in the medium and long term. It also can produce short-term political and social benefits, such as increased community participation in school management and reform. The analysis highlights the strong conviction that education reform is a powerful tool for social justice. A history of successful reforms over the past decade, and the heightened engagement in education of the for-profit and not-for-profit private sectors will influence positively Central America's ongoing education reform efforts.

Reducing the Vulnerability to Natural Disasters

The tragedy of Hurricane Mitch highlighted another crucial element for successful development in Central America: the need to reduce its vulnerability to natural disasters. Chapter 18 points out the necessity of developing an expanded safety net that may help to cope with natural disasters and which should include environmental, economic, and social elements. This chapter makes clear that reducing social, environmental, and economic vulnerability and improving inclusion and equity through such an extended safety net will be a fundamental part of a meaningful equation for sustainable development and competitiveness.

Pension Reform

There are, to be sure, many steps that the Central American countries can take on their own to foster development. One pending issue that may bring important positive effects in several areas is the reform of the social security systems. This issue is analyzed in detail in Chapter 19. So far, reform of the social security system has only been implemented in El Salvador. Pensions systems currently cover a very low fraction of the population, with the exception of Costa Rica. Their financing basis—a pay-as-you-go formula—provides inadequate incentives and delivers low returns. This is exacerbated by the demographic context in Central America, characterized by low fertility ratios and increasing life expectancies. The moment seems appropriate for countries to move to schemes based on the funding of contributions and on private management. The cost of such a move is low now, precisely because the coverage of current social security systems is very low.

Such a reform will have multiple benefits. Funded systems can obtain larger rates of return than the systems they replace. The rates of contributions can be reduced, which benefits workers directly. At the same time, distortions in the labor market are reduced and coverage of a larger fraction of the population becomes more feasible. Pension funds also can play a crucial role in the development of financial markets, as the experience of countries that have gone through this reform, such as Chile, attests. In Central America, where financial markets have low levels of development, private pension funds can constitute a cornerstone for their expansion. The regional operation of pension funds is an important goal for Central America, enabling it to attract world-class operators and to benefit from the scale economies of an expanded market.

Deepening Financial Markets

Finally, Chapter 20 reviews the current status of financial markets in Central America. Recent empirical studies have shown that financial markets may contribute significantly to the development process. For a long time, however, financial markets were repressed in Central America. There were severe limits to the fluctuations of interest rates, and government intervention in the allocation of credit was common throughout the region until the 1980s. In Costa Rica, El Salvador, and Nicaragua, the whole banking sector was public. During the 1990s, financial liberalization proceeded. Interest rates were freed and credit allocation was significantly reduced, thus allowing for increased private sector participation.

The liberalization of the financial sector has required substantial improvements in the regulatory skills of governments. In some countries, the expansion of financial activities has gone faster than the capacity of the government to respond to the changes and provide appropriate supervision of financial institutions. Beefing up the regulatory capacity at the national and, especially, the regional level is crucial to reaping the benefits of financial markets.

2

Central American Development in Perspective

FELIPE LARRAÍN B. AND JOSÉ TAVARES

It is striking how many things the Central American republics have in common. Costa Rica, El Salvador, Guatemala, Honduras, and Nicaragua were all former Spanish colonies that seceded as a unit in the 1820s. Their strategic location in the path of major world trade routes awarded the region an importance in world affairs despite its lack of economic and political influence. The international community's interest in the area's economic and political circumstances alternated between interference and indifference. All Central American countries have been affected, for better and for worse, by the overwhelming importance of the United States, both economically and politically. In the words of Coatsworth (1994, p.3), "Early in the twentieth century the United States succeeded in its drive to secure unilateral strategic, political, and economic dominance in the Caribbean, including the Central American republics."[1] Central American countries have tried to counterbalance this overwhelming dominance of the United States by attempting to enlist the interest of other countries and regions such as the European Community.[2]

The region's long search for connectivity to the world economy resulted in the development of a model of growth based on the export of primary agricultural products. Reliance on this model, however, has made Central America overly dependent on a few products characterized by high price volatility. Over time, this growth model has proven to be insufficient to promote for-

---

1. Coatsworth continues: "except for its colonies . . . the United States has dominated the small states in the Caribbean more completely and for a longer time than any other part of the globe."

2. This applies to Japan and Taiwan most recently, and also to the Communist bloc in past decades and to Germany in the 1930s. See Coatsworth (1994).

ward and backward linkages between the export sectors and the rest of the region's economies.

Central American culture integrates indigenous and immigrant elements. Most countries are host to indigenous groups such as Afro-Caribbeans. The local political systems, all at different levels of development, are characterized by a relatively low level of participation and by the traditional influence of private interests on the export sectors.

Central America is divided into Atlantic and Pacific regions, which differ according to climate and settlement patterns. The climate near the Atlantic coast helps produce banana crops, while the areas near the Pacific are host to large coffee plantations. In earlier times, the denser settlement on the Pacific coast determined the location of major cities and infrastructure, and thus political power and influence. In the twentieth century, the economic fortunes of Central American countries fluctuated sharply. Costa Rica has generally maintained the lead in terms of per capita GDP, and in Nicaragua and Honduras income levels have both soared and lagged. Income inequality, compounded by ethnic inequality, discourages access to education, health, and other public services.

Finally, Central America can be studied both within the Latin American context and as a separate case. Central America, Mexico, and South America share similar historic experiences, as well as turbulent processes of integration into the world markets. However, because of the size of its countries, its unique location, and its involvement with the United States economy, Central America warrants special attention. To address the issues facing Central America adequately, we must first describe its geography, history, and institutions, and analyze how these have affected regional development. Only then can one extract practical lessons that will help the countries attain higher levels of income. This chapter addresses the first issue, by broadly characterizing the region in historical, geographical and social terms.

Figure 2-1 presents the evolution of average GDP per capita for Central America and East Asia decade by decade, from 1966 to 1996. The contrast is dramatic: economic growth in East Asia was sustained through the 1970s and 1980s whereas Central America's income levels did not change. During the 1980s East Asia almost doubled its income levels.

East Asia certainly differs from Central America in several important respects, first of all, country size. East Asian territories are either much smaller (Singapore and Hong Kong) or significantly larger (South Korea and Taiwan, not to mention Japan). Second, Central America has historically depended on the export of a few primary crops. Third, the level of human capital in East Asia has been historically higher. Last but not least, there were substantial land redistributions in East Asian countries such as Japan, South Korea and Taiwan. Dramatic growth in Asia was not an accident but the end result of an

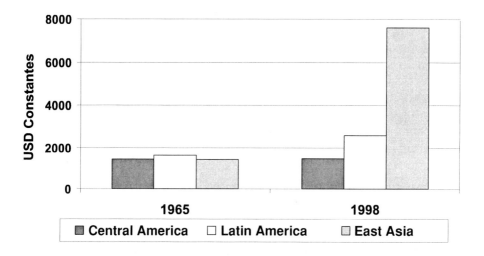

Figure 2-1.   Average GDP Per Capita

economic strategy based on internationalization, liberalization, and human and physical capital accumulation. In spite of the obvious differences between the two regions, therefore, a strategy for economic growth in Central America should certainly take East Asia's experience into account.

GEOGRAPHY AND CENTRAL AMERICA

The relationship between a country's economic performance and its geographic characteristics is receiving increasing attention from academics and policymakers. A country's geographic characteristics, such as easy access to the coast or its latitude, are clearly related to its economic fortunes or misfortunes. A country's latitude, for instance, may affect sanitary and health conditions or demographic patterns. These, in turn, influence economic performance.[3] Regions around the equator are those with lower per capita GDP. Gallup, Sachs, and Mellinger (1998) find that tropical regions, in comparison

---

3. Recently, Jared Diamond (1997) tried to account for the preeminence of Europe in economic development by relying almost solely on geographical explanations: the ability of peoples in the Eurasian land mass to trade and share innovations; the sharing of an ecological zone by the inhabitants of Eurasia, which allowed technological diffusion; advantages in native plants and domesticated animals.

to temperate regions, are slow to develop.[4] In the Americas, the distribution of per capita GDP, by latitude, fits the above pattern remarkably well.[5] Hall and Jones (1999), in an attempt to explain differences in productivity across countries, find that a country's distance from the tropics is the strongest predictor of its economic success, accounting for a full one-third of the variation in social infrastructure.[6] In his classic study, *An Inquiry into the Nature and Causes of the Wealth of Nations*, Adam Smith stresses the importance of a country's location to its integration into world markets.[7] He points out the significance of navigable rivers and waterways in the development of the British and American economies. Easy access to the coast is required in order to take advantage of world markets, which provide market size and allow specialization of production. In turn, these are a source of technological and economic progress.[8] Landlocked countries, on the other hand, are at a severe economic disadvantage. Radelet and Sachs (1999) show that none of the major exporting countries are landlocked. Almost all countries with successful economies are located in the path of major shipping routes or are close to major markets such as the United States, Western Europe, or Japan. Central America is in a geographic position that will allow it to benefit from both of these advantages.

Radelet and Sachs (1999) find that having access to the sea and being located close to major markets decrease shipping costs and facilitate the promotion of manufactured exports. The impact of high shipping costs on exports, these authors suggest, is hard to neutralize by removing tariff or nontariff barriers or by lowering wage costs. In industries such as apparel, the effect of high shipping costs is heightened by the fact that imported materials are a substantial part of the final product's value and by the fact that the average wage level is relatively low. Barberia (1999) notes that the costs of shipping apparel exports between the United States and its trading partners are influenced by a particular country's distance from the United States. Better port quality in Central America would also decrease shipping costs.

Overall, Central America is at a significant disadvantage relative to other

---

4. They also contend that of the top thirty countries ranked by per capita GDP, only two are tropical and these are very special cases: Hong Kong and Singapore.

5. See Bloom and Sachs (1999).

6. The authors measure social infrastructure as the extent to which governments do not engage in diversionary policies (such as expropriation and repudiation of contracts, corruption and inadequate legal and bureaucratic provision) and the extent to which the country is open to international trade.

7. See Smith (1991)

8. Thus, as verified empirically by Bloom and Sachs (1999), coastal regions are able to support more people with higher average incomes.

areas of the world in terms of shipping costs. The contrast with East Asia is particularly shocking: whereas East Asia is at least four times farther away from the United States, the combined cost of shipping materials to and from South Asia is slightly lower than for Central America. This is an important fact, since shipping costs determine how much apparel can be exported from developing countries to the United States.[9]

Geography and infrastructure are related. Better infrastructure, for example, may help overcome poor geographic location or compound the benefits of good location. Central American countries with extensive coastlines should focus on developing good infrastructure.

The Land

Geographically, Central America is an isthmus between North and South America. The adversity of its geography is highlighted by the fact that there is only one navigable river, the San Juan River, located between Costa Rica and Nicaragua. The characteristics of the coast have not facilitated the development of natural deep-water seaports. Moreover, coastal shipping was used less extensively than might have been expected, given the geography of the region. This was because the largest population centers have been concentrated in the isolated highlands.

Central American countries are prone to natural disasters; earthquakes and volcanic eruptions strike the Pacific coast while hurricanes hit the Atlantic side. Santiago de Guatemala was devastated in 1541. Between 1700 and 1773 there were no less than ten eruptions of the Fuego volcano on the outskirts of Santiago de Guatemala, and in 1776 the colonial administration moved the city.[10] Earthquakes destroyed Managua, Nicaragua, in 1931 and 1972. When hurricanes originating in the Caribbean hit the Central American coast, the damage tends to be very high. As Hurricane Mitch amply demonstrated, Honduras and Nicaragua are particularly vulnerable.[11]

Natural disasters have had a major impact on the region's agriculture. Volcanos release material that mixes with soil and is ideal for growing specific agricultural products. The central highlands alone have sustained most of the region's population from pre-Colombian times. The mountainous core, made up of highlands descending toward the Pacific and the Atlantic plains, extends across Central America like a geographic spinal cord. Most

9. See Barberia (1999).

10. See Perez-Brignoli (1989).

11. For an evaluation of the vulnerability of the region and estimates of the damages caused by Mitch, see Barahona, Doryan, Larraín, and Sachs (1999).

natural-disaster activity has been concentrated on the Pacific coast; the constant drainage problems of the Atlantic lowlands, have meant that these coastal areas are traditionally disease-prone and unhealthy. The Atlantic Coast was settled differently from the Pacific: since there were few indigenous people in the region, the need for labor was met by bringing in Africans from Jamaica and elsewhere in the Caribbean. The development of the banana economy and the construction of railroads reinforced this pattern of population settlement.

Central America's greatest competitive advantage is that it is located close to North America, the largest import market in the world. Table 2-1 compares the transport costs of Central America and East Asia to the United States. It shows that although Central American countries are two-thirds closer to the United States than is East Asia, their transport costs are greater than East Asia's. Table 2-2 compares Central America's distance to import markets. It shows that Central America is relatively close to world markets and that, with the exception of MERCOSUR, Central America is the most natural trade area.

Table 2-3 shows the total area of five Central American countries and delineates what the land was used for in 1960 and 1995. In terms of land area, Guatemala, Honduras, and Nicaragua are the largest countries, all with areas slightly above ten million hectares. Costa Rica's area is roughly half that of Guatemala, and El Salvador's area is less than half of Costa Rica's. The amount of land used for agriculture increased substantially in all countries between 1960 and 1995, with the exception of El Salvador. While the area of arable

Table 2-1.   *Central American and East Asian Transport Costs to the United States*

	Distance to the U.S. (in miles)	*Container Cost[a] (U.S. to Region)*	*Container Cost (Region to U.S.)*	*Total Cost*
Costa Rica	2047	1589	1743	3332
El Salvador	2851	2610	2593	5203
Guatemala	1804	2197	2240	4437
Honduras	1764	2128	1845	3973
Nicaragua	2701	2973	3243	6216
Central America	**2233**	**2299**	**2333**	**4632**
Hong Kong	6380	2062	1024	3086
South Korea	5229	2092	1024	3116
Malaysia	8234	2473	1625	4098
China (Shanghai)	6350	2879	1424	4303
East Asia	**6548**	**2376**	**1560**	**3936**

Source: Lorena Barberia, "Central America's Export Competitiveness: The Impact of Shipping Costs on the Apparel Industry." Mimeo (1999). Harvard Institute for International Development.
[a]Costs in 1998 US$.

Table 2-2. *Regional Trade Agreements and Distance to Markets[a]*

	Distance to Markets *(1)*	*Distance to Partners* *(2)*	*Ratio* *(2)/(1)*
CACM	9073	1225	0.14
Andean Pact	9702	1813	0.19
MERCOSUR	10265	1120	0.11
NAFTA	8777	2459	0.28
EU	6072	1404	0.23
EFTA	6184	1645	0.27
East Asia	10125	2650	0.26

Source: José Tavares, "The Access of Central America to Export Markets: Diagnostic and Policy Recommendations," *HIID Development Discussion Paper 693* (April 1999). Cambridge, MA: Harvard Institute for International Development.
[a]Distances, in miles, to the seventy top import markets and to partners in regional trade agreements.

land increased little in this period, the irrigated land area grew substantially, denoting the greater importance of intensive agriculture. Table 2-4 documents the portion of land used in Central America, Latin America as a whole and East Asia as cropland and pasture in 1960 and 1995.

The population of Central America is unevenly distributed, both within and between countries. Table 2-5 shows the population density of Central American countries for each decade starting with the 1920s. El Salvador has five times less area yet a larger population than Nicaragua The populations of Guatemala and Honduras have increased, while El Salvador's has decreased substantially. Although most of Central America has a low population den-

Table 2-3. *Land Area and Its Uses*

		Costa Rica	*El Salvador*	*Guatemala*	*Honduras*	*Nicaragua*
Total Area (sq. mi.)	—	19,652	8,260	42,042	43,277	50,180
Total Area (sq. km.)	—	50,900	20,935	108,889	112,088	118,358
Total Area (thou. has)	—	5,106	2,085	10,843	11,189	12,140
Agricultural Land[a]	1960[b]	1,395	1,252	2,646	2,980	5,080
	1995	2,870	1,345	4,512	3,570	7,384
Arable Land	1960	285	488	1,100	1,345	1,030
	1995	285	544	1,355	1,695	2,457
Irrigated Land	1960	26	18	32	50	18
	1995	126	120	125	74	88
Cereal Production[c]	1960	103	298	695	302	244
	1995	54	438	639	476	399

Source: World Bank (1998).
[a]Agricultural Land computed for 1994.
[b]The 1960 data actually refer to 1961.
[c]Cereal Production computed for 1996.

Table 2-4. *Land Use[a]—Central America, Latin America, and East Asia*

	Cropland[b]		Permanent Pasture[c]		Other[d]	
	1960	1994	1960	1994	1960	1994
Costa Rica	9.4	10.4	17.9	45.6	72.7	43.8
El Salvador	31.1	36.4	29.0	29.4	40.0	35.1
Guatemala	14.2	17.6	10.2	23.0	75.6	58.4
Honduras	13.2	18.1	13.4	13.4	73.4	68.1
Nicaragua	9.7	21.2	32.1	39.7	58.2	39.2
East Asia	11.1	11.9	24.8	34.1	64.1	54.4
Latin America	5.1	7.8	25.2	29.4	69.7	62.7

Source: Based on World Bank (1998). Data for 1994.
[a]As a percentage of land area. Land area is a country's total area, excluding inland water bodies. In most cases, the definition of "inland water bodies" includes major rivers and lakes.
[b]Cropland includes temporary and permanent crops, temporary meadows, market and kitchen gardens, and land that is temporarily fallow. Permanent crops are those that do not need to be replanted after each harvest, excluding trees grown for wood or timber.
[c]Permanent pasture is land used for five or more years for forage crops (cultivated or wild).
[d]Other land includes forest, woodlands, areas to be forested in the near future, uncultivated land, grassland not used for pasture, wetlands, wastelands, built-up areas (residential, recreational, and industrial), and areas covered by roads and other infrastructure.

sity, El Salvador in particular has a high population density by international standards. In fact, in El Salvador the unavailability of land has sparked conflicts with neighbors and led to substantial emigration. Table 2-6 shows the population densities of Central America, Latin America as a whole, and East Asia. All countries in Central America have higher population densities than the average population density in Latin America. Nicaragua and Honduras have particularly low densities due to extensive tracts of uninhabited Atlantic

Table 2-5. *Population—Central America*

	Costa Rica	El Salvador	Guatemala	Honduras	Nicaragua
1920	0.42	1.17	1.27	0.72	0.64
1930	0.50	1.44	1.76	0.95	0.68
1940	0.62	1.63	2.20	1.15	0.83
1950	0.80	1.86	2.81	1.43	1.06
1960	1.24	2.58	3.96	1.94	1.50
1970	1.73	3.60	5.25	2.63	2.06
1980	2.28	4.55	6.92	3.66	2.80
1990	3.04	5.03	9.20	5.11	3.75
1998	3.84	5.81	10.93	6.10	4.50

Source: Bulmer-Thomas (1987), World Bank (1998), and IADB (1999). Data for the years 1920 to 1950 are based on Bulmer-Thomas (1987), statistical appendix. Data from the 1960s on derived from World Bank (1998). Data for 1998 are from IADB (1999). Note: figures are in millions of inhabitants. Total population includes all residents regardless of legal status or citizenship. Refugees not permanently settled in their new country are generally considered to be part of the population of their country of origin.

Table 2-6. *Population Density[a]—Central America, Latin America, and East Asia*

	Costa Rica	El Salvador	Guatemala	Honduras	Nicaragua	Latin America	East Asia
1950	18	90	27	13	8	—	—
1960[b]	25.1	127.4	37.6	17.9	12.8	11.1	56.7
1970	33.9	172.6	48.4	23.5	17.0	14.1	70.5
1980	44.7	219.4	63.8	32.7	23.1	17.9	85.7
1990	59.4	242.8	84.8	45.6	30.9	21.8	100.7
1996	67.4	280.4	100.8	54.5	37.1	24.2	109.2

Source: Perez-Brignoli (1989, p.32) for 1950 data and World Bank (1998) for other years.
[a]Population density is mid-year population divided by land area in square kilometers. Land area is a country's total area, excluding inland water bodies. In most cases, the definition of "inland water bodies" includes major rivers and lakes. Total population includes all residents regardless of legal status or citizenship. Refugees not permanently settled in the country of asylum are generally considered to be part of the population of their country of origin.
[b]The 1960 data are for 1961.

Table 2-7. *Rural Density[a]—Central America, Latin America, and East Asia*

	Costa Rica	El Salvador	Guatemala	Honduras	Nicaragua	Latin America	East Asia
1960[b]	284.1	335.2	249.5	114.3	89.9	225.5	518.7
1970	366.2	484.5	307.6	135.3	105.1	213.7	654.1
1980	459.2	474.2	340.9	152.8	113.4	197.6	775.1
1990	563.3	499.5	438.6	188.0	77.6	213.1	833.7
1995	600.2	572.4	478.9	196.4	67.5	230.4	853.7

Source: World Bank (1998).
[a]Figures are number of inhabitants in rural areas divided by arable land area in square kilometers. Arable land refers to temporary crops, temporary meadows, and market and residential gardens.
[b]The 1960 data are for 1961.

lowlands.[12] Population growth more than doubled in all Central American countries between 1950 and 1980, giving Central America a higher population density than all of Latin America combined—and in some cases higher than all of East Asia (see Table 2-7).

Table 2-8 presents population growth in Central America, Latin America, and East Asia. While Guatemala, Honduras, and Nicaragua have the highest growth rates in the region in the later periods, Costa Rica and El Salvador reached their peak in the 1950s and 1960s respectively and then witnessed decreases in their rate of population growth. The conflicts of the 1980s in El Salvador caused that country's growth rate to plummet to 1%, the lowest growth rate ever in the region.

For most of its history, Central America's typical agglomeration has been the town. The many isolated mountain villages hindered connectedness be-

12. See Table 2-1.

Table 2-8. *Population Growth[a]—Central America, Latin America, and East Asia*

	Costa Rica	El Salvador	Guatemala	Honduras	Nicaragua	Latin America	East Asia
1920s[b]	1.7	2.0	3.5	2.9	0.6	—	—
1930s	2.2	1.2	2.2	1.8	1.9	—	—
1940s	2.4	1.3	2.4	2.1	2.4	—	—
1950s	4.9	2.8	3.2	3.2	2.9	—	—
1960s[c]	3.4	3.3	2.8	3.1	3.2	2.6	2.7
1970s	2.8	2.5	2.8	3.2	3.1	2.4	2.1
1980s	2.9	1.0	2.8	3.4	2.9	2.1	1.6
1990s[d]	2.2	2.3	2.9	3.0	3.1	1.7	1.4

Source: Bulmer-Thomas (1987), statistical appendix; World Bank (1998); and IADB (1999).
[a]Annual population growth rates are expressed as percentages. Population includes all residents regardless of legal status or citizenship. Refugees not permanently settled in the country of asylum are generally considered part of the population of the country of origin.
[b]Data for the 1920s to the 1950s are based on Bulmer-Thomas (1987), statistical appendix.
[c]Data for the 1960s are based on World Bank (1998).
[d]Up to 1996 and based on IADB (1999).

tween the different localities. Since colonial times, travel by land has been extremely difficult; construction of the Inter-American Highway only began during World War II and the highway did not reach Panama City until 1964. Larger cities appeared only in the second half of the twentieth century. As Table 2-9 shows, the urban population in the early twentieth century typically did not surpass ten percent of any Central American country's total population. In the 1960s there was a noticeable increase of the population concentrated in cit-

Table 2-9. *Urban Population[a]—Central America, Latin America, and East Asia*

	Costa Rica	El Salvador	Guatemala	Honduras	Nicaragua	Latin America	East Asia
1910	7.9	8.8	8.9	6.3	10.9[b]	—	—
1930	13.2	10.4	10.3	4.7	17.9	18	—
1940	15.4	12.4	9.8	6.1	21.8	—	—
1950	17.7	13.0	11.2	6.8	15.2	29	—
1960	36.6	38.3	32.4	22.7	39.6	49.3	16.5
1970	39.7	39.4	35.5	28.9	47.0	57.4	18.5
1980	43.1	41.6	37.4	34.9	53.4	64.9	21.2
1990	47.1	43.9	38.0	40.7	59.4	71.0	27.6
1996	49.8	45.3	39.2	44.4	62.6	73.7	32.2

Source: Weaver (1994), World Bank (1998), and Perez-Brignoli (1989). Data for 1910 to 1950 are from Weaver (1994). Data from 1960 onwards are from World Bank (1998). Figures for Latin America before 1960 are from Perez-Brignoli (1989).
[a]Urban population is the mid-year population of areas defined as urban in each country and reported to the United Nations. It is defined as the percentage of people living in agglomerations of more than 20,000 inhabitants.
[b]Figure actually refers to 1920. Urban population is the mid-year population of areas defined as urban in each country and reported to the United Nations.

Table 2-10. Urban Population Growth[a]—Central America, Latin America, and East Asia

	Costa Rica	El Salvador	Guatemala	Honduras	Nicaragua	Latin America	East Asia
1980s	3.8	1.5	3.0	4.9	3.9	3.0	4.6
1990s[b]	3.1	2.9	3.3	4.4	4.0	2.4	3.7

Source: Data based on World Bank (1998).
[a]Annual population growth rate.
[b]Data for the 1990s are computed up to 1996.

ies. In 1980, the percentage of the urban population in the country's largest city ranged from 64 percent for Costa Rica and 47 percent for Nicaragua to a low of 22 percent for El Salvador.[13] Urban population has increased continuously in Central America since 1910 and is today higher than in East Asia but it is substantially lower than in Latin America as a whole. Central America's growth rate reflects the continuous move toward larger agglomerations.

Central America has suffered from a lack of raw materials and energy on which to base industrial development. Nevertheless, wood supplies have long been systematically exploited, first by the British and later by the United States.[14] Overall, in spite the region's location and strategic importance, Central America's limited economic resources and peripheral character have meant that agriculture has remained the main area of economic activity in the region, whether in the planting of corn for domestic consumption or coffee and bananas for export.

The People

Spaniards arriving in Central America encountered indigenous cultures. Whether in Mexico or northern Costa Rica, these cultures shared some common experiences. For example, they had traded with one another for centuries. The Spanish administrative apparatus mirrored this commonality by organizing the region into the unified *Virreinato* of Mexico.

Race and ethnicity tend to reinforce social distinctions; indigenous people and such groups as the Africans and the mestizos experienced diminished social status. After independence, those of "Spanish ancestry" were replaced at the top of the social structure by the mestizos, at least in formal terms. Indians, Africans, and later the Chinese were relegated to the bottom of the social scale and usually were employed in more menial tasks. Table 2-11 presents an overview of the ethnic composition of the different Central American coun-

---

13. See Weaver (1994, 162).

14. According to Perez-Brignoli (1989), the woods of Honduras and Belize were the main source of materials for London's reconstruction after the Great Fire of 1666.

Table 2-11.   *Ethnic Composition of the Population—Central America*

	Costa Rica	El Salvador	Guatemala	Honduras	Nicaragua
Mixed or Unspecified	97.6	75.0	46.4	89.9	65.3
Indigenous	0.3	20.0	53.6	6.7	9.5
European	1.9	—	—	2.1	13.3
African	—	5.0	—	1.2	11.1
Other	0.1	—	—	—	0.7

Source: Weaver (1994). Note: Data refer to the 1940s for El Salvador and Nicaragua, 1945 for Honduras, and 1950 for Guatemala and Costa Rica.

tries in the 1940s and 1950s. The group labeled "mixed or unspecified" is remarkably large, which demonstrates the high degree of racial mixing that has occurred since the first European settlements. Guatemala stands out due to the size of its indigenous population, which continues to account for about half of its total population. The size of Nicaragua's African population is also striking.

Tables 2-12 and 2-13 present the age structure of the population and the level of participation of women and children in the labor market in 1960 and 1995. The youngest group of the population in Central America is bigger than in Latin America as a whole, at levels around 45 percent of the population for all countries except Costa Rica. The age-dependency ratios, though decreasing, are nevertheless high by international standards due to the low percentage of individuals above sixty-four years of age. As for children in the labor

Table 2-12.   *Population Age Structure—Central America, Latin America, and East Asia*

	Costa Rica	El Salvador	Guatemala	Honduras	Nicaragua	Latin America	East Asia
Population 0–14 years							
1960	0.47	0.46	0.46	0.46	0.48	0.42	0.40
1995	0.34	0.37	0.44	0.44	0.43	0.33	0.28
Active Population (15–64 years)[a]							
1960	0.49	0.51	0.51	0.51	0.50	0.54	0.56
1995	0.61	0.58	0.52	0.54	0.54	0.62	0.66
Age-Dependency Ratio[b]							
1960	1.02	0.95	0.95	0.95	1.01	0.87	0.79
1995	0.64	0.71	0.90	0.87	0.85	0.62	0.52

Source: Data based on World Bank (1998).
[a]Active population is the number of people who could potentially be economically active. Population includes all residents regardless of legal status or citizenship except for refugees who, not permanently settled in the country of asylum, are generally considered part of the population of the country of origin.
[b]The Age-Dependency ratio is the ratio of dependents (the population under age fifteen and above age sixty-five) to the working-age population (those aged fifteen to sixty-four). For example, 0.7 means there are seven dependents for every ten people of working age.

Table 2-13. *Women and Children in the Labor Force—Central America, Latin America, and East Asia*

	Costa Rica	El Salvador	Guatemala	Honduras	Nicaragua	Latin America	East Asia
Children 10–14 in Labor Force[a]							
1960	15.61	18.38	22.68	20.72	20.19	14.63	38.53
1995	5.21	14.83	15.81	8.23	13.59	9.46	10.81
Female Labor Force Participation[b]							
1960	15.79	16.97	12.22	12.31	18.12	19.03	39.39
1995	29.92	34.58	26.71	30.18	36.50	33.44	44.34

Source: World Bank (1998).
[a]Share of children from ages ten to fourteen that is active in the labor force. Labor force comprises all people who meet the International Labor Organization's definition of the economically active population.
[b]As a percentage of the total labor force. Labor force comprises all people who meet the International Labor Organization's definition of the economically active.

force, only Costa Rica has a lower share of the youngest age group working. Women are decidedly less likely to be in the labor force in Central America than they are in the other areas. However, in the last thirty-five years the change toward increased female participation has been remarkable.

In the highlands of Guatemala, the pre-Colombian culture of the Maya still survives. The Mayans (around half of the country's population) remain relatively isolated from the rest of the economy and have little access to the education and health systems. In other areas of Central America, few members of the indigenous population remain. From the southern Pacific plains of Guatemala to the border of Nicaragua and Costa Rica, the mestizos (people who exhibit both European and indigenous features) are the most prevalent. The culture of the *criollos* (people of Spanish descent who are born in Spanish America), however, scarcely remains in the urban middle and rural landed classes. From the early years of the coffee booms, the arrival of non-Spanish businessmen and the ascendancy of the United States have left a strong cultural imprint. Along the Pacific, European traits are more prominent as a result of the early settlements. African traits are more noticeable along the Atlantic coast from Belize south to Costa Rica among people isolated from the mainstream.

A Strategic Passage

The strategic importance of Central America as a point of passage of commercial flows has indelibly marked its history and fate. As Perez-Brignoli (1989) put it, "In the giant chess game of shipping lanes, naval power, and military might, Central America has always been perceived geopolitically, its significance as purely strategic." At the southernmost tip of Central America lies Panama, which has pursued a separate destiny from other countries in the region. Panama's history is associated with the fact that the country occupies the narrowest strip of land between the Atlantic and the Pacific Oceans. Panama was the first point of passage of the Spanish galleons carrying gold and silver from South America. Shortly after independence, it became the site chosen by the United States for the construction of a transoceanic canal.

The master game of the transoceanic passage began in the nineteenth century. Foreign powers soon identified two feasible routes for the canal. The first, through southern Nicaragua, would make use of the navigable stretch of the San Juan River and Lake Nicaragua. The second, which was eventually chosen, was the Panama route. Britain, the first important foreign player in the region, established settlements in Belize and on the Atlantic coasts of Honduras and Nicaragua. British interest in a transoceanic canal eventually collided with U.S. interests. In 1849, the California gold rush heightened U.S. interest in a shorter route, and thus less expensive communications, between the Atlantic and the Pacific.[15] In the 1850s, the Clayton-Bulwer Treaty forced the British government to renounce unilateral control of a future canal.[16] More significantly, Britain eventually freed the United States from the commitment that had prohibited both powers from obtaining unilateral control of the canal.

The context of American involvement in the region was set by the Monroe Doctrine (1823), which can be summarized by the phrase "America for the Americans." This encouraged a bellicose attitude by the United States *vis à vis* the European powers, an attitude that was further compounded by the United States' growing strategic interests in the region.[17] President Taft explicitly introduced the diplomatic and military option in the defense of U.S. interests, specifically U.S. investments in Latin America. This led to what would be dubbed "dollar diplomacy," and to an enduring ambiguity regarding the interests of the American government and American companies in Latin America. During Theodore Roosevelt's presidency, U.S. interest in the region grew.[18] The United States refinanced Central American debt to Europeans so that it would be owed, instead, to U.S. bondholders. At the beginning of the

---

15. The connection between the eastern and western states initially was by way of the San Juan River and Lake Nicaragua and, after 1855, the transoceanic railroad across Panama.

16. Also, both the United States and Britain agreed not to colonize any part of Central America.

17. Woodrow Wilson (and later Franklin Delano Roosevelt) pursued a Good Neighbor policy, which somewhat softened the spirit of the Monroe doctrine.

18. This "Roosevelt Corollary" committed the United States to maintaining peace and order in the region, with the aim of reducing the likelihood of European intervention.

twentieth century, the United States had established a dominant presence in the Caribbean, not least through annexation of Cuba and Puerto Rico in the wake of the Spanish American War. The 1907 Washington Peace Conference, which brought together the United States, Mexico, and Central America, proposed a commitment to mutual noninterference and nonrecognition of governments that emerged by force.[19] The mention of noninterference was clearly proposed in the expectation that nonetheless U.S. interests would be appropriately taken into account. A Central American court of justice was put in place to arbitrate conflicts. Most recommendations emerging from the conference, however, would not hold. Frequent challenges by Zelaya in Nicaragua led to U.S. intervention and the eventual occupation of Nicaragua by U.S. marines in 1912. An ulterior motive for the invasion was the need to preclude the creation of a transoceanic canal as an alternative to Panama's. Nicaragua had been pinpointed as the most promising site for a canal in the nineteenth century, but by 1903, with the independence of Panama, the attention of the United States had moved south.[20] The Panama Canal, which would become a focus for U.S. defense concerns, was completed by 1914, following on Panama's independence from Colombia in 1903 and the signing of an agreement with the United States.

CENTRAL AMERICAN ECONOMIES IN PERSPECTIVE

Society

The importance of societal factors and institutions for economic performance has been noted extensively in the economic literature. Factors such as political instability, income inequality, corruption, the availability of education, and level of democracy have been found to relate to economic performance. Some authors go as far as suggesting an association between culture and economic development.[21]

Hall and Jones (1999) find that most of the difference in the level of output per worker across economies is explained by institutions and government policies. Higher rates of investment in physical and human capital, and a more efficient use of those resources, are driven by a social infrastructure that

---

19. Under the 1922 Treaty of Peace and Amity.

20. The Bryan-Chamorro Treaty of 1916 included the right in perpetuity to construct a canal crossing Nicaragua, as well as territorial concessions that facilitated the strategic defense of access to the Panama canal. See Perez-Brignoli (1989).

21. Most recently David Landes (1998) has argued that cultural factors are key to understanding why some countries develop and others fail to do so.

encourages the accumulation of capital and skill as well as the creation and use of new technologies.[22] Important features of this beneficial social infrastructure include the capability of individuals to capture the private returns of their effort.

The negative correlation between population growth and growth of income per capita is well documented. It has given rise to several theories explaining the causal relationship between the two variables. In societies with limited amounts of human capital and high mortality, parents choose large families and invest little in each child. As a result, there is little physical and human capital accumulation and income per capita is relatively stagnant.[23]

Democracy is very important for social peace and economic development. This social stability is "bought" by higher wages, low income inequality, and a higher level of educational provision.[24] Low income inequality and high provision of education have been shown to have a positive effect on the rate of economic growth.[25] Another potential benefit of democratic institutions is their ability to face exogenous shocks: democratic societies may be more able to redistribute income and implement the necessary painful adjustments to changing economic circumstances.[26]

In 1821, the areas that would become Central America gained independence from Spain, contemporaneously with most countries in Latin America. The two regions almost immediately split from Mexico, and formed a unified political unit. This, however, was to be a short-lived experience. After 1838, the five Central American countries parted to become separate republics. The first fifty years of independence were characterized by relative political and social turmoil, which abated around 1870. Bulmer-Thomas (1987) maintains that the problem of order was progressively being resolved in the nineteenth

---

22. Differences in output per worker relate to the use of physical and human capital and efficiency with which they are used. Hall and Jones (1999) find that the difference (a factor of 35) between the United States and Niger, has to do with different capital intensities (a factor of 1.5) and different education levels (a factor of 3.1). The "productivity residual," which accounts for a factor of 7.7, is thus the most important. It is this that correlates with "social infrastructure," according to the authors.

23. See Becker et al. (1990). Galor and Weil (1996) have recently developed the following argument: increases in capital per worker raise women's wages more than men's; since women's wages increase more than total household income, fertility is reduced through a rise in the opportunity cost of having children, sparking a virtuous cycle of higher capital per worker, higher growth and lower fertility.

24. See Rodrik (1999) for the link between democracies and higher wages. Tavares and Wacziarg (1999) present evidence of the link between democracy, higher education levels and lower income inequality.

25. See Alesina and Perotti (1996) and Larrain and Vergara (1998) for evidence of the negative link between income inequality and economic growth.

26. This is suggested, for instance, in Rodrik (1998).

century, while little changed in the sphere of liberty. In 1870, an era of progress dubbed the "liberal era" was initiated. Its basis was the export of coffee and bananas.

Since colonial times, the region and its political leaders had looked for a solid link to the international economy on which to base sustainable progress. Members of the coffee and banana elite, who had progressively gained preeminence, now took hold of the state. Their influence was used to pass legislation that would facilitate the supply of land and labor to the export sector. The former landowner class, whose wealth was based on cattle interests, has now faded from the limelight. There were few explicit clashes between the old and the traditional elite since their respective spheres of business barely overlapped. A politically liberal period in the nineteenth century, saw increased secularization and a stronger presence of public administration in society. However, the conservative and liberal periods did not differ much as far as the conduct of politics and governmental affairs were concerned. The overriding features of the Central American nation-states forming in the nineteenth century were a centralization of power in the fiscal, legal, and administrative arenas; the creation of military and police institutions; the definition of national borders; and a certain degree of integration of the indigenous peoples into the life and image of the nation.

During the years of primary export booms, an outstanding feature of the region's image was the instability of its political system.[27] Political competition took place in the context of a nominal split between liberals and conservatives until 1870, after which personality politics gained importance. The local political system in every country was modelled on the U.S. system, but frequent manipulation 'of the ballot prevented the emergence of democratic alternation between the ins and outs. Moreover, outsiders tended to lay claim to political power through violent armed insurgencies. The tendency for power to be held by *caudillos* was evident in the late 1800s, when press freedom and independent labor were still not a reality.

According to Bulmer-Thomas (1987), the differences between Costa Rica and other countries in the region in this period have been somewhat exaggerated. In Costa Rica the political system was similarly underdeveloped, and participation only increased as education took hold. Given the difficulties of a legitimate change of power, cabinet turnover tended to be associated with outbursts of violence. The fact that Central American countries had once been part of a single unit encouraged meddling in each other's internal af-

---

27. In the early twentieth century, political instability, coupled with the economic influence of the banana monoculture, led to the popularization of the term "banana republic," first used in Henry (1917).

fairs, which led to further instability. Nevertheless, the success of coffee exports favored social stability by making public revenues available and by creating a vested interest in social peace among the landowners.

Differences in social status and hierarchy have historically been very conspicuous in Central America. The basis of the differences has been land ownership. Conflict over land has led to several violent outbursts. Central American countries remain rural societies, with only a fraction of the labor force specializing in export crops. The seasonal demand for labor has been a source of personal income instability, which leads directly to social instability. In the wake of the World War II boom, basic social needs began to feature in national agendas, in part because of the influence of United Nations missions that diagnosed local problems.

Private business interests began to organize explicitly in the 1970s. Labor, by contrast, already organized after World War I, when strikes and other conflicts became common in the banana-producing areas. The first communist parties were created following the depression of the 1930s; but a conservative reaction led to their effacement from civic life shortly thereafter. Government has progressively gained autonomy relative to the export interests.

The prestige and power of the Catholic Church has frequently contrasted with the weakness of civil institutions in Central America. For example, state control of education and the establishment of freedom of religion came to the region relatively late. In the 1960s, the Church became a more complex institution and its conservative character was diluted by grassroots activism. Intended as a response to the communist threat, this led to a new emphasis on the economic and social needs of the poor. The Church's legitimacy among the conservative sectors of society gave a new authority to its pleas for social justice and broader participation,

Honduras was for many years the country most vulnerable to manipulation by its Central American neighbors, due to the lack of an export commodity and a cohesive ruling class. The rise of banana exports provided an economic basis, but the country remained vulnerable to outside political influence. The ambiguous relationship between the American administration and American commercial interests, namely the fruit companies, compounded the problem.[28]

The professionalization of the military took place in the late nineteenth century in Guatemala, the early twentieth century in El Salvador and Nicaragua, and as late as the 1950s in Honduras. In Costa Rica, it never really materialized. The Costa Rican army was discredited after the brief dictatorship of

---

28. Even if the strategic interests of the United States and the economic interests of the companies did not exactly coincide. See Munro (1964).

Federico Tinoco from 1917 to 1919. The consequent loss of status led to its dismantling in 1949. Costa Rica is an oddity within Latin America in that it is a country without an army. Although beneficial for the country's civic and economic development, Costa Rica's lack of an army is thus largely an accident of history. Nonetheless, it has turned into a rewarding national policy.

Costa Rica's social development was very peculiar. The colonial inheritance was one of small, independent-minded farmers in a sparsely populated corner of the isthmus.[29] Far from the regional centers of power, devoid of a substantial natural resources, and isolated from the internal uprisings of the federation, Costa Rica was able to experiment and then start the export of coffee to England. Its success further attenuated internal divisions, already mild by Central American standards. The country held regular elections with direct suffrage from 1912 on, and the labor movement was allowed to develop. The 1948 upheaval led to a number of substantial reforms—of which the elimination of the army was the most conspicuous. Civil services reform, the promotion of general education, and the development of social security assured that the benefits of the high prices for coffee and the boom of the 1950s were more evenly distributed. This, in turn consolidated political participation and the civic traditions of the country. In the 1970s, social security was further extended to become almost universal.

The Economy

Economic growth in Latin America has lagged behind that of Europe and of countries such as Canada, the United States, Australia, and New Zealand. The difference in per capita GDP was already present in the 1820s.By 1980, the industrialized world had incomes three times as large as those of Latin America.[30] In the early1990s, after the crisis of the 1980s that hit Latin America the hardest, the incomes of the industrial world were four times as large.

The income of the Central American countries has generally lagged behind that of Latin America, with the exception of Costa Rica. All the economies of Central America experienced substantial progress from the early twentieth century to the onset of the crisis of the 1980s. Figure 2-2 presents the value of GDP per capita for the five Central American countries since 1920. For a brief period in the late 1940s, Guatemala had the highest income per capita of the region, but the rest of the time Costa Rica enjoyed that distinction and after that the difference between Costa Rica's average income level and other Central American countries progressively increased.

---

29. The country had no more than 50,000 inhabitants in the early 1800s.
30. See, for instance, Bloom and Sachs (1999).

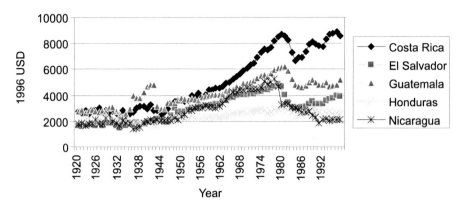

Figure 2-2. GDP Per Capita 1920–1998

The small size of all five Central American economies and their reliance on commodity exports have led to substantial fluctuations in national incomes. On the eve of the Great Depression, Honduras' GDP per capita was second to Costa Rica's, but, overexposed to price fluctuations and with 40 percent of the national product totally dependent on bananas, the Honduran per capita GDP was the lowest in the region by 1942. The crisis of the1930s (1940s for Guatemala) left its mark. Nicaragua and Honduras recovered their 1929 income-per-capita levels only in the early 1950s and the mid-1960s, respectively. Nicaragua went from the lowest GDP per head in the 1920s to the second highest in the postwar period.[31] By then, Nicaragua had become the most specialized in export commodities.

Tables 2-14 and 2-15 show the average growth rates for each country and decade from 1920 to 1980. Costa Rica has been the most successful, growing at the highest rates, both in absolute terms and per capita. Honduras has experienced the lowest growth, while the other three countries approach Costa Rica's progress.[32] The 1950s and 1960s for Costa Rica, El Salvador, and Nicaragua, and the 1960s and 1970s for Guatemala and Honduras have witnessed the highest growth in absolute GDP. In per capita terms, Costa Rica's progress in the seventies became more noticeable as population growth slowed down

---

31. And to the bottom again, in the wake of the crisis of the 1980s.

32. Honduras' performance can not be explained by higher rates of population growth, since the five countries are very similar in this respect. See Table 2-14 above.

Table 2-14.   *Growth of GDP PPP[a]—Central America*

	Costa Rica	El Salvador	Guatemala	Honduras	Nicaragua
1920s	1.37	3.45	4.84	5.20	4.71
1930s	4.02	1.08	6.81	−1.59	0.82
1940s	4.95	5.50	−0.48	3.64	3.36
1950s	8.32	5.15	4.18	3.66	6.47
1960s	8.03	6.81	6.16	5.35	9.31
1970s	7.26	4.89	6.55	5.02	−0.09
1980s	1.95	−1.01	0.39	2.42	−0.95
1990s	3.55	5.23	4.00	2.09	4.81

Source: Bulmer-Thomas (1987) and World Bank (1998). Data for 1920 to 1980 based on
Bulmer-Thomas (1987), statistical appendix. Data from 1980 from World Bank (1998).
[a]GDP PPP is gross domestic product converted to international dollars using purchasing power parity
rates. An international dollar has the same purchasing power over GDP as the U.S. dollar in the United
States. GDP measures the total output of goods and services for final use that occurs within the domestic
territory of a given country, regardless of the allocation to domestic and foreign claims. Gross domestic
product at purchaser values (market prices) is the sum of gross value added by all resident and nonresident
producers in the economy plus any taxes and minus any subsidies not included in the value of the products. It is calculated without making deductions for depreciation of fabricated assets or for depletion and
degradation of natural resources. Data are in constant international dollars.

Table 2-15.   *Growth of Per Capita GDP[a]—Central America*

	Costa Rica	El Salvador	Guatemala	Honduras	Nicaragua
1920s	−0.25	1.15	1.02	1.76	3.85
1930s	1.49	−0.10	3.75	−2.87	−0.90
1940s	2.04	3.73	−2.30	1.30	0.77
1950s	2.31	1.79	0.71	0.34	2.74
1960s	3.34	2.26	2.33	1.35	5.21
1970s	3.76	1.54	2.38	1.12	−2.68
1980s	−0.77	−1.71	−1.96	−0.83	−3.01
1990s	1.44	2.61	1.11	−0.59	1.62

Source: Bulmer-Thomas (1987) and World Bank (1998). Data for 1920 to 1980 based on Bulmer-
Thomas (1987), statistical appendix. Data from 1980 from World Bank (1998).
[a]GDP per capita based on purchasing power parity (PPP). GDP PPP is gross domestic product converted
to international dollars using purchasing power parity rates.

significantly. Nicaragua's income per capita, on the other hand, dropped substantially in the seventies as fertility rates rose and economic crisis set in.

As Bulmer-Thomas[33] states, there was an unwritten "article of faith among both colonial and republican administrators that no one would work for wages as hired labor unless he or she were compelled." Economic development was associated with the use of force to control the workers and restrict their access to land. Communal lands were closed and antivagrancy laws enforced in El Salvador, Nicaragua, and Guatemala. The idea of a positive wage-elasticity for the labor supply was foreign to the region. One result was that local markets for nascent manufactures never developed. The population was unwilling to migrate from the highlands to the Atlantic coast, which was seen as unhealthy and unsafe, and so the banana companies were allowed to import black laborers from the West Indies.[34] The advent of the Central American Common Market (CACM) in the 1960s lowered resistance to wage increases by employers as new goods were sold in markets less subject to exogenous price fluctuations. Until the early twentieth century, manufacturing remained limited to a very few areas, and the development of a home market for manufactures was affected by exchange rate instability.[35] Foreign direct investment was confined to a few sectors: bananas, railways, and mining.[36] Bursts in manufacturing occurred in the 1930s in Costa Rica and Nicaragua, the 1940s in El Salvador and Guatemala, and the 1950s in Honduras. The import substitution policies of the 1960s, which were initially put forward in the context of implementing the CACM, led to the most significant coordinated effect to develop manufacturing. The share of manufactures in the national product rose in the 1960s. However, manufacturing stagnated again in the 1970s, revealing the limitations of the import-substitution model.[37] In the event, manufacturing has not exceeded 18 percent of total product in most countries, the exception being Nicaragua on the eve of the 1980s crisis.

Land ownership and land use are key factors in understanding Central America. In the 1800s, the system of *colonato* guaranteed the peasantry some access to the land while providing the emerging export economy with a stable

---

33. Bulmer-Thomas (1987, 11).

34. According to Bulmer-Thomas (1987), black laborers were actually better remunerated than the coffee laborers in the highlands, but market segmentation precluded any general increase in wages.

35. In spite of the existence of a rudimentary textile industry, Bulmer-Thomas (1987) mentions that even coffee bags were imported in this period.

36. Estimates of the stock of foreign direct investment put it at $112.5 million: 36 million in agriculture, 43.3 million in railroads and 13.5 million in mining, with public utilities a mere 0.5 million. This contrasts with the experience of Latin America in general (Bulmer-Thomas 1987).

37. See Table 2-16.

Table 2-16. *Manufactures as Share of GDP—Central America*

	Costa Rica	El Salvador	Guatemala	Honduras	Nicaragua	Latin America	East Asia
1920[a]	7.27	10.22	14.17	6.69	9.06	—	—
1930	8.71	10.62	13.95	4.80	5.17	—	—
1940	13.20	10.32	7.30	6.81	11.02	—	—
1950	11.56	12.89	11.10	9.08	10.81	—	—
1960	12.50	13.94	11.95	15.28	13.06	—	—
1970	15.15	17.60	14.60	13.99	19.18	25.13	23.63
1980	16.93	17.15	15.57	15.07	23.05	26.64	31.86
1990[b]	19.38	21.71	—	16.34	16.88	23.54	29.21
1996[c]	18.46	20.95	13.97	18.28	16.05	20.79	32.81

Source: Bulmer-Thomas (1987) and World Bank (1998).
[a]Data for 1920 to 1980 are based on Bulmer-Thomas (1987), statistical appendix.
[b]Data for 1990 are from the World Bank (1998).
[c]East Asia figure is for 1995.

Table 2-17. *Agriculture as Share of GDP—Central America*

	Costa Rica	El Salvador	Guatemala	Honduras	Nicaragua	Latin America	East Asia
1920[a]	47.38	48.76	41.99	49.46	55.78	—	—
1930	43.26	48.33	37.54	55.20	66.19	—	—
1940	33.54	47.43	45.31	50.61	46.72	—	—
1950	38.54	40.96	36.55	44.83	36.59	—	—
1960	29.66	36.02	33.43	32.83	29.50	—	29.21
1970	25.04	30.62	30.12	34.61	27.01	12.68	34.56
1980	19.15	30.18	27.65	25.13	25.75	10.05	28.03
1990[b]	15.94	17.10	26.12	22.44	31.52	9.67	24.64
1996[c]	15.52	13.13	24.06	21.71	34.17	10.48	19.89

Source: Bulmer-Thomas (1987) and World Bank (1998).
[a]Data for 1920 to1980 are based on Bulmer-Thomas (1987), statistical appendix.
[b]Data for 1990 are from the World Bank (1998).
[c]East Asia figure is for 1995.

supply of labor.[38] Agrarian reform was rare and limited in scope, so the question of land remained important. By 1920, agriculture dominated the export market. In the 1920s and 1930s, the rise of export agriculture compensated for the decline in domestic agriculture, so that the overall share of agriculture increased.[39] In the twentieth century as a whole, agriculture experienced a secular decline from about 50 percent of GDP to an average of 25 percent. Since this decline slowed in the 1970s, the agricultural sector remains important.

---

38. This system consisted in granting a family of peasants the use of a parcel of land against the commitment to do a certain amount of work.

39. The banana export boom in Honduras in the 1920s is an example: agriculture for domestic use declined by 8.6 percent in the decade, to 16.8 percent of GDP, while agricultural exports rose 14.8 percent in the same period. See Bulmer-Thomas (1987), statistical appendix.

Table 2-18. *Government Spending as Share of GDP*

	Costa Rica	El Salvador	Guatemala	Honduras	Nicaragua
1920	2.92	5.64	2.78	4.82	0.74
1930	4.75	6.54	8.35	3.25	0.57
1940	5.08	5.50	2.98	3.44	2.73
1950	5.92	7.33	8.36	4.05	10.68
1960	10.74	8.92	8.80	4.75	10.93
1970	11.95	8.43	7.03	3.63	7.53
1980	11.21	10.78	7.58	5.22	11.93

Source: Bulmer-Thomas (1987), statistical appendix.

Central American governments emerged in the late 1800s as guarantors of the export-related interests. This support was informal but important, and consisted of both direct incentives and the development of infrastructure.[40] Foreign interests, particularly in banana production, always feared that stronger states might appropriate some of their rents. Yet, in spite of high profit levels, banana production was not subject to significant direct taxation until the 1950s, by which time this activity had begun to lose economic preeminence.

As Table 2-18 shows, the level of public spending in all Central America remained relatively low for most of the twentieth century. Even in the wake of the 1948 revolution and the social democratic policies of the 1950s,[41] the Costa Rican government did not account for more than 12 percent of GDP. In the 1960s, the fiscally conservative governments of the northern republics managed to actually decrease the already low levels of public spending.[42] Thus, the low levels of public spending reflected both the simple character of the economies and ideological choices.[43] The education budgets remained low—generally half to one-third of military budgets—in spite of low literacy rates. Taxation was strongly resisted by organized special interests. As a result, the most dynamic sectors of the economy tended to be undertaxed, which led to severe distortions as well as to equity problems in tax-system design. Governments generally relied on tariffs as a source of revenue and resisted direct taxation.[44]

---

40. Only with the crisis of the 1980s did the coffee producers feel the need to organize formally in order to make themselves heard by the state.

41. Mostly under the second Figueres administration.

42. This was reversed in the 1970s, in response to military needs and the availability of international loans.

43. The extremely low levels of public spending in Nicaragua during the 1920s and 1930s relate to the phase of the U.S. protectorate that lasted until 1937.

44. In the wake of the CACM tariff disarmament, the San José protocol of 1968 raised average tariffs by 30 percent, a knee-jerk response to a fiscal crisis. All governments resisted consideration of serious tax reform.

Deficits in the public sector were common but not substantial enough to affect the level of debt as share of GDP. Though the latter was relatively low, the debt problem gained preeminence and was assigned high priority by contemporaries. The reason was simple: because debt was contracted in gold-standard currencies, a commodity export crisis would lead to serious default problems. Moreover, bondholders had sufficient influence to use the diplomatic and even military weight of their governments. Foreign bondholders tended to claim trade-tax revenues as guarantees of repayment.

The coffee boom led to the creation of the first banks and other financial developments in the region.[45] Ownership was controlled firmly by nationals, and only in the early twentieth century did British and American banks gain some standing. Banks did not relate closely to the banana industry. This was due to two factors: non-overlapping ownership and the fact that the banana industry was vertically integrated and thus less dependent on financial transactions external to the firms. The financial system generally did not respond to the interests of the nonexport sector, which delayed industrialization. Some observers claim that bank nationalization in Costa Rica (1948) and in El Salvador and Nicaragua (1980s) was an excessive governmental reaction to the banks' unresponsiveness to the interests of the non-coffee economy.[46]

Exchange rate instability was a serious problem in Central America until the 1920s, derived from fluctuations in export earnings as well as from unfortunate monetary choices. El Salvador and Honduras had been on the silver standard since 1873, but the depreciation of silver led to a depreciation of the currencies and domestic inflation.[47] On the other hand, Guatemala and Nicaragua suffered from inflation at the same time as bankers found the pleasures of printing money irresistible. This led to the loss of convertibility and to further monetization of the economies.[48] In the 1920s, financial reforms were initiated that led to a period of exchange rate stability lasting to the 1980s.

---

45. The first banks opened in Costa Rica in the 1860s, Guatemala in the 1870s, and elsewhere in the 1880s. (Bulmer-Thomas 1987).

46. In Costa Rica, the banks then became an important promoter of the small-farm sector and the cooperative sector.

47. It is likely that coffee growers were actually interested in depreciation, as they sold in a gold market and made payments in pesos. Moreover, the wages of coffee workers adjusted with a lag. The fruit companies, on the other hand, were mostly isolated from fluctuations as they contracted few expenses locally, much less so than coffee growers. The monopsonistic power of banana producers over local growers led the latter to receive low but stable prices, isolating them from market fluctuations. On the other hand, this price stability meant that the national economy would not benefit from rises in banana prices which could compensate for a fall in coffee prices.

48. Nicaragua went on the gold standard following the United States occupation, and Costa Rica made a timely switch to the gold standard in 1896. In these countries, exchange rate stability was the norm until the loss of export markets with World War I.

The development of transportation followed the export boom. The avowed objectives were to promote trade and national integration.[49] The 1860s saw the development of the Pacific ports, benefiting from proximity to the main population centers. The Panamanian transoceanic railway allowed these ports to become an access route to markets in the eastern United States. Beginning in the 1870s, the main effort was directed to the creation of national railway systems. The involvement of foreign companies became necessary as difficulties in construction emerged. A system of concessions was put in place. By 1920, most of the lines were foreign-owned and operated.

Export-Led Growth

The importance of natural resources for economic development has been exaggerated. There is in fact mounting evidence that the economies of countries with abundant natural resources grow at lower rates than other economies. Historically, the economies of resource-poor countries have frequently outperformed the economies of resource-rich ones. Japan, Germany, and Switzerland in the postwar period, and the Asian Tigers more recently, are all resource-poor countries characterized by substantially higher-than-average growth rates. On the other hand, the performance of Mexico, Venezuela, Russia, and a great number of other oil exporters' performance in the twentieth century has left much to be desired, in spite of frequent efforts by these countries to push for diversified investments and industrial development. Sachs and Warner (2000) have shown that economies with high ratios of natural-resource exports to GDP tended to grow more slowly than others.[50] If a natural resource has high transport costs, its transformation in the local economy may be a path for industrialization. However, the secular trend to a decrease in transport costs makes it even less crucial for countries to be rich in resources.[51]

There are several explanations for the resource-to-poverty link.[52] An obvious one is "moral hazard," or the idea that wealth leads to lack of diligence in production and in institution building. A second explanation is the lack of

---

49. The republics with an Atlantic coast had local Afro-Caribbean communities that were fairly isolated.

50. They measured resource-abundance in 1970 according to the share of resource-based exports, defined as agriculture, minerals, and fuels. Growth rates were computed in 1950 for the next 20 years.

51. Sachs and Warner (2000) provide the example of the steel industry. In the nineteenth century, when transport costs were high, it was Germany, Britain, and the United States, rich in coal and iron ore deposits, that developed the steel industry. By contrast, as costs decreased in the 20th century, it was possible for resource-poor countries such as Japan and Korea to become major steel exporters.

52. See Sachs and Warner (2000).

backward and forward linkages of resource extraction, as compared to manufacturing. In an influential volume on development focusing on Latin America, Hirschman (1958) suggested that linkages between primary exports and the rest of the economy are small. A closely related possibility is that, unlike manufacturing and agriculture, natural resources benefit less from learning-by-doing and greater productivity.[53]

Macroeconomic policy may respond negatively to commodity export booms, in a "Dutch-disease" phenomenon.[54] This refers to the deindustrialization of a resource-rich economy because of overvaluation of the local currency, which leads to lack of competitiveness of non-natural resource exports. The volatility of primary resource prices may also be a problem in itself since it increases risk and discourages investment. A better-known explanation for the resources-to-poverty link is that of Prebisch (1950) and Singer (1950). Their explanation rests on the idea that primary commodities experience a secular decline in their terms of trade as a result of a decline in world demand.[55]

Another explanation is that dependence on natural resources fosters interest groups that negatively affect economic development. These groups either have a direct negative effect (Gelb 1988) or are part of the "feeding frenzy" that occurs during export booms. The volatility of export revenues, namely occasional windfall revenues, may also lead to perverse behavior by interest groups.[56] Governments may also become more corrupt and generally less efficient because the ease of taxing natural resources diverts them from growth-enhancing pursuits.[57]

The discussion above is relevant for Central America in two ways. First, it highlights the importance of diversification after this region has gone through at least a century of growth based on traditional exports of agricultural products. Second, it shows that the otherwise resource-poor countries

---

53. An example is Matsuyama (1992) who proposes a model where the social return to manufacturing exceeds the private return and the rate of capital accumulation is proportional to total sectoral production.

54. The "Dutch-Disease" was so named after the pernicious side effects on the rest of the economy of the substantial increase in exports of natural gas following its discovery in the The Netherlands.

55. This hypothesis was to have a tremendous impact on the economic policies of Latin America. Because it links growth and industrialization with a severance of ties with the international economy through import-substitution policies, it has been pinpointed as one of the explanations of recent Latin American stagnation.

56. As in Lane and Tornell (1996).

57. Larraín and Tavares (1999) find that oil producing countries tend to be more corrupt than the average.

of Central America should expect no particular difficulties in their growth process due to a lack of natural resources.

From the late 1800s, the economies of Central America have based exports and growth on a few commodities. Until the 1940s, they relied on coffee and bananas. El Salvador specialized almost exclusively in coffee and Honduras almost exclusively in bananas. This was a natural response to the geographical locations and climates of these countries—the Atlantic coast favoring banana plantations and the Pacific coast coffee growing. After the war, a few other primary commodities were added, namely cotton, sugar, and beef.[58] As the economies became more exposed to international trade, (see Table 2-19), they became less vulnerable to any specific commodity's price.

The coffee plant was introduced to the region in the eighteenth century. The initial experiments with producing coffee for export were conducted in the first half of the nineteenth century, but full-fledged development of coffee export production was delayed by the poor road connections between the coffee zones in the highlands and the coast. The main export markets, which were Europe and the eastern states of the United States, were very distant. Several authors point to Costa Rica's resource poverty as the root cause of its lead in moving to coffee exports. Since independence, Costa Rica has conducted a particularly desperate search for an export crop. The backwater of the vice-royalty of Guatemala in colonial times, it had no "traditional exports" on which to rely. At the time, Guatemala and El Salvador enjoyed moderate booms with exactly the same products that had been produced since colonial times, requiring no innovations in the transport or financial systems. Nicaragua maintained its role as regional provider of cattle.[59]

Costa Rica's visible success became a beacon for other countries in the region, and by the 1880s coffee production was established in El Salvador, Guatemala, and Nicaragua. Spectacular export growth ensued. Honduras did not follow their lead, partly due to a shortage of labor, partly to the climate. In the 1890s, coffee exports constituted 96 percent of export earnings in Guatemala, 91 percent in Costa Rica, 71 percent in Nicaragua, and 66 percent in El Salvador. Figures of this magnitude remained in the early twentieth century—Central American countries having the highest percentage of coffee in total exports in all of Latin America.[60] Labor-rich El Salvador and Guatemala became the major coffee exporters in the region by the end of the 1800s, based on large landholdings and more repressive labor conditions.[61]

---

58. The domestic market was always the most important in the case of beef.

59. See Perez-Brignoli (1989).

60. See Bulmer-Thomas (1987) and Topk and Wells (1998).

61. While in these countries laborers were recruited from the landless masses, in Costa Rica family members supplied a considerable part of the labor used in the small holdings.

Table 2-19.   *Exports Plus Imports as Share of GDP—Central America, Latin America, and East Asia*

	Costa Rica	El Salvador	Guatemala	Honduras	Nicaragua	Latin America	East Asia
1920[a]	88.61	48.45	38.54	47.54	45.97	—	—
1930	73.00	48.86	30.59	66.86	46.93	—	—
1940	53.16	23.94	15.55	37.91	26.43	—	—
1950	49.88	40.31	24.54	43.56	36.10	—	—
1960[b]	47.59	45.05	27.18	44.42	49.79	25.84	20.07
1970	63.21	49.38	36.35	62.02	55.27	23.39	18.56
1980	63.30	67.41	47.11	80.30	67.50	32.48	31.87
1990	75.96	49.79	43.47	76.13	71.36	31.06	44.39
1996	91.09	54.35	40.33	99.72	106.44	33.14	58.25[c]

Source: Bulmer-Thomas (1987) and World Bank (1998).
[a]Data for 1920 through 1960 are based on Bulmer-Thomas (1987), statistical appendix.
[b]Data for 1960 on are from World Bank (1998).
[c]Figure is for 1995.

In an attempt to ward off the cost of the impending conflict, Central American countries declared their neutrality early in World War I. However, Central America's exports declined dramatically with the onset of that war. The region experienced a downward adjustment in prices and diverted coffee exports to the U.S. market, which remained unscathed by the hostilities in Europe. The United States increased its role as both client and supplier. Between 1913 and 1920, its imports from the region went from 55 percent to 70 percent of the total, and exports to the region increased from 40 percent to 80 percent.[62] By 1930, Central America supplied 10 percent of the world's coffee, up from 5 percent in the late nineteenth century, in a market that had tripled in the same period.[63] The export of coffee was consolidated in the 1940s, when several bilateral trade treaties between the region and the United States were signed. The coffee agreements of 1940 between the United States and Latin America as a whole guaranteed an export market to Central America precisely at the time the European markets were closing.

Concessionaires called to build infrastructure in Central America created interesting responses to the issue of financing. In Costa Rica, the concessionaire Minor Keith assigned most of the land bordering the railroad line to banana production.[64] As the rail line progressed, so did revenues from exports.

---

62. See Bulmer-Thomas (1987, 9).
63. Latin America provided 89 percent of the world total. See Topik and Wells (1998, 53).
64. His railroad endeavor being in serious financial difficulties, he decided to raise the capital by producing bananas. See Wilson (1947) for an account of this important development.

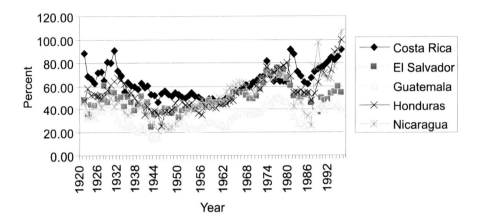

Figure 2-3.   Trade as Share of GDP in Central America

Until the end of the nineteenth century, banana exports originated in small plantations and were sold directly to the shipping lines. The growth in exports was spectacular, which led to the use of the interior landmass and to increases in the scale of production. Refrigeration allowed better handling of a very perishable fruit. Guatemala and Honduras followed in Costa Rica's footsteps and the banana industry became an alternative source of local income. The Atlantic coast was most appropriate for growing bananas due to soil conditions and the proximity to the large North American market. Thus development of plantations on the Pacific coast was not attempted until the 1930s.[65] The banana industry did provide some diversification—coffee exports went to Europe and bananas to the United States. The switch from the *Gros Michel* to the *Cavendish* banana (the latter being more resistant to diseases but more costly to ship) led to the boxing of shipments and a more efficient use of ship space.

The banana and coffee industries are often contrasted. Whereas banana companies remained under foreign control, coffee was always a local endeavor. In the banana industry, vertical integration led to monopsonistic tendencies. The creation in 1899 of the United Fruit Company (UFCO) led to a monopoly in Costa Rica and Guatemala. The Cuyamel Fruit Company and Standard Fruit created a monopoly in the other countries. Why did banana production fall into foreign hands in the first place? To blame, among other things, were the shortage of money to build much- needed railroads and

---

65. See Bulmer-Thomas (1987, 338).

Table 2-20. *Export Agriculture as Share of GDP*[a]—*Central America*

	Costa Rica	El Salvador	Guatemala	Honduras	Nicaragua
1920	28.38	21.61	22.71	22.51	9.95
1930	27.07	27.07	18.68	39.19	19.79
1940	14.68	21.00	9.70	24.73	11.68
1950	20.85	18.40	10.59	18.28	9.87
1960	11.64	16.49	11.84	11.88	10.25
1970	11.84	15.73	9.39	14.33	12.88
1980	8.41	15.63	9.44	12.25	11.04

Source: Data based on Bulmer-Thomas (1987), statistical appendix.
[a]Export Agriculture is defined as coffee, bananas, sugar, and cotton.

ports and insufficient capability to market the fruit. The banana industry was run by locals until the 1900s and the state was not willing to finance the infrastructure to develop it further. When foreign companies offered to build the infrastructure and recruit laborers abroad, they found institutional support. After all, it meant the development of vast areas of the countries and an opportunity cost of essentially zero. The banana companies ended up running virtual economic and political enclaves that managed health, education, and transportation systems.

Table 2-20 shows the importance of export agriculture in GDP. Exports of the four main products (coffee, bananas, sugar, and cotton) always accounted for a significant portion of the total, although the importance of these exports generally declined after World War II. This matches a general decrease in the trade intensity (measured by exports plus imports in GDP after World War II) that has been reversed only recently.[66]

The early twentieth century was characterized by the transformation of trade surpluses into deficits in the import-substitution decade of the 1960s and, even more acutely, in the 1970s. This change is convincing evidence for the limited value of import-substitution policies. In the 1970s, Costa Rica and El Salvador ran trade deficits of more than 7 percent of GDP, increasing their vulnerability to the coming debt crisis that was to dramatically reverse the flow of foreign financing to Latin American countries.

The export-led model of growth based on primary commodities has entailed the extreme vulnerability of Central America to external shocks that is palpable in the region's history. Figure 2-4 presents the evolution of the terms of trade, by country, from the 1920s to the 1980s. The magnitude of fluctua-

---

66. See Table 2-19

Table 2-21.   *Trade Balance as Share of GDP—Central America*

	Costa Rica	El Salvador	Guatemala	Honduras	Nicaragua
1920–29	15.32	12.32	4.84	17.40	1.80
1930–39	15.28	20.95	5.91	20.48	7.87
1940–49	3.75	13.53	4.81	9.07	−0.74
1950–59	−4.10	1.39	−4.43	−0.30	−2.53
1960–69	−4.56	4.96	−0.76	−1.31	−1.68
1970–79	−7.51	−7.57	1.36	−3.77	−2.16

Source: Data based on Bulmer-Thomas (1987), statistical appendix.

tions in the terms of trade in Honduras in the 1930s, Nicaragua in the 1940s, and El Salvador in the 1970s, is remarkable. Also noteworthy is the co-movement of terms of trade between countries (excluding the episodes above), which is evidence for the similarity of trade composition. All the countries experienced a major positive shock in terms of trade in the 1950s and the extent of the fluctuations in the period studied is very high: from indices averaging 50 to 100 in the 1920s, back to 50 in the 1930s and 1940s, up to 150 in the 1950s and back to 100 in the 1960s and 1970s. Table 2-22 presents the yearly average rate of change in terms of trade for every decade since the 1920s and the 1980s.

Export-led growth did not fully deliver on its promise of long-term growth. The need for diversification first appeared in the early twentieth century, but certain facts worked against it: the close association between banks and coffee that discouraged financing of new activities; the capture of the state by coffee interests; the operation of the railroad to the almost exclusive benefit of banana exports; and the low density of population. In general, for export-led growth to be successful, it needs a dense web of backward and

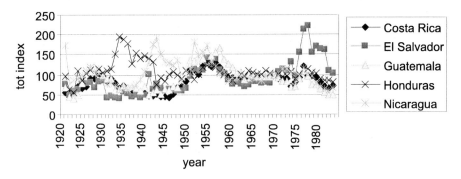

Figure 2-4.   *Terms of Trade in Central America*

Table 2-22. Yearly Rate of Change in the Terms of Trade[a]—Central America

	Costa Rica	El Salvador	Guatemala	Honduras	Nicaragua
1920s	6.78	1.15	4.57	0.69	−4.52
1930s	−3.45	1.82	−2.10	3.47	3.81
1940s	8.06	−3.40	11.50	−2.24	−1.45
1950s	−1.28	−0.84	−0.78	−0.83	−2.56
1960s	−0.59	0.30	−1.96	1.97	0.67
1970s	−0.32	5.42	−2.44	0.58	−0.25
1980s	−3.97	−7.87	−6.92	−4.21	−2.74

Source: Data based on Bulmer-Thomas (1987), statistical appendix.
[a]Terms of trade is the ratio of the price index for exports divided by the price index for imports.

forward linkages that Central America has lacked,[67] due to ownership, the nature of the commodities, or other reasons. Complementary sectors such as transportation, banking, and government did not fully develop because of strategic limitations deriving from ownership and the low level of taxation. In the second half of the twentieth century, the Central American Common Market compounded the problem by concentrating its attention on tariff disarmament on final products, largely bypassing intermediate and capital goods and thus precluding the development of linkages.

Tables 2-23 and 2-24 document how Central America lags behind Latin America as a whole in diversification toward manufacturing. Note that in 1965, only 8 percent of Latin American exports came from the manufacturing sector, and in the 1980s, Central America moved from leading to lagging in this respect. It is remarkable how little the export structure in the region changed in the 1980s. Nicaragua and Honduras actually saw a decrease in the importance of manufacture. In the 1990s, Central America started diversifying again, though only Nicaragua and Honduras have outpaced Latin America in that respect.

A Short History of Regional Integration

Shortly after winning independence from Spain, the countries of Central America were annexed to Mexico. Hopes of progress toward rational administration soon abated as the localities vied for influence and for autonomy

---

67. In the words of Perez-Brignoli (1989), the region's products were "only desserts" on the tables of Europe and America.

Table 2-23. *Manufacturing Exports as Share of Exports—Central America*

	Costa Rica	El Salvador	Guatemala	Honduras	Nicaragua	Latin America
1965	14.59	16.33	13.99	4.42	5.30	8.20
1970	18.65	28.67	27.98	8.08	16.04	14.53
1980	28.32	35.37	24.16	12.49	13.79	19.44
1990	26.81	37.74	24.47	9.34	8.28	34.93
1996	24.46	41.18	30.71	30.51	33.68	45.43

Source: World Bank (1998).

Table 2-24. *Growth in Per Capita Income[a]—Central America, Latin America, and East Asia*

	1970s	1980s	1990s
Central America	1.22	−1.65	1.24
Latin America	7.39	1.41	2.95
East Asia	8.70	10.2	10.9

Source: World Bank (1998).
[a]Growth of income per capita based on GDP at market prices in constant U.S. dollars averaged for the period.

from the remote center of power. Independence movements arose in the region and on July 1, 1823, a congress in Guatemala City declared Central America's independence. This declaration was ratified by delegates from the entire region. On November 22, 1824, a General Constituent Assembly promulgated a constitution based in part on that of the United States. The new federation of Central America was made up of Costa Rica, El Salvador, Guatemala, Honduras, and Nicaragua. The United Provinces of Central America was proclaimed to be "sovereign, free, and independent of old Spain, of Mexico, and of all other powers whether of the Old or the New World."[68]

Some of the initial difficulties of the federation related to the isolation of the different states, which was made worse by the nonexistence of proper transportation. The concentration of the population in Guatemala, which accounted at the time for half of Central America's one million inhabitants, compounded the problem. The British presence grew concomitantly with the issue of the transoceanic canal, which tended to aggravate local rivalries. Such matters as the creation of new bishoprics (religious autonomy being easily associated with political autonomy) and disagreements over borders made relations within the federation difficult. In 1825, the first president of the federa-

---

68. See Perez-Brignoli (1989, 67).

Box 2-1.

An Early View of Central American Integration

The possibilities of Central American integration inspired academic interest outside the region as early as 1922. In an article in the American Economic Review, the economist Harry Collings tried to determine whether the economic environment in Central America justified federation and how a federation could favor economic development (Collings 1922). Collings draws the attention of readers to the "similarity in religion, interests, aptitude and . . . ability." According to him, the connections went beyond culture: "Economically all the countries are confronted with the same problems—the development of their natural resources, which are largely agricultural, and the creation of facilities for placing their products more readily in the hands of the ultimate consumer, either at home or abroad."

Collings also refers to the major hindrances to the development of the region. The priority list reads well as a current checklist for the promotion of trade:

1. Government stability
2. Reduction of government expenses
3. Reform of the currency and banking system
4. Creation of better conditions for borrowers and lenders in foreign investments
5. Development of transportation—both railroad and shipping
6. Stimulation of foreign trade

The author concluded that regional integration can be instrumental in promoting Central America's political stability, its autonomy vis-à-vis the external world, and the development of its exports.

---

tion was elected but disputes between the liberal and the conservative wings of the federation led to civil war (1825–1829). Debt to a British bank was used by England as a lever to vie for control of Atlantic possessions.[69] In 1835, a reform movement emerged, but by 1838, as Congress proposed to take control of customs revenues, the union had disintegrated.[70]

The federation's demise left it associated with ambitious but not always realistic projects of reform that aimed to curtail the traditional sources of power,

---

69. Conveniently, the loan had been made to all republics, on a pro-rata basis.

70. Several different reforms, some clearly utopian in nature, faced opposition from the traditional sources of power, but the reaction was never stronger than to changes in taxation, which are deemed responsible for several uprisings by the *mestizo* and Indian populations. See Perez-Brignoli (1989).

bridge the European and indigenous communities, and most important, connect Central America to the world economy.[71]

Central American countries united forces again in the 1850s, this time against William Walker, an American mercenary who attempted to annex Nicaragua. The prompt recognition of Walker's republic by the United States alarmed the countries in the region. Together, with the material help of the British, they finally defeated the invaders.[72] In 1885, the Guatemalan ruler Rufino Barrios proclaimed the unification of Central America into a new republic, of which he would be the supreme military commander.[73] This was promptly rejected by El Salvador, Nicaragua, and Costa Rica. Whereas in the 1840s liberals tended to support some form of Central American unification, later in the century they had moved away from the idea, distracted by the wave of commodity export booms. However, several intellectuals kept the flame of future union lit.[74]

The major developments in economic integration can be traced to the 1950s, when Central American countries initiated a formal process of regional integration by agreeing to several bilateral trade agreements. The explicit aim was a regional free trade area, to evolve to a customs union. The five countries signed the general agreement creating the Central American Common Market in 1960.[75] The freeing of trade was the main objective. As well, it created several regional institutions that would have an important role in the coming years. The Central American Bank for Economic Integration (BCIE) became a conduit for financing infrastructure with mainly American funds. The increase in intraregional commerce and growth rates in the 1960s led to hopes of rapid industrialization and completion of what was seen as part of a long road to full economic integration. In 1971, however, Honduras retreated from the CACM in the wake of the so-called Soccer War with El Salvador.[76]

---

71. As Perez-Brignoli (1989, 77) ably puts it, "The Liberals believed in a utopia of progress: to bring forth to these lands the . . . lame lit by the French Revolution and the independence of the United States. . . . The Conservatives longed for the colonial way of life. They had boundless respect for the Church and they feared any social change they could not control." The contrast between ineffective grandiloquence and overanxious reaction is an enduring element of Central American political life.

72. This war effort has been curiously named the "National Campaign."

73. In his words, "divided and isolated we are nothing, united we can become something and united we shall be." See Perez-Brignoli (1989).

74. In 1899, Guatemalan students organized the Central American Union Party (Partido Unionista Centroamericano), under the influence of Salvador Mendieta, a Nicaraguan enthusiast. His book, *La Enfermedad de Centro-América*, proposes union as a cure for the Central American "disease." See Perez-Brignoli (1989).

75. Costa Rica adhered in 1963.

76. This war, sparked by a soccer competition between the two countries, originated in the movement of landless Salvadoran peasants to occupy empty land in southern Honduras; Honduras remained an observer of the CACM for an extended period.

In the 1970s, the model calling for integration and import substitution was exhausted as local industries moved to produce consumer nondurables for the local market but at the cost of tremedous increase in the imports of intermediate goods. The reduction in growth rates and the emergence of large trade imbalances after decades of surpluses are evidence for the limitations of the model.[77] Coatsworth (1994) puts the incipient development of regional integration into the context of the relationship with the United States, suggesting that the United States discouraged the integration efforts of the 1960s. Among others who had second thoughts about the direction, if not the value, of regional economic integration were the institutions of integration themselves, who advocated better coordination between governments and the inclusion of agriculture in the integration process.[78]

Conclusion

Geography has played, and is likely to continue to play, an important role in Central America's development. Central America's strategic position as the isthmus separating the Atlantic and Pacific oceans has been both a liability and an asset. The geo-strategic value of the region has historically attracted the attention of the United States and other international powers. This political interest has fueled a relationship with the outside world that, however intense, has seldom contributed to the political and economic development of Central America. Nonetheless, the position of the region, close to large markets and in the way of sea routes, has made possible an early integration with the world market for specific commodities. The challenge is for Central America to fully use its proximity to the major markets to extend and deepen economic integration, which must be the cornerstone of its development strategy.

The region's climate and proximity to markets have encouraged its reliance on an export-led model of growth based on a few primary products. This model worked well as an early source of capital: local elites developed and diversified away from traditional colonial products, while foreign investment flowed in, furthering access to technological and managerial know-how unavailable in the region. In addition, the export-led model of growth promoted the integration of national markets through the development of transport infrastructure and the establishment of a basic administrative structure. However, the heavy reliance on the export of products such as coffee and bananas, which were subject to large fluctuations in world market prices, has left the

---

77. See Table 2-21.
78. See SIECA (1972).

Central American economies vulnerable to economic and political events beyond their control. A new development model is actively being sought.

Political instability has compounded economic instability. The countries in the region have lived through some of the worst episodes of internal conflict and civil war in the whole of Latin America. Their effects on the regional economy have been nothing less than catastrophic. Income inequality and a lack of pluralism and transparency in the political sphere are the main causes of social instability, with deep roots in the history of the region. History strongly points to the role of solid, open and efficient political institutions in promoting economic growth and satisfying the basic needs of the whole population.

Finally, their small size and the closeness of the Central American to one another suggest the potential benefits of regional integration. Larger and more competitive markets, shared transport infrastructure, and a stronger voice in international fora are just a few of these benefits. The cultural and historical commonalities also lower the cost of regional integration. However, several attempts at political and economic integration have either failed or delivered results well below expectations. The Alliance for Sustainable Development of 1994 is an interesting development, but it is still too early to judge its long-term impact. The lessons from past history in the region is that any serious effort at regional integration needs to be thoroughly understood in its economic and political consequences and the costs and the gains for individual countries explicitly and openly negotiated. What is more, the overall gains to the region need to materialize in ways that compensate potential losers. Given its geographical, historical and social characteristics, Central America stands out as one of the world regions where integration holds the highest promise. That promise has yet to be fulfilled.

REFERENCES

Alesina, A., and R. Perotti. 1996. "Income Distribution, Political Instability, and Investment." *European Economic Review* 40 (6): 1203–28.

Barberia, Lorena. 1999. The Impact of Shipping Costs on the Apparel Industry. Cambridge, MA: Harvard Institute for International Development. Mimeographed.

Barahona, J. Doryan, F.Larraín and J. Sachs. Chapter 10 in this volume.

Becker, G., Murphy, K., and Tamura, R. 1990. "Human Capital, Fertility, and Economic Growth." *Journal of Political Economy*, 98 (5), Part 2: The Problem Of Development: A Conference of the Institute for the Study of Free Enterprise Systems: 12-37.

Bloom, D., and J. Sachs. 1999. "Geography, Demography, and Economic Growth in Africa: Development in Africa." Brookings-Papers-on-Economic-Activity; 0(2), 1998, pages 207-73.

Bulmer-Thomas, V. 1987. *The Political Economy of Central America Since 1920.* Cambridge, England, Cambridge University Press.

Coatsworth, John. 1994. *Central America and the United States: The Clients and the Colossus.* New York: Twayne Publishers.

Collings, Harry. 1922. "The Economic Basis of Federation in Central America." *American Economic Review Papers and Proceedings* 12 (1): 168–76.

Galor, O., and D. Weil. 1996. "The Gender Gap, Fertility, and Growth." *American Economic Review* 86 (3): 374-87.

Gallup, J., J. Sachs, and A. Mellinger. 1999. "Geography and Economic Development." *International Regional Science Review* 22 (2): 179-232.

Gelb, A. 1988. *Windfall Gains: Blessing or Curse?* New York: Oxford University Press.

Hall, R., and C. Jones. 1999. "Why Do Some Countries Produce So Much More Output Per Worker Than Others?" *Quarterly Journal of Economics* 114 (1): 83-116.

Henry, O. 1917. *Cabbages and Kings.* New York, NY: Doubleday.

Hirschman, A. 1958. *The Strategy of Economic Development.* New Haven, CT: Yale University Press.

Inter-American Development Bank. 1999. "Basic Socio-Economic Data for 19 July 1999, Statistics and Quantitative Analysis Unit." *http://www.iadb.org/.*

Larraín, F., and J. Tavares. 1999. Can Openness Deter Corruption? Cambridge, MA: Harvard Institute for International Development. Mimeographed.

Larraín, F., and R. Veraga. 1998. "Income Distribution, Investment, and Growth." In A. Solimano, ed. *Social Inequality Values: Growth and the State.* Michigan: University of Michigan Press.

Lane, P., and A. Tornell. 1996. "Power, Growth, and the Voracity Effect." *Journal of Economic Growth* 1(2): 213-41.

Landes, David. 1998. The Wealth and Poverty of Nations: *Why Some are So Rich and Others So Poor?* New York: W. W. Norton.

Matsuyama, K. 1992. "Agricultural Productivity, Comparative Advantage, and Economic Growth." *Journal of Economic Theory* 58 (2): 317–34.

Munro, D. 1964. Intervention and Dollar Diplomacy in the Caribbean, *1900–1921.* Princeton: Princeton University Press.

———. 1918. *The Five Republics of Central America.* Oxford University Press, Oxford, England.

Perez-Brignoli, H. 1989. *A Brief History of Central America.* Berkeley, CA: University of California Press.

Prebisch, Raul. 1950. "The Economic Development of Latin America and Its Principal Problems." Haggard,-Stephan, ed. The international political economy and the developing countries. Volume 1. Elgar Reference Collection. Library of International Political Economy vol. 7. Aldershot, U.K.: Elgar; distributed in the U.S. by Ashgate, Brookfield, Vt., 1995, pages 47-105. Previously published: [1950].

Radelet S., and J. Sachs. 1999. Shipping Costs, Manufactured Exports, and Economic Growth. Cambrdge, MA: Harvard Institute for International Development. Mimeographed

Rodrik, D. 1999. "Where Did All The Growth Go? External Shocks, Social Conflict, and Growth Collapses", Journal-of-Economic-Growth; 4(4), December 1999, pages 385-412.

Rodrik, D. 1999. "Democracies Pay Higher Wages." *Quarterly-Journal-of-Economics*; 114(3), August 1999, pages 707-38.

Sachs, J., and A. Warner. 2000. "The Big Push, Natural Resource Booms and Growth." *Journal of Development Economics*. Forthcoming

SIECA (Secretaría de integración económica de Centro América). 1972. Report.

Singer, H. 1950. "The Distribution of Trade between Investing and Borrowing Countries." *American Economic Review* 40: 473–85.

Smith, Adam. 1991. An Inquiry into the Nature and Causes of the Wealth of Nations. Everymans Library.

Tavares, J. and Wacziarg, R. 2000. "How Democracy Affects Growth." *European Economic Review*. Forthcoming.

Topik, S., and A. Wells, eds. 1998. *The Second Conquest of Latin America—Coffee, Henequen, and Oil during the Export Boom 1850–1930*. Austin: University of Texas Press.

Weaver, F. 1994. Inside the Volcano: *The History and Political Economy of Central America*. Boulder, CO: Westview Press.

Wilson, C. 1947. *Empire in Green and Gold - the Story of the American Banana Trade*. New York, NY: Henry Holt.

World Bank. 1998. *World Development Indicators*. CD-ROM.

3

Crisis and Recovery: Central America from the Eighties to the Nineties

JOSÉ TAVARES

Central America and Latin America experienced high rates of economic growth through the 1960s and the 1970s. In Latin America as a whole, per capita income grew at average rates similar to those in East Asia. However, the region experienced a dramatic reversal of fortune in the 1980s: from 1982 to 1992, per capita GDP growth in the region averaged −0.8 percent in what has been dubbed Latin America's "lost decade."[1] The poor policy choices of Latin American governments in the 1970s, including inward-looking protectionist policies and policies leading to substantial external indebtedness, made the region vulnerable to the external shock triggered by a halt in international lending in 1982.[2] Recurrent public deficits and the use of inflationary finance compounded the problem. In most Latin American countries structural reform was undertaken only after a descent into severe macroeconomic crisis.[3] The lack of adequate policy responses by the international financial community and by national governments following the freeze of international lending in the early 1980s exacerbated the situation.

Central America generally underperformed relative to Latin America, even though its broad economic fluctuations tended to coincide with Latin America's. Table 3-1 presents the growth rates for five-year periods in Latin America, East Asia, and each of the countries in Central America.[4] Central America's average per capita growth rate was stagnant in the 1975–79 period; and

---

1. See Edwards (1995, 7).

2. For an overview of the Latin American crisis see Edwards and Larraín (1989).

3. Colombia and Costa Rica were the exceptions. See Loayza and Palacios (1997, 1).

4. Chapter 2 in this volume provides a wider assessment, in comparative perspective, of the determinants of Central America's growth experience from the 1960s.

Table 3-1. *Growth in Per Capita GNP[a]—Central America, Latin America[b], and East Asia (1975–1998)*

	1975–79	1980–84	1985–89	1990–94	1995–98[a]
Costa Rica	2.11	−3.07	1.82	3.22	0.25
El Salvador	0.96	−6.01	0.10	3.84	1.78
Guatemala	2.92	−3.48	−0.66	−0.11	1.55
Honduras	3.55	−2.61	0.75	0.14	1.08
Nicaragua	−7.24	−1.17	−8.54	−3.73	1.65
Central America	**0.46**	**−3.27**	**−1.31**	**0.67**	**1.26**
Latin America & Caribbean	**2.06**	**−1.75**	**1.33**	**0.74**	**1.35**
East Asia & Pacific	**4.88**	**5.41**	**6.53**	**8.06**	**—**

Source: World Bank (1998) and IADB (1999) for the period 1995–1998.
[a]GDP per capita growth for 1995–1998.
[b]Latin America includes Central America, the Caribbean, and Mexico.

Nicaragua was almost wholly responsible for the this figure, since its per capita income decreased at a rate of −7.24 percent annually. All other countries, with the exception of El Salvador, were growing at rates of 2 percent to 3.5 percent a year, close to the Latin American average. These intercountry differences disappeared in the 1980–84 period, as Central America slumped into a major recession. Income per capita decreased at an average of −3.27 percent a year—almost double the rate of yearly decrease of Latin America's per capita income. El Salvador, sinking into internal strife, was the hardest hit.

In the second half of the 1980s, Latin America as a whole experienced positive growth, but Central America was still stagnant. Costa Rica outperformed the rest of Latin America in this period, but Nicaragua, which was in the midst of military conflict, took the hardest hit: its average income decreased at an astounding rate of 8.5 positive percent annually.[5] Finally, though Central American economies regained positive growth rates in the 1990s, the region still trailed behind the rest of the hemisphere. By contrast, all through the 1980s and 1990s the economies of East Asia grew at robust rates of 5 percent to 8 percent a year. The crisis of the 1980s simply did not exist in East Asia.

As expected, the behavior of investment affected national income. Table 3-2 shows the growth rates of gross domestic fixed investment in Central America, Latin America, and East Asia.[6] The contrast between the late 1970s

5. In a cross-country comparison of growth performance from 1965 to 1985, Barro and Lee (1994) report that El Salvador and Nicaragua were placed in the lowest growth quintile in a sample of 116 economies for the 1970–90 period.

6. Gross domestic fixed investment includes both private and public investment. Central America's averages are presented with and without figures for Nicaragua, since these seem doubtful.

Table 3-2.   *Growth in Gross Domestic Fixed Investment—Central America, Latin America[b], and East Asia (1975–1998)*

	1975–79	1980–84	1985–89	1990–94	1995–98
Costa Rica	11.66	−5.54	7.87	7.61	0.7
El Salvador	8.30	−11.90	7.53	11.60	3.5
Guatemala	11.63	−9.94	6.59	5.50	−1.3
Honduras	9.57	−2.90	5.30	11.65	0.1
Nicaragua	−15.59	40.08	−6.84	5.87	14.8
Central America	5.11	1.96	4.09	8.45	3.55
Central America w/o Nicaragua	**10.29**	**−7.57**	**6.82**	**9.09**	**0.75**
Latin America & Caribbean	**5.44**	**−4.33**	**3.58**	**3.90**	**5.37**
East Asia & Pacific	**6.01**	**8.59**	**6.91**	**14.54**	

Source: World Bank (1998) and IADB (1999) for the period 1995–98.
[b]Latin America includes Central America, the Caribbean, and Mexico.

and the 1980s is stark: average increases of 10 percent a year in the late 1970s were transformed into decreases of 7.5 percent as the crisis struck. Latin America experienced a total reversal in the investment rate. In the second half of the 1980s, higher expectations in the hemisphere led to a recovery in investment.

In Costa Rica, El Salvador, and Guatemala, income decreased between 20 and 36 percent in the five years between 1980 and 1984, as Figure 3-2 testifies. In Nicaragua the income drop occurred earlier and led to a 45 percent decline in average income per capita between 1977 and 1984. Honduras, starting at lower income levels, experienced milder fluctuations. During the recovery of the 1990s, only Costa Rica attained its precrisis income levels. The considerable decline in the early 1980s occurred in spite of other factors that could have lessened the shock. First, regional trade was growing at very high rates in the early 1980s.[7] Second, unlike what occurred elsewhere in Latin America, and mainly for political reasons, credits by foreign governments remained available to Central America throughout the decade. The region's poor economic performance in the 1980s thus has to be ascribed substantially to the violent conflicts in which it became enmeshed and to a model of economic growth based on exports of primary commodities, a model that made Central America particularly vulnerable to fluctuations in world markets.

7. This growth was due to purchases by Nicaragua on credit. According to Bulmer-Thomas (1987), later difficulties in repaying these debts would harm the cause of regional integration.

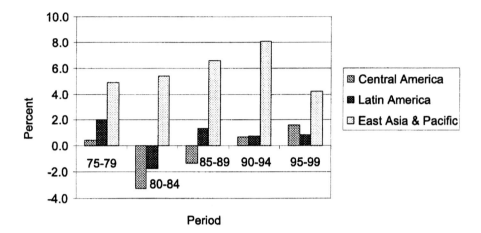

Figure 3-1.   Growth in Per Capita GNP—Central America, Latin America, and East Asia

THE CRISIS OF THE EIGHTIES

Three dimensions to the Central American crisis of the 1980s are worth examining. The first is the interruption of international capital flows, resulting in the debt crisis. The second is the external trade shock, related to import-substitution policies in Latin America as a whole but compounded, in

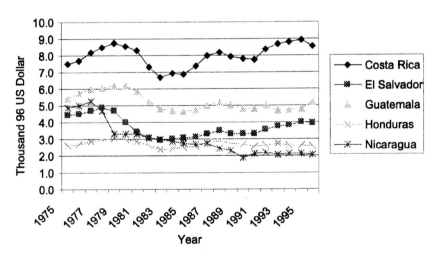

Figure 3-2.   Income Per Capita—Central America 1975–1998
Source: World Bank (1998) and IADB (1999).

Central America, by a negative terms-of-trade shock. Finally, most countries in Central America were directly or indirectly affected by political instability in the region, which evolved into severe military conflicts with a major economic impact.

The Debt Crisis

In the wake of the oil crises of 1973–74 and 1978, Latin America found itself flooded with foreign capital. The influx of petrodollars into the global credit markets, as well as low real interest rates, increased the supply of international loans available to developing countries. The demand for foreign capital, on the other hand, was encouraged by the increases in petroleum prices (in the case of Mexico and Venezuela) and of commodity prices (in the case of Central America). Throughout the 1970s, both private and public sectors in Latin America accumulated substantial obligations in floating-interest-rate external debt with commercial banks. Between 1975 and 1982, Latin America's ratio of foreign debt to GDP increased from 21 percent to 44 percent of GDP.[8] In the same period, Central America's average external-debt obligations increased from 31 percent to 77 percent of GDP. These dramatic increases in indebtedness were further influenced by the liberal way in which the international financial community, including commercial banks, made funds available to Latin American countries.

In 1982, an exogenous shock in the form of recession in the industrialized countries led to a rapid rise in interest rates and a subsequent appreciation in the dollar, as the prices of commodities in world markets fell sharply.[9] The Latin American crisis began in 1982, when Mexico suspended its debt service payments. Commercial banks refused to "roll over" credits to developing countries, which were considered to be at severe risk of defaulting. The reduction in the availability of funds could hardly have been more swift, decreasing by almost 40 percent between 1981 and 1983.[10] Governments in industrialized countries saw Latin America's situation as a short-term liquidity problem and thus refused to "bail out" their commercial banks. As governments and banks in industrialized countries mulled over a possible resolution of the crisis, Latin America continued to accumulate debt. Debt-to-GDP ratios in the region continued to increase until the late 1980s, the result of a vicious cycle whereby devalued currencies and higher interest rates led to costlier interest

---

8. Computations based on World Bank (1998).

9. See Dooley (1994) for an overview of the onset and the development of the debt crisis and Sachs (1985) for the macroeconomic response to indebtedness.

10. See Edwards (1995, 23).

payments. Edwards (1995) estimates that, by 1986, fully 5.3 percent of Latin America's GDP was being spent on interest payments alone. In 1989, voluntary debt-rescheduling agreements under the Brady Plan were signed with several Latin American governments. The amount of debt reduction, however, was limited, especially when new official debt was added to net debt reduction.[11] By 1992, the average ratio of debt to GDP for Latin America had fallen to 38 percent, and to 56 percent for Central America (excluding Nicaragua).[12] However, as new official debt was added to net debt reduction, the amount of debt reduction was limited.[13] Low interest rates in the 1990s facilitated debt repayment but high external indebtedness levels remain a problem for several Latin American countries.

Figures 3-3 to 3-5 and Tables 3-3 to 3-5 present the evolution of overall external debt and its short-term and private nonguaranteed components for Central America, Latin America, and East Asia. The most noticeable feature in Table 3-3 is the substantial jump in external debt as a percentage of GDP in Central America and Latin America. However, even when the atypical case of Nicaragua is excluded, the increase in external debt is more pronounced in Central America than in Latin America—over 27 percent of GDP between the last half of the 1970s and the first half of the 1980s. Costa Rica and Nicaragua (and Honduras later) witnessed the largest increases of external-debt obligations in the region in the 1980s. By the early 1990s, Latin America, unlike Central America, saw its external indebtedness decrease to precrisis levels. (see Figure 3-3). While Costa Rica managed to control the burden of foreign debt in recent years, Nicaragua and Honduras remain largely hostage to their debt obligations.[14] Interestingly, East Asia's external debt obligations increased, slowly but steadily, throughout the decade. By the mid-1990s, East Asia's indebtedness levels were ominously close to those of Latin America in the late 1970s, a strong sign of the crisis to come.

The behavior of short-term and of private, nonguaranteed external-debt flows is probably a better indicator of the radical character of the change in international availability of capital to the Americas. As the crisis developed, the likelihood of countries in Latin America repaying their external debts progressively faded. Domestic and international investors were less and less

---

11. See Dooley (1994, 31).

12. Nicaragua, with a debt-to-GDP ratio in 1992 of 6 percent, raised the regional average to 167 percent of GDP.

13. See Dooley (1994, 31).

14. Costa Rica's external debt decreased at the expense of its domestic debt, which is the highest among countries in the region. Chapter 8 analyzes how high levels of indebtedness affect Honduras and Nicaragua's economic performance and presents the argument for debt relief.

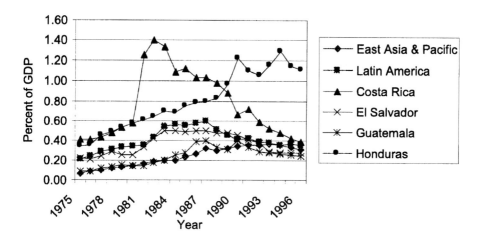

Figure 3-3.   External Debt—Central America, Latin America, and East Asia

willing to hold Latin American currencies or government debt, and short-term as well as nonguaranteed debt fell accordingly. The decrease in private nonguaranteed flows as a fraction of total external debt is particularly drastic in Central America, falling from a high of 33 percent to less than 5 percent by the mid-1980s. Latin America experiences a similar drop a few years later. These nonguaranteed flows start regaining their importance in Latin America and East Asia by 1989, and by 1996 they have tripled to 16 percent, reflecting the renewed international confidence in these economies. Interest-

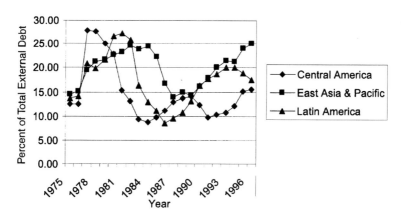

Figure 3-4.   Short-Term Debt—Central America, Latin America, and East Asia

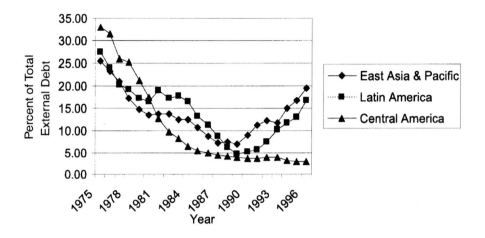

Figure 3-5. *Private Nonguaranteed Debt—Central America, Latin America, and East Asia*

Table 3-3. *External Debt (1975–1998)—Central America, Latin America, and East Asia*

	1975–79	*1980–84*	*1985–89*	*1990–94*
Costa Rica	45.10	113.01	101.28	58.76
El Salvador	24.36	40.12	48.71	35.94
Guatemala	11.59	18.42	34.12	31.25
Honduras	43.11	63.87	82.65	116.80
Nicaragua	66.11	124.79	374.67	717.11
Central America	38.05	72.04	128.29	191.97
Central America w/o Nicaragua	31.04	58.86	66.69	60.69
Latin America & Caribbean	27.46	44.54	53.74	38.84
East Asia	10.24	17.57	28.75	35.21

Source: World Bank (1998).

ingly, this recovery does not occur in Central America, and nonguaranteed private flows remain dormant in the 1990s.[15]

The evolution of short-term debt as a fraction of total foreign debt confirms that the crisis hit Central America before Latin America and had more long-lasting effects. Central America, riding on the export price boom of the late 1970s, dramatically raised its exposure to short-term indebtedness only to see the indebtedness halved in just five years. Latin America's access to

---

15. See Figures 3-3 and 3-4.

Table 3-4. *Short-Term External Debt (1975–1998)ᵃ—Central America, Latin America and East Asia*

	1975–79	1980–84	1985–89	1990–94
Costa Rica	15.86	16.28	11.93	9.39
El Salvador	19.48	13.75	8.89	6.61
Guatemala	29.80	12.06	11.01	15.01
Honduras	12.13	11.24	11.96	5.74
Nicaragua	28.24	16.15	17.93	18.21
Central America	**21.10**	**13.90**	**12.35**	**10.99**
Central America w/o Nicaragua	**19.32**	**13.33**	**10.95**	**9.19**
Latin America & Caribbean	**18.06**	**21.76**	**10.64**	**18.50**
East Asia	**18.40**	**23.80**	**16.42**	**19.34**

Source: World Bank (1998).
ᵃAs a percent of total external debt.

Table 3-5. *Private Nonguaranteed Debt (1975–1998)ᵃ—Central America, Latin America, and East Asiaᵇ*

	1975–79	1980–84	1985–89	1990–94
Costa Rica	24.72	10.59	6.71	7.44
El Salvador	34.64	10.63	3.65	0.69
Guatemala	30.41	12.93	4.26	4.67
Honduras	19.74	9.58	3.68	2.18
Central America w/o Nicaragua	**27.38**	**10.93**	**4.58**	**3.75**
Latin America & Caribbean	**21.66**	**17.36**	**8.94**	**8.11**
East Asia	**20.32**	**13.18**	**8.27**	**11.86**

Source: World Bank (1998).
ᵃAs a percent of total external debt.
ᵇData for Nicaragua are not available.

short-term credit drops by similar amounts a few years later, but recovers in the early 1990s.[16] This recovery is more decisive than Central America's.[17]

The first sign of impending crisis was the loss in reserves held by financial institutions (see Table 3-6). Costa Rica, Guatemala, and Honduras experienced the first losses just before 1980. The Salvadoran and Nicaraguan institution lost reserves only after 1982, but the Nicaraguan reversal was significantly larger than that of its regional partners, with losses of international reserves amounting to 3 percent of national product. Following close on the reserve reversal, capital flight took hold. Net foreign assets became negative, first in Costa Rica and El Salvador, and later in the other countries in the re-

16. See Larraín (1997).
17. See Figures 3-3 to 3-5.

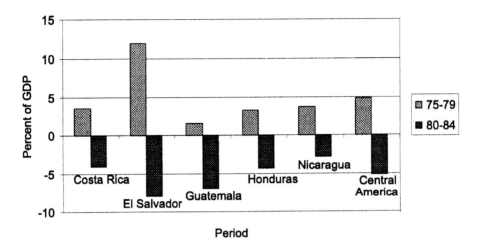

Figure 3-6. *Change in Terms of Trade*

gion. Again, Nicaragua seemed to suffer the most, with terms-of-trade shocks and the debt crisis being compounded by the closing down of commercial relations with the United States. The decline in capital flows exposed the deficit in the current account. In addition to a decrease of inflows there was an increase in the outflow of capital to the United States. In Central America, the determinants of these flows were the expectation of exchange-rate devalua-

Table 3-6. *Change in Reserves and Foreign Assets—Central America, Argentina, and Brazil*

	Change In Net Reserves[ab]			Net Foreign Assets[ac]		
	1977–79	*1980–82*	*1983–85*	*1977–79*	*1980–82*	*1983–85*
Costa Rica	−0.48	−1.62	−0.51	4.06	−8.19	5.81
El Salvador	0.23	1.69	−0.53	6.04	−4.65	0.06
Guatemala	−1.36	2.40	−0.61	11.43	2.64	−3.43
Honduras	−1.65	2.82	0.73	6.83	0.43	−4.57
Nicaragua	1.31	1.49	−3.09	−6.56	−16.22	−50.52

Source: World Bank (1998).
[a]Change in net reserves and net foreign assets as percentage of gross domestic product at market prices.
[b]Change in net reserves is the net change in a country's holdings of international reserves resulting from transactions on the current, capital, and financial accounts. These include changes in holdings of monetary gold, SDRs, foreign exchange assets, reserve position in the International Monetary Fund, and other claims on nonresidents that are available to the central authority. The measure is net of liabilities constituting foreign authorities' reserves, and counterpart items for valuation changes and exceptional financing items.
[c]Net foreign assets is the sum of foreign assets held by monetary authorities and deposit money banks, less their foreign liabilities.

Table 3-7. *Inflation Rate (1975–1998)—Central America, Latin America, and East Asia*

	1975–79	1980–84	1985–89	1990–94	1995–98
Costa Rica	8.05	37.98	16.21	18.57	16.4
El Salvador	13.17	13.74	23.30	15.74	6.7
Guatemala	11.17	6.10	18.03	21.42	8.9
Honduras	7.92	9.89	4.91	19.71	21.8
Nicaragua	14.86	29.06	3368.10	2096.43	11.9
Central America	**11.03**	**19.35**	**686.11**	**434.37**	**13.14**
Central America w/o Nicaragua	**10.07**	**16.93**	**15.62**	**18.86**	**13.45**
Latin America & Caribbean	—	—	—	—	**21.7**

Source: World Bank (1998); IADB (1999) for the period 1995–1998.

tion and the higher political risk associated with the heightening of social tensions. The first reason is clearly not the whole story since capital flight was important in El Salvador and Guatemala despite their history of exchange-rate stability.[18] Thus, much of the capital flight responded to political instability and was not temporary in nature.[19]

The crisis of the 1980s found many Latin American governments running primary budget deficits to finance large public sectors, namely public industries and utilities, which had come to rely on public support.[20] Quasi-fiscal deficits had also increased as central banks became each economy's "borrower of first resort." Commercial banks were forced to hold government debt through compulsory reserve requirements. The external obligations of the private sector were assumed by the monetary authority lest there be a collapse of the domestic financial system. Fiscal deficits can be financed by a combination of different financing sources.[21] In the case of Latin American countries in the 1980s, since the stock of public debt relative to GDP had grown to dramatic levels by the early 1980s, financing through domestic or international borrowing was not available. Governments therefore increasingly turned to seigniorage to finance budget deficits.[22] The inflation rate in Latin America shows how the re-

18. The Guatemalan and Salvadoran currencies had not seen their rates change against the dollar since 1925 and 1934, respectively. See Chapter 9 for a description of exchange-rate regimes in the region.

19. A related issue is the role of emigrant's remittances as a source of capital during the crisis, which was particularly relevant in the case of El Salvador. See Funkhouser (1992).

20. See Larraín and Selowsky (1991) for the responses of Latin American countries to the economic shocks of the 1970s, focusing on the adjustment of the public sector.

21. The three sources of finance to withstand fiscal deficits are the increase of short- and long-run debt through the sale of bonds; the increase of net foreign debt; and the increase of high-powered money by extending central bank credit to the government.

22. In the extreme case of Argentina, Rodriguez (1994) estimates that 70 percent of the country's primary fiscal deficit was financed through money creation in the period between 1980 and 1989. Although money creation may be noninflationary, its rate of growth, if above the rate of growth of real income, is likely to cause prices to increase.

gion relied on inflationary finance to withstand the shock of the 1980s. In Central America, Costa Rica was the first to experience relatively high rates, and, together with Honduras, still has to lower its inflation rate to single digit levels. As seigniorage became a major source of deficit financing, an inflationary spiral ensued in many Latin economies.[23] This led to hyperinflation in Argentina, Bolivia, Brazil, Nicaragua, and Peru. In the case of Nicaragua, average annual inflation reached 2,151.3 percent between 1987 and 1992, whereas the Latin American average for the same period was 148 percent per year.[24]

Table 3-8 presents the rates of growth of money and prices in Central American countries, Argentina, and Brazil. With the exception of Nicaragua, the Central American countries relied much less on money creation than the Latin American countries. Table 3-8 brings to light the clear correspondence between money growth and inflation, across countries and over time.

The macroeconomic imbalances in Latin America were addressed by stabilization programs. In a first stage, governments experimented with heterodox reforms, emphasizing exchange-rate and price controls that aimed at directly controlling inflation. These policies failed; they led only to short-term declines in the inflation rates. By the mid-1980s, a new consensus favored orthodox programs of inflation stabilization, including fiscal restraint and demand management. Similarly, in a first phase of adjustment after the debt crunch, Central American countries paid only lip service to the International Monetary Fund's demand for fiscal and monetary restraint.[25] Central American governments opted for accommodating the outflow of capital and letting foreign reserves run down. This phase came to an end in late 1980 in Costa Rica and El Salvador, 1981 in Honduras, and 1982 in Guatemala.

A second phase of adjustment, adjustment without conditionality,[26] lasted until 1982 in El Salvador, Costa Rica, and Honduras, and until 1983 in Guatemala. Governments tried to stem the outflow of reserves and balance trade flows by relying on the use of import controls such as prior deposits, licenses, and quotas. Several countries introduced systems of multiple exchange rates that awarded the privilege of inexpensive access to imports to special sectors of the economy. These measures, of a clearly interventionist and distortionary character, were not favored by the International Monetary Fund (IMF). Central American governments also exposed themselves to criticism by not showing as much zeal in promoting exports as in suppress-

---

23. Seigniorage refers to the revenue obtained by governmental authorities from the printing of new money.

24. See Edwards (1995).

25. See Bulmer-Thomas (1987).

26. Conditionality refers to the imposition by external actors of important and relevant prerequisites in the process of adjustment, usually as a the counterpart of external assistance.

Table 3-8. *Money^a and Inflation^b—Central America, Argentina, and Brazil*

	Money Growth		Inflation	
	1980–82	1983–85	1980–82	1983–85
Costa Rica	43.39	23.22	48.44	19.87
El Salvador	7.66	18.63	14.63	15.72
Guatemala	12.55	14.26	7.52	8.88
Honduras	12.40	8.50	12.15	5.45
Nicaragua	30.81	99.02	28.02	87.09
Central America	**21.36**	**32.73**	**22.15**	**27.40**
Argentina	110.43	494.77	140.00	546.92
Brazil	77.85	242.80	—	182.10

Source: World Bank (1998).
^aYearly change in money and quasi-money growth for the period. Average annual growth rate in money and quasi-money. Money and quasi-money comprise the sum of currency outside banks, demand deposits other than those of the central government, and the time, savings, and foreign currency deposits of resident sectors other than the central government. This definition is frequently called M2.
^bInflation as measured by the consumer price index reflects the annual percentage change in the cost to the average consumer of acquiring a fixed basket of goods and services.

ing imports. As a result of the measures taken during this adjustment phase, international transactions decreased, and an economic downturn soon followed Simultaneously, the fiscal situation deteriorated as public revenues declined and budget deficits increased. By 1982, Costa Rica's total public revenues had fallen to 82 percent of their 1979 level. Revenues in El Salvador and Guatemala were down to about 62 percent their 1979 levels by, respectively, 1983 and 1984. These dramatic changes occurred in spite of a stable share of public revenues in the national product for Costa Rica and El Salvador and a small decrease of 2.5 percent in Guatemala. In Nicaragua, the situation was entirely different: in spite of a much larger fall in the national product, the share of current public revenues increased from a mere 14 percent to a full 39 percent between 1979 and 1984.[27] Efforts to decrease expenditure were cut short by increased military needs so that the public deficit rose continually.

A third phase of adjustment in Central America saw the IMF giving its approval to stand-by credit facilities as a response to macroeconomic adjustment programs that were comprehensive and eventually included substantial fiscal measures. Agreements were reached with El Salvador (July 1982), Honduras (November 1982), Costa Rica (December 1982), and Guatemala (September

---

27. Revenues as share of GDP fluctuated between 36 percent and 39 percent and back to 36 percent in the years 1983 to 1985, but real revenues barely changed. This may be an instance of

1983).[28] In all these adjustments, the focus became the budget deficit and the emphasis was thus put on raising revenues and decreasing expenditures. The IMF showed its eagerness to restrain the operations of government-owned companies, in recognition of their role in increasing external indebtedness.[29] In spite of the willingness of the local cabinets to comply with the IMF's program, support in congress tended not to materialize as there was little public acceptance of the austerity measures. The norm was for fiscal measures to be reversed soon after they were implemented. On the external front, more emphasis this time was put on promoting exports. This resulted in part from the launch of the Caribbean Basin Initiative in 1984, which offered duty-free entry into the U.S. market of exports from most Central American and Caribbean countries for a period of twelve years.[30] The use of tax-credit certificates became a popular government initiative, promoting nontraditional exports to countries outside Central America. Costa Rica introduced the most conspicuous scheme to subsidize extraregional exports, known as Certificados de Abonos Tributários (CATs). All of these programs, however, entailed costs.[31]

The Central American countries expected the painful phase of adjustment to open the door to new credits and the rescheduling of old debts on more favorable terms. This promise did not materialize. Official lending, mostly from the United States, partially compensated for the lack of capital resources available to respond to the intensity of conflicts in the region. However, a measure of the legacy of the lost decade in Central America is given in Table 3-9, which shows how interest payments as a share of national product tripled in the region in the decades after 1975.

Import-Substitution Policies and Terms-of-Trade Shocks

In the mid-1980s, Latin America undertook aggressive trade reforms targeted at eliminating protectionist and government-led industrialization policies that had been in place since the mid-1940s. The crisis of the 1980s

---

reaching the flat portion of the Laffer curve, which proposes an inverse U relationship between tax rates and tax revenues.

28. No agreement was reached with Nicaragua.

29. The so-called investment corporations in Costa Rica, Guatemala, and Honduras supported inefficient private companies and were notable loss-makers. See Bulmer-Thomas (1987).

30. The countries which were excluded, for political reasons, included Cuba and Nicaragua.

31. This scheme was introduced in 1972 and gained momentum in 1984. By 1992, almost all nontraditional exports were subsidized, even though only exports to countries outside the region benefited from tax exemptions. Nontraditional exports indeed rose sharply but the fiscal cost, rising to around 1.2 percent of GDP in 1989, raised doubts about the program. Willmore (1997) shows how the rise in extraregional exports was mostly due to a substitution away from intraregional exports. Nevertheless, some observers credit this program for the degree of diversification of Costa Rican exports, which are the highest in the region.

Table 3-9. Interest Payments (1975–1998)[a]—Central America and Latin America

	1975	1985	1994
Costa Rica	6.62	8.95	16.24
El Salvador	2.19	9.11	13.28
Guatemala	5.99	8.95	11.70
Nicaragua	10.27	6.32	20.31
Central America w/o Honduras	**6.27**	**8.33**	**15.38**
Latin America & Caribbean	**6.31**	**9.03**	**13.42**

Source: World Bank (1998).
[a]In percent of current government revenue. Data for Honduras are not available.

brought a new consensus based on the need to restructure import-substitution industrialization. Latin America's external sector had become the most distorted in the world and the growth of exports was found lacking.[32] The dramatic reversal in trade policy has been characterized as the area where stabilization reform programs had their deepest and most long-lived effects.[33]

Import-substitution policies had originated in a reaction to the exogenous shocks experienced by Latin America in the 1930s and 1940s. The drop in commodity prices during the Great Depression, and the capacity shortages caused by World War II, suggested the adoption of inward-looking policies as the region's strategy to escape from dependence on unstable, "unfair" world markets. Policymakers maintained that developing countries needed to diversify their trade portfolios by reducing the focus on primary commodity exports and instituting temporary protection of the manufacturing sector. In addition, proponents of import substitution argued that a successful strategy to develop a manufacturing base required state intervention to promote investment and growth.[34] Though the intent of import substitution had been to promote nontraditional exports, the net effect was to discourage export activities altogether. The main tools of import-substitution policies were high average levels and dispersion of tariffs and paratariffs for imported intermediate materials, the adoption of nontariff barriers, and the promotion of appreciated exchange rates.[35] The high levels of effective protection and over-

32. Edwards (1994, 1) presents tariff and nontariff rates for the region.
33. See Loayza and Palacios (1997).
34. See Cardoso and Helwege (1992).
35. Import substitution led to overvalued exchange rates as a result of several specific policies. First, Latin American governments preferred to use exchange rates, rather than interest rates, to fight inflation in the post–World War II period. The idea was to subsidize interest rates in order to promote investment in capital goods and manufactured exports. Second, heavy borrowing from abroad during the 1970s and 1980s contributed to the appreciation of the real exchange rate. Finally, policies such as multiple exchange rates were intended to give targeted support to key industries but also led to the rise of the black-market premium on foreign exchange.

valued exchange rates in Latin America resulted in a lack of export competitiveness.

By the mid-1980s, protectionist policies had expanded to most sectors of the economy: the average non-weighted total tariff rate on imports was over 50 percent in 1985, and roughly 28 percent of imports were subject to non-tariff barriers.[36] There was also great dispersion between the minimum and maximum import tariff rate. Central America was the region with the highest degree of protection in terms of tariff and nontariff rates. In the 1980s, the coverage of nontariff barriers reached almost 100 percent and tariff protection averaged 66 percent in Central America.

The world recession of the early 1980s, following on the heels of the oil crisis of 1979–1980, had a substantial impact in Central America. The impact of higher world interest rates, which increased the debt burden precisely as foreign credit dried up on Latin America and, reflexively, on Central America, is not to be ignored. Central America experienced a major boom in export prices followed by a significant bust. Table 3-10 presents the change in terms of trade, in purchasing power of exports, and in export intensity for Central America beginning in the mid-1970s (see also Figures 3-3 through 3-6). All the countries in Central America experienced positive terms-of-trade shocks in the late 1970s that were reversed in the early 1980s. This was the result of a dramatic fall in the price of coffee, as the price of oil increased in the wake of the second oil shock. While the price of bananas remained relatively stable, the price of coffee went from $5,174 per metric ton in 1977 to $3,400 in 1980 and $2,902 in 1983.[37] El Salvador and Guatemala, the most dependent on coffee exports, indeed experienced the most radical negative terms-of-trade shocks in the 1980–84 period.

The change in the purchasing power of exports is more pronounced than the change in the terms of trade. The fall in the purchasing power of exports reflects both the diminished volume of exports and the negative shock to terms of trade. Since gross national product was falling in the first half of the 1980s, the fall in exports as a share of national product implies a major fall in absolute export volume. The countries in the region, which share very similar export structures, were subject to contemporaneous external shocks. The deterioration in the terms of trade led to a balance-of-payments crisis and a liquidity crisis in the region. By contrast, in the aftermath of the oil crisis of 1973–74, adjustment had been averted thanks to the increase in coffee prices.[38]

---

36. See Edwards (1994, 19).
37. See Urrutia (1991).
38. $1,109 per metric ton in 1972 to $5,174 in 1977. See Urrutia (1991).

Table 3-10. *External Shocks—Central America*

	Exports[a]		Terms-of-Trade Shocks[b]		Purchasing Power Parity[c]	
	1975–79	1980–84	1975–79	1980–84	1975–79	1980–84
Costa Rica	−0.63	1.58	3.61	−3.97	7.05	−2.51
El Salvador	0.79	−2.48	11.93	−7.87	11.69	−9.20
Guatemala	−0.08	−1.84	1.54	−6.92	5.45	−7.98
Honduras	1.19	−2.30	3.23	−4.21	17.15	−4.10
Nicaragua	2.75	−1.56	3.72	−2.74	7.42	−2.88
Central America	**0.80**	**−1.32**	**4.80**	**−5.14**	**9.75**	**−5.33**

Source: Exports as share of GDP from World Bank (1998). Terms of trade and purchasing power of exports based on Bulmer-Thomas (1987), statistical appendix.
[a]Change in exports as share of GDP between the two end dates.
[b]Change in terms of trade and change in purchasing power of exports is the yearly average for the period.

The adjustment programs of the 1980s eventually put the emphasis on the promotion of nontraditional exports, a move promptly accepted by the multilateral institutions such as the World Bank and the I M F. The ratification of the Caribbean Basin Initiative and regional industrial policies helped to diversify exports, initiating the rise of textiles and apparel as major export sectors in Central America. But regional trade integration was not furthered for two reasons: the development of the Central American Common Market (CACM) was not on the United States' agenda (mainly for political reasons),[39] and the import-substitution policies of the CACM did not appeal to international organizations. The withering of regional integration in the 1980s had the effect of depriving Central American entrepreneurs of access to a wider market between their protected national markets and the world.[40] Although intraregional trade boomed in the early 1980s, it later declined in response to the introduction of import restrictions in the first adjustment programs. These restrictions tended, for the most part, to affect consumption goods, which constituted the bulk of regional trade transactions. Other factors, such as unpaid intercountry trade-related debts, increased exchange-rate instability. Political instability also affected trade flows. Finally, the mere fall in incomes had a significant negative effect on trade flows. As far as trade policy goes, the interests of the countries in the region and those of the external powers did not always coincide. In the fiscal policy area, by contrast, a broader consensus was more easily achieved.

The change in reserves alluded to in the previous section could be due to a

39. According to Bulmer-Thomas (1987), there was a perception that a revival of the CACM would benefit all countries, including Nicaragua.
40. See Chapter 5 in this volume for an account of the development phases of the CACM.

Table 3-11.   *Trade Balance—Central America, Latin America, and East Asia*

	1975–79	1980–84	1985–89	1990–94
Costa Rica	−7.61	−2.54	−2.17	−4.65
El Salvador	−3.04	−4.78	−7.20	−14.42
Guatemala	−3.98	−3.37	−3.40	−6.60
Honduras	−5.50	−5.63	−4.28	−7.52
Nicaragua	0.75	−14.43	−18.01	−27.28
Central America	−3.88	−6.15	−7.01	−12.09
Central America w/o Nicaragua	**−5.03**	**−4.08**	**−4.26**	**−8.30**
Latin America & Caribbean	**−1.89**	**1.16**	**2.85**	**0.30**
Argentina	1.69	1.37	3.48	0.33
Brazil	−2.05	0.95	3.85	2.13
East Asia & Pacific	**0.36**	**−0.13**	**−0.69**	**0.12**

Source: World Bank (1998).

deterioration in the trade balance or in the current account balance. The difference is that a deficit in the trade balance signals the country's inability to obtain foreign currency by exporting more than it imports. In other words, a possible response to the lower availability of foreign funds is to turn the trade balance into a surplus. By definition, a deficit in the current account must be covered by either a surplus in the capital account or by foreign exchange reserve losses. In the absence of changes in reserves, the current account deficit is therefore equivalent to a net inflow of capital. As Table 3-11 highlights, a move toward a trade surplus was the response to the lower availability of capital in Argentina, Brazil, and Latin America at large: the trade balance in these countries progressed toward greater surpluses through the 1980s. That was not the case in Central America: the trade deficit as a share of GDP remained high in all Central America in the 1980s and this situation only became more pronounced in the 1990s. This fact points to the less-diversified export base of the region, correspondingly less capable of responding to external stimuli.

Table 3-11 presents values for the current account balance and shows that, in Central America, only El Salvador partially compensated for the trade deficit with inward flows of capital. Though also in deficit, the current accounts of Argentina and Brazil in the 1980s were closer to balance than Central America's. In Central America, there is evidence that the change in short-term capital flows was responsible for most of the change in reserves for El Salvador, Guatemala, and Nicaragua, probably in response to political as well as economic factors.[41]

The failure of a short-term solution to the debt crisis and the need to ignite

---

41. See Bulmer-Thomas (1987, 238).

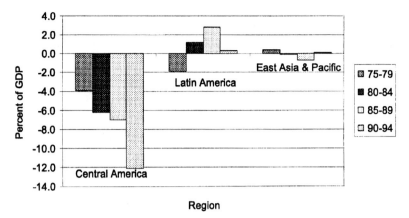

Figure 3-7. **Trade Balance**

Table 3-12. *Current Account Balance—Central America, Latin America, and East Asia*

	1975–79	*1980–84*	*1985–89*	*1990–94*
Costa Rica	−10.53	−10.53	−4.50	−5.06
El Salvador	−1.42	−2.43	0.39	−1.89
Guatemala	−2.69	−3.95	−3.73	−4.49
Honduras	−8.43	−9.52	−4.15	−6.73
Nicaragua	0.55	−20.33	−25.68	−31.69
Central America	**−4.50**	**−9.35**	**−7.53**	**−9.98**
Central America w/o Nicaragua	**−5.77**	**−6.61**	**−3.00**	**−4.55**
Argentina	1.43	−4.10	−2.08	−1.19
Brazil	−4.19	−3.81	−0.22	0.05

Source: World Bank (1998).

export growth led to a search for fundamental changes and, eventually, to the adoption of radical trade-policy reforms. Successful reform programs were characterized by a multitiered approach. For example, Costa Rica promoted its export sector in the early 1990s by using a combination of policies that was part of a larger manufacturing strategy. The plan included a sustained depreciation of the exchange rate, low nontariff barriers, and the implementation of a battery of export promotion schemes, such as tax credits. However, the extent of reform and timing varied across countries. Amongthe reformers were Bolivia, Chile, and Mexico. On the other end of the spectrum, El Salvador, Guatemala, Honduras, and Nicaragua adopted trade reforms only fifteen years after Chile, in the early 1990s. But late reformers were not necessarily less radical in their pursuit. Nicaragua, for instance, cut import tariffs from 110 percent to 15 percent in less than two years. The evidence is that countries that undertook the most radical reforms tended to witness the greatest recovery in the 1990s.[42]

Latin America's trade policy reforms have been unique for many reasons. First, reforms were achieved in a relatively short period of time. Second, contrary to the sequencing advised by several economists, most governments undertook an aggressive reform effort on the trade front prior to achieving macroeconomic stabilization.

Political Instability and Violent Conflict

Central America in the 1980s experienced a progressive descent into political instability and violent conflict, the economic consequences of which paralleled those of the debt crisis. Although the crises did not evolve into full-fledged intercountry conflicts, they nevertheless affected the whole region. Particularly hit were El Salvador, Guatemala, and Honduras, whose internal conflicts took center stage for much of the 1980s. The deterioration in the terms of trade and the closing of access to international finance, in conjunction with political instability, led to a fall in living standards similar to that of the 1930s world depression. As George Irvin (1991) said, "It is generally agreed that the crisis of the 1980s is the most serious Central America has known since the 1930s and, arguably, century. The crisis has combined internal political upheaval and external economic shock in historically unprecedented proportions."

In July 1979, the Somoza dynasty lost its hold on power in Nicaragua after decades of tight grip on the country's political and economic life. This event was seen as a watershed in the region, experienced with a sense of hope but also. Soon after the Nicaraguan revolution the government in El Salvador fell and civil war erupted there in early 1980. In Guatemala dormant internal conflict evolved into full-fledged civil war between 1979 and 1982.

The expropriation of property and the nationalization of mines and banks in Nicaragua only radicalized the regional crisis. More ominous for the region's fortunes in the year to come, a counterrevolutionary army was set up in Nicaragua in 1981, with ample support from the United States. This development coincided with the change from the Carter to the Reagan administration, which froze aid and credit for wheat purchases. The conflict became inextricably linked to the Cold War and, even though there were few substantial U.S. interests at stake, a large symbolic weight was awarded by policymakers to maintaining U.S. dominance in the region.[43]

---

42. See Edwards (1995).

43. As highlighted in Coatsworth (1994), "no U.S. government has ever devoted as much of its own political capital and the nation's resources to Central America as did the Reagan administration between 1981 and 1989."

Other responses were more benign. Economic aid to the region increased and the United States exerted subtle pressures on the IMF for favorable country credit assessments.[44] The most important reaction to Central America's descent into instability was the creation of the Caribbean Basin Initiative, which allowed Central America to export goods free of duties to the United States. Mexico and Venezuela, flooded with increased oil revenues in the wake of the second oil shock, offered special price agreements to Central American countries through the San José oil facility, initiated in 1980.[45] Mexico and Venezuela also supplied substantial bilateral aid.[46] In 1983, these countries joined Colombia and Panama in the Contadora group, a Latin American political initiative to suggest solutions to the regional crisis in Central America. The European Economic Community (EEC) also offered increased aid and political support for a peaceful solution of the conflict.[47] Nicaragua was more and more enmeshed in the Soviet bloc: imports from COMECON countries accounted for 30 percent of imports in 1984, up from 1 percent in 1980. The rest of Nicaragua's financial needs were addressed by the Central American partners through regional indebtedness.

U.S. policies had a "two-track" nature: they both responded to left-wing insurgency and promoted economic and social development. The economic and military objectives were often at odds, not least because of divisions within the U.S. administration itself.[48] U.S. policies toward the region were clearly delineated in the Kissinger report, which emphasized less state intervention, openness to international markets, and general liberalization of the economy.[49] The report recognized the need for social development but was criticized for largely ignoring the potential impact of issues such as the revival of the CACM, broader political and labor participation, and regional vulnerabilities related to food security and dependence on primary exports.[50]

In addition to the economic crisis that affected Latin America as a whole, Central America experienced economic devastation due to civil wars and natural disasters. El Salvador was struck by an earthquake in 1986 and Nicaragua was hit by Hurricane Joan in 1988.[51] As for violent conflict, all the countries

---

44. See Bulmer-Thomas (1987).

45. These agreements included guarantee of oil supplies as well as long-term loans on up to 30 percent of the value of purchases for energy saving projects. See Grayson (1985).

46. Mexico's aid to Guatemala amounted to $500 million in the first five years, a figure not exceeded any other country.

47. The solution was an agreement signed in November 1985 and later supported by Argentina, Brazil, Peru, and Uruguay.

48. See Baloyra (1985) for a critique of the "two-track" policy, and Whitehead (1983) for an examination of the determinants of U.S. policy toward Central America.

49. See Kissinger (1984).

50. See Romero (1985) and Bulmer-Thomas (1988).

51. See Chapter 18 for an evaluation of the region's vulnerability to natural disasters since Hurricane Mitch in 1999.

Table 3-13. *The Cost of War in Central America: 1980–1989*

	Duration of Conflict (years)	Internally & Externally Displaced Persons	Civilian and Military Fatalities	Direct and Indirect Losses (in billions of U.S. dollars)
El Salvador	12	458,600	70,000	1.076
Guatemala	36	—	—	—
Nicaragua	11	487,100	45,000	2.520

Source: Crosby (1990).

with the exception of Costa Rica experienced its direct effects. All of these conflicts were incredibly long-lasting, from eleven years in Nicaragua to a protracted conflict in Guatemala that by 1989 had lasted for 36 years. The human and material costs have been enormous and their effects on human life, migrations, and property still mark Central America today.

Table 3-13 presents figures that quantify the costs of war in Central America in human as well as economic terms. At 1990 levels, roughly 9 percent of El Salvador's population and 14 percent of Nicaragua's population were displaced by war. While some refugees remained within domestic borders, many migrated to the United States and nearby countries such as Mexico and Costa Rica. The major cities in war-torn countries experienced significant population increases a rural inhabitants tried to diminish their exposure to the conflict zones. These large population shifts also reduced the supply of skilled and white-collar labor.

The deterioration in infrastructure and property has been substantial in El Salvador and Nicaragua. El Salvador's educational crisis provides a glimpse of the repercussions of war on the provision of government services and the functioning of institutions. During the conflict, over six hundred schools were closed in rural conflict areas. Students interrupted their studies or flooded into crowded urban schools. The educational institutions that did remain in operation were severely constrained since the state had significantly reduced its spending for social services.[52] As for the production sectors, agriculture was the hardest hit. In the case of Nicaragua, the economic losses were even greater due to the U.S. embargo. Of the $2.5 billion in total damages, nearly 1.1 billion has been estimated as the indirect cost of the loss of Nicaragua's access to the U.S. market. During the Sandinista years, the country was forced to find alternative markets for its exports, and to import goods at higher costs from the Soviet bloc. Lacking repair supplies, many of these goods became obsolete, further reducing productivity. In the countries affected by war, a smaller percentage of foreign aid was committed to recon-

---

52. See Crosby (1990, 108).

struction relative to military assistance. Crosby (1990) estimates total military and economic assistance to Central America between 1981 and 1990 to be $12 billion.

On the political front, formal elections were run but progress toward democratization came to a halt in the region, the exception being Costa Rica. While the Reagan administration emphasized the need for democratization, the U.S. armed forces in El Salvador, Guatemala, and Honduras pursued policies that often ran contrary to democratization.[53]

The Recovery of the Nineties

Macroeconomic Stabilization and Reform

Beginning in the second half of the 1980s, Central America gradually began to recover from the economic and political crisis. The recovery took various forms in the different countries. Even though macroeconomic reforms have been put in place in several sectors of the economy, much remains to be completed. As was the case in other Latin American countries, Central American countries that responded early came out of the contraction of the 1980s earlier. Costa Rica and El Salvador are the most striking examples in Central America in the areas of trade liberalization and the deepening of the financial system. The growth rates of per capita GNP in these countries were in excess of 3 percent a year in the first half of the 1990s (see Table 3-1).

Positive rates of GDP growth in the post–1982 period were usually the first indication of economic recovery. This was the case in Costa Rica, which, as early as 1983, experienced an economic turnaround with annual growth equal to 2.7 percent. After a brief slowdown in 1985, Costa Rica grew consistently from 1986 onward. Honduras' recovery began in 1984 at a slightly lower growth rate than that of Costa Rica. The countries in conflict, El Salvador, Guatemala and Nicaragua, experienced very low to negative growth rates throughout the 1980s. Nicaragua lived through one of the worst growth experiences, its per capita GNP decreasing at rates of 8 percent and 3 percent annually in the second half of the 1980s and the first half of the 1990s, respectively. By 1995, all five Central American economies were growing at positive rates. The regional average growth rate went from 0.67 percent to 1.26 percent in the 1990–94 and 1995–98 periods.

The reform process in Central America included the liberalization of trade

---

53. The increased importance of the military did not stifle political development in the case of Honduras, where the military was a stabilizing influence. See Bulmer-Thomas (1987).

flows in the context of a general outward orientation of the economies, as well as macroeconomic stabilization. Both policies contrasted with the previous era of trade protectionism and deficit spending.

Trade Liberalization

Trade liberalization comprised lowering tariff barriers, promoting nontraditional exports, unifying exchange rates, and allowing exporters to access intermediate and capital goods at international prices. In terms of trade liberalization, Central America followed Latin America in what Loayza and Palacios (1997) have named the "deepest and most generalized" of the areas of economic reform, and came quite close to the Asian Newly Industrialized Countries in terms of export orientation. In 1986, Costa Rica became the first country in Central America to liberalize trade and one of the first in Latin America.[54] Costa Rica's trade strategy included avoiding an appreciation of the exchange rate,[55] lowering nontariff barriers, and implementing a battery of export-promotion schemes. Costa Rica drastically reduced its average level of tariff protection from 92 in 1985 to 16 in 1992.[56] Tariff dispersion was also cut: whereas tariffs were between 1 percent and 100 percent of import value in 1986, they had decreased to between 5 percent and 20 percent by 1991. Nontariff barriers, even though covering only 0.8 percent of imports in Costa Rica, were eliminated in 1991.[57] The remaining component in Costa Rica's successful program was the real devaluation against the dollar, which reduced the country's antiexport bias and helped to sustain a relatively constant real exchange rate.[58]

El Salvador, Guatemala, Honduras, and Nicaragua followed trade liberalization strategies similar to those adopted by Costa Rica. Several special features should be noted, however. First, the initial levels and coverage of nontariff barriers were higher in these countries, and reductions in nontariff barriers were more gradual. Honduras, for instance, opted for converting trade-protection schemes into equivalent import tariffs before phasing them out entirely. Second, El Salvador, Guatemala, Honduras, and Nicaragua were latecomers to the wave of liberalization reforms occurring in Latin America.

54. The first Latin American country to initiate trade liberalization was Chile in 1975. Uruguay followed in 1978. Bolivia, Costa Rica, and Mexico were the next line of reformers in 1986. For details see Edwards (1994a) and Edwards (1995).

55. Costa Rica opted for abandoning the fixed exchange rate with the U.S. dollar after the 1974 and 1981 oil shocks. In each case, the country underwent a large devaluation.

56. Tariffs and paratariffs, as estimated in Edwards (1994a, 23).

57. Compared with tariffs in other Central American countries of almost 100 percent in the eighties, which were also reduced in the early nineties.

58. See Chapter 9 in this volume for the evolution of real exchange rates in Central America.

Third, real exchange-rate management policies diverged from those of Costa Rica. Devaluations in these other countries occurred later in the 1980s.[59] Guatemala and El Salvador abandoned their fixed-exchange-rate regime with the U.S. dollar in 1986, while Honduras preserved its fixed exchange rate with the U.S. dollar until 1990. Nicaragua maintained fixed exchange rates throughout the 1980s, which resulted in an effective real-exchange-rate appreciation that reduced the country's competitive position.

The result of Central America's successful trade liberalization was an increase in overall export volumes and some diversification of the export base. In the five years after 1982, Costa Rica increased its nontraditional exports by almost 50 percent, from 23 percent to 34 percent of total exports.

Macroeconomic Stabilization

In order to restore macroeconomic stability and generate sufficient revenues to honor their external-debt obligations, Latin American governments adopted several policies to reestablish fiscal balance. The reduction of budget deficits and inflation were the avowed goals of these programs. Policies to increase public-sector revenues were unfeasible, so governments initially focused their efforts on decreasing budget deficits and halting money creation. Central American governments, with the exception of Costa Rica, introduced fiscal austerity measures as part of stabilization.[60] The most remarkable turnaround in public-sector balances in Central America took place in Nicaragua. The Chamorro administration transformed a 17.8 percent deficit in 1990 into a 4 percent surplus in 1991. In terms of reducing public-sector bureaucracy, the performance of El Salvador was also remarkable, leading Loayza and Palacios (1997) to classify it as one of the top three Latin American countries to significantly decrease public-sector employment between 1985 and 1995.

The debt crisis had caused a rise in inflationary financing as governments scrambled for alternative sources other than external borrowing to finance fiscal deficits. A critical component in the stabilization period thus became

---

59. For decades, Central America had effectively used fixed nominal exchange rates relative to the U. S. dollar as a way to maintain low inflation levels. The crisis of the 1980s caused an appreciation in the real exchange rate for all five countries, but Central American governments were reluctant to devalue for fear of further inflation. Nevertheless, Costa Rica's earlier devaluation resulted in a faster resumption of economic growth. The other four Central America nations that chose to maintain nominal fixed-exchange-rate regimes required larger devaluations (in magnitude) and recovered less quickly.

60. Costa Rica continued to run fiscal deficits and spent a fairly large proportion of government expenditures on public salaries throughout the 1980s and early 1990s. For example, Loayza and Palacios (1997) report that nearly 50 percent of Costa Rica's primary government expenditures went toward public employees' salaries in the mid-1990s.

the reduction of inflation. Nicaragua illustrates the extreme case of inflation stabilization in Central America. The combination of a trade embargo by the United States and the halt in international lending[61] caused Nicaragua to rely increasingly on money creation so that, by the late 1980s, hyperinflation spiraled out of control. The end of the trade embargo and the offer of substantial foreign aid in the wake of Violetta Chamorro's election in 1990 allowed a tightening of monetary policy and the institution of a currency peg versus the U.S. dollar.[62] The importance of foreign aid flows in ameliorating Nicaragua's macroeconomic crisis should not be overlooked. In 1991, Nicaragua received $715 million in donations from foreign governments and multilateral organizations. This amount represented more than "three times the value of the total gross international reserves of the country's financial reserves at the end of the previous year."[63] These actions curbed Nicaragua's annual inflation an average of 11 percent a year in the late 1990s (see Tables 3-3 to 3-7).

As liberalization and stabilization programs were pursued, Central American governments became acutely aware of their overreliance on seigniorage and trade taxes as the primary sources of revenue. The five countries undertook structural reforms aimed at reducing the distortionary effects of taxation, increasing revenue collection efforts, and fighting tax evasion.[64] Although reforms varied between countries, there were common themes. Governments tried to rely more on indirect taxes than on domestic goods, and by 1992, all five Central American countries had adopted a value-added tax (VAT).[65] The major benefit of a value-added-tax regime is that it is relatively more effective at revenue collection, especially in countries with weak tax-administrative systems such as those in Central America. Because VAT regimes tax transactions between agents, they are more effective instruments in environments where tax evasion is a problem. Yet, in an analysis of the effectiveness of VAT systems, Loayza and Palacios (1997) conclude that few Cen-

---

61. Starting in 1985, the United States imposed a trade embargo on Nicaragua, a significant blow to its ability to earn foreign currency, since the United States had been Nicaragua's major trading partner.

62. In the 1980s, the cordoba had become appreciated against the U.S. dollar. Before instituting a currency peg, the Nicaraguan government devalued the cordoba by 80 percent during the first phase of stabilization in 1991.

63. Economist Intelligence Unit (1998, 25).

64. See the Chapter on Fiscal Policy for an account of these fiscal reform programs.

65. El Salvador was the last country in the region to adopt the VAT; it did so in 1992. Costa Rica, Honduras, and Nicaragua had adopted the VAT in the mid-1970s, and Guatemala adopted it in 1983.

tral American countries have achieved acceptable collection levels measured in terms of trade-adjusted productivity.[66]

Central American governments also undertook significant reforms of their corporate and personal income-tax systems. All five countries reduced the top corporate income tax rate, and Costa Rica, El Salvador, and Guatemala also cut the top rate for personal income taxes. The minimum personal tax rate was increased in Costa Rica and El Salvador, while it remained unchanged or fell in the remaining Central America republics. In most countries, tax laws were instituted to treat capital gains as ordinary income.[67] Withholding taxes on foreign remittances were increased in all countries except El Salvador.

The experience of Central America in the 1990s demonstrates that economic reforms had an impact on the resumption of economic growth in the region. Trade liberalization and fiscal and monetary stabilization, in particular, provided economic agents with the proper signals in the form of undistorted international prices and reasonable interest and exchange rates. These are the basis of an economic environment that is conducive to investment and growth. However, the relatively low growth rates in Central America, when compared with Latin America and East Asia, suggest that much more needs to be done if higher rates of growth are to be attained.

How Competitive is Central America?

In this section we will evaluate Central America's competitiveness relative to Latin America and East Asia. The objective is to assess the recent progress of the regions in different policy sectors and point to the areas most in need of reforms. The successful economies of East Asia and other Latin American countries will provide a benchmark.

In this section we will use the Central American Global Competitiveness Reports for the years 1997 through 1999, which rank the competitiveness of Costa Rica, El Salvador, Guatemala, Honduras, and Nicaragua in comparison with 57 other countries.[68] These reports construct an index of competitiveness from a considerable number of economic indicators. The objective is to obtain an index that correlates closely with economic growth so that the more

---

66. The authors note that only two out of five countries in the region, El Salvador and Guatemala, have achieved trade-adjusted VAT productivity rates over 40 percent, which is the threshold level for effective tax collection.

67. Edwards (1995) has argued that a particularly important benefit of tax reform in Latin America during the late 1980s and early 1990s was that it eliminated the uncertainty surrounding capital gains.

68. See Warner (1997) and Warner, Moore, and Tavares (1998; 1999).

Table 3-14.   Competitiveness Ranking 1999—Central America, Latin America, and East Asia

	Costa Rica	El Salvador	Guatemala	Honduras	Nicaragua	Central America	Latin America[a]	East Asia[b]
Global Competitiveness	34	44	50	55	56	48	41	18
Openness	29	48	39	54	37	41	42	21
Government	23	6	9	13	27	16	31	8
Finance	48	42	59	55	52	51	45	17
Infrastructure	48	40	44	56	55	49	40	26
Technology	29	53	55	61	59	51	44	27
Management	35	44	49	57	56	48	36	28
Labor	30	55	60	56	62	53	42	21
Institutions	50	46	55	56	58	53	44	31

Source: Warner, Moore, and Tavares (1999).
[a] Latin America average computed with the rankings for Argentina, Brazil, Chile, Colombia, Mexico, Peru, and Venezuela.
[b] East Asia average includes Hong Kong, Indonesia, Korea, Malaysia, Philippines, Singapore, Taiwan, and Thailand.

competitive a country, the better its prospects for medium-term economic growth.[69] The Global Competitiveness Index builds on the results for eight indexes, relying on both macroeconomic and survey data:

- *Openness.* Measures openness to foreign trade and investment, foreign direct investment and financial flows, exchange rate policy, and ease of exporting.
- *Government.* Measures the role of the state in the economy. This includes the overall burden of government expenditures, fiscal deficits, rates of public saving, marginal tax rates, and the overall competence of the civil service.
- *Finance.* Measures how efficiently the financial intermediaries channel savings into productive investment, the level of competition in financial markets, the perceived stability and solvency of key financial institutions, levels of national saving and investment, and credit ratings given by outside observers.
- *Infrastructure.* Measures the quality of roads, railways, ports, telecommunications, the cost of air transportation, and overall infrastructure investment.
- *Technology.* Measures computer usage, the spread of new technologies, the ability of the economy to absorb new technologies, and the level and quality of research and development.
- *Management.* Measures overall management quality, marketing, staff training and motivation practices, efficiency of compensation schemes, and the quality of internal financial control systems.
- *Labor.* Measures the efficiency and competitiveness of the domestic labor market. It combines a measure of the level of a country's labor costs relative to international norms, together with measures of labor market efficiency, such as obstacles to hiring and firing of workers, the level of basic education and skills, and the extent of distortionary labor taxes.
- *Institutions.* Measures the extent of business competition, the quality of legal institutions and practices, the extent of corruption, and vulnerability to organized crime.

For each factor, the index was built by aggregating the data on several questions pertaining to a certain subindex. We present the results for the 1999 competitiveness rankings in Table 3-14. East Asia ranks better than Central America or Latin America in all subindexes and thus, naturally, in overall competitiveness.[70] While East Asian countries are ranked on average 18th out

---

69. There is indeed a positive relationship on average between the competitiveness index and economic growth: the coefficient on the competitiveness index is significant and this variable accounts for about 40 percent of the cross-country variation in economic growth rates, after the initial level of income is taken into account.

70. The world's most competitive economy is Singapore's, followed by that of the United States, and then Hong Kong. Singapore and Hong Kong owe their position in the ranking to high levels of openness in trade and finance, small government, superb infrastructure, and low levels of corruption. At the other end of the spectrum are Ukraine and Russia, whose rankings reflect the erratic nature of these countries' reforms as they emerge from socialist systems.

of 62 countries, the average Central American ranking is 48, compared to 41 for Latin America. Even if Central America tends to be ranked below the major Latin American countries for the subcategories, it ranks slightly better in international openness and substantially better in the government category.

An analysis by country reveals that Costa Rica tends to fare better than, and El Salvador comes close to, the typical Latin American country. Costa Rica's strengths are openness, government, and technology. El Salvador's are government, finance, and infrastructure. In all these categories, Costa Rica and El Salvador fare better than Latin America as a whole. Guatemala's relative strengths are openness, government, and infrastructure. Honduras and Nicaragua, though close to the bottom of the scale in the competitiveness ranking, fare relatively well in openness and government.

Table 3-15 presents changes in the competitiveness index and its subindexes between 1997 and 1999, the years for which the ranking is available. All the countries in the region have shown progress in their rankings.[71] Guatemala, El Salvador, and Honduras have progressed the most: four and three positions respectively in the ranking. Costa Rica, which started from a substantially better position, shows less progress, and Nicaragua moved up only by one position. Guatemala's improved ranking stems mostly from investment in infrastructure; in this category, the country moved up thirteen places. El Salvador's improvement, on the other hand, derives from a jump of ten positions in the area of finance. Also remarkable are Costa Rica's improvements in the area of government and technology, and Nicaragua's in openness. These are balanced by a degradation of both countries' competitiveness indexes on labor and Costa Rica's on institutions. Central American countries as a whole have tended to improve in the areas of government, infrastructure, finance, and management, and maintained their relative position as far as openness of the economies to trade, in which they fare relatively well. On the other hand, most of the regional losses are in the areas of labor markets, and this factor alone is responsible for the deterioration of the overall ranking.

Finally, Table 3-16 shows selected competitiveness rankings that illustrate some of the strengths and weaknesses of the region and that may determine its economic performance in the medium term. We can see, for example, that El Salvador and Guatemala rank high in the world as far as the character of its administrative regulations goes. They are better positioned than the typical

---

71. Changes are computed after correcting for the addition of Bolivia, Ecuador, and Mauritius in 1999, which influences the relative position of the countries. I ignored the additions and reranked the countries so that any improvement in ranking reflects only a bettering of the country's position relative to the countries in the 1997 sample.

Table 3-15. *Change in Competitiveness Ranking 1997–1999—Central America*

	Costa Rica	El Salvador	Guatemala	Honduras	Nicaragua	**Central America**
Global Competitiveness	2	3	4	3	1	**3**
Openness	−3	−3	2	−7	16	**1**
Government	12	1	4	7	6	**6**
Finance	−1	10	1	1	5	**3**
Infrastructure	0	6	13	3	−3	**4**
Technology	13	4	−5	−1	−1	**2**
Management	4	5	5	0	2	**3**
Labor	−10	4	−3	−6	−26	**−8**
Institutions	−17	6	3	0	−3	**−2**

Source: Warner (1997) and Warner, Moore, and Tavares (1999).

East Asian country in this respect. Central American tax systems are relatively poor and tend to hinder business competitiveness. The composition of public spending is not appropriate in most countries. In regard to the alignment of the exchange rate with economic fundamentals, Costa Rica and El Salvador fare better than East Asia, and Nicaragua is on the Latin American average. In openness to foreign investors and building a competitive advantage based on unique products and processes, only Costa Rica fares better than East Asia. Finally, and somewhat surprisingly, Central American respondents have pointed out unequivocally that strained diplomatic relations with neighbors impose significant costs on business activity. Given the current state of peace, both between and within Central American countries, these answers suggest that business leaders expect benefits from cooperation and integration that are not being reaped.

The analysis of competitiveness rankings reveals that Central American countries share common strengths, namely relatively lean and nonintrusive governments and a high degree of openness to international goods and financial markets. It also reveals country-specific strengths such as the good exposure of Costa Rica to technology, the Salvadoran lead in financial markets, and the Guatemalan success in building proper transport infrastructure.[72] The different success areas of different Central American countries suggest the benefits of sharing experiences and designing policies at the regional level. The overall message is that Central America has managed to make some progress in most areas relevant to a country's competitiveness. This is true

---

72. Chapter 6 in this volume analyzes the consequences of the establishment of Intel, a chip manufacturer, in Costa Rica. Chapters 12 and 20 in Volume II present the infrastructure- and financial-sector developments in the region.

Table 3-16. Selected Competitiveness Rankings 1999—Central America, Latin America, and East Asia

	Costa Rica	El Salvador	Guatemala	Honduras	Nicaragua	Central America	Latin America[a]	East Asia[b]
Regulations	31	8	15	38	48	28	37	26
Tax System	53	45	42	51	55	49	48	24
Public Spending	37	23	43	39	29	34	43	18
Exchange Rate	23	31	53	36	45	38	45	35
Foreign Investors	26	38	54	39	45	40	28	42
Competitive Advantage	27	37	49	42	53	42	36	35
Neighbors	43	45	56	54	49	49	33	38

Source: Warner, Moore, and Tavares (1999).

[a]Latin America average computed with the rankings for Argentina, Brazil, Chile, Colombia, Mexico, Peru, and Venezuela.

[b]East Asia average includes Hong Kong, Indonesia, Korea, Malaysia, Philippines, Singapore, Taiwan, and Thailand.

The questions are: 1. Administrative regulations that constrain business are *pervasive / minimal.* 2. The composition of government spending in your country is *wasteful / provides necessary goods and services that the market does not provide.* 3. The tax system in your country *hinders business competitiveness/ promotes business competitiveness.* 4. The exchange rate of your country is *too high or too low / properly reflects economic fundamentals.* 5. Foreign citizens in your country *are prohibited from investing in stocks and bonds in your country / are free to invest in stocks and bonds in your country.* 6. Competitive advantages of your nation's companies in international markets *are due to low cost labor or natural resources / are due to unique products and processes.* 7. The state of diplomatic relations of your country with neighboring countries *imposes significant costs on business activity in your country / facilitates business activity in your country.*

even when the countries in the region are ranked relative to the most competitive in the world. However, the uneven pace of progress in the same area for different countries as well as the poor absolute positioning of most Central American countries, suggests that much more can be done to improve the region's economic performance.

CONCLUSION

In this chapter, we have reviewed the recent macroeconomic experience of Central American countries, in the context of the Latin American crisis of the 1980s and the subsequent recovery. WEhave found that, beginning with the 1980s, Central America's economic growth has parallels but lags behind Latin American growth, and falls well below East Asian growth rates. The crisis of the 1980s hit Central America particularly hard. The positive rates of absolute and per capita GDP growth in the 1990s are a good sign, but higher growth rates are necessary.

Central America, unlike Latin America, suffered a large positive trade shock in the late 1970s and a negative one in the early 1980s. This is the result of the region's vulnerability to export price fluctuations, which suggests the need for export diversification as insurance against external shocks.

Central America incurred higher levels of indebtedness sooner than the rest of Latin America, and in the 1990s it has not decreased its indebtedness by nearly as much as Latin America. In particular, the high levels of short-term and private nonguaranteed indebtedness were incurred earlier in Central America. These capital flows dried up sooner and did not recover as much in the 1990s. As for the response to the crisis, Central America did not move to positive trade balance, unlike the rest of Latin America, and its policies relied less on money finance and more on international aid. The conclusion from this experience is that Central American countries are especially vulnerable to financial flows and need to focus on attracting long-term capital.

Finally, the crisis of the 1980s and the recovery of the 1990s in the region have demonstrated the huge costs of political instability and war. Countries with serious internal conflicts had larger negative fluctuations in income per capita and lower growth throughout the 1980s. Economic growth has resumed only as peace is attained. The economic benefits of social stability and democratization in Central America have been amply demonstrated and can only be ignored at a substantial cost to the material well-being of the countries in the region.

REFERENCES

Baloyra, E. 1985. "Central America on the Reagan Watch: Rhetoric and Reality." *Journal of Interamerican Studies and World Affairs*: 295–319.

Barro,-Robert-J.; Lee,-Jung-Wha. 1993. "Losers and Winners in Economic Growth." Bruno,-Michael; Pleskovic,-Boris, eds. Proceedings of the World Bank Annual Conference on Development Economics, 1993: Supplement to The World Bank Economic Review and The World Bank Research Observer. Washington, D.C.: World Bank, 1994, pages 267-97.

Bulmer-Thomas, V. 1987. *The Political Economy of Central America Since 1920.* Cambridge: Cambridge University Press.

Bulmer-Thomas, V. 1988. "The Kissinger Report." In *Studies in the Economics of Central America,* edited by V. Bulmer-Thomas. New York: St. Martin's Press.

Cardoso, Eliana, and Ann Helwege. 1992. *Latin America's Economy: Diversity, Trends, and Conflicts.* Cambridge, MA: The MIT Press.

Coatsworth, John. 1994. *Central America and the United States: The Clients and the Colossus.* New York: Twayne Publishers.

Crosby, Benjamin L. 1990. "Central America." In *After the Wars: Reconstruction in Afghanistan, Indochina, Central America, Southern Africa, and the Horn of Africa,* edited by Anthony Lake. New Jersey: Overseas Development Council.

Dooley, Michael. 1994. "A Retrospective on the Debt Crisis." National Bureau of Economic Research (NBER) Working Paper No. 4963.

Economist Intelligence Unit. 1998. "Nicaragua EIU Country Profile 1997–1998."

Edwards, S. 1995. *Crisis and Reform in Latin America: From Despair to Hope.* New York: Published for World Bank by Oxford University Press.

———. 1994a. "Trade Liberalization Reforms in Latin America." In *Latin America's Economic Future,* edited by Graham Bird and Ann Helwege. San Diego: Academic Press.

———. 1994b. "Trade and Industrial Policy Reform in Latin America." National Bureau of Economic Research (NBER) Working Paper, Series No. 4772.

———. 1993. "Exchange Rates, Inflation, and Disinflation: Latin American Experiences." National Bureau of Economic Research (NBER) Working Paper No. 4320.

Edwards, S. and Larraín, F. 1989. "Debt, Adjustment, and Recovery in Latin America: An Introduction." In *Debt, Adjustment and Recovery: Latin America's Prospects for Growth and Development,* edited by S. Edwards and F. Larraín. Oxford and Cambridge, MA.: Blackwell.

Funkhouser, E. 1992. "Mass Emigration, Remittances, and Economic Adjustment: The Case of El Salvador in the 1980s." In *Immigration and the Work Force: Economic Consequences for the United States and Source Areas,* edited by G. Borjas and R. Freeman. National Bureau of Economic Research Project Report. Chicago and London: University of Chicago Press.

Grayson, G. 1985. "The San José Oil Facility." *Third World Quarterly*

Irvin, George. 1991. "New Perspectives for Modernization in Central America." *Development and Change* 22: 93–115.

Kissinger, H. 1984. "Report of the National Bipartisan Commission on Central America." Washington, D.C.: Government Printing Office.

Larraín, F. 1997. "El Retorno de los Capitales Privados a America Latina en la Decada de los Noventa." *Cuadernos-de-Economia* 34 (103): 267-75.

Larraín,, F. and M. Selowski. 1991. *The Public Sector and the Latin American Crisis,* An International Center for Economic Growth Publication. San Francisco, CA: ICS Press.

Loayza, Norman, and Luisa Palacios. 1997. "Economic Reform and Progress in Latin America and the Caribbean." World Bank Policy Research Working Paper No. 1829.

Pearce, Jenny. 1998. "From Civil War to 'Civil Society': Has the End of the Cold War Brought Peace to Central America?" *International Affairs* 74

Robinson, William I. 1998. "Mal-Development in Central America: Globalization and Social Change." *Development and Change* 29: 467–497.

Rodríguez, Carlos. 1994. "Argentina: Fiscal Disequilibria Leading to Hyperinflation." In *Public Sector Deficits and Macroeconomic Performance,* edited by William Easterly, Carlos Alfredo Rodríguez, and Klaus Schmidt-Hebbel. New York: Oxford University Press.

Romero, A. 1985. "The Kissinger Report and the Restoration of U.S. Hegemony." *Millenium* 116–129.

Sachs, J. 1991. "External Debt and Macroeconomic Performance in Latin America and Asia." *Brookings Papers on Economic Activity* 1985:2.

Urrutia, Miguel. 1991. "Long-Term Trends in Latin American Economic Development." Washington, D.C.: Inter-American Development Bank.

Warner, A. 1997. "The Central America Competitiveness Report 1997." Cambridge: Harvard Institute for International Development.

Warner, A., C. Moore, and J. Tavares. 1998. *The Central America Competitiveness Report 1998.* Cambridge: Center for International Development.

———. 1999. *The Central America Competitiveness Report 1999.* Cambridge: Center for International Development.

Whitehead, L. 1983. "Explaining Washington's Central American Policies." *Journal of Latin American Studies* 15 (2): 321–63.

Willmore, Larry. 1997. Promotion of Exports in Central America: An Analysis of Second-Best Policies. New York: United Nations.

4

Economic Growth in Central America: A Long-Run Perspective

GERARDO ESQUIVEL[1]

Central America has undergone major economic, social, and legal changes in the past few years. A number of economic reforms in the region have attempted to transform the natural resource-based economies of this group of small countries into more diverse, outward-oriented ones. The idea underlying these reforms is that the previous pattern of economic development has exhausted any economic growth possibilities and, in fact, has been at the root of some of the economic problems that these countries faced during the 1980s and early 1990s.

In this chapter, the performance of the Central American economies (in terms of both per capita GDP growth and productivity performance) will be viewed from a long-run perspective. In order to understand the factors that may have determined the economic performance of the economies of the region, a determinants-of-growth analysis for a wide sample of countries was conducted and then applied to Central America. In particular we studied how different institutional, political, and economic factors have shaped the pattern of economic growth in Central America since 1960. A series of international comparisons of economic progress with other countries and/or regions of the world were carried out in order to provide a more precise assessment of the long-run performance of the Central American economies. This exercise provided a benchmark to evaluate the performance of each particular Central American country and the region as a whole. Finally, we discussed the use of

1. I wish to acknowledge the helpful comments of Rodrigo Cifuentes, Cristina García-López, Luis Felipe López-Calva and José Tavares, and the excellent research assistance of Ximena Clark.

higher input volumes and technological progress as potential sources of economic growth in Central America.

THE STARTING POINT:
CENTRAL AMERICA'S ECONOMIC SITUATION IN 1950

By 1950, Central American economies were textbook examples of small, open, and agriculture-based developing economies. World War II had recently ended and the region's agricultural products were experiencing an export boom.[2] The terms of trade for these countries were at relatively high levels, and large inflows of foreign exchange allowed them to sustain their fixed exchange rates vis-à-vis the U.S. dollar and to afford the imported manufactured goods they needed to keep growing. A succinct characterization of the Central American countries around this time would certainly emphasize the following elements: their economies were predominantly agricultural, they all had strong U.S. commercial and political ties, their political regimes were relatively unstable, and they all experienced large amounts of external trade relative to their domestic output.[3]

Central American countries in 1950 had an income per capita in 1985 international dollars (that is, using purchasing power parity prices) that ranged between 981 for Honduras and 1532 for Guatemala. Costa Rica, El Salvador, and Nicaragua had an income per capita of 1457, 1206, and 1152 international dollars, respectively. Central America's position relative to other economies in 1950 is shown in Table 4-1.[4] Among other results, this table shows that, by 1950, Central America was already lagging behind certain other regions of the world. Indeed, per capita income in the region was only about one-seventh that of the United States, and about one-third that of some of the richest European countries. Also, the per capita income of Central America was about half the average per capita income of Argentina, Brazil, Chile, and Mexico. However, the Central American countries did not fare as badly when compared to other regions or groups of countries. For example, Central America's average per capita income represented more than 80 percent of the per capita income of the poorest European countries (Greece, Spain, and Portugal), and it was very close to the average of another group of eight Latin

---

2. See Bulmer-Thomas (1987a). The reader is referred to Chapter 2 in this volume for a more detailed analysis of the economic history of Central America.

3. More details on each of these aspects can be found in Bulmer-Thomas (1987a), Perez-Brignoli (1989), Lindenberg (1990), and Weaver (1994).

4. The groupings were defined based on geographical location and data availability. They will be described in more detail later.

A

Table 4-1. Output per Capita in Central America Relative to other Regions, 1950 (in percentages)

	USA	Rich Europe	Latin America 1	Poor Europe	Latin America 2	Asia	Africa
Costa Rica	16.6	33.8	58.7	96.5	113.9	171.1	230.5
El Salvador	13.7	28.0	48.6	79.9	94.3	141.6	190.8
Guatemala	17.5	35.6	61.7	101.5	119.7	179.9	242.3
Honduras	11.2	22.8	39.5	65.0	76.7	115.2	155.2
Nicaragua	13.1	26.8	46.4	76.3	90.0	135.3	182.2
Central America	14.4	29.4	51.0	83.8	98.9	148.6	200.2

Note: Countries were selected based on data availability in 1950 and on population size.
Regional data are unweighted averages and they include the following countries:
Rich Europe: Austria, Belgium, Denmark, Finland, France, Germany, Ireland, Italy, Netherlands, Norway, Sweden, Switzerland, and UK.
Latin America 1: Argentina, Brazil, Chile, and Mexico
Poor Europe: Greece, Portugal, and Spain
Latin America 2: Bolivia, Colombia, Dominican Republic, Ecuador, Paraguay, Peru, Uruguay, Venezuela
Asia: India, Japan, Pakistan, Philippines, and Thailand
Africa: Egypt, Kenya, Morocco, Nigeria, and Uganda.
Source: Calculated from Penn World Table v. 5.6.

merican economies. Moreover, Central America was on average 50 percent and 100 percent richer than a selected group of Asian and African countries, respectively.

LONG-RUN MACROECONOMIC PERFORMANCE

Economic Growth, 1950 to 1997

Figure 4-1 shows the GDP per capita in 1985 international dollars for each of the five Central American countries and the region as a whole from 1950 to 1997.[5] One can identify a common pattern of growth in the region during this period. Most countries in the region grew relatively rapidly between 1950 and the late1970s. The only country that does not completely fit this description is Nicaragua, which showed some signs of instability in the early1960s. In any event, sometime around 1980 all countries in the region had reached a peak in their level of output per capita, and had begun a period of sharp economic decline. This period of negative economic performance lasted for about four or five years in the majority of cases, and coincided with the debt crisis that afflicted most of Latin America. Not quite unexpectedly, this period also coincided with the presence of negative terms-of-trade shocks and with the end of exchange rate stability in the region.[6] By the end of the 1980s, most countries in the region, after a brief period of relative stagnation, had begun a steady process of economic recovery that still continues. Again, the main exception to the pattern just described is Nicaragua, whose economy deteriorated throughout the 1980s as a result of non–market-oriented economic policies, internal conflicts, and an economic embargo imposed by the United States. In spite of this, Nicaragua has been part of the regional economic recovery that began in 1990, and its growth rate even has surpassed the rest of the region in recent years.

An interesting but unfortunate fact is that only one country in the region, Costa Rica, has been able to recover its late-1970s level of per capita output. The remaining countries of the region still fall short of the maximum level attained sometime during the late 1970s or early 1980s. This situation is also evident in the regional averages displayed in the bottom-right graph of Figure 4-1.

Between 1950 and 1997, Central America's output per capita grew on aver-

---

5. These series were obtained by combining 1950-1992 data from the Penn World Table v. 5.6 with annual real GDP growth-rate data from the World Bank (1999).

6. See Chapters 9 and 10 in this volume for a more detailed review of Central America's exchange rate history. Bulmer-Thomas (1987b) discusses the balance-of-payments crises that affected the region during these years.

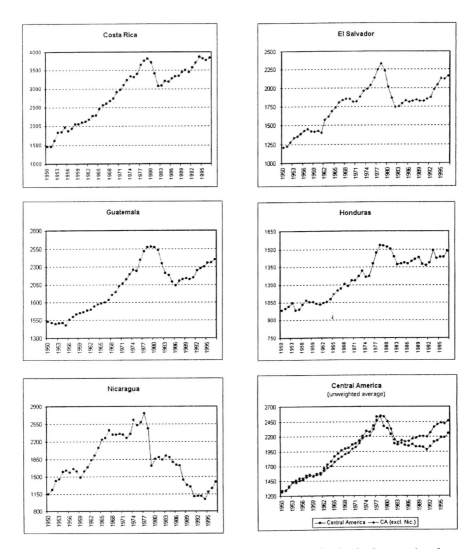

Figure 4-1.   Central America Gross Domestic Output per Capita (at international prices)
Source: Penn World Table v. 5.6 and World Development Indicators, World Bank (1999).

age at a rate of 1.25 percent per year. Country performance fluctuated between a maximum annual average growth rate of 2.1 percent for Costa Rica and a minimum of 0.4 percent for Nicaragua. On the other hand, El Salvador, Guatemala, and Honduras grew at the rates of 1.25, 1.0, and 0.9 percent per year during this period, respectively. As of 1997, no Central American country other than Costa Rica had yet recovered its 1980 level of output per capita.

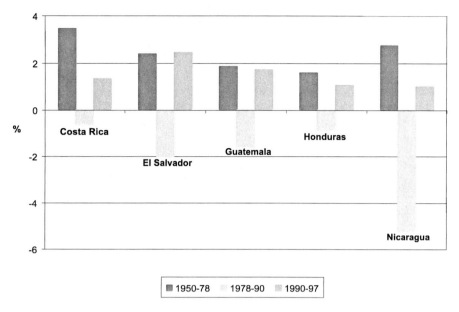

Figure 4-2.   Per Capita GDP Growth (annual average growth rate)

Nicaragua is the most extreme case: its level of output per capita in 1995 was essentially the same as it had been in 1950.

Economic growth throughout the period was far from constant. In fact, we can distinguish three markedly different subperiods. The first runs from 1950 through 1978, when most countries in the region reached a peak in their level of output per capita. The second subperiod starts in 1979 and ends in 1990. It includes the so-called "lost decade" that characterized most of Latin America, and also the years of most intense military conflicts in the region. Probably as a result of these conflicts, Central America seems to have fared worse than the rest of Latin America during these years. The last subperiod, from 1990 to the present, is characterized by positive economic growth. Figure 4-2 shows this trend clearly. It depicts the annual average growth rates for these three subperiods for each Central American country. It is noteworthy that, with the exception of El Salvador, economic growth during the 1990s has proceeded at lower rates than during the 1960s and 1970s.

The period that began in 1979 was one of relative macroeconomic instability throughout Central America. Figure 4-3 shows growth volatility for the three subperiods defined above. Output volatility is measured by the standard deviation of annual output-per-capita growth rates. In four countries of the region, the volatility of growth was greater during the 1979–90 period

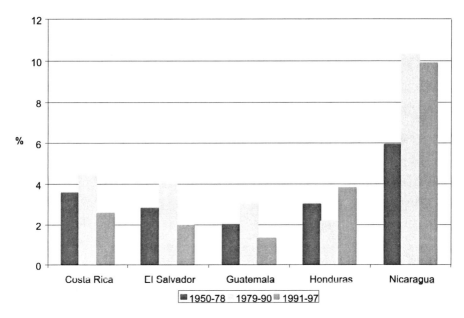

Figure 4-3.   Volatility of GDP Growth (standard deviation of annual GDP growth rate)

than in the other two subperiods. This is especially evident in the cases of El Salvador and Nicaragua, but it is also true for Costa Rica and Guatemala. The relative importance of the various factors affecting the macroeconomic performance of Central American countries differs across countries. However, all the factors are related to the debt crisis that afflicted the entire Latin American region in this period, as well as to the intensification of internal political conflicts throughout the region. As expected, Nicaragua is the Central American country that shows the greatest volatility in all subperiods. Guatemala, on the other hand, seems to be the most stable country in the region during this period.

Interregional Convergence, 1950–1997

A topic that has recently attracted the attention of numerous economic analysts is whether or not there is absolute convergence of income per capita across a group of economies. There is evidence of *absolute* convergence when several economies tend to converge with each other in terms of output per capita. In other words, there is absolute convergence when the dispersion of regional output declines over time. These two definitions imply that, in order to observe absolute convergence across countries, poor countries need to grow at higher rates than rich ones.[7]

According to recent studies, there is strong evidence in favor of the hypothesis of economic convergence across countries belonging to the same region. For example, Barro and Sala-i-Martin (1991) have provided empirical evidence of economic convergence across several European countries and regions. Similarly, Orozco (1994) and Rincon (1998) have found evidence in favor of the hypothesis of absolute convergence across the economies of Latin America. Other studies have also produced evidence of strong absolute convergence at the regional, provincial, or state level in several countries.[8]

Figure 4-4 shows a conventional measure of absolute economic convergence within Central America. It plots the standard deviation of the log of output per capita across the countries of the region.[9] The figure has two lines. One shows the dispersion of output per capita among the five countries of the region. The other line does the same for the whole region without Nicaragua. The conclusion is straightforward: *There is no evidence of absolute economic convergence within the region during the entire period.* In fact, when the five Central American countries are included in the estimation of the per- capita-income dispersion, we observe a continuous process of economic divergence that started in the early 1950s and accelerated sometime around 1982. This steady process of economic divergence started to reverse in 1993.

On the other hand, when we exclude Nicaragua from our calculations of the regional dispersion of income per capita, we observe a somewhat different picture. Now, the trend in economic divergence in Central America stops somewhere around the mid-1970s. The dispersion of income per capita in the region remains relatively stable thereafter. However, even in this situation, *there is no evidence of absolute convergence within the region during the second half of the century.* It must be emphasized that this result contrasts sharply with the experience of other closely integrated regions such as Europe.

---

7. This discussion should not be confused with the ongoing debate about the existence and speed of *conditional* convergence. There is conditional convergence when an economy grows at lower rates, the closer it is to its own steady-state level. Note that conditional convergence does not necessarily imply that poorer countries will grow faster than richer ones. In fact, in the presence of conditional convergence, a poor economy may grow at a lower rate than a rich one, as long as the poorer economy is closer to its own steady state. See Sala-i-Martin (1996a) for a further discussion of these two concepts.

8. See, for example, the results surveyed in Sala-i-Martin (1996b) and Esquivel (1999).

9. This indicator is also known as σ-*convergence*. See Sala-i-Martin (1996a) for a discussion of the characteristics and properties of this indicator.

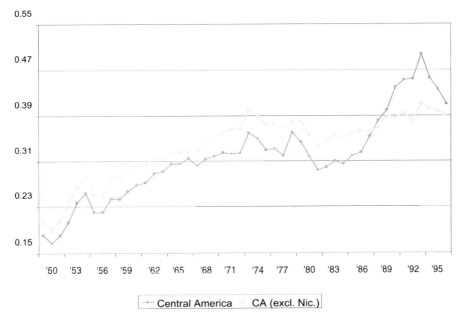

Figure 4-4. *Regional Dispersion of Output per Capita (standard deviation of logs of GDP per capita*

Central America's Tragedy: Per Capita Income in Comparative Perspective

So far I have described the pattern of economic growth in Central America between 1950 and 1997. However, in order to evaluate Central America's performance over the long run, a benchmark is needed, and it must be chosen and defined with care. It is relatively easy to find a country or a group of countries that may lead to a serious under- or overestimation of Central America's economic performance during this period. Therefore, to minimize this type of problem, several groups of countries will serve as points of comparison.

The countries and/or regions that will be used in the comparisons are as follows:

1. *United States of America.*
2. *Latin America I.* Argentina, Brazil, Chile, and Mexico. This group includes some of the largest economies in the subcontinent.
3. *Latin America II.* Bolivia, Colombia, Dominican Republic, Ecuador, Paraguay, Peru, Uruguay, and Venezuela. This group includes relatively small Latin American countries as well as Latin American countries that had an income per capita similar to Central America's average in 1950.

4. *Europe I.* Relatively rich European countries such as Austria, Belgium, Denmark, Finland, France, Germany, Ireland, Italy, Netherlands, Norway, Sweden, Switzerland, and the United Kingdom.

5. *Europe II.* The three European countries that were relatively backward at the beginning of our period of analysis: Greece, Portugal, and Spain.

6. *Asia.* Hong Kong, China, India, Indonesia, Japan, Korea, Pakistan, Philippines, and Thailand.

7. *Africa.* Algeria, Cameroon, Egypt, Ghana, Kenya, Malawi, Morocco, Nigeria, Senegal, Sudan, Togo, Tunisia, Uganda, Zambia, and Zimbabwe.[10]

Table 4-2 shows the results of this comparative exercise for each Central American country and for the regional average. The results displayed in this table clearly illustrate Central America's economic tragedy: in spite of having grown at positive rates throughout the 1950–97 period (see Figure 4-1), Central America's relative economic position deteriorated continuously *vis-à-vis* each of the previously defined regions. Moreover, Central America's income per capita in 1997 is lower in absolute terms than all the other regions used as benchmarks, with the sole exception of Africa.

By comparing Central America with other regions, one can evaluate the magnitude of Central America's disastrous economic performance. Some European economies (*Europe II*), for example, were relatively poor in 1950; in that year, Central America had an income per capita that represented about 83 percent of the income per capita of these countries. In fact, Guatemala even had a slightly higher level of income than the average of the three European countries included in this group. By 1997, Central America's per capita income was on average only about one-fourth the income of these countries. The second comparison is against the group of Asian countries. While in 1950, Central America had an income per capita that was 48 percent higher than that of this group of Asian economies, by 1997 Central America's per capita income was less than one-third that of the Asian countries. Finally, one can compare Central America and Africa. Although Central America's level of income continues to be higher than the African average, its relative advantage has been diminishing over time: whereas in 1970 Central America's income was more than twice the African average, by 1997 it was only about 60 percent higher. The decline is even more drastic considering that Africa has gone through a very difficult economic period, and that its negative economic performance in the last decades has been a matter of concern to numerous analysts.[11]

---

10. No data were available for some countries in specific years. In 1950, for example, we only had data for five countries in the Asia region.

11. See, among others, Easterly and Levine (1997) and Collier and Gunning (1999).

Table 4-2.   *Output per Capita in Central America Relative to other Regions (in percentages)*

	1950	1960	1970	1980	1990	1997
1.- Relative to USA						
Costa Rica	16.6	21.2	22.4	24.3	19.4	19.2
El Salvador	13.7	14.4	14.0	13.2	10.1	10.8
Guatemala	17.5	16.8	15.6	16.8	11.8	12.0
Honduras	11.2	10.5	9.5	9.9	7.6	7.4
Nicaragua	13.1	16.2	18.2	12.1	7.2	7.0
Central America	14.4	15.8	16.0	15.3	11.2	11.3
2.- Relative to Latin America 1						
Costa Rica	58.7	70.1	74.2	71.6	74.0	64.7
El Salvador	48.6	47.7	46.2	38.8	38.6	36.4
Guatemala	61.7	55.5	51.8	49.6	45.0	40.4
Honduras	39.5	34.7	31.6	29.3	29.1	25.0
Nicaragua	46.4	53.7	60.2	35.7	27.4	23.4
Central America	51.0	52.3	52.8	45.0	42.8	38.0
3.- Relative to Latin America 2						
Costa Rica	113.9	144.8	154.8	140.0	147.9	140.1
El Salvador	94.3	98.6	96.5	75.9	77.1	78.8
Guatemala	119.7	114.7	108.1	97.0	89.9	87.5
Honduras	76.7	71.8	65.9	57.2	58.2	54.2
Nicaragua	90.0	111.0	125.7	69.8	54.7	50.7
Central America	98.9	108.2	110.2	88.0	85.6	82.2
4.- Relative to Europe 1						
Costa Rica	33.8	34.7	33.0	33.3	25.8	25.7
El Salvador	28.0	23.6	20.6	18.1	13.4	14.5
Guatemala	35.6	27.5	23.1	23.1	15.7	16.1
Honduras	22.8	17.2	14.1	13.6	10.2	9.9
Nicaragua	26.8	26.6	26.8	16.6	9.5	9.3
Central America	29.4	25.9	23.5	20.9	14.9	15.1
5.- Relative to Europe 2						
Costa Rica	96.5	88.8	65.1	61.0	44.1	43.5
El Salvador	79.9	60.4	40.5	33.1	23.0	24.4
Guatemala	101.5	70.3	45.4	42.3	26.8	27.1
Honduras	65.0	44.0	27.7	24.9	17.3	16.8
Nicaragua	76.3	68.0	52.8	30.4	16.3	15.7
Central America	83.8	66.3	46.3	38.3	25.5	25.5
6.- Relative to Asia						
Costa Rica	171.1	164.0	122.5	101.8	61.1	53.1
El Salvador	141.6	111.7	76.4	55.2	31.8	29.9
Guatemala	179.9	129.9	85.6	70.5	37.1	33.2
Honduras	115.2	81.3	52.2	41.6	24.0	20.5
Nicaragua	135.3	125.7	99.5	50.7	22.6	19.2
Central America	148.6	122.5	87.2	64.0	35.3	31.2
7.- Relative to Africa						
Costa Rica	230.5	254.0	293.2	287.6	272.4	275.6
El Salvador	190.8	172.9	182.8	155.8	142.0	154.9
Guatemala	242.3	201.1	204.8	199.2	165.6	172.1
Honduras	155.2	125.9	124.9	117.5	107.2	106.6
Nicaragua	182.2	194.6	238.2	143.4	100.7	99.7
Central America	200.2	189.7	208.8	180.7	157.6	161.8

Sources: Own calculations based on 1950-90 data from the Penn World Table v. 5.6 and 1997 data from World Bank (1999).

At the country level, comparative performance does not look much better.

In general, all countries in the region fell behind each of the benchmark regions. The only exception was Costa Rica, which improved its relative level of income between 1950 and 1997 *vis-à-vis* the United States and the two Latin American groups. However, no Central American country achieved any relative gains between 1970 and 1997. That is, during these twenty-seven years, all Central American countries lagged behind most other regions in the world. As expected, the country that fared worst in economic terms was Nicaragua. In fact, by 1997 Nicaragua had an income-per-capita level that was slightly below the African average. This result is even more dramatic if one considers that Nicaragua had an income-per-capita level in 1950 that exceeded the African average by 80 percent.

Cross-Country Evidence on the Determinants of Economic Growth and Central America's Growth Performance

In this section we carry out an empirical analysis on the determinants of economic growth in a wide sample of countries in the period 1970–1996. We then use our results to evaluate the economic performance of Central America and to investigate which factors help to explain the recent pattern of economic growth in this region.

The Determinants-of-Economic-Growth Approach

Following the seminal contributions of Barro and Sala-i-Martin (1992) and Mankiw, Romer, and Weil (1992), a spurt of empirical studies about the determinants of economic growth on a cross-country basis has appeared in recent years. The enormous number of studies on the topic have been surveyed recently by Durlauf and Quah (1999) and Temple (1999). For this reason, only a brief description of the more widely used approach will be presented here.

The framework used is similar to the one popularized by Barro and Sala-i-Martin (1995). It is based on the following expression:

$$Dy = f(y_{-1}, x)$$

where Dy is the growth rate of income per capita in a given period, y_{-1} is the income per capita in the initial year, and x is a vector of determinants of the steady state income level. The vector x may include a series of economic, politic, and/or institutional variables, which are expected to affect the relative position of an economy's steady state. These variables usually enter in two different formats: either as beginning-of-period variables or as period averages. In any event, these variables are assumed to be predetermined and they are supposed to affect the position of the steady-state level of an economy's income per capita.

Cross-Country Economic Growth: An Empirical Exercise

Although a large number of variables has been found to be statistically significant in some regressions, one of the few stylized facts that has emerged from the empirical literature on economic growth is that only a relatively small number of the variables is actually robust.[12] Therefore, what follows will use an empirical specification with relatively few explanatory variables.[13]

The determinants-of-growth exercise begins by replicating the results of Sachs and Warner (1997). This specification was chosen because it includes several explanatory variables that are considered relevant for the specific case of Central America. For example, the Sachs-Warner specification includes right-hand-side variables that provide information on natural resources, institutional characteristics (rule-of-law index), the investment rate, and an index of trade openness that is not based solely on external trade data.

The first column of Table 4-3 simply replicates the Sachs-Warner results by using their original data and country sample. This column shows that the selected explanatory variables do a relatively good job at explaining cross-country income growth differences during the 1970–89 period (the adjusted R-squared is 0.60), and most of the estimated coefficients are statistically significant. The second column updates the original Sachs-Warner regression. Now, the dependent variables are the income-per-capita growth rate between 1960 and 1997. The explanatory variables are adjusted accordingly. Despite the change of period, the results in Column 1 are still qualitatively similar to those in Column 2.

All coefficients in regression (2) have the expected signs and most of them are also statistically significant. The only exception is the coefficient associated with the terms-of-trade variable, which is no longer significant at any standard level. The new regression fits even better than the original Sachs-Warner regression: the new adjusted R-squared is 0.75. When comparing Columns 1 and 2 we also see that there are a few seemingly important changes in the magnitude of some of the coefficients. However, these are most probably due to the loss of some countries, which occurred when we updated

---

12. See, for example, Levine and Renelt (1992) and Sala-i-Martin (1997).

13. Some of the explanatory variables used in this exercise might also be considered as endogenous variables. To avoid endogeneity problems in our specification, we mostly use past values of these variables, so as to have only predetermined variables in the right-hand side of the equations to be estimated.

Table 4.3. *Estimated Growth Regressions*

Variables	Original Sachs-Warner 1970-89		Extended Period: 1960-97			
			+ Antigovernment demonstrations	+ assassinations	+ change in cabinet	+ natural disasters
	(1)	(2)	(3)	(4)	(5)	(6)
Log GDP on initial year (1970 or 1960)	-1.79 (-8.20)	-0.83 (-5.20)	-0.76 (-4.61)	-0.78 (-4.68)	-0.75 (-4.58)	-0.93 (-5.20)
Primary Resource Intensity (primary exports / GDP)	-10.26 (-6.89)	-7.99 (-6.85)	-7.83 (-6.51)	-7.77 (-6.74)	-7.87 (-6.84)	-8.28 (-5.15)
Openness Index (variable lies between 0 and 1)	1.34 (3.44)	1.44 (4.70)	1.43 (4.71)	1.40 (4.61)	1.39 (4.35)	0.98 (3.80)
Log (INV/GDP)	0.81 (2.63)	1.88 (4.11)	1.81 (3.99)	1.84 (4.02)	1.79 (3.97)	1.47 (3.53)
Rule of Law	0.40 (3.94)	0.17 (2.04)	0.14 (1.69)	0.15 (1.71)	0.15 (1.72)	0.26 (3.11)
Terms of Trade Growth	0.09 (1.85)	0.004 (0.11)	0.020 (0.52)	0.022 (0.58)	0.020 (0.53)	-0.06 (-1.74)
Political Instability			0.007 (0.10)	392.17 (0.45)	0.064 (0.31)	
Natural Disasters Index						-0.0041 (-1.778)
Adjusted R-squared	0.60	0.75	0.74	0.73	0.74	0.86
Sample Size	73	67	64	65	64	30
Standard Error	1.52	0.708	0.694	0.697	0.694	0.423

Note: Numbers in parentheses are *t*-statistics.

the Sachs-Warner regression, rather than to a break in the data or to an important change in the relationship among variables.

Before extending the empirical analysis, let us discuss some of the results in Column 2. These results show that a higher share of primary exports on domestic GDP tends to have a negative and significant effect on the per-capita-income growth rate. There are several non–mutually excluding explanations for this negative effect of primary-resources intensity on economic performance.

An often-cited explanation is the one championed by the economists associated with the Economic Commission for Latin America (ECLAC). This explanation, known as the Prebisch-Singer hypothesis, argues that there is a long-term declining trend in the terms of trade for economies based on natural resources.[14] The argument is then extended to suggest that these type of economies will naturally tend to grow at lower rates than industrialized economies.

An alternative explanation focuses on the large external vulnerability implicit in all economies that obtain an important amount of foreign-exchange reserves from their primary exports. In this case, it is the variability or the uncertainty in the terms of trade that affects macroeconomic performance.[15] Yet another likely explanation focuses more on the behavior of interest groups that attempt to expropriate the economic gains of sudden favorable terms-of-trade shocks (Lane and Tornell 1999). These authors suggest a way that even positive shocks on the terms of trade may generate a negative effect on economic growth. The authors offer a myriad of examples as well as some anecdotal evidence in support of their analysis.

All the previous explanations assume that the negative effect of primary exports on GDP occurs through the terms of trade. However, our regressions in Table 4-3 already control for this variable and it was found to be nonsignificant. In this context, it seems relevant to mention an alternative explanation that does not use the terms of trade as a channel. This is the explanation offered by Leamer, et al. (1999), which suggests that permanent agriculture and mineral exploitation tends to absorb the scarce savings of a country rich in natural resources, thus delaying the emergence of manufacturing industry. All in all, it is very likely that a combination of the above-mentioned factors plays a role in explaining the negative association between natural resources and economic growth that is found in Table 4-3, Column 2.

Table 4-3 also shows a positive effect of the openness index on economic

14. To get a flavor of the recent debate about this hypothesis, see Lutz (1999) and Leon and Soto (1997). These authors present strong empirical evidence in favor of the Prebisch-Singer hypothesis using modern econometric techniques. On the other hand, Cuddington and Urzua (1989) arrive at a different conclusion. Leon and Soto (1995) found no empirical evidence supporting the Prebisch-Singer hypothesis for Latin American exports.

15. See, for example, Mendoza (1997).

growth. According to Sachs and Warner (1995), the openness index is measured as the fraction of the 1970-1992 period that a country was integrated
into the world economy. The positive effect of trade openness on economic
growth is compatible with previous findings by Sachs and Warner (1995;
1997) and Edwards (1998). The magnitude of this coefficient shows that a
country that was open throughout the whole 1970–1992 period would have
grown 1.44 percentage points per year faster than a country that remained
closed during the whole period.

Results in Column 2 also show that an adequate institutional environment
matters for economic growth. This interpretation is suggested because the coefficient associated to the rule-of-law index is positive and statistically significant at the 5 percent level. Of course, this aspect is strongly related to the
choices and behavior of the economic and political elites of the region during
these years. It would be interesting to discuss in detail the political economy
aspects that underlie the rule-of-law index in Central America. However, this
topic is beyond the objective of this chapter and it has already been discussed
by a number of authors.[16]

Column 2 in Table 4-3 also shows two other well known results: a strong
evidence of conditional convergence across countries (which is captured by
the negative coefficient associated to the initial level of income per capita), as
well as the positive effect of the investment rate on the growth rate of income
per capita. As mentioned before, the terms-of-trade growth variable is not
significant in this specification.

Columns 3, 4, and 5 in Table 4-3 add some political variables to the specification in Column 2. The idea is to see whether political variables have played
a role in determining rates of economic growth.[17] This seems especially important in the context of Central America, since this region was very unstable
in political terms during the period under analysis (Lindenberg 1990). The
political variables added to our specification are the average number of anti-
government demonstrations per year, the number of assassinations per thou-
sand people, and the number of unexpected changes in the official cabinet.[18]
Columns 3 to 5 in Table 4-3 show that including these variables does not add
any explanatory power to our previous specification. More importantly, the
inclusion of these variables does not affect the magnitude nor the statistical
significance of our original explanatory variables. Therefore, these results
suggest that political variables do not affect economic growth through channels other than the ones already considered in Column 2. In this sense, it is ir-

---

16. See, for example, Weaver (1994).
17. This hypothesis has received empirical support from Alesina et al. (1996).
18. The source of these variables is Easterly and Rebelo (1993).

relevant whether political instability is correlated with lower rates of economic growth, since its effect may already have been captured by lower rates of investment or relatively low levels of the rule-of-law index.

Anecdotal evidence, as well as the recent negative impact of both Hurricane Mitch and the climatological phenomenon known as El Niño, suggest that Central America's economic performance may be negatively affected by a disproportionate number of natural disasters.[19] This hypothesis will now be tested by including a natural-disaster index as an additional explanatory variable in our determinants-of-economic growth regression. The index was prepared by the United Nations Environment Programme (UNEP) and is designed to reflect the proneness of some countries to natural disasters (UNEP 1993). Unfortunately, because the natural-disaster index is available only for a selected number of countries, the test cannot be performed over a wide sample. In fact, when the new variable is included, data for only thirty countries (including the five countries of Central America) remain. The results of adding the natural-disasters variable in our analysis are shown in Table 4-3, Column 6.

Several interesting results are obtained. On the one hand, the natural-disasters index turned out to be significant at the 10 percent level, and its associated coefficient was, as expected, negative. This suggests that a country that is more prone to suffer from natural disasters (such as the Central American countries) also tends to have lower rates of economic growth. Interestingly, however, the other estimated coefficients in the regression are still highly significant, and more important, their magnitude does not change drastically in comparison to previous regressions. These results can be interpreted as suggesting that while geography matters, so do institutional and policy factors.

Unfortunately, regardless of the relatively good fit of the specification which includes the natural-disasters index (the adjusted R-squared is 0.86, significantly larger than in alternative specifications), the fact that these results are obtained using data from a reduced sample of countries may cast doubt on any conclusion based on them. Therefore, in what follows, the results obtained in Table 4-3, Column 2 will be used to evaluate Central America's economic performance. In any case, the reader should always keep in mind that Central American countries have often been affected by natural events, which were absolutely beyond the control of the economic authorities.

---

19. Chapter 18 in Volume II of this series provides a detailed account of the damage in Central America provoked by Hurricane Mitch.

How Well Does the Model Explain Central America's Growth?

In this section we analyze the appropriateness of the regression analysis of the previous section in evaluating Central America's recent macroeconomic performance.

Figure 4-5 presents a country-by-country comparison between the observed 1960–97 income-per-capita growth rates and the predicted values that are obtained when using the econometric estimates shown in Table 4-3, Column 2. Figure 4-5 shows two interesting results. First, fitted values for Central American countries capture relatively well the observed pattern of income-per-capita growth rates in the region. The main exception is Nicaragua, whose predicted growth rate was positive (around 0.5 percent per year), whereas it actually had a negative economic performance during the period under analysis. As discussed before, between 1979 and 1989 Nicaragua implemented a series of non–market-oriented policies that seems to have undermined its economic prospects.[20]

A second interesting result shown in Figure 4-5 is the fact that most Central American countries grew faster than predicted between 1960 and 1997 (again, with the exception of Nicaragua). This conclusion seems paradoxical since we have just documented how Central America fell behind many other regions of the world during this period. According to our empirical estimates,

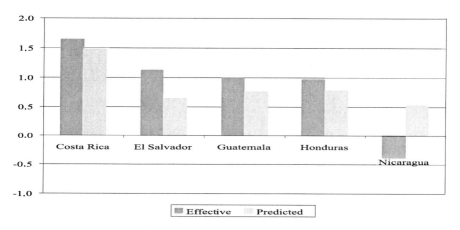

Figure 4-5. Predicted vs. Effective Growth Rates in Central America, 1960–1997

---

20. See Ocampo (1991) for a detailed account of the macroeconomic policies implemented by the Sandinista regime in Nicaragua during this period.

however, most Central American economies should have lagged behind even more than they did. That, instead, they experienced relatively rapid growth certainly invites us to investigate the relative weight of the different factors that appear to have hampered economic progress in Central America.

Which Factors have Hampered Economic Growth in Central America?

This section addresses the following question: Which factors explain the relatively bad macroeconomic performance of Central America since 1960? We have already identified some of the factors that have influenced economic growth rates in a wide sample of countries. We now want to determine the relative weight of each of these factors in explaining the observed per-capita-income growth rates in Central America. In order to do so, we apply a sources-of-growth decomposition analysis.

The approach is as follows: Define a number of regions to serve as reference points, and then compute the contribution each independent variable makes to explaining the difference in growth rates between two given regions, using the following expression:

$$Dy_{i,j} = b_i (x_{i,j} - x_{i,CA})$$

where $Dy_{i,j}$ is the contribution of factor i to explaining the difference in growth rates between region j and Central America (CA), b_i is the estimated coefficient associated with variable i, and $x_{i,j}$ $(x_{i,CA})$ is the average value of variable i in region j (Central America).

The first step consists of defining the regions that will be used as benchmarks. For brevity's sake, only four regions are defined: Latin America I (Argentina, Brazil, Chile, and Mexico), Latin America II (Bolivia, Colombia, Ecuador, Paraguay, and Peru), Asia I (Korea, Indonesia, and Thailand), and Asia II (Singapore, Hong Kong, and Taiwan). These groups partially resemble the ones that we defined earlier. However, we now consider only those countries that were included in the estimation of the regressions described in Table 4-3.

Table 4-4 shows the average values of the explanatory variables for Central America and for the regions that will be used as benchmarks. Central America's averages do not include Nicaragua. The rationale is that Nicaragua's performance is so negative that its inclusion would bias the results.

The bottom part of Table 4-4 shows the average regional growth rates. We can see that Central America grew at much lower rates than other regions of the world during this period. A quick look at Table 4-4 also shows that Central America is the region with the highest share of primary exports to GDP (primary-resource intensity), the lowest values of both the openness- and

Table 4-4. *Average Values of Explanatory and Dependent Variables by Region*

Variable	Central America	LA1	LA2	Asia1	Asia2
Log (initial GDP)	7.32	7.95	7.29	6.70	7.71
Primary resource intensity	0.17	0.07	0.13	0.07	0.02
Openness index	0.13	0.24	0.39	0.88	1.00
Log (INV/GDP)	2.96	3.06	3.03	3.37	3.48
Rule of law	1.75	3.75	2.00	2.33	6.00
Terms of trade change	-2.25	-1.99	0.20	0.93	-0.61
Annual average per capita income growth rate (1960-97)	1.18	1.95	1.63	4.99	5.58

Note: Groups of countries are: CA= Costa Rica, El Salvador, Guatemala, Honduras; LA1= Argentina, Brazil, Mexico, Chile; LA2= Paraguay, Colombia, Ecuador, Peru, Bolivia; Asia1= Korea, Indonesia, Thailand; Asia2= Singapore, Hong Kong, Taiwan.

the rule-of-law indexes, and the lowest investment rate. As found in our empirical exercise, each of these factors negatively affects economic-growth rates. Combined, they help to explain the poor economic performance of the region during the 1960–97 period.

Table 4-5. *Sources of Growth Rate Differences between Central America and Selected Regions*

Source	CA vs LA1 level	(%)	CA vs LA2 level	(%)	CA vs Asia1 level	(%)	CA vs Asia2 level	(%)
Log (initial GDP)	-0.53	-68.1	0.02	5.5	0.51	13.4	-0.32	-7.4
Primary resource intensity	0.83	107.2	0.38	84.2	0.80	21.1	1.23	27.9
Openness index	0.70	21.6	0.39	86.3	1.09	28.6	1.26	28.6
Log (INV/GDP)	0.18	23.5	0.12	27.9	0.77	20.3	0.98	22.3
Rule of law	0.33	43.0	0.04	9.3	0.10	2.5	0.71	16.1
Terms of trade change	0.00	0.1	0.01	2.3	0.01	0.3	0.01	0.2
Unexplained difference in growth rate	-0.21	-27.2	-0.52	-115.4	0.52	13.7	0.54	12.3
Observed difference in growth rate	0.77	100.0	0.45	100.0	3.81	100.0	4.40	100.0

Note: Groups of countries are: CA= Costa Rica, El Salvador, Guatemala, Honduras, Nicaragua; LA1= Argentina, Brazil, Mexico, Chile;   LA2= Paraguay, Colombia, Ecuador, Peru, Bolivia; Asia1= Korea, Indonesia, Thailand;   Asia2= Singapore, Hong Kong, Taiwan.

The results of the sources-of-growth decomposition analysis described above are shown in Table 4-5. There are four sets of comparisons. They all show the contribution of each independent variable to the interregional difference in growth rates. Results are shown both in levels (or percentage points per annum) and in percentages of total growth-rate differences.

Table 4-5 shows that the single most important element explaining why Central America grew at lower rates than other Latin American countries is its heavy dependence on primary exports. This single element explains 107 percent and 84 percent of the difference in growth rates between Central America and countries grouped in Latin America I and II, respectively. In addition, the variable "rule-of-law" explains an important part (43 percent) of the lower growth rate in Central America as compared with Latin America I.

With respect to the Asian countries, Table 4-5 also shows some interesting results. In the comparisons with the two Asian groups, there is not a single dominant explanatory factor. Instead, interregional growth-rate differences between Central America and Asia are explained by a combination of different elements. In both cases, the most important factor is the openness index, closely followed by the primary-resource intensity and the investment-rate variables. Taken together, these three variables explain more than 70 percent of the difference in growth rates between the Asian countries and Central America. The openness index, for example, explains 29 percent of the interregional differences in both comparisons. This variable alone explains why the two Asian groups grew 1.1 and 1.3 percentage points per annum more than Central America, respectively. These results confirm that there is no simple explanation for the recent economic performance of Central America; the performance is instead the result of various elements combined.

GROWTH AND TOTAL-FACTOR PRODUCTIVITY

In this section, economic growth is viewed from a somewhat different perspective. The issue is whether the observed economic growth in Central America is better explained by the accumulation of production inputs or by increases in productivity. The results described in this section are drawn from Robles (2000) and were obtained using a standard growth-accounting methodology.[21]

Table 4-6 shows the results of deconstructing growth in Central American into three main components: accumulation of capital, accumulation of labor, and total-factor productivity (TEP) gains. These results are computed for

---

21. See Harberger (1998) for more details on the methodology.

Table 4-6.   *Central America 1960–1996—Sources of Economic Growth for Central American Countries*

	GDP Growth	TFP	Contribution of Capital	Contribution of Labor
Costa Rica				
1960–1965	5.2%	0.7%	1.7%	2.7%
1965–1970	7.0%	3.1%	2.1%	1.8%
1970–1975	6.1%	2.0%	2.8%	1.3%
1975–1980	5.3%	0.5%	2.6%	2.2%
1980–1985	0.4%	−2.8%	1.9%	1.4%
1985–1990	4.6%	2.3%	1.9%	0.4%
1990–1996	3.8%	0.1%	1.7%	1.9%
1960–1996	4.7%	0.9%	2.1%	1.6%
Nicaragua				
1960–1965	10.1%	6.4%	1.3%	2.4%
1965–1970	3.8%	0.3%	1.7%	1.8%
1970–1975	5.2%	0.9%	1.9%	2.3%
1975–1980	−3.2%	−5.5%	0.5%	1.8%
1980–1985	0.7%	−2.3%	0.9%	2.1%
1985–1990	−3.2%	−5.7%	0.4%	2.1%
1990–1996	2.0%	−0.3%	0.3%	2.0%
1960–1996	2.2%	−0.9%	1.0%	2.1%
Honduras				
1960–1965	5.5%	2.8%	1.4%	1.3%
1965–1970	3.6%	−1.0%	2.4%	2.2%
1970–1975	3.7%	−0.4%	2.0%	2.2%
1975–1980	7.2%	1.8%	2.7%	2.8%
1980–1985	1.8%	−1.5%	0.9%	2.4%
1985–1990	3.2%	−0.1%	1.3%	2.0%
1990–1996	3.6%	1.1%	3.0%	−0.4%
1960–1996	4.1%	0.4%	2.0%	1.7%
El Salvador				
1960–1965	6.9%	2.7%	2.7%	1.5%
1965–1970	4.5%	0.1%	2.6%	1.7%
1970–1975	5.5%	0.3%	3.7%	1.4%
1975–1980	1.2%	0.6%	2.9%	−2.4%
1980–1985	−1.8%	−4.0%	0.3%	1.9%
1985–1990	1.9%	−5.0%	0.6%	6.2%
1990–1996	5.5%	1.6%	1.9%	2.0%
1960–1996	3.4%	−0.4%	2.1%	1.8%
Guatemala				
1960–1965	5.3%	2.3%	1.5%	1.5%
1965–1970	5.8%	2.3%	2.0%	1.5%
1970–1975	5.6%	1.7%	2.6%	1.3%
1975–1980	5.7%	0.4%	3.3%	2.0%
1980–1985	−1.1%	−3.1%	0.9%	1.1%
1985–1990	2.9%	0.8%	0.8%	1.3%
1990–1996	4.1%	0.9%	1.5%	1.7%
1960–1996	4.0%	0.8%	1.8%	1.5%

Source: Robles (2000)

five-year intervals between 1960 and 1996,[22] as well as for the whole 1960–96 period.

Before describing the main results of this exercise, it is important to mention two characteristics of the data used in this section. First, growth rates in Table 4-6 correspond to total output, not per-capita output. Second, most data come from domestic sources (e.g. Ministries, Institutes, etc.) and they may differ from data compiled and processed by international organizations. Therefore, information and data used in this section are not immediately comparable to the data we have used before.

Table 4-6 shows that the main contribution to economic growth in Central America throughout the 1960–96 period came from capital and labor accumulation. In all countries, these two components alone account for more than 80 percent of total growth. In two cases (El Salvador and Nicaragua), input accumulation accounts for more than 100 percent of total output growth. This result is explained by the fact that these two countries had negative productivity gains during all these years. In fact, Nicaragua has had negative changes in its total-factor productivity in every five-year subperiod during the last twenty years. In the case of El Salvador, productivity losses took place only between 1980 and 1990, but they were large enough to outweigh the moderate productivity gains that had been achieved in previous years.

On the other hand, Costa Rica and Guatemala have had the largest annual average gain in total-factor productivity among Central American countries during the 1960–96 period: 0.9 and 0.8 percent, respectively. Indeed, both countries had a continuous increase in productivity during the whole period except for the 1980–85 subperiod. In spite of such gains, the most striking result in Table 4-6 is the fact that Central American countries have had remarkably low TFP growth rates since 1960. Such growth rates stand in sharp contrast with those that have been obtained for other regions in similar periods.

For example, studies by Jorgenson (1995) and Young (1995) have shown that recent TFP growth in Asian countries has been around 3 percent or 4 percent per year. This fact, together with the casual observation that Central American countries with higher TFP have also had the largest output growth, suggest that there is a link between productivity growth and GDP growth. This possibility is explored Figures 4-6a to 4-6f.

Figure 4-6a plots both GDP and TFP five-year average growth rates for Central American countries. There are seven data points per country, or thirty-five observations. The figure shows that there is a very strong correlation between both variables. The results of a simple regression between both variables is also shown. The fit of the regression is very good, as shown by the

---

22. The only exception is the last subperiod, which goes from 1990 to 1996.

a. Central America
(Five-year Average Growth Rates)

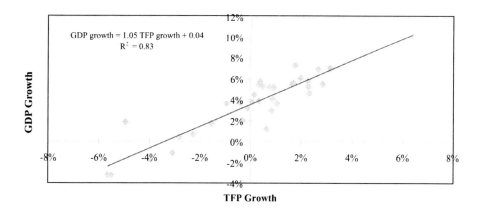

b. Costa Rica (Yearly Growth)

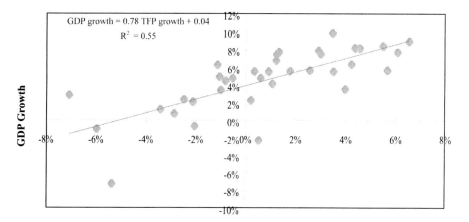

Figure 4-6.   Relationship Between GDP and TFP Growth

c. Nicaragua (Yearly Growth)

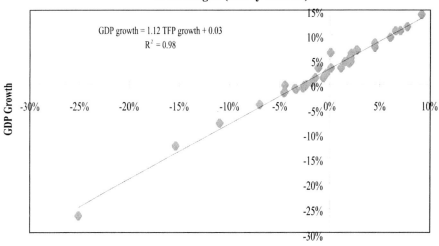

GDP growth = 1.12 TFP growth + 0.03
$R^2 = 0.98$

TFP Growth

d. El Salvador (Yearly Growth)

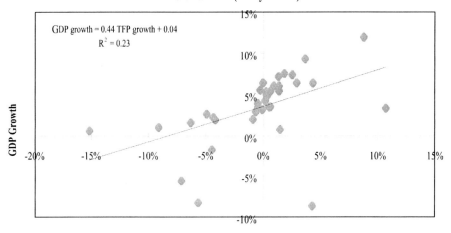

GDP growth = 0.44 TFP growth + 0.04
$R^2 = 0.23$

TFP Growth

Figure 4-6. *Continued*

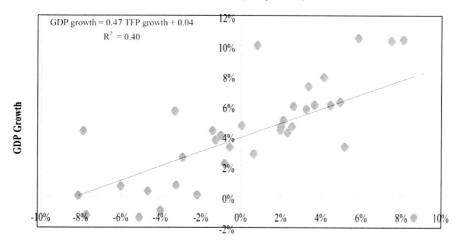

e. Honduras (Yearly Growth)

GDP growth = 0.47 TFP growth + 0.04
$R^2 = 0.40$

GDP Growth

TFP Growth

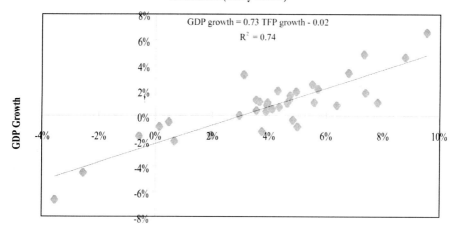

f. Guatemala (Yearly Growth)

GDP growth = 0.73 TFP growth - 0.02
$R^2 = 0.74$

GDP Growth

TFP Growth

Figure 4-6. *Continued*

fitted line and by the R-squared of 0.83 that is obtained with the regression. More interestingly, the estimated slope is 1.05, which is not statistically different from 1.0. This suggests that output growth increases one-to-one with productivity increases in Central America.

Figures 4-6b to 4-6f plot the yearly growth rates of both GDP and TFP for each Central American country. All graphs show a positive and significant relationship between both variables, thus confirming our previous finding. Data for Nicaragua and Guatemala show the strongest correlation, whereas data for El Salvador show the weakest. Although the evidence for a one-to-one association between productivity growth and TFP growth is weaker in these figures, this result can be easily explained by two factors: the presence of business-cycle effects when using yearly data and the exacerbation of measurement errors that tends to occur when using annual information instead of five-year averages.

Conclusion

This chapter discussed the macroeconomic performance of Central America from a long-run perspective. Analysis shows that countries in this region have had a common pattern of growth since 1950. This pattern began with a period of economic progress that lasted from the early 1950s through the late 1970s. This was followed by a period of economic decline and political instability in most countries, a decline that lasted for most of the 1980s. Since 1990, the region has entered into a phase of renewed economic growth. However, in spite of having had a relatively long period of economic expansion, Central America has fallen behind almost all other regions in the world.

Comparative analysis of the macroeconomic performance of Central America illustrates the true magnitude of the economic tragedy that has afflicted most countries in the region. As shown above, between 1970 and 1997 no single country in the region has achieved a relative economic gain vis-à-vis any other region in the world.

A detailed analysis of the factors that have hampered economic growth in the region has shown that there is no single explanatory factor behind the slow growth rate. Instead, the explanation consists of a number of factors that include economic elements (low investment rates), institutional elements (rule of law), policy elements (trade-openness), and structural elements (high primary-exports intensity).

Finally, the relationship between productivity and growth has shown that most of the growth gains achieved since 1960 were due to the rapid accumulation of inputs rather than to productivity increases. This suggests that there is a fundamental flaw in the process of economic development of Central American economies. Central American countries have tended to inhibit productivity gains and instead promote economic growth through the simple accumulation of production factors. Our findings suggest that an adequate combination of policies and structural reforms oriented toward the promotion of a more stable institutional, political, and economic environment is essential if the countries of Central America are going to achieve the relatively high rates of economic growth required to raise their standard of living. Fortunately, although clear and decisive steps forwards are still much needed, most of the recent reforms in the region have been heading in the right direction.

REFERENCES

Alesina, Alberto, Sule Ozler, Nouriel Roubini, and Phillip Swagel. 1996. "Political Instability and Economic Growth." *Journal of Economic Growth* 1 (2): 189–211.

Barro, Robert J., and Xavier Sala-i-Martin. 1991. "Convergence Across States and Regions." *Brookings Papers on Economic Activity* 1: 107–58.

Barro, Robert J., and Xavier Sala-i-Martin. 1992. "Convergence." *Journal of Political Economy"* 100 (April): 233–51.

———. 1995. *Economic Growth.* New York: McGraw Hill.

Bulmer-Thomas, Victor. 1987a. *The Political Economy of Central America since 1920.* New York: Cambridge University Press.

———. 1987b. The Balance-of-Payments Crisis and Adjustment Programmes in Central America. In *Latin American Debt and the Adjustment Crisis,* edited by R. Thorp and L. Whitehead. Pittsburgh Latin American Series: University of Pittsburgh Press.

Collier, Paul, and Jan W. Gunning. 1999. "Explaining African Economic Performance." *Journal of Economic Literature* 371 (March): 64–111.

Cuddington, John T., and Carlos M. Urzua. 1989. "Trends and Cycles in the Net Barter Terms of Trade: A New Approach." *Economic Journal* 99 (June): 426–42.

Durlauf, Steven N. and Danny Quah. 1999. "The New Empirics of Economic Growth." In *Handbook of Macroeconomics,* edited by John B. Taylor and Michael Woodford. Oxford: North-Holland Elsevier Science .

Easterly, William and Sergio Rebelo. 1993. "Fiscal Policy and Economic Growth: an Empirical Investigation." *Journal of Monetary Economics* 32 (3): 417-58.

Easterly, William, and Ross Levine. 1997. "Africa's Growth Tragedy: Policies and Ethnic Divisions." *Quarterly Journal of Economics* 112 (4): 1203–50.

Edwards, Sebastian. 1998. "Openness, Productivity, and Growth: What Do We Really Know?" *Economic Journal* 108 (447): 383–98.

Esquivel, Gerardo. 1999. "Convergencia Regional en Mexico: 1940-95", *El Trimestre Económico* LXVI (4):725-761.

Harberger, Arnold C. 1998. "A Vision of the Growth Process." *American Economic Review* 88 (1): 1–32.

Jorgenson, Dale W. 1995. *Productivity*. In Volume 2 of *International Comparisons of Economic Growth*. Cambridge and London: The MIT Press.

Juan-Ramon, Victor-Hugo. 1999. "Honduras' Growth Performance During 1970–97." *Policy Discussion Paper 99/1*. Washington, D.C.: International Monetary Fund.

Lane, Philip R., and Aaron Tornell. 1999. "The Voracity Effect." *American Economic Review* 89 (1): 22–46.

Leamer, E. E., H. Maul, S. Rodriguez, and P. K. Schott. 1999. "Does Natural Resource Abundance Increase Latin American Income Inequality?" *Journal of Development Economics* 59 (1): 3–42.

Leon, Javier, and Raimundo Soto. 1995. "Terminos de intercambio en la America Latina: Una cuantificacion de la hipotesis de Prebisch y Singer." *El Trimestre Economico* 62 (2): 171–99.

———. 1997. "Structural Breaks and Long-Run Trends in Commodity Prices." *Journal of International Development* 9 (3): 347–66.

Levine, Ross, and David A. Renelt. 1992. "A Sensitivity Analysis of Cross-Country Growth Regressions." *American Economic Review* 824: 942–63.

Lindenberg, Marc. 1990. "World Economic Cycles and Central American Political Instability." *World Politics* 42 (3): 397-421.

Lutz, Matthias G. 1999. "A General Test of the Prebisch-Singer Hypothesis." *Review of Development Economics* 3 (1): 44–57.

Mankiw, Romer, and Weil. 1992. "A Contribution to the Empirics of Economic Growth.." *Quarterly Journal of Economics* 107 (2): 407-37.

Mendoza, Enrique G. 1997. "Terms-of-Trade Uncertainty and Economic Growth." *Journal of Development Economics* 54 (2): 323–56.

Ocampo, José Antonio. 1991. "Collapse and (Incomplete) Stabilization of the Nicaraguan Economy." In *The Macroeconomics of Populism in Latin America*, edited by Rudiger Dornbusch and Sebastian Edwards. Chicago and London: University of Chicago Press.

Orozco, Fernando. 1994. *Convergence Hypothesis: The Latin American Experience*. Ph.D. diss., Rice University.

Perez-Brignoli, Hector, 1989. *A Brief History of Central America*. Berkeley: University of California Press.

Rincon, Augusto. 1998. "Crecimiento Económico en la America Latina. Estudio Basado en el Modelo Neoclasico." *El Trimestre Económico* 65 (3): 339–62.

Robles, Edgar. 2000. "Economic Growth in Central America: Evolution of Productivity in Manufacturing." *HIID Development Discussion Paper* no 749. February. Cambridge, MA.: Harvard Institute for International Development.

Sachs, Jeffrey D., and Andrew Warner. 1995. "Economic Reform and the Process of Global Integration." *Brookings Papers on Economic Activity* 1: 1–117. Washington, D.C.: Brookings Institution.

————. "Natural Resource Abundance and Economic Growth." Revised version. Cambridge, MA.: Harvard Institute for International Development. Unpublished manuscript.

————. 1999. "The Big Push, Natural Resource Booms, and Growth." *Journal of Development Economics* 59 (1): 43–76.

Sala-i-Martin, Xavier. 1996a. "The Classical Approach to Convergence Analysis." *Economic Journal* 106 (437): 1019-36.

————. 1996b. "Regional Cohesion: Evidence and Theories of Regional Growth and Convergence." *European Economic Review* 40(6): 1325–52.

————. 1997. "I Just Ran Two Million Regressions." *American Economic Review* 872: 178–83.

Temple, Jonathan. 1999. "The New Growth Evidence." *Journal of Economic Literature.* 37 (1): 112-56.

Thorp, Rosemary. 1998. *Progress, Poverty, and Exclusion: An Economic History of Latin America.* Washington, D.C.: Inter-American Development Bank.

United Nations Environment Programme (UNEP). 1993. *Environmental Data Report 1993–94.* Cambridge, Eng.: Blackwell.

Weaver, Frederick Stirton. 1994. Inside the Volcano: The History and Political Economy of Central America. Boulder, CO: Westview Press.

World Bank. 1999. *World Development Indicators.* CD-ROM. Washington, D.C.: World Bank.

Young, Alwyn. 1995. "The Tyranny of Numbers: Confronting the Statistical Realities of the East Asian Growth Experience." *Quarterly Journal of Economics* 110 (3): 641–80.

5

Trade, Investment, and Regional Integration: Patterns and Strategic Recommendations

JOSÉ TAVARES

The economic history of Central America is indelibly linked with international trade and investment. For better or worse, Central America has been associated with the export of commodities since at least the early coffee and banana booms of the nineteenth century. Today, it is widely understood that Central America's economic future rests on being able to exploit fully old and new connections with the international economy. The small size of the regional economies, added to their location next to major world markets and in the path of major trading routes, underlines the importance and potential of international linkages.

In the last two decades, Central America has abandoned the pursuit of protectionist import-substitution policies and moved decisively to liberalize the international flows of goods, services, and capital. The 1990s brought peace and democratization to Central America and provided it with a new goal: achieving sustained growth. The region has now reached reasonable levels of macroeconomic stability, which is the first necessary condition for economic growth. However, macroeconomic and political stability are insufficient in themselves. Governments and individuals have begun to realize that a structural economic transformation is needed if the region is to enjoy long-term growth. The liberalization of trade and investment, including but not limited to the diversification of export products and markets, should be given top priority in the quest for structural reform in Central America.

Obtaining wide and secure access to the U. S. market through long-term binding agreements is a pivotal issue. The North American Free Trade Agreement (NAFTA), which liberalized trade flows between the United States, Canada, and Mexico, has made salient to Central America the importance of secure access to the U.S. market. Several Central American products compete directly with Mexican products for the U.S. market. Competition can only increase, given Mexico's preferential access to the U.S. market. Central America has yet to formulate a consistent strategy for sustainable trade access to the U.S. market. The small size of the economies in the region and the lack of geographical contiguity to the U.S. will impede Central America from becoming a high priority for the United States. Thus, and in spite of the continued key role of the United States, private and public sector leaders in the region are slowly recognizing the importance of other export markets. Mexico and South America, which are both large and geographically close are just such untapped export markets.

Regional trade integration has experienced a relative revival since the early 1990s, following a marked decline in intraregional trade flows after the crises of the 1980s. Trade integration efforts should be directed toward increasing the effective size of the Central American "home market" so that companies, investors, and consumers can use it to good advantage. A major obstacle to the deepening of the integration process is a lack of political commitment from Central American governments and policymakers. The deregulation of internal markets and the reform of the public sector must advance in parallel with the trade and investment liberalization.

This chapter evaluates the status of Central America in the policy areas of international trade and investment. It starts with an overview of the existing trade agreements between Central America and other countries and regions, in which we emphasize the significance of bilateral trade flows. Next, we survey the recent rise in foreign direct investment (FDI) to the region in the context of the developing world. The objective is to highlight the factors that are most effective in attracting international investment flows, such as infrastructure and market size. A final section argues for, and presents guidelines to develop, a successful trade and investment strategy for the region.

GAINS FROM INTERNATIONAL TRADE AND INVESTMENT

In the last two decades, several developing countries have undertaken trade policy reform. The stated aim has generally been to promote the liberalization of internal markets and further growth in income per capita. Liberalization has occurred at a bilateral level and, increasingly, also at a multilateral level. It has taken the form of a reduction or elimination of tariff and nontariff barriers, taxes, subsidies, and other restrictions on the free flow of imports and ex-

Box 5-1
Trade with Central America: The View from the United States

Every year, the U.S. Department of Trade submits to the House Committee on Foreign Affairs a report on the trade practices of individual countries.*
Reading these reports is a very good way to understand how the U.S. government sees trade with Central America and to identify what the region has to
do to become more attractive to the United States. The structure of the reports is revealing: there are sections on each country's macroeconomic environment, including exchange-rate and debt policy, but the most voluminous
sections are called "Significant Barriers to U.S. Exports," "Protection of U.S.
Intellectual Property," and "Worker Rights."

Each Central American country is a case in itself, but there are issues that
recur in most of the individual country reports. These issues are generally
positive as far as the overall macroeconomic environment is concerned, and
all acknowledge that change is occurring in all areas and in the right direction. A shift from nontariff barriers to tariffs and the ongoing tariff disarmament under the CACM are recognized and applauded. However, even if the
changes are moving in the right direction, the current situation is still seen as
problematic and warranting policy action in key areas. The most problematic
areas are:

Protection of Intellectual Property Rights. Enforcement of international
standards is a problem. Counterfeits are widely available. Speculators
register trademarks with the purpose of extracting compensation from
international companies. The litigation needed to remove the trademarks is long and expensive.

Customs Procedures. Customs specialists cost money. Customs brokers enjoy a monopoly and must be nationals. Formulas lead to overvaluation
of exports. Occasional arbitrary customs valuations and delays add to
cost and lead to destruction of perishables. In some countries steep secondary customs costs exist.

Special Taxes. Luxury, consumption, and sales taxes are levied. Some taxes
on imported goods are charged in cascading fashion.

Sanitary Regulations. These eliminate some markets and impede the
growth of others.

Government Procurement. Disqualifying foreign bidders for failure to comply with detailed procedures with no possibility of change is one issue.
There are also lengthy and costly appeals processes and a general lack of
transparency.

Worker's Conditions. Poor enforcement of child-labor laws and occasional
lay-offs of union organizers are concerns.

The U.S. products that are most affected are varied. Property rights issues affect mostly video and sound recordings, books, trademark clothing, cable broadcasts, and medicines; sanitary regulations harm imports of fresh food, and meat and poultry; and special taxes tend to fall on fruit, tobacco, soft drinks, and imported goods not considered basic foodstuffs. In sum, bureaucratic expediency and transparency, simplification of sanitary regulation, streamlining of the tax system, and enforcement of property rights seem to be the policies that could lead to the best improvement in the image of Central American countries as trade partners of the United States.

* See U.S. Trade Department, Bureau of Economic and Business Affairs. "1997 Country Reports on Economic Policy and Trade Practices." Http://www.state.gov/www/issues/economic/trade_reports/index.html.

ports. Such policies are often classified as "free trade" initiatives. A second area of reform is the strengthening of existing regional trade agreements and the creation of new ones to provide preferential access to regional partners. Prime examples are the creation of MERCOSUR and NAFTA in the 1990s, as well as the revival of older agreements such as the Central American Common Market (CACM) and the Andean Pact. Finally, a third area of reform is the liberalization of capital flows, and especially of Foreign Direct Investment (FDI). The internationalization of production and the move to privatization in developing countries make investment policy a key area of action for governments. This section reviews the benefits of trade liberalization with particular attention to trade agreements. It also sets out the benefits associated with FDI inflows.

The Benefits of Trade Liberalization

The economics literature has considered at least five important benefits of trade liberalization:

1. Static-efficiency-gains associated with better allocation of factors across sectors.
2. Economies of scale, derived from access to a larger market.
3. Acquisition and development of more appropriate technologies.
4. Increased ability to cope with external shocks.
5. Reduction in rent-seeking activities.

The static-efficiency-gains argument maintains that the benefits of trade liberalization stem from exposure to undistorted world market prices. Trade barriers tend to raise the domestic price of import-competing products relative to the domestic price of exportables, making imports relatively more expensive. The reduction in tariffs, subsidies, and quotas eliminates this wedge, aligning domestic prices with world prices so that the correct incentives are given to domestic producers and consumers. Countries with open-trade policies thus benefit from more efficient price systems and can exploit their comparative advantage to attain the highest possible value for their output.[1] Economists have analyzed extensively the effect of import-substitution policies and documented the deleterious effects on developing countries of the trade protectionism of the 1960s and 1970s.[2] The next four arguments relate to the dynamic benefits of trade.

Economies of scale are a second important argument in favor of liberalizing trade. Small economies such as those of Central America can especially benefit from access to the larger sales base afforded by the world market. In protected markets with restricted entry, the benefits of scale economies are not achieved: firms are lured by the high prices they can charge for their products in the closed market, the number of firms tends to be above the optimal, and the scale of production falls below the optimum level. The expansion in production, driven by export growth, allows firms to reduce costs through economies of scale. Murphy, Shleifer, and Vishny (1989) argue convincingly that trade liberalization can have a sort of "big-push" effect on capital accumulation, one capable of furthering industrialization and overcoming low income in developing countries.

Third, open economies are particularly well positioned to benefit from technology transfers, which are a source of innovation and growth. A series of models developed by Grossman and Helpman (1991) has demonstrated that the combination of technical change and liberalized trade may provide the stimulus for countries to specialize in nontraditional goods.[3] Endogenous growth models tend to complement the evidence provided by country- and

---

1. See Dollar (1992).

2. See Bhagwati (1993) and Svedberg (1991) for case studies of India and Sub-Saharan Africa that document the rise in inefficient, high-cost industries spawned by domestic prices in excess of world prices. Balassa (1971) estimated the cost of protection in Brazil at that time to be as high as 9.5 percent of gross national product. In the case of South Korea, Gunasekera and Tyers (1991) reported welfare gains equivalent to 7 percent of GDP resulting from the liberalization of Korea's trade.

3. As noted by Rodriguez and Rodrik (1999), this result holds for countries that have a comparative advantage in specific activities, driven by economies of scale and technological progress, precisely the ones able to deliver long-run growth.

industry-level case studies and to show that trade is associated with technological progress and growth.[4]

Fourth, the argument that open economies are more apt to respond to negative external shocks has been supported empirically in work by Balassa (1981a and 1981b) and Sachs (1985). Sachs argues that open economies in East Asia were able to avoid Latin America's debt crisis because their export sectors recovered quickly and generated the funds necessary to avoid balance-of-payments crises. Thus, even if open economies are more vulnerable to shocks from abroad, their outward orientation also allows them to recover more quickly.

Finally, trade liberalization has important institutional effects. Protectionist policies in the form of import quotas and licenses give government officials significant discretionary powers which tend to be improperly used. Domestic firms respond to the incentives in place by increasing their rent-seeking activities, and these further drive up the costs associated with protectionist policies. Krueger (1974) and Bhagwati (1982) have examined the links between protectionist trade policies and rent-seeking activities. Larraín and Tavares (1999) have shown that openness to trade is an important deterrent of corruption. In sum, trade liberalization is likely to be a simple and highly effective way to discipline economic and political players in otherwise insulated economies.

Gains from Regional Trade Agreements

Most regional trade agreements have followed the establishment in 1947 of the General Agreement on Tariffs and Trade (GATT).[5] The "new regionalism" of the 1990s has led to more than a hundred regional agreements, signed by both developed and developing countries and covering more than half of world trade.[6] These agreements take the form of custom unions, free trade areas, and nonreciprocal preferential agreements, and they generally establish that the tariffs applied to products that originate in the region are subject to lower rates than products from nonparticipating countries. In some cases, such as that of the European Union (EU), the treaties have evolved to encompass other areas, such as labor and capital mobility, and monetary unification.

Economists have traditionally criticized regional trade agreements as a second-best alternative to free trade. Regional integration has the beneficial effect of expanding the market size and reducing trade barriers within the area,

---

4. See Romer (1992), Amsden and Hikino (1991), and Young (1991).
5. See World Trade Organization (1995).
6. See Ethier (1998).

but often at the expense of increasing trade barriers with outside countries. These two effects are referred to as "trade creation" and "trade diversion." Krugman (1991) argues that the European Community's enlargement was suboptimal since southern European countries would divert grain purchases from inexpensive suppliers in South America and Australia to more expensive European suppliers.

Recent research, on the other hand, has argued in favor of trade agreements on the basis of the numerous benefits that are harder to compute using economic analysis. The nontraditional benefits from regional trade agreements, which include the reduced uncertainty and increased policy credibility, may be more important than traditional benefits from trade openness.

Ethier (1998) presents a model in which regional trade agreements benefit small developing countries by providing a signal of commitment to reform and increasing the bargaining power of contracting parties internally and externally. Fernandez (1997) argues that the government's commitment to trade liberalization is stronger under regional trade agreements due to better enforcement of penalties and the association of trade with other bilateral agreements. Regional treaties function as political tools that bind future governments, increase bargaining power with nonparticipant countries, and improve regional coordination through the establishment of formal institutions.

Perroni and Whalley (1994) argue that, especially for small countries, regional trade agreements function as an insurance against the risk of costly trade wars and trade disputes. Fernandez (1997) contends that regional trade agreements amongst developing countries do not mitigate risk as well as do agreements between developing and developed countries.

There is evidence that regional trade agreements can lead to dynamic effects by attracting FDI. Blomstrom and Kokko (1997) offer such evidence in a study of the impact of NAFTA, MERCOSUR, and the Canada-U.S. Free Trade Agreement.

Foreign Direct Investment and Economic Growth

The recent expansion of multinational production has led to an increase in FDI, defined as the flow of equity capital from a firm and its associates or subsidiaries abroad. The impact of FDI flows has been particularly important for developing countries because alternative sources of international lending are not always available. Foreign direct investment aids recipient countries through static and dynamic channels. A review of the case-study and cross-country literature by Blomstrom and Kokko (1996) concludes that foreign multinationals have contributed to productivity growth in host countries. Blomstrom and Kokko stress that a host country's "industry and policy environment are the most important determinants of the net benefits of FDI."[7] Borensztein, Gregorio, and Lee (1995) report a positive and statistically significant correlation between FDI and the rate of total capital accumulation in the host economy.

FDI allows firms to finance projects that could not be financed through domestic savings. In countries with undeveloped financial markets, minor stock market activity, or controlled credit markets, FDI flows are often the primary source of private sector capital investment. Several arguments have established the impact of FDI through increased technological transfers and diffusion, and the fostering of internal market competition. Blomstrom (1989) has noted that international transfers of technology can have important spillover effects on the local economy. The basis for the argument is that the benefits of the international technology extend beyond the proprietary firm through external effects. Multinationals can funnel modern technologies downstream to local suppliers and upstream to local clients. In addition, a "demonstration effect" can stimulate local firms to refine technologies introduced by multinational affiliates. FDI can also have positive spillovers by furthering international trade. In developing countries, multinational affiliates may finance many of the startup costs required to establish trade links. Domestic firms can learn from these effective international networks how to connect with foreign buyers and suppliers.[8]

TRADE

In spite of reversals and pace changes, Central American countries have been involved in a process of regional integration since the 1950s, when several bilateral trade agreements were signed. These were seen as paving the way for a regional trade area. In the early 1960s, the CACM was established through regional trade agreements. The aim was to build a common market that would evolve into a free-trade zone and ultimately, with the adoption of a common external tariff, into a customs union. The integration process, however, evolved into a scheme to promote industrialization through import substitution. In the early 1990s, with political stabilization and democratization in the region, integration revived under a different guise. After the Guatemala Protocol of 1993, the CACM changed gears toward liberalization of regional

---

7. See Blomstrom and Kokko (1996, 33).

8. For instance, Blomstrom (1990) reports that multinational affiliates played a key role in linking exporters of light consumer goods in developing countries to final buyers.

and international trade.[9] However, regional trade integration is an unfinished endeavor, and several private actors in Central America allude to its incomplete and imperfect character, saying that it is not "for real." The main shortcomings are the exclusion of important sectors such as agriculture, the ad hoc choice of "exceptions" to overall liberalization, the existence of cartels in air and sea transportation, and the poor road infrastructure. The large number of trade agreements within the region and with third parties stretch the capabilities of national and regional administrations and decrease the credibility of the liberalization process.[10]

The coordination of foreign trade policy has met with some success, particularly when Central America has presented a common front in hemispheric trade talks, such as the the Free Trade in the Americas meetings and negotiations with the Dominican Republic. The fact that the external tariff is not truly common, and the ubiquitous tendency to exclude certain products from liberalization, have led to the break up, in practical terms, of the Central American common front.[11]

Partners, Flows, and Products

Central America has developed a number of regional institutions in order to facilitate progress in trade integration and trade openness in general. One of the earliest institutions that has remained central to the provision of logistical and technical support is the Secretariat for Central American Economic Integration, known by its Spanish initials as SIECA. SIECA was created by the General Treaty of Central American Economic Integration, signed in 1960, to coordinate the integration effort. The Protocol of Tegucigalpa in 1991 created the Central American Integration System (SICA) but kept SIECA as the body responsible for the economic matters within this system. In 1993, the Guatemala Protocol created the Subsystem of Central American Economic Integration.

The integration process is led by the Central American presidents, who make joint decisions in the context of regional presidential summits. The executive element of the integration process depends on a series of ministerial meetings. The Council of Ministers of Economic Integration involves only those specifically responsible for the integration process (Ministers of the Economy) and the presidents of the central banks. The Inter-Sectoral and

---

9. See Chapter 2 in this volume.

10. See Tavares (1999).

11. In the case of the Dominican Republic, agreement to elaborate five bilateral lists has compounded the problems of treaty implementation.

Table 5-1.   *Economic Integration in Central America*[a]

Institution	Who Sits?	Mission	Responds To
Council of Ministers of Economic Integration	—Ministers of economy —Presidents of central banks	Policy decision and coordination	Presidents Summit
Intersectoral Council of Ministers of Economic Integration	—Ministers of economy —Ministers of other branches	Policy decision	
Sectoral Council of Ministers	—Ministers of one branch	Policy decision on specific area	
Executive Committee of Economic Integration	—Representative of each country	Execution of the policy decisions	Council of Ministers of Economic Integration
SIECA[b]	—Secretary General (nominated by the Council of Ministers of Economic Integration) and technicians	Technical and administrative functions; policy proposals	Council of Ministers of Economic Integration
Consultative Committee of Economic Integration	Representatives of the private sector	Consultative	SIECA
Central American Bank for Economic Integration (BCIE)		Project financing	

[a]Does not include education and research institutions such as the Central American Public Administration Institute (ICAP) and the Central American Institute for Industrial Research and Technology (ICAITI).
[b]Includes the Secretariat of Agriculture and Poultry (SCA), the Secretariat of the Monetary Council (SMCA) and the Secretariat for Tourism Integration (SITCA).

Sectoral Council of Ministers asssemble only the ministers involved with the particular issues being discussed—agriculture or banking, for example. The Executive Committee of Economic Integration, made up of nominees of the ministers of the Economy and reporting to the Council of Ministers, approves specific projects and programs. SIECA provides logistical and technical support. The Consultative Committee of Economic Integration is a mainly consultative body made up of representatives of the private sector. Table 5-1 presents an outline of the framework of Central American integration, broken down by institution.

It is useful to look at the CACM in the context of the major trade agreements in the world. Tavares (1999) presents data on absolute and per capita

Table 5-2. *A Typology of Central America's Trade Negotiations*

	Type of Negotiation		
Number of Parts	*Coordinated*	*Converging*	*Unified*
Multilateral	World Trade Organization		
Plurilateral	Free Trade in the Americas		
Bilateral			United States
		Mexico	
			EU, CARICOM, MERCOSUR, Canada, Panama, Dominican Republic, Chile and the Republic of China
	Colombia and Venezuela		

Source: SIECA (1998).

gross domestic product, and distance to major markets for several regional trade agreements.[12] Central America is the smallest market: its total product is about six times smaller than the total product of the next smallest area, that encompassed by the Andean Pact. As a trade group, the CACM displays the lowest average GDP per capita of all trade areas (comparable only to the region of the Andean Pact), three times smaller than that of MERCOSUR, and twelve times smaller than the NAFTA average. Central America displays the second lowest ratio of average intraregional distance to average distance to all markets, suggesting the potential for regional integration.[13] Intraregional inequality in per capita GDP is high relative to average per capita GDP.[14]

The countries of Central America, individually or in groups, have ratified free trade agreements with a number of countries and trade areas. The scope and degree of completeness of these agreements varies substantially. Table 5-2 presents a list of the most important agreements being negotiated.[15]

The conclusion one derives from Table 5-2 may be misleading in that, in spite of the large number of "unified" trade negotiations, Central American

---

12. The agreements include the CACM, NAFTA, MERCOSUR, and the Andean Pact in the Americas; and the European Free Trade Association (EFTA) and the European Union in Europe.

13. The region with the lowest ratio is MERCOSUR, suggesting it is a natural trade bloc likely to deepen its ties in the future.

14. Interestingly, the regions involved in the NAFTA have a high value in this inequality index, certainly due to the large absolute difference between the GDP of Mexico and that of its partners.

15. Agreements can be classified as coordinated, converging, and unified. In coordinated agreements, there is an exchange of information between countries. In converging negotiations, the type of reciprocity expected from the outside partner is discussed in advance so that countries aim at similar results—even if progress is pursued individually. Unified agreements are jointly undertaken. See SIECA (1998).

policymakers frequently refer to the difficulties of coordinating trade policy between national governments. One contentious issue is the appropriate rate of liberalization. In the case of an agreement with Mexico, Costa Rica has been much more interested and active than the other countries in the region.[16] Another issue affecting the content of agreements as well as the speed of reaching them is the close integration of the private sector in negotiations. This results in a tendency to mix private and public priorities, a recognized lack of technical expertise, and a lack of continuity in the negotiating teams.[17] Private participation in policymaking in the trade area is an expedient way to give the government negotiation teams a sense of the priorities of the economic agents, and to obtain invaluable feedback from civil society.[18]

All Central American countries are currently full members of the General Agreement on Tariffs and Trade (GATT). Accession negotiations were pursued independently; thus each country has different end-agreements.[19] Countries in the region are also members of the World Trade Organization (WTO), created in 1994, and have ratified subsidiary agreements including those on trade in services and on intellectual property as it relates to commerce. Central America has thus committed to tariff cuts and harmonization in the 1995–2004 period. There is a specific agreement on agriculture that commits countries to convert nontariff barriers into tariff barriers, as well as an agreement on services.

However, the key multilateral agreement prompting trade liberalization in Central America is the Free Trade in the Americas (FTAA) initiative. An attempt by the United States to encourage trade openness in the American continent and respond to pleas for access to the U.S. market. In 1998 the FTAA negotiations were relaunched at the Summit of the Americas in Santiago de Chile. Ultimately, the agreement was meant to encompass, in some form, the various regional agreements in the Americas.[20] Its inclusiveness was, however, also a weakness; the need to accommodate a large number of countries that desire to liberalize different speeds is a potential handicap. Important for Central America (and the Caribbean) was the creation of a committee to analyze issues specific to small economies. Presently, there is a commitment to conclude negotiations by 2005 but the most important hurdle to FTAA advancement is clearly the concrete political will in the United States to pursue it to its fullest consequences.

---

16. See Gonzalez (1998).

17. See Gonzalez (1998).

18. See Estrada (1998).

19. Nicaragua has belonged to the GATT since 1950, Costa Rica since 1990, El Salvador and Guatemala since 1991, and Honduras since 1994.

20. Such as NAFTA, MERCOSUR, the Andean Pact, CARICOM, and the CACM.

An important issue in the characterization of Central American trade is the degree of diversification, both of clients and suppliers. Central American exports are very concentrated in a few client economies, and the countries in the region are remarkably similar in the relative importance of the different client markets. Between 67 percent and 92 percent of Central America's exports in 1998 flowed to developed economies, and these figures have increased since.[21] Table 5-3 presents the share of Central American exports to and imports from the major partners, as well as the growth rates, using 1996 data.[22] The salient feature is the importance of the countries involved in NAFTA, and more specifically, the United States, as a client and supplier. In 1996, the United States absorbed 38.5 percent of total exports from Central America and supplied 45 percent of the region's imports. The countries in NAFTA supplied more than half of Central America's imports. In addition to this high level of transactions, exports from Central America to NAFTA countries are growing at substantial rates.[23] The overall pattern of trade flows has been very stable and, after a slight decrease in the share of exports to the United States in 1994 and 1995 (in the wake of NAFTA), previous levels were quickly resumed.[24]

Although there has been an upward shift in recent years, the level of transactions with Mexico, in sharp contrast with the United States, has been very disappointing: Mexico has typically acquired only 2 percent to 3 percent of total Central American. In spite of its geographical and cultural proximity, Mexico has been less important as a client than South America and Asia. Trade between Mexico and Central America tends to display a surplus in favor of Mexico, which, unlike Central America, relies on a diverse set of exports. Costa Rica was the first country in Central America to liberalize trade with Mexico in a comprehensive trade agreement that addressed tariff and nontariff barriers and created a set of side agreements on services, investment, intellectual property, and business travel. Bilateral trade increased substantially, as did the bilateral deficit. The negotiations between El Salvador, Honduras, and Guatemala on the one hand, and Mexico on the other, have been dragging on for years and it is unclear when they will be finalized.

Canada, the other NAFTA partner, drafted a framework agreement on trade and investment with the region in 1998, outlining joint objectives. Costa Rica has already signed a bilateral investment agreement with Canada, which is meant to complement a future trade agreement. Panama, a country

---

21. See Inter-American Development Bank (1999).

22. See Inter-American Development Bank (1999).

23. This is only surpassed by the growth in exports to the G-3 group (Colombia, Mexico, and Venezuela), probably reflecting the emergence of Mexico as a client.

24. See Tavares (1999).

Table 5-3. *Central America—Exports and Imports as Share of Total CACM Flows*

	Andean Community	CACM	CARICOM	G–3	MERCOSUR	NAFTA	USA	EU–15	Pacific
Exports	1.7	20.9	0.7	3.1	0.2	42.1	38.5	24.8	2.6
Imports	6.4	12.3	0.3	12.6	2.1	53.8	45.5	9.7	7.5

Source: Inter-American Development Bank (1999). Data for 1996.

whose contiguity to Central America and control of the Panama Canal is key to the development of Central American trade, has so far pursued its very own trade and investment objectives. This is the result of its special political and economic ties with the United States. The potential exists for Panama to exploit its canal infrastructure and relatively advanced financial sector to become a service provider for Central America.

After NAFTA, the two most important markets for Central America are the European Union (EU) and the CACM itself, each responsible for purchasing between 20 percent and 25 percent of total Central American exports. Unlike the countries in NAFTA, which are important as both a client and a supplier, the EU is more important as a client. Exchanges with the EU are mostly under the Generalized System of Preferences. So far, trade agreements between Central America, the countries in the Andean Pact and the countries in MERCOSUR have not borne much fruit. With MERCOSUR the situation is less auspicious; there is a 1998 framework agreement to facilitate trade and investment between the regions, but no formal trade agreements have been signed.[25]

Trade flows between Central America and the rest of the world are a determinant of the region's economic performance. Export and import flows in both absolute terms and relative to GDP increased for all Central American countries in the 1990s after the decrease of the 1980s. Table 5-4 displays the growth rates of GDP, exports, imports, and the change in trade intensities in the 1990s. We see that exports and imports tended to grow at substantially higher rates than GDP, sometimes twice as high.[26] Nicaragua, after the lifting of the U.S. embargo in the early 1990s, saw exports grow almost four times faster than GDP. As a result, indicators of export and import intensity grew across the region.

The structure of trade flows in products is also very similar between coun-

---

25. Chile, a country associated with MERCOSUR, has proposed to sign a trade agreement with Central America as part of its general pursuit of free trade with all countries in the Western Hemisphere.

26. The exception is Honduras.

Table 5-4. *Growth of Trade and GDP in the 1990s—Central America and Latin America*

	GDP Growth	Exports			Imports		
		Growth	Percent of GDP		Growth	Percent of GDP	
	1990–98	1990–98	1990	1998	1990–98	1990	1998
Costa Rica[b]	4.0	9.1	34.2	46.2	9.0	41.1	46.9
El Salvador	5.0	12.2	18.6	22.7	14.1	31.2	35.7
Guatemala	4.1	7.0	19.7	17.8	10.3	23.7	26.2
Honduras[ab]	3.1	2.3	37.2	46.2	2.9	39.9	52.2
Nicaragua	2.4	9.7	24.9	37.8	8.3	43.4	77.6
Central America	**3.7**	**8.1**	**26.9**	**34.1**	**9.0**	**35.9**	**47.7**
Latin America[a]	**3.3**	**8.3**	**15.0**	**20.7**	**13.2**	**7.6**	**24.3**

Source: Inter-American Development Bank (1999).
[a]For Latin America and Honduras, GDP export and import growth rates refer to 1990–1997.
[b]For Costa Rica and Honduras, export and import shares are for 1997.

tries in Central America, reflecting a long-lasting specialization in agricultural goods.[27] The importance of coffee and fruits as export products tends to decrease slowly but has far from subsided. Table 5-5 presents the share of the five most important export products for each of the Central American countries and for Latin America, contrasting the 1991 and 1996 figures.[28] It is noticeable that the Central American export of products is more concentrated than that of Latin America as a whole. This reality remained substantially unchanged in the 1990s, as shown by the figures for 1991 or 1996. Honduras stands out as the least diversified in both years. However, during this period, Central America progressed more than the rest of Latin America America toward greater diversification; the share of the five top products decreased by an average of 7 percent in Central America, compared to 3 percent in Latin America as a whole. An examination of some of the specific products reveals just how concentrated exports from Central America are. Coffee is the main export product in four countries, its share in total exports ranging from 14 percent to 36 percent; fruit and nuts are important for Costa Rica, Honduras, and Guatemala. Of the other export products displayed, only Medicaments is not part of the primary exports category. The importance of medicaments, as well as of crustaceans and mollusks, suggests what may become a new pattern of regional specialization.

Countries that have developed successfully have been able to shift from agricultural products to labor-intensive manufactures. Several countries with

---

27. Chapter 2 in this volume presents an overview of the economic history of regional export specialization.

28. See Inter-American Development Bank (1998).

Table 5-5. *Central America and Latin America—Share of Top Five Export Products in Total Exports*

	Share of the Top Five Export Products		Share of Some Top Five Export Products by Country				
			1996				
			071 Coffee and Substitutes	057 Fruits and Nuts	061 Sugar and Molasses	036 Crustaceans and Mollusks	542 Medicaments
	1991	1996					
Costa Rica	60.3	56.8	14.1	23.1	—	—	—
El Salvador	55.8	51.2	34.1	—	4.3	4.1	4.6
Guatemala	51.6	49.8	23.3	9.1	10.9	—	3.5
Honduras	77.4	70.7	26.1	19.7	—	6.8	—
Nicaragua	69.9	49.7	19.4	—	—	9.7	—
Latin America	45.0	41.7	—	—	—	—	—

Source: Inter-American Development Bank (1998). Note: The full product designations are 071 Coffee and Coffee Substitutes, 057 Fruit and Nuts (not including oil nuts), fresh or dried, 061 Sugars, Molasses and Honey, 036 Crustaceans, Mollusks and Aquatic Invertebrates, whether in shell or not, fresh (live or dead) and 542 Medicaments (including veterinary medicaments). The percentages of total exports are only displayed when the product is one of the top five export products for the country in question.

levels of GDP per capita similar to Central America have much larger net exports of manufactures.

What Drives Central American Exports?

In devising a trade strategy for Central America, it is important to understand the determinants of the region's export flows. Clark and tavares (1999) analyze Central American exports in the context of the "gravity equation" approach. This empirical approach proposes that bilateral trade flows are affected positively by the importer and exporter countries' economic sizes and stages of development[29] and negatively by geographical and cultural "resistance" factors, such as bilateral distance and use of different official languages.[30] Intuitively, higher volumes of economic transactions (indicated by higher GDP levels) lead to a higher likelihood of transactions across borders, i.e., international trade. As for per capita GDP, a higher level tends to be associated with a more diversified economy, which also leads to more frequent

29. Measured, respectively, by absolute and per capita GDP.
30. The term "gravity equation" comes from an analogy to Newton's Law of Universal Gravitation that says matter attracts other matter with a force that is proportional to the product of their masses and inversely proportional to (the square of) the distance between them.

cross-border trade. The association between distance and less trade is also in-tuitive, relying on transport costs or other resistance factors.[31]

Even though the gravity approach started as no more than a successful em-pirical relationship,[32] researchers progressively recognized that most available models of international trade deliver predictions that are compatible with it. Helpman (1987) added to its theoretical legitimacy by using the significance of gravity-type variables in empirical trade studies to support the reasonable-ness of theories of trade relying on monopolistic competition. More recently, Deardorff (1995) has shown how the problem of the gravity equation is not lack but overabundance of theoretical support. For our purposes, what is rel-evant is that the gravity approach delivers high predictive power, making it the appropriate instrument for the study of the determinants of bilateral trade flows.

The basic specification studied in Clark and Tavares (1999) is:

$$X_{ij} = \alpha(POP_iPOP_j)^{\beta}(PGNP_iPGNP_j)^{\delta}(DIST)^{\gamma}\exp(\gamma BORD + \eta LANG + \mu BLOCS + \varepsilon)$$

where X_{ij} denotes the dependent variable (bilateral exports from country i to country j), POP denotes total population, PGNP denotes per capita GNP, DIST refers to the distance between countries i and j, BORD takes the value of one if countries are adjacent and zero otherwise, LANG takes the value of one if countries share the same language and zero otherwise. BLOCS is a vector including dummies for regional blocs, each of these taking the value of one if countries belong to the corresponding regional bloc and zero otherwise.[33] The sample is composed of sixty-eight countries, which include the major trading countries in the world as defined in Wei and Frankel (1995) along with the Central American countries. Trade flows are measured for 1970, 1980, 1990, and 1995.[34]

The first appropriate questions are whether Central American exports are reasonably well explained by the gravity variables and whether they show any specificity. Clark and Tavares (1999) approach these issues by analyzing, in ad-

---

31. The introduction of a control for whether countries share a common language or a common land border accounts for these additional trade resistance factors and allows the dis-tance variable to capture more precisely the effect of transport costs on trade volume.

32. See Tinbergen (1962).

33. Given that the dependent variable is bounded below by zero—and many observations achieve this bound— Clark and Tavares (1999) present this gravity equation using the Tobit procedure instead of the usual Ordinary Least Squares. This method avoids bias in the esti-mates by taking into account the large subsample of observations that are zero due to the fact that many pairs of countries do not trade among themselves.

34. See Clark and Tavares (1999) for a detailed presentation of the data sources and empiri-cal procedure.

dition to the full sample, the subsample in which any of the Central American countries is an exporter, and comparing the results with those of the subsample of East Asian (EA9), nonindustrial (NIND), and industrial (IND) exporters.[35] On the importer side, the sample is divided into industrial (IND) and nonindustrial (NIND) country groups. Estimation results are presented in Table 5-6. Notice first how the negative coefficient on distance in the Central America sample is higher than that of any other group of countries, which shows that Central American exports go to other countries in the region and to the United States, i.e., to importers that are geographically close. The distance coefficient for nonindustrialized, East Asian, and industrialized countries gets progressively closer to zero, suggesting that the higher the level of an exporter's income, the less important distance is in determining bilateral export volume.[36] While the coefficient for the border dummy is larger for Central America, the coefficient on common language comes out as insignificant.[37]

With respect to the size and income effect, the overall results make sense: when the importer is a nonindustrial country, an increase in its size does not affect exports as much as an increase in the exporter's size. The reverse is true when the importer country is industrialized. As for the effect of income per capita, it seems that the exporter's characteristics are the main determinants of flows. The exceptions are Central America and East Asia, whose exports to industrial countries depend more on the latter's income per capita. The effect of size on the importer economy in the large sample is smaller for Central America than for any other subsample of exporters. The split of the sample into industrial and nonindustrial countries reveals that while an increase in the size of nonindustrial economies has a very small effect on Central America's exports (0.217 in column 3, the increase in size of the industrial clients has a very strong effect on Central America's exports (0.926 in column seven). The increase in the size of Central American exporters, on the other hand, strongly affects exports to nonindustrial countries (1.271 in column three six) and has little effect

---

35. EA9 includes continental China, Hong Kong, Indonesia, Malaysia, the Philippines, Singapore, South Korea, Taiwan, and Thailand. Japan is included in IND. Industrialized and nonindustrialized correspond to the Organization for Economic Cooperation and Development (OECD) member states and non-OECD member states, respectively, with Mexico considered a non-OECD state.

36. For most exporter groups, the distance coefficient is higher when the importer is nonindustrial, again suggesting a negative relationship between one of the partner's level of development and the importance of distance. As expected, the stage of development reveals a host of a country's characteristics, including good transport infrastructure.

37. Its negative sign indicates that, if anything, Central America trades less with Spanish speaking countries than with other countries, probably a result of the relatively low volume of exports from Central America to other countries in Latin America.

Table 5-6. *Determinants of Bilateral Exports—Is Central America Different?*

Variables	General	Non-industrial Countries as Importers				Industrial Countries as Importers			
		CA	NIND	IND	EA9	CA	NIND	IND	EA9
Distance	−0.889*	−1.799*	−1.285	−0.703*	−1.515*	−1.524	−0.655*	−0.728*	−0.486*
	(0.020)	(0.176)	(0.049)	(0.035)	(0.099)	(0.201)	(0.038)	(0.017)	(0.158)
Size Effect									
Exporter	1.013*	1.271*	1.159*	1.134*	0.892*	0.251	0.832*	0.801*	0.645*
	(0.012)	(0.287)	(0.029)	(0.017)	(0.103)	(0.165)	(0.020)	(0.012)	(0.075)
Importer	0.919*	0.217**	0.877*	0.777*	0.737*	0.926*	1.121*	0.778*	1.023*
	(0.011)	(0.103)	(0.028)	(0.019)	(0.058)	(0.049)	(0.018)	(0.012)	(0.034)
Income Effect									
Exporter	1.308*	1.876*	1.466*	1.666*	1.518*	0.853*	1.021*	1.070*	0.861*
	(0.012)	(0.233)	(0.037)	(0.053)	(0.141)	(0.126)	(0.026)	(0.040)	(0.102)
Importer	1.198*	0.762*	1.015*	0.984*	0.861*	1.673*	0.834*	0.678*	1.064*
	(0.012)	(0.132)	(0.036)	(0.024)	(0.070)	(0.155)	(0.056)	(0.040)	(0.108)
Border	0.752*	1.939*	1.213*	0.769**	1.335*	–	0.495	0.372*	–
	(0.094)	(0.499)	(0.169)	(0.325)	(0.442)		(0.350)	(0.076)	
Language	0.802*	−0.808**	0.920*	0.746*	0.183	−0.054	0.466*	0.634*	0.947*
	(0.043)	(0.378)	(0.092)	(0.073)	(0.192)	(0.318)	(0.079)	(0.060)	(0.141)
# Observations	17828	885	8016	3982	1593	440	3982	1848	792
Log Likelihood	−30747.96	−793.10	−12360.84	−6648.09	−2835.52	−647.73	−6986.90	−2113.47	−1323.14
Year Dummies	Yes	Yes	Yes	Yes	Yes	Yes	Yes	Yes	Yes

Source: Based on Clark and Tavares (1999), Table III. Note: A constant was included in each specification.
(*): significant at 1 percent, (**): significant at 5 percent.
The first row indicates the coefficient value and the second its standard error.

on exports to industrial countries (0.251 in Column 7), Central America's exports, it seems, are particularly sensitive to growth in developed economies.[38]

As for the income effect, Central America is very sensitive to increases in its own and in its client's income per capita. Moreover, in line with results on size, an increase in Central America's own income per capita has a larger effect on exports to nonindustrial countries than for industrial countries. When results for industrial importers are compared, the differences are striking: increases in the client's income per capita have an elasticity of 1.673 in the case of Central America and at most 1.064 for other exporter groups.[39] Since, as seen above, the largest share of Central America's trade is with industrialized countries, these results suggest that growth in Central America will tend to diversify its client base.[40]

The message seems to be twofold. First, growth in rich countries affects Central America's exports more than growth in poor countries, irrespective of whether the growth is in the economy's sheer size or in income per capita. Second, growth of the Central American economies provides more exports to nonindustrial countries than to industrial countries, again irrespective of whether the growth is in the size of the economy or in income per capita.

Trade Creation and Trade Diversion

One of the questions that is particularly suited for study through the gravity approach is the extent to which trade agreements affect trade flows. Trade blocs are groups of countries that share institutional mechanisms that can favor or hamper imports from certain countries outside the bloc. The creation of trade blocs can lead to trade creation, the increase in trade between countries within the bloc due to the decrease in intrabloc barriers to trade. However, trade blocs can also lead to trade diversion when the decrease in internal barriers to trade leads to the substitution of suppliers outside the bloc for less efficient suppliers inside the bloc. Trade creation and trade diversion are studied through the introduction of dummy variables. These dummy variables take the value of one when both countries belong to the trade agree-

---

38. It is true that for all subsamples of exporters, their own size effect tends to be larger than the client size effect when the client is nonindustrial, and the reverse when the client is industrial. For Central America, however, the difference is starker.

39. For all other exporter groups, their own income effect is higher than the client's income effect when the importer country is industrialized.

40. The results on distance, language, size, and income are confirmed when samples isolating each of the Central American countries are analyzed. The only exception is the high value of the coefficient on border, which is entirely due to Nicaragua.

ment and zero otherwise (trade creation); or they take the value of one when
one country does and the other does not belong to the trade agreement
(trade diversion).

Naturally, most of the gravity literature on trade creation and trade diversion tends to focus on trade agreements between developed countries.[41]
Brada and Mendez (1985) use one of the few applications of the gravity
framework on a sample including the CACM: they attempt to quantify the
increase of trade by comparing the CACM with other trade agreements[42] in
the years 1970, 1973, and 1976. Trade creation effects are divided into an
"environment effect," which is related to average distance and per capita
GDP, and a "policy effect," which measures directly the effectiveness of the
trade agreement in promoting trade creation. The CACM stands out for two
different reasons. First, the environment effects are of the same order of
magnitude as those in the European Economic Community (EEC) and the
European Free Trade Association (EFTA) and much larger than those in the
Andean Pact and the Latin American Free Trade Association.[43] Second, trade
creation due to policy factors is higher for the CACM than for any other
trade area, which may be interpreted as evidence that policies favoring Central American integration are likely to have a large impact on regional trade
flows.

Table 5-7 presents the results from Clark and Tavares (1999) on trade creation and trade diversion for the whole sample (1970–95), and for each of the
four subperiods. Since the issue of interest is the relationship between Central
America and each of the trade blocs, a dummy variable was introduced to account for cases where the exporter was from Central America and the importer from a specific bloc. This is designated "TD-CA." The CACM is the
area with the most trade-creation effects, even though trade creation is found

---

41. Bayoumi and Eichengreen (1995) find that the European Economic Community (EEC)
and the European Free Trade Association (EFTA) areas are responsible for an increase in trade
volume that cannot be attributed to the member countries' economic characteristics. Frankel,
et al. (1993) find evidence in favor of the existence of three trading blocs (Americas, Europe,
and Eastern Asia) since intraregional trade exceeds what can be explained by the usual gravity
variables. Wei and Frankel (1995) attempt to evaluate whether emerging trade blocs are
trade-reducing or trade-enhancing. They find that both East Asia and Western Europe were
more open in the 1970s and 1980s, but while East Asia's openness increased with time, the opposite happened in Europe.

42. The other trade agreements include the EEC, the EFTA, and the Andean Pact.

43. This is due to the fact that the average distance between Central American economies is
the shortest for the sample of trade pacts and compensates for the fact that Central American
countries are relatively poor and thus, all else being equal, would tend to trade less with each
other.

for the East Asia, EFTA and Andean Pact blocs.[44] As for trade diversion, the results show that most blocs are actually open to imports from the outside, as evidenced by a positive coefficient on TD for the bloc. For the CACM, there is no evidence that it negatively affected the volume of trade between Central America and outside countries.

As mentioned above, the coefficients of the TD-CA dummies estimate whether a particular bloc is closed or open with respect to Central America, *over and above* its degree of openness to all countries. Openness toward Central America differs from overall openness in the cases of East Asia and MERCOSUR, which are more closed to Central America than to other countries. EFTA and the EC, on the other hand, are more open to Central American exports than is predicted by the basic gravity framework. When we look at 1995 only, the same evidence emerges. In 1995, NAFTA seems more open to imports from Central America than from other regions.[45] Clark and Tavares (1999) tested whether each bloc was closed or open to Central American exports in absolute terms.[46] They show that only for MERCOSUR (whole period and 1995) and East Asia (1995) is there conclusive statistical evidence that there is trade diversion with respect to Central America.

The Importance of U.S. Duties

In the wake of the NAFTA agreement, exports from Central America and Mexico have been subject to different import duties as they enter the United States. This divergence is intensifying and is unlikely to subside unless trade access by Central American countries is written into a new trade agreement. Table 5-8 displays the evolution of import duties to which Central American exports are subject relative to Mexican import duties, for both manufactures and for all goods. The impact of the NAFTA agreement, which came into effect in 1994, is noticeable: relative charges on manufactures more than doubled for all countries in the region from two times the Mexican levels to four times the Mexican levels; for all, the same effect is present, even if slightly less

---

44. No evidence is found of trade creation for the European Community in the 1970–1995 period or for MERCOSUR and the NAFTA. The high volume of trade between the countries in these areas is thus fully explained by gravity factors such as distance and income per capita.

45. This probably reflects the high historical volume of trade between the two regions; it is not an estimate of the specific impact of the NAFTA.

46. This corresponds to testing whether the sum of the coefficients TD and TD-CA is smaller or larger than zero.

Table 5-7. *Trade Blocs and Trade Creation (1970–1995)*

Variables	1970–1995	1970	1980	1990	1995
Constant	−14.248*	−14.543*	−18.591*	−15.836*	−16.425*
	(0.255)	(0.496)	(0.658)	(0.519)	(0.476)
Distance	−0.794*	−0.688*	−0.815*	−0.760*	−0.820*
	(0.022)	(0.041)	(0.050)	(0.044)	(0.040)
Population (size)	0.961*	0.832*	0.983*	0.952*	1.036*
	(0.009)	(0.017)	(0.020)	(0.017)	(0.015)
Per Capita GNP	1.234*	1.239*	1.388*	1.178*	1.224*
	(0.010)	(0.022)	(0.025)	(0.017)	(0.016)
Border	0.667*	0.626*	0.723*	1.217*	0.181
	(0.093)	(0.173)	(0.209)	(0.181)	(0.170)
Language	0.780*	0.553*	0.868*	0.746*	1.011*
	(0.043)	(0.081)	(0.098)	(0.084)	(0.073)
EA (TC)	1.673*	1.785*	1.339*	2.273*	1.388*
	(0.106)	(0.200)	(0.245)	(0.211)	(0.178)
EA (TD)	0.489*	0.460*	0.417*	0.810*	0.151b
	(0.049)	(0.095)	(0.112)	(0.096)	(0.088)
EA (TD-CA)	−0.819*	0.044	−0.559	−1.576*	−0.788*
	(0.174)	(0.370)	(0.407)	(0.344)	(0.254)
NAFTA (TC)	0.561	—	—	—	0.273
	(0.776)	—	—	—	(0.652)
NAFTA (TD)	−0.033	—	—	—	−0.490*
	(0.152)	—	—	—	(0.135)
NAFTA (TD-CA)	0.956b	—	—	—	1.018**
	(0.510)	—	—	—	(0.426)
EC (TC)	0.079	0.689b	0.143	0.276	−0.271b
	(0.113)	(0.416)	(0.320)	(0.208)	(0.150)
EC (TD)	0.738*	1.170*	1.076*	0.892*	0.011
	(0.051)	(0.115)	(0.119)	(0.094)	(0.081)
EC (TD-CA)	0.465*	0.286	0.788**	0.033	0.800*
	(0.147)	(0.371)	(0.371)	(0.276)	(0.203)

pronounced.[47] The evolution of relative duties between 1994 and 1998 shows that they doubled in this short period following the creation of NAFTA. In some countries, the figure actually is closer to a fourfold increase. Exports from Central America to the United States are thus subject to duties close to ten times the level of duties on Mexican exports.

Clark and Tavares estimate the effect of U.S. import duties on the level of Central American exports to the United States. As Table 5-9 shows, relative import duties have a statistically significant negative effect on the level of Central American exports to the United States. The effects are strongest for Honduras, Guatemala, and El Salvador, in decreasing order of magnitude.

---

47. Costa Rica is the exception, probably due to the fact that its exports to the United States are not so dependent on manufactures.

Table 5-7. *Continued*

Variables	1970–1995	1970	1980	1990	1995
EFTA (TC)	0.909*	1.345*	0.781	−0.187	0.278
	(0.216)	(0.284)	(0.499)	(0.561)	(0.647)
EFTA (TD)	0.408*	0.755*	0.779*	0.092	−0.557*
	(0.064)	(0.101)	(0.141)	(0.137)	(0.138)
EFTA (TD-CA)	1.156*	0.425	1.666*	1.315*	1.318*
	(0.209)	(0.327)	(0.462)	(0.451)	(0.453)
MERCOSUR (TC)	1.060b	—	—	—	1.020**
	(0.552)	—	—	—	(0.473)
MERCOSUR (TD)	0.077	—	—	—	−0.196b
	(0.136)	—	—	—	(0.119)
MERCOSUR (TD-CA)	−2.920*	—	—	—	−2.835*
	(0.589)	—	—	—	(0.495)
CACM (TC)	3.733*	3.780*	3.996*	3.383*	3.726*
	(0.225)	(0.419)	(0.520)	(0.450)	(0.377)
CACM (TD)	0.201*	0.060	0.189	0.240b	0.147
	(0.068)	(0.140)	(0.156)	(0.133)	(0.111)
ANDEAN (TC)	1.753*	—	—	—	1.431*
	(0.428)	—	—	—	(0.365)
ANDEAN (TD)	−0.073	—	—	—	−0.329*
	(0.125)	—	—	—	(0.110)
ANDEAN (TD-CA)	−0.419	—	—	—	−0.531
	(0.434)	—	—	—	(0.368)
# Observations	17828	4556	4556	4556	4556
Log Likelihood	−30331.41	−6553.14	−8155.39	−8091.34	−7140.37
Year Dummies	Yes	No	No	No	No

Source: Clark and Tavares (1999), Table V.
Note: (*): significant at 1 percent, (**): significant at 5 percent. First row indicates the coefficient value and the second its standard error. The abbreviations are as follows: EA – East Asia; NAFTA – North American Free Trade Agreement; EC – European Community; EFTA – European Free Trade Agreement; MERCOSUR – South American Common Market; CACM – Central American Common Market; ANDEAN – Andean Pact. TC and TD refer to trade creation and trade diversion, respectively.

Table 5-8. *Relative U.S. Import Duties—Central America versus Mexico*

	All Commodities			Manufactures		
	1990	1994	1998	1990	1994	1998
Costa Rica	3.2	3.1	3.7	2.0	3.9	9.8
Guatemala	1.9	4.3	13.3	2.0	6.1	25.3
Honduras	1.6	4.2	9.1	2.1	4.8	13.5
El Salvador	1.9	5.6	12.2	1.8	5.6	16.8
Nicaragua	0.1	3.4	13.7	0.1	7.9	27.2

Source: U.S. International Trade Commission (1999) Note: Figures represent the average import duty on each Central American country's exports divided by the equivalent Mexican magnitude.

Table 5-9.   *Effect of Relative Import Duties on Central American Exports (1989–1996)*

	Estimates by Country					
	Central America	Costa Rica	El Salvador	Guatemala	Honduras	Nicaragua
Relative Duties	-0.992**	-1.050	-1.839**	-2.454**	-3.332*	0.134
	0.457	0.902	0.912	1.018	1.282	0.970

Source: Clark and Tavares (1999) Table X.
Note: (*): significant at 1 percent, (**): significant at 5 percent. The first row indicates the coefficient value and the second its standard error. Only the results on the variables of interest have been reported. All specifications include a constant, the product of importer and exporter country's population, and the product of their per capita GDP, bilateral distance, border, language, and year dummies.

The fact that Nicaraguan exports are not significantly affected by the increase in import duties is due to the fact that in the period under consideration, exports to the United States were increasing at a strong rate following the lifting of the trade embargo.

FOREIGN DIRECT INVESTMENT

Direct Investment Inflows to Developing Countries

Foreign investment flows have played a preeminent role in the economy and politics of developing countries. Much of the FDI previous to World War II was in industries related to natural resources.[48] Since the liberalization of the late 1980s and early 1990s, investment has become more diversified and in the last decade only 5 percent of total FDI outflows from the United States, Germany, Japan, and the U.K. have been of this kind. The flows of FDI to developing countries, particularly to Latin America, have gained a renewed importance in the 1990s. In 1997, world FDI has increased by 18 percent in real terms, compared with a 7 percent average growth rate for the 1990s. In this decade, developed countries accounted for the overwhelming share of FDI outflows (90 percent) as well as inflows (60 percent). [49] However, the share of developing countries' total inflows has been growing, reaching 38 percent in 1997. The increase in FDI inflows to Latin America has been remarkable, almost doubling between 1995 and 1997. In 1998, inflows to Latin America seemed to stabilize at the new, higher level. Compared to the 1980s average, annual FDI inflows to Latin America in the 1990s have increased almost five-

---

48. Around 60 percent of total stock, according to Dunning (1993).
49. See Cepal (1998).

fold. The average FDI-to-exports ratio increased from 5.6 percent in 1980 to 19.4 percent in 1999; the ratio is even larger for the top destinations.

The increase in FDI flows to Latin America was a broad phenomenon, even if Brazil accounted for almost half of the upswing, and emerged as the destination of 30 percent of all investments in 1997, as compared with 15 percent in the first half of the 1990s. The relative shares of Argentina, Chile, and Mexico shrank, even though all three (especially Argentina and Mexico) recorded sizeable increases in FDI inflows in absolute terms.[50] The reemergence of FDI to Latin America resulted in a considerable increase in the region's stock of FDI—47 percent of it being accumulated since 1990.[51] FDI inflows to countries in the Caribbean Basin climbed by 24 percent in 1997, the lion's share being destined to financial centers (57 percent in 1997).

Caribbean countries exceeded Central American countries in FDI growth for 1997. The steep ascent of FDI flows to Central America in the 1990s is the result of a number of factors, including new business opportunities resulting from economic liberalization accompanied by political and institutional stability. Costa Rica has probably been the most successful in attracting FDI to its high technology electronics and tourism areas. Table 5-10 presents FDI flows to Central America in the context of Latin America.

Table 5-11 presents the accumulated stock of FDI for Central American countries as of 1997. Costa Rica stands out as the best able to attract FDI flows, with foreign investment assets accounting for 35.5 percent of GDP. Most of the other countries in the region display a figure of around 15 percent.

Three factors seem to have contributed to FDI inflows into the Caribbean region. The first, which has been particularly important in the case of the Central American countries and the Dominican Republic, is the development of maquila industries in the Export Processing Zones (EPZs). The second, and more recent, factor is the privatization of telephone companies, electric companies, and financial firms, which gathered momentum in El Salvador, Guatemala, and Panama. The third factor is the establishment of high-technology electronics and computer firms catering to international markets or the construction of hotels and tourist facilities. The paradigmatic example is Costa Rica's successful bid for the Intel plant. Policymakers in the Dominican Republic appear to be heading in the direction of Costa Rica's example.

---

50. Colombia and Venezuela were also increasingly attractive destinations for foreign investors. The main exception to this overall increase of FDI flows to Latin America was Peru, where flows decreased considerably.

51. See Cepal (1998).

Table 5-10. *Central America, Latin America, and the Caribbean—Net Inward Foreign Direct Investment (1990–1997)*

	1990	1991	1992	1993	1994	1995	1996	1997
Argentina	1836	2439	4012	3261	3107	4783	5090	6326
Brazil	989	1103	2061	1292	3072	4859	1120	19652
Chile	661	822	935	1034	2583	2978	4724	5417
Mexico	2549	4742	4393	4389	10973	9526	9185	12477
Costa Rica	163	178	226	247	298	396	427	446
El Salvador	2	25	15	16	23	38	25	—
Guatemala	48	91	94	143	65	75	77	84
Honduras	44	52	48	27	35	50	91	122
Nicaragua	—	1	15	39	40	75	97	173
Central America	**257**	**347**	**398**	**472**	**461**	**634**	**717**	**825**
Central America and Caribbean Total	**938**	**1,244**	**1,140**	**1,318**	**1,726**	**1,865**	**2,044**	**2,892**
Share of Central America	**0.27**	**0.28**	**0.35**	**0.36**	**0.27**	**0.34**	**0.35**	**0.29**
Latin America	**7,297**	**11,841**	**13,390**	**12,783**	**26,280**	**28,535**	**40,048**	**58,500**
Share of Central America	**0.04**	**0.03**	**0.03**	**0.04**	**0.02**	**0.02**	**0.02**	**0.01**

Source: Cepal (1998). Note: 1998 estimates.

Table 5-11.   *FDI Stocks in Central America (1997)*

	FDI Stock as Share of GDP
Costa Rica	35.3
El Salvador	3.0
Guatemala	14.4
Honduras	16.4
Nicaragua	17.4

Source: Ramirez and Sullivan (1999). Note: 1998 estimates.

Determinants of FDI Inflows

There are a number of important determinants of FDI inflows, from general macroeconomic conditions such as economic growth and exchange-rate policy to microeconomic issues such as the quality of infrastructure and the regulatory and bureaucratic environment. Among the factors that have been recognized as key in attracting FDI are the size of the internal market and the rate of growth of the economy.[52] Trade liberalization has also been shown to be important. Moreover, the experience of small East Asian countries such as Singapore, Hong Kong, and Taiwan, has shown that a liberal export regime can eliminate the shortcomings of a limited internal market.[53] Before World War II, the existence of natural resources was a main determinant of FDI, but the focus has since changed to human capital and physical infrastructure, and there is evidence that good conditions in these areas can overcome higher labor costs.[54] Though labor costs are frequently mentioned as a determinant of FDI flows, evidence that this is the case is scarce.[55] As for tax incentives, the results are mixed, with Lim (1983) actually suggesting that overly generous benefits may have a negative impact since they provide the wrong signal as to the investment climate in the country. Higher levels of corruption and uncertainty have been robustly associated with lower FDI inflows.[56] EPZs seem to be well-fitted policy instruments for the attraction of FDI.[57]

Ramirez and Sullivan (1999) studied the determinants of foreign direct investment with special reference to Central America. Their econometric speci-

---

52. See, for instance, Agarwal (1980) and Torrisi (1985).

53. See Kravis and Lipsey (1982).

54. See Amirahmadi and Wu (1994) and Root and Ahmed (1979).

55. It seems that low labor costs are an important factor for the subsample of developing countries, but most FDI is directed at developed countries so that when a complete sample is used, countries with higher wage costs actually attract more FDI.

56. See Wei (1997a) and Wei (1997b).

57. In Korea, over 27 percent of total inward FDI was located in EPZs in the early 1970s, while in Costa Rica in the late 1980s, about 70 percent of all foreign companies that established operations did so in EPZs. See Esquivel, Jenkins and Larraín (1998).

fication had net FDI inflows, in absolute terms and as a percentage of GDP, as the variable to be explained by a series of macroeconomic and microeconomic determinants. They found that FDI inflows are associated with higher GDP growth, the size of the economy, stable real exchange rates, good infrastructure, human capital, and political stability.[58] Moreover, the authors found evidence that economies that are open can overcome their size disadvantage. Their main conclusions are that investment in infrastructure and increases in market size through international liberalization and regional integration encourage higher levels of FDI to Central America.

Central America vs. Mexico: Characterizing Differential Access to the U.S. Market

Central America enjoyed considerable prominence on the U.S. agenda at the height of the Cold War, since local insurgencies were considered a potential threat to U.S. interests. Security concerns were important enough to prompt a unilateral effort to expand access to the U.S. market for Central American and Caribbean countries and this led to the Caribbean Basin Initiative (CBI).[59] Then, the political climate in the United States changed, the prominence of the region faded, and the area was left with the challenge of securing trade relations with the northern market.

The United States is the most important client of Mexico and the majority of Central American countries. The signing of a free-trade agreement between the three large economies of North America in 1994 has led to diverging conditions of access to the U.S. market for Mexican and Central American exports.

Determinants of Differential Access

The main difference between the economies of Mexico and Central America is the absolute difference in market size. Mexico is one of the ten most populous countries in the world, with over 80 million people, compared with a total of around thirty million in Central America. This translates into even greater differences in GDP: Mexico's per capita GDP is considerably higher than the average for Central America. This difference has consequences. Mexico is the third-largest supplier of U.S. imports after Canada and Japan. Mexico is also important as a client of the United States. The sheer size of the Mexican market, its geographical proximity, and strong migratory flows, all contribute to extend the range of American products that look for a market in Mexico.

Mexico also has an advantage over Central America because it is closer to

58. War is a major deterrent of FDI inflows.
59. See Pastor (1993).

the United States and because most of the Mexican maquilas are located in northern Mexican states, a short haul away from the populous U.S. states of Texas and California. Basically, air and maritime freight from Central America has to compete with trucks hauling goods from northern Mexican states. Better road links with and easier transit through Mexico are important elements of any Central American strategy to improve access to the U.S. market.

Political reality works to reinforce the difference in economic standing in the U.S. market between Mexico and Central America. Mexico and the United States share a common border, one of the most porous in the world, which implies cooperation. Through this border large numbers of Mexicans cross to find employment in the United States; this has made Mexico the main source of migrant labor, legal or illegal, in the United States. This population forms the backbone of an increasingly vocal Hispanic community.

Mexico has been the focus of American attention in the wake of the NAFTA treaty negotiations, in particular as Mexico's political institutions feel the need to become more responsive to economic and policitcal demands. Mexico is undergoing important institutional changes, the recent election of a president not affiliated with the PRI (Institutional and Revolutionary Party) being just the most conspicuous. U.S. public opinion recognizes that NAFTA was and is the catalyst of those changes. Central America is also undergoing economic and political liberalization, but unlike Mexico, it is seen essentially in the same light as in the years of Cold War. This may easily be the most important fact affecting Central America's access to U.S. markets. Any Central American strategy should focus on establishing the connection between political reforms in Central America and improved economic conditions with access to the U.S. market as the key.

Whereas some political realities that have allowed Mexico to play a larger role in U.S. affairs are unchangeable, other realities may be counterbalanced by intelligent and purposeful policies on the part of Central America.

Two different legal frameworks set the stage for trade between the United States and Mexico on the one hand and Central America on the other. The main difference between NAFTA and the CBI is that the former is a treaty between countries and the latter is a U.S. law, brought into force unilaterally and thus revocable at will. NAFTA resulted from bilateral negotiations involving both interested parties, resulting in characteristics of permanence and coverage that the CBI lacks.[60] Significantly, NAFTA establishes mechanisms to

---

60. The broader coverage of the NAFTA is patent in its inclusion of provisions on trade in services, public-sector procurement rules, and intellectual property rights and investment. Moreover, two additional agreements on labor law and the environment were signed in parallel with the main NAFTA treaty. The CBI, on the other hand, mentions protection of labor rights as a precondition for country eligibility, but only in the context of international norms. It ignores environmental issues.

solve disagreements over labor and environmental issues, precisely those questions that have the greatest potential to lead to U.S. protectionist pressures in the future.[61] As far as anti-dumping actions are concerned, NAFTA establishes a mechanism that replaces national courts with a commission including specialists from the three countries. CBI countries have to appeal to U.S. courts, a more costly and lengthy process. As nontraditional barriers become more important in international trade relations, these conflict-resolution mechanisms are an invaluable asset to Mexican exporters.

Another nonquantifiable but important benefit of NAFTA over the CBI is the added credibility it lends to liberalization in Mexico. The United States bailed out Mexico following the 1994 exchange rate crisis. The possibility of a slowdown in Mexico's liberalization path was averted. In the eyes of the international community, it is necessary for Central America to display sources of credibility. Given the region's recent economic history, these are much harder to find internally than through closer economic ties with the United States.

Central American products enter the U.S. market under less favorable conditions than Mexican products. Textiles, apparel, shoes, and canned tuna are affected most. Tables 5-12 through 5-15 present Central American and Mexican exports to the United States during the 1990s. Both Mexico and Central America have seen the value of their exports to the U.S. rise in the period, particularly in manufacturing and total U.S. imports. The increase in agricultural exports has been more modest. The access of Central American agricultural products is free of tariffs but subject to other types of restrictions, including quotas and quantity restrictions. No future relaxation of these nontariff restrictions is agreed. Mexico, on the other hand, benefits from the progressive lowering of trade barriers on agricultural products.[62]

Textiles are likely to remain the most important export sector for Central America and Mexico in their transactions with the United States. Taken together, the five Central American countries exported almost as much textiles to the United States in 1996 as did Mexico—10 percent and 12 percent, respectively of total U.S. imports.[63] After NAFTA ratification, the Central American share of the U.S. market has increased at a lower rate than the Mex-

---

61. The general conflict-resolution mechanism unfolds in three predetermined stages: consultation, reference to the Free Trade Commission, and creation of an arbitration panel. This minimizes the possibility of Mexico being threatened by Section 301 of the Foreign Trade Law, which allows the United States to unilaterally sanction countries that violate trade law or discriminate against U.S. exports.

62. See INCAE (Instituto Centroamericano de Administracíon de Empresas) (1997) and Gonzalez (1998) for a list of products and their conditions of access within the CBI and the NAFTA.

63. See INCAE (1997).

Table 5-12. Central American and Mexican Exports to the United States—1988–1997

	1988	1989	1990	1991	1992	1993	1994	1995	1996	1997
Costa Rica	774	962	1005	1154	1412	1541	1647	1843	1974	2323
El Salvador	284	245	238	303	384	488	609	812	1074	1346
Guatemala	433	609	794	899	1081	1194	1283	1527	1673	1990
Honduras	441	461	491	557	782	914	1098	1441	1796	2322
Nicaragua	1	0	15	60	69	128	167	239	350	439
Central America	**1933**	**2277**	**2543**	**2972**	**3727**	**4266**	**4804**	**5862**	**6774**	**8421**
Mexico	—	27186	30172	31130	35211	39917	49494	62101	74297	85938
World	—	473396	496028	488453	532665	580659	663256	743445	795289	870671

In millions of 1996 U.S. dollars. *Source:* Tavares (1999).

Table 5-13. *Central American and Mexican Manufactured Exports to the United States—1990–1996*

	1990	1991	1992	1993	1994	1995	1996
Costa Rica	564	639	839	951	1049	1162	1229
El Salvador	116	157	233	332	493	694	931
Guatemala	250	389	535	632	682	812	914
Honduras	156	242	423	574	733	1033	1366
Nicaragua	1	2	6	24	43	95	192
Central America	**1085**	**1429**	**2036**	**2513**	**3000**	**3796**	**4743**
Mexico	**21236**	**23000**	**27098**	**31382**	**40357**	**50528**	**60966**
World Exports	**389584**	**393820**	**434256**	**480016**	**557871**	**629632**	**659867**

In millions of 1996 U.S. dollars. *Source:* Tavares (1999).

Table 5-14. *Central American and Mexican Agricultural Exports to the United States—1990–1996*

	1990	1991	1992	1993	1994	1995	1996
Costa Rica	400	475	535	552	550	637	682
El Salvador	109	130	134	134	92	89	101
Guatemala	497	472	503	510	548	648	660
Honduras	260	213	251	231	238	280	277
Nicaragua	8	40	44	74	77	71	80
Central America	**1274**	**1329**	**1466**	**1501**	**1505**	**1724**	**1800**
Mexico	**2632**	**2514**	**2385**	**2707**	**2860**	**3780**	**3713**
World Exports	**22426**	**22184**	**23447**	**23664**	**25949**	**29261**	**32568**

In millions of 1996 U.S. dollars. *Source:* Tavares (1999).

Table 5-15. *Central American and Mexican Textile Exports to the United States—1990–1996*

	1990	1991	1992	1993	1994	1995	1996
Costa Rica	381.4	438.8	589.2	652.6	684.8	756.9	7100
El Salvador	54.4	90.3	165.8	251.2	397.9	582.2	748.1
Guatemala	190.6	329.7	451.1	545.7	591.2	682.3	805.9
Honduras	112.8	195.5	365.0	506.2	644.8	918.5	1222.6
Nicaragua	—	—	—	—	28.5	73.9	142.1
Total CA	**739.2**	**1054.3**	**1571.1**	**1955.7**	**2347.2**	**3013.8**	**3628.7**
Mexico	**—**	**—**	**—**	**1127.0**	**1594.0**	**2565.8**	**4231.5**
World	**—**	**—**	**—**	**—**	**31386.5**	**34648.6**	**36389.5**

In millions of 1996 U.S. dollars. *Source:* U.S. Trade Department.

ican share.[64] Whereas most categories of textile exports from Central America may be subject to quantitative restrictions in case the United States invokes the need for safeguards, similar Mexican exports are explicitly free from this threat.

The rules of origin that apply to Mexican exports are more lax and easier to evaluate, thus leading to a lower likelihood of trade disputes. To benefit from an expedited entry into the U.S. market, Mexican products have to comply with two main criteria: a "change-in-tariff classification," and the amount of regional content.[65] Articles from a CBI country, on the other hand, are subject to stricter rules: they must be cultivated, produced, or manufactured in a CBI country or, alternatively, be turned into a "new and different" product. Moreover, CBI products only benefit if exported directly from the beneficiary country to the United States. The rule that applies to CBI goods is more subjective in nature than the one that applies to Mexican exports.

Trade Access to the United States: The Options for Central America

It is important to examine the options open for Central America in improving trade access to the United States. The 1992 election in the United States ignited a debate over NAFTA and U.S. trade policy. Extreme positions emerged. Political events in Mexico, as well as the financial crisis, associated NAFTA with the idea of a somewhat ill-conceived concession on the part of the United States. The debate over "fair" trade, once focused on Japan, now included NAFTA as a "straw man." While it is not foreseeable that these anti-NAFTA currents will threaten the treaty, they certainly make it harder to pursue enlargement.[66] Congress has denied fast-track authority to the President on the issue[67] and politicians do not seem interested in spending any po-

---

64. Almost contemporaneously with the NAFTA ratification, a study by the World Bank suggested that Central America stood to lose about 4 percent of its earnings from the export of apparel as a result of the NAFTA. See World Bank (1994, 4).

65. The first criterion applies to a large part of the goods and is effective when a product is classified in a tariff category different from the inputs that entered its production. The criterion of regional content is stricter in that it demands a higher percentage—50 percent to 60 percent—of the value; but it is only applicable in some cases, and there are no restrictions in terms of the percentage of value added in each country.

66. Chile's inability to become a NAFTA member in spite of its image as a model economy suggests the enormous difficulties any reforming economy will have in accessing the NAFTA, particularly when one considers that Chile even had the support of the U.S. business community.

67. The fast-track procedure is meant to facilitate trade agreements between the U.S. and other countries. It has to be preapproved by Congress and, under its provisions, Congress binds itself to approve agreements presented by the executive without amendments and within a certain period of time.

litical capital on it. Moreover, the NAFTA extension requires the acceptance of the three current members of the treaty, which may or may not be automatic. It is unlikely, however, that most resistance will come from countries other than the United States.

Another possibility is the development of a free trade agreement between Central American countries and the United States. Its greatest advantage would be flexibility. A separate free trade agreement would not raise the issue of NAFTA access in U.S. politics but it would make possible a formal tie with NAFTA later on; it would enable the degree of trade liberalization to be as close as possible to current NAFTA standards. A free trade agreement implies mutual concessions, which increase the expected life of the agreement. However, the feeling among observers and policymakers has been summarized in Gonzalez (1997): "Neither a free trade agreement nor NAFTA adhesion are, at this moment, valid options, and they should not be considered at this moment."[68] The situation has not changed in this regard.

The CBI, which came into effect in January 1984, and was created because the United States wanted to counter the influence of left-wing movements in the region. Given the United States' national security justification and the small size of the countries involved, the initiative did not spur much internal debate in the United States. The high number of countries involved in the CBI, and their diversity, complicated the issues and the building of a "case" with the U.S. administration.[69] In the aftermath of Hurricane Mitch, the fate of the region has attracted enough interest in Central America to create support for CBI-enhancement as part of a relief package for the region. There is a good chance that the urgency of the disaster favors passage of CBI enhancement, whereas the passage of an omnibus trade bill is not likely at all.

The political and economic costs that would arise if the United States does not keep its word on trade integration with Latin America are very high, and the economic costs from loss of credibility are important, too. This increases the likelihood that the Free Trade Area of the Americas (FTAA) will see progress in the future, however much it may be delayed. However, the U.S. administration probably would pursue a strategy of delay if it is not interested in the FTAA. This initiative is not only vague in terms of its timetable, however. Its continental scope makes it vulnerable to many pitfalls due to the diversity of

---

68. Translated from Spanish.

69. Whereas Central American countries are connected by land to Mexico and the other NAFTA countries, the Caribbean countries are island economies; Caribbean countries draw most of their sustenance from tourism while tourism is still a nascent industry in the Central American countries, whose economies are comparatively diversified. The Caribbean countries draw substantial amounts of financial aid from former colonizing powers; the GDP per capita of the Caribbean countries is actually higher than that of the Central American countries.

the countries concerned and their varying degrees of involvement with the United States. A potential threat is the emergence of MERCOSUR as an alternative to NAFTA, shouldered by the former's promising ties with the EU. A highly undesirable result would be for Central America to be left between NAFTA and MERCOSUR, without secure access to either of the two agreements.

Last but not least, by being bundled with such a diverse array of countries, Central American nations may lose their capacity to build the independent case warranted by their small size and their geographical proximity to the United States. Central America, considered within the Latin American context, is likely to have very little bargaining power. The division of Central American countries into different positions, with self-defeating consequences, is a real possibility.

The recent history of the trade bills that consider enhancing Central America's access to the U.S. market illustrates the difficulties to come. Two recent trade bills put forward to Congress were HR 984 IH by and the CBI. The first bill addressed aid and relief measures to Central America in the wake of Hurricane Mitch as well as trade enhancement. It was split in two for lack of support; the relief portion was approved but the trade measures were not. The CBI bill was split into five separate bills to improve flexibility and the likelihood that some trade enhancement measures would be approved, possibly as part of other bills. The most likely outcome is that some trade enhancement measures will pass, but that no full access similar to NAFTA will be granted. The fact that an election is approaching complicates the issue, since trade agreements have become an unpopular issue on which divisions are politically exploited. The sentiment is that trade benefits are a "giveaway" by the U.S., with no corresponding benefits for the American economy.

In contrast, a trade bill awarding certain African countries access to the U.S. textile market was much more popular, even though it, too, eventually failed. Thus, Central America draws sympathy for its interests as far as they relate to overcoming tragedy but not yet for achieving sustainable, export-based growth. Central America is still perceived as lacking in macro-economic-policy performance, and its credibility as a partner needs to be greatly enhanced. Moreover, the text of the bills mentions that benefits would be awarded to countries planning to become parties to the FTAA and the effectiveness of the agreement in promoting drug-related crop eradication would be considered. This indicates that in order to maximize the probability of obtaining access to the U.S. market, the best policies available to Central American countries may be to pursue credible trade liberalization with other countries in the hemisphere and to improve their image as civil societies.

A Central American Trade and Investment Strategy

Central America in the 1990s has decidedly evolved toward a strategy of international trade and investment liberalization. The countries in the region are pursuing a multifrontal approach in which trade and investment agreements with different countries are pursued simultaneously.[70] Given the relatively low levels of trade flows with large economies that are geographically close, such as Mexico and South America, this strategy is a sensible one. However, the scarce technical and political resources of the region and its past difficulties with implementing a de facto liberalization in the context of the CACM, mean that it is essential to set priorities. From the number of studies referred to in previous sections, we can derive a list of priorities for Central America.

Gaining Access to the U.S. Market

Central American economies are small. Thus, the creation of a truly common market in Central America is the most credible bargaining chip in trade negotiations with the United States, which has understandably rejected trade negotiations with Central America on a nation-by-nation basis. Currently there is very poor coordination among Central American countries in the presentation of their "case" for access to the U.S. market. This is a major shortcoming that needs to be addressed. Both "coherence of policy" and "size of the market" arguments are considerable parts of a successful case for access to the US market. In regard to the "coherence of policy" argument, Gonzalez (1997) mentions that "the nature of the commercial relationship between the different Central American countries and the United States is very similar across the region." The strong similarities among Central American economies should facilitate joint negotiation of trade liberalization with the United States.

Given the importance of Central America as an export market for Mexican products, regional market integration can be a particularly effective card to play in negotiations with Mexico. Regional integration can also increase the region's bargaining power in the Free Trade in the Americas' initiative, allowing Central American countries to focus on their common interests. The "size of the market" argument should be addressed in Central America's case. A larger market size would encourage investment flows to the region, one of the key benefits of trade integration. Given the origin of the largest share of exports in the maquila industry, facilitating foreign investment is necessary to

---

70. See above.

maintain external balance in further liberalization. Central America's attractiveness to foreign investors should become a top policy goal. This is particularly important since Mexico's increased attractiveness threatens the flow of international investment to Central America. Free trade between Central America and various regional country groups guarantees investors in the region access to larger markets, which is one of the most important determinants of FDI inflows. The other key factor in attracting investment inflows is a solid transportation and telecommunications infrastructure, which is also a fundamental element in building the region's internal market.

The most obvious instrument to attain a larger market is regional integration. Some may see the process of regional integration as a poor substitute for increased access to foreign markets—the U.S. market in particular. But regional integration is a natural complement to any strategy to increase access to the U.S. market. The CACM, however, is far from a perfect free market. There are important exceptions to the free movement of essential goods. Governments in the region need to convey their interest in the process of regional integration. Trade integration should be accompanied by substantial harmonization of national regulations. Other countries will find it much more palatable to negotiate with a single Central American institution and a single set of market regulations than with a series of diverse national institutions.

In a certain sense, the regional economies already have some features of an integrated region. Willmore (1997) reports that some export processors moved from Guatemala to El Salvador as soon as the war ended there. The migratory flows, namely between Nicaragua and Costa Rica, are substantial. Perhaps it is because Central America is already partially integrated and experiences its benefits that the region is slow to bring about full regional integration.

Create Credible Institutions

One key benefit from regional integration is that it would enable Central American countries to demonstrate their institution-building capabilities. Strong and credible regional institutions can easily be the most important step for the region to earn overall credibility—especially in the eyes of the United States.[71] Regional institutions need a thorough redesign and a clearer mandate. Another way to develop a good institutional track record is to sign free trade agreements with the NAFTA countries (Mexico and the United States in particular). Joint institutions can thus be in place, as the conditions for improved and secure trade access are met.

---

71. Mexico's experience as a member of NAFTA has made clear the importance of being perceived as a credible, reliable partner capable of institutional reform.

Regional institutions are the most obvious way to build a more favorable image of the region with American policymakers and the public. At this time, Central American countries are strongly associated with fratricide and are also thought to be antagonistic toward the United States.[72] Creating a new regional image based on cooperation may be the best way to replace the current negative one.

Regional integration could also help countries avoid harmful competition. There is a tendency for countries and regions to compete for FDI inflows by according extensive benefits to foreign investors. Regional institutions may be the best way to set policies that will attract investment at the lowest possible cost.

It is likely that labor and environmental issues will be prominent in negotiations leading to increased access of Central American products to the U.S. market. These issues are voiced by strong political constituencies and have been responsible in the past for stalling the approval of "fast-track procedures.[73] Creating a strong regional reputation for valuing labor rights and environmental protection is one of the best ways to strengthen the case for trade integration with the United States.

Diversify Markets

The United States is the largest customer of the region and, given its size, is likely to remain so. The top priority for Central America is to extend the current trade agreements with the United States and prepare the groundwork for future NAFTA parity. This corresponds to taking full advantage of one of the region's most important characteristics: its location. In their strategy to improve access to the U.S. market, it is crucial for Central American countries to further trade and investment agreements with the other two NAFTA members—Mexico and Canada. This will facilitate future agreements with NAFTA as a whole, and preempt potential problems with the United States' NAFTA partners.

The countries of the CACM should continue to encourage the trade initiative with the Americas. In this context, the pursuit of closer ties with South America is an insurance against regional isolation. MERCOSUR is a natural trade area in that the ratio of the average distance to partner over the average distance to markets is the lowest for the any trade area in the world. Moreover,

---

72. The possible exception is Costa Rica, though it is unclear whether the regional image dominates even there.

73. See Gonzalez (1998).

MERCOSUR is the only area in the Americas whose major partner is not NAFTA. If an incipient U.S.–Brazilian rivalry is added to the picture, there is a real risk that Central America will find itself lost between two large trade areas. Looking exclusively to the north is not the best way to avoid this risk.

Central America is contiguous to one of the largest markets in the world— Mexico. Central America is an important client for Mexico's manufactures, and Mexico is a potentially important market for Central America's exports. Trade creation resulting from the NAFTA agreement can lead to higher levels of Central American exports if Mexican producers find it more profitable to export to the United States, and Central America's exporters are able to undercut them in unattended niches of the Mexican market. [74]

Mexico seems very interested in promoting political and social stability in Central America.[75] Cultural ties, including a common heritage and a shared Hispanic culture, can be the generator in Mexico of a genuine interest in Central America's fate. On some occasions, Mexico has already acted as an advocate for Central America before the United States. Central America should nurture this important relationship. Trade liberalization with Mexico can further attract Mexican investors to Central America, creating a constituency sensitive to the region's interests in future negotiations for NAFTA access. Central America is an important client for Mexico's manufactures. In other words, the share of Central American products in total Mexican imports is larger than its share in total U.S. imports. This is not likely to change.

Diversify Products

Even as traditional agricultural exports remain important, a consensus has emerged that economic growth in the region will need to rely more on diversification into textiles and other manufactures. As mentioned above, the light-manufactures sectors have been a stepping stone to continued growth. Diversification will make Central American countries less vulnerable to

---

74. This process is more likely, the lower the elasticity of supply of the Mexican manufacturing sector and the higher the elasticity of the Central American producers. Leamer et al. (1997) document that Central American exports are a much larger share of total Mexican imports than of total U.S. imports. These authors, using alternative-growth scenarios in North America, show that there are incentives for Mexico to increase both its exports and imports under NAFTA. They also show that the higher the growth rate of Mexico, the more important Central American exports to this country become.

75. Given the need to overcome its own social instability to consolidate the gains from NAFTA, Mexico is very conscious of the potential for internal conflicts in Central America to spill over the border. The ease with which migratory flows to and through Mexico can emerge is another factor joining the political fates of the Mexican Federation and Central America.

terms-of-trade shocks and natural disasters. Given Central America's proximity to the U.S. market, the region should aim produce goods and services that are more "sensitive" to transportation costs and delivery time.

Modernize Infrastructure

The importance of modernizing transport infrastructure cannot be exaggerated. It is the most important instrument in the promotion of regional trade and investment flows. Given the small distances between the countries in the region, only the lack of coordination in infrastructure policy and the low quality of some structures stand in the way of trade promotion. In this context, the completion of a road that cuts across the five countries, connecting main export-producing areas to ports and airports, should be a priority. Infrastructure can lead to substantial improvements in port and airport efficiency as competition between existing structures is facilitated. As seen above, one of the most important determinants of FDI location is the quality of the infrastructure.

Table 5-16 presents the connection between the priorities mentioned above and the benefits from international trade and investment summarized in the early part of this chapter. Only by pursuing these objectives can Central America take advantage of its extremely advantageous location and its historical ties.

CONCLUSION

Central America is a region with a high degree of openness to international trade. In the wake of NAFTA ratification and at a time of increasing global integration, Central America needs to make strategic choices regarding the direction of its trade and investment policies. The region has a short list of very important clients. The United States, its major trading partner, is responsible for approximately half of the exports from Central America. The NAFTA countries as a whole, together with the European Union and the CACM, absorb 80 percent of Central American exports.

Central American exports are highly concentrated in a few products. Between 80 percent and 90 percent of the exports of countries in the region arise in the Food and Live Animals and the Miscellaneous Manufactures categories (Standard International Trade Classifications categories zero and eight).

The rising weight of maquila exports in Central America is driven by foreign investment, known to be extremely sensitive to factors such as market

Table 5-16. *A Central American Trade and Investment Strategy—From Priority Actions to Economic Benefits*

	Static Efficiency Gains	*Economies of Scale*	*Economic Growth*	*Coping with External Shocks*	*Reforming Institutions*	*Upgrading Technology*
Increase Market Size	Market Size Promotes Better Allocation of Resources	Producers Benefit from Economies of Scale			Further Institutions Appropriate to Larger Market	
Create Credible Institutions	Institutions Lower Transaction Costs				Protect Intellectual Property	Respect Environment and Labor Regulations
Diversify Markets				Lower Dependence on External Business Cycles		
Diversify Products			Light Manufactures to Access Higher Growth Sectors	Lower Dependence on Specific Commodity Shocks		Better Technology Absorbtion by Manufacturing Sector
Modernize Infrastructure		Lower Transport Costs Increase Market Size	Transportation Capital Benefits Productivity			

size, infrastructure and labor costs. The regional market is still an incomplete free-trade zone and an imperfect customs union, which delays the benefits for the regional firms and consumers of a larger "home" market.

Central America's internationalization strategy needs to address and counteract specific risks. The Caribbean Basin Initiative, giving Central America's textiles access to the U.S. market, can be easily reversed unilaterally in response to substantial domestic protectionist pressure in the U.S. Central America is thus highly vulnerable to U.S. policies it cannot control and that can have an overwhelming impact on the region. The resulting uncertainty has certainly limited the attractiveness of Central America as a foreign investment destination. Furthermore, in a region where NAFTA and MERCOSUR are emerging as solid trade areas, Central America risks finding itself outside both blocs, with no large export market to rely on.

Central America's internationalization strategy is evolving simultaneously on many fronts. It should focus on clearer priorities. These are the increase in market size through regional integration and international openness, the creation of credible regional institutions, the diversification of markets and products, and the development of transport infrastructure as an instrument for increasing the effective size of the "home market."

The negative image of Central America in U.S. eyes has barely changed since the Cold War period. Dramatically reversing this image of instability and lack of credibility may yet be the hardest and most important task facing Central America before it can attract substantial trade and investment flows.

REFERENCES

Agarwal, Jamuna. 1980. "Determinants of Foreign Direct Investment: A Survey." Weltwirtschaftliches Archiv 116: 737–773.

Amirahmadi, Hooshang, and Weiping Wu. 1994. "Foreign Direct Investment in Developing Countries." *Journal of Developing Areas* 28: 167–189.

Amsden, A. and T. Hikino. 1991. "Borrowing Technology or Innovating: An Exploration of Two Paths to Industrial Development." New York, NY: New School for Social Research. Mimeographed.

Balassa, Bela. 1971. *The Structure of Protection in Developing Countries.* Baltimore: The Johns Hopkins Press.

———— 1981a. The Newly Industrializing Countries in the World Economy. New York: Pergamon Press.

———— 1981b. "Adjustment to External Shocks in Developing Economies." *World Bank Working Paper No. 472.* Washington, D.C.: World Bank.

Barberia, Lorena. 1999. "Central America's Export Competitiveness: The Impact of Shipping Costs on the Apparel Industry." Cambridge, MA: Kennedy School of Government. Mimeographed

Basile, A., and D. Germidis. 1984. "Investing in Export Processing Zones." Paris: Organization for Economic Cooperation and Development.

Bayoumi, Tamin, and Barry Eichengreen. 1995. "Is Regionalism Simply a Diversion? Evidence from the Evolution of the EC and EFTA." *National Bureau of Economic Research (NBER) Working Paper No. 5283.*

Bhagwati, J. 1982. "Directly and productive, profit-seeking activities." *Journal of Political Economy* 90: 988–1002.

——— 1993. *India's Economy: The Shackled Giant.* Oxford: Clarendon Press.

Blomstrom, Magnus. 1989. Foreign Investment and Spillovers: a Study of Technology Transfer to Mexico. London: Routledge.

——— 1990. Transnational Corporations and Manufacturing Exports from Developing Countries. New York: United Nations.

Blomstrom, Magnus, and Ari Kokko. 1996. "The Impact of Foreign Investment on Host Countries: A Review of the Empirical Evidence."

——— 1997. "Regional Integration and Foreign Direct Investment." *National Bureau of Ecobnomic Research (NBER) Working Paper No. W6019.*

Borensztein,-E.; De-Gregorio,-J.; Lee,-J.-W. 1998. "How Does Foreign Direct Investment Affect Economic Growth?" Journal-of-International-Economics; 45(1), June 1998, pages 115-35.

Brada and Mendez. 1985. "Economic Integration Among Developed, Developing, and Centrally Planned Economies: A Comparative Analysis." *Review of Economics and Statistics* 67 (4): 549–56.

Burns, J. G. 1995. "Free Trade Zones: Global Overview and Future Prospects." *Industry Trade and Technology Review.* (September): 35–47.

CEPAL. 1998. "Foreign Investment in Latin America and the Caribbean." Santiago de Chile: Choi, I. 1995. Export-Oriented Foreign Direct Investment in East Asia and Latin America: Determinants of Location. Ph.D. diss., Department of Economics, University of South Carolina.

Clark, Ximena, and José Tavares. 1999. "Determinants of Central American Exports: A Quantitative Approach Using the Gravity Equation." Development Discussion Paper. Cambridge: Harvard Institute for International Development.

Deardorff, Alan. 1995. "Determinants of Bilateral Trade: Does Gravity Work in a Bilateral World?" *National Bureau of Economic Research (NBER) Working Paper 5377.*

Dollar, David. 1992. "Outward-oriented Developing Economies Really Do Grow More Rapidly: Evidence from 95 LDCs, 1976–85." In *Economic Development and Cultural Change,* by Dunning, John. 1993. *Multinational Enterprises and the Global Economy.* Reading, PA: Addison-Wesley.

Economist, The. 1997. "Central America Opens for Business." 21 June 1997.

Estrada, Fanny de. 1998. Personal Interview. Agexpront, Guatemala City, Guatemala.

Ethier, Wilfred J. 1998. "Regionalism in a Multilateral World." Economics, Energy Environment Working Paper from Fondazione Eni Enrico Mattei.

Fernandez, Raquel. 1997. "Returns to Regionalism: An Evaluation of Non-Traditional Gains from RTAs." *National Bureau of Economic Research (NBER) Working Paper No. 5970.*

Frankel, Jeffrey, Ernest Stein, and Shang-Jin Wei. 1993. "Continental Trading Blocs: Are They Natural or Super-Natural?" *National Bureau of Economic Research (NBER) Working Paper 4588.*

Fröbel, Folker, Jurgen Heinrichs, and Otto Kreye. 1980. The New International Division of Labour: Structural Unemployment in Industrialised Countries and Industrialisation in Developing Countries. New York: Cambridge University Press.

Gonzalez, Anabel. 1998. Personal Interview. Vice-Ministra de Comercio Exterior, Ministerio de Comercio Exterior. San José, Costa Rica.

Grossman, Gene, and Elhanan Helpman. 1991. *Innovation and Growth in the Global Economy.* Cambridge: The MIT Press.

Gunasekera, H. D. B. H., and R. Tyers. 1991. "Imperfect Competition and Returns to Scale in a Newly Industrializing Economy: A General Equilibrium Analysis of Korean Trade Policy." *Journal of Development Economics* 34: 223–47.

Hamada, K. 1974. "An Economic Analysis of the Duty-Free Zone." *Journal of International Economics* 4: 225–41.

Hamilton, C., and L. Svensson. 1982. "On the Welfare Effects of a 'Duty-Free Zone.'" *Journal of International Economics* 13: 45–64.

Helpman, Elhanan. 1987. "Imperfect Competition and International Trade: Evidence from Fourteen Industrial Countries." *Journal of the Japanese and International Economies* 1: 62–81.

ILO/UNCTC. 1988. Economic and Social Effects of Multinational Enterprises in Export Processing Zones. Geneva: International Labor Organization.

INCAE (Instituto Centroamericano de Administración de Empresas).1997. "Estudio sobre la Paridad con el NAFTA para los Paises Centroamericanos." San José, Costa Rica: Instituto Centroamericano de Administración de Empresas.

Inter-American Development Bank. 1998. *Integration and Trade in the Americas.* Periodic Note, August 1998.

Inter-American Development Bank. 1999. Statistics. Http://www.iadb.org/.

Kravis, Irving, and Robert E. Lipsey. 1982. "The Location of Overseas Production and Production for Export by U.S. Multinational Firms." *Journal of International Economics 12 (3–4): 201–23.*

Kreye, Otto, Jurgen Heinrichs, and Folker Fröbel. 1987. "Export Processing Zones in Developing Countries: Results of a New Survey." *Working Papers/Multinational Enterprises Programme, No. 43.* Geneva: International Labour Office.

Krueger, Anne. 1974. "The Political Economy of the Rent-Seeking Society." *American Economic Review* 64: 291–303.

Krugman, Paul. 1991. "Is Bilateralism Bad?" In *International Trade and Trade Policy*, edited by E. Helpman and A. Razin. Cambridge, MA: The MIT Press.

Larraín, F. and J. Tavares. 1999. "Can Openness Deter Corruption?" Cambridge, MA: Harvard Institute for International Development. Mimeographed

Lim, David. 1983. "Fiscal Incentives and Direct Foreign Investment in Less Developed Countries." *The Journal of Development Studies* 19 (2): 2–12.

Miyagiwa, K. 1986. "A Reconsideration of the Welfare Economics of a Free-Trade Zone." *Journal of International Economics* 21: 337–50.

Murphy,-Kevin-M.; Shleifer,-Andrei; Vishny,-Robert. 1989. "Industrialization and the Big Push." Journal-of-Political-Economy; 97(5), October 1989, pages 1003-26.

Pastor, Robert. 1993. "The North American Free Trade Agreement: Hemispheric and Geopolitical Implications." Inter-American Development Bank.

Perroni, C. and J. Whalley. 1994. "The New Regionalism: Trade Liberalization or Insurance?" *National Bureau of Economic Research (NBER) Working Paper No. 4626.*

Ramirez, Manuel, and Craig Sullivan. 1999. "Determinants of Foreign Direct Investment: Policy Implications for Central America." Kennedy School of Government, Harvard University. Mimeographed.

Roberts, M. 1992. Export Processing Zones in Jamaica and Mauritius: Evolution of an Export Oriented Development Model. San Francisco, CA: Inquiries.

Rodriguez, Francisco, and Dani Rodrik. 1999. "Trade Policy and Economic Growth: A Skeptic's Guide to the Cross-National Evidence." *National Bureau of Economic Research (NBER) Working Paper Series No. 7081.*

Romer, Paul. 1992. "Two Strategies for Economic Development: Using Ideas and Producing Ideas." *Proceedings of World Bank Annual Conference on Development Economics.* Washington, D.C.: World Bank.

Root, F., and A. Ahmed. 1979. "Empirical Determinants of Manufacturing Foreign Direct Investment in Developing Countries." *Economic Development and Cultural Change* 27: 751–67.

Sachs, Jeffrey. 1985. "External Debt and Macroeconomic Performance in Latin America and East Asia." *Brookings Papers on Economic Activity* 2: 565–573.

SIECA (Secretaria de Integración Económica Centro Americana). 1998.Http://www.sieca.org.gt/publico/

Svedberg, P. 1991. "The Export Performance of Sub-Saharan Africa." *Economic Development and Cultural Change* 39: 549–66.

Tavares, José. 1999. "The Access of Central America to Export Markets: Diagnostic and Policy Recommendations." *HIID Development Discussion Paper 693.* Cambridge, MA: Harvard Institute for International Development.

Tinbergen, J. 1962. Shaping the World Economy: Suggestions for an International Economic Policy. New York: The Twentieth Century Fund.

Torrisi, C. 1985. "The Determinants of Foreign Investment in a Small LDC." *Journal of Economic Development* 10: 29–45.

UNCTC. 1985. "Export Processing Free Zones in Developing Countries: Implications for Trade and Industrialization Policies." Geneva: United Nations Conference on Trade and Development.

Urizar, Carmen. 1998. Personal Interview, Cien, Guatemala City, Guatemala.

U.S. Trade Department, Bureau of Economic and Business Affairs. "1997 Country Reports on Economic Policy and Trade Practices." Http://www.state.gov/www/issues/economic/trade_reports/index/html

Warr, P. 1987. "Export Promotion via Industrial Enclaves: The Philippines' Bataan Export Processing Zone." *The Journal of Development Studies* ?(?): 220–41.

———— 1989. "Export Processing Zones: The Economics of Enclave Manufacturing." *World*

Bank Research Observer 4 (1): 65–88.

Warr, P., and B. D. Wright. 1981. "The Isolation Paradox and the Discount Rate for Benefit-Cost Analysis." *Quarterly Journal of Economics* 96(?):

Wei, Shang-Jin. 1997a. "How Taxing Is Corruption on International Investors?" *National Bureau of Economic Research (NBER) Working Paper No. 6030.*

———— 1997b. "Why Is Corruption So Much More Taxing Than Tax? Arbitrariness Kills." . Harvard University. Mimeographed.

Wei, Shang-Jin, and J. Frankel. 1995. "Open Regionalism in a World of Continental Trading Blocs." *National Bureau of Economic Research (NBER) Working Paper 5272.*

Willmore, Larry. 1997. Promotion of Exports in Central America: An Analysis of Second Best Policies. New York: United Nations.

World Bank. 1994. "Central America and the North American Free Trade Agreement." Latin America and the Caribbean Regional Office. September 1996.

World Bank. 1992. *Export Processing Zones.* Washington, D.C.: World Bank.

World Trade Organization. 1995. *Regionalism and the World Trading System.*

Young, Alwyn. 1991. "Learning By Doing and the Dynamic Effects of International Trade." *Quarterly Journal of Economics* 106: 369–405.

6

Intel: A Case Study of Foreign Direct Investment in Central America

FELIPE LARRAÍN B., LUIS F. LÓPEZ-CALVA, AND
ANDRÉS RODRÍGUEZ-CLARE[1]

INTRODUCTION

The attraction of foreign direct investment (FDI) constitutes a fundamental element to support strategies that aim to achieve sustained economic growth in developing countries. This is because globalization and the attendant opening of the economies to competition require increased financial resources and technology, which would be impossible to obtain under a policy of autarky.[2] Though relatively well-established principles exist to explain why a multinational company may decide to move into a specific country, each experience has its idiosyncratic elements from which both theorists and policymakers can learn important lessons. There is less consensus, however, on the potential positive or negative effects that FDI may have on the host economy, and on what factors determine these effects.

This chapter presents a case study of foreign direct investment (FDI) going into a small country. It analyzes the advent of Intel, manufacturer of microprocessors, to Costa Rica, a country that is very small indeed when compared with other potential locations for a company of that nature.

The literature on FDI contains theoretical formulations on the factors that

1. We are grateful to Gerardo Esquivel, Cristina García-López and José Tavares for very useful comments on an earlier draft. We received valuable assistance and comments from Ricardo Monge and Maritza Arroyo at CINDE-San José. Ricardo Matarrita provided useful information available from PROCOMER databases.

2. See the discussion on international trade and investment in the region, contained in Chapter 5 of this volume.

attract FDI and on policies oriented towards increasing FDI flows to a country.[3] There are also models of the effects that such investment has on the host country at both the micro- and macroeconomic levels (see Blomstrom and Kokko 1997). Recent attempts to use cross-country data to analyze the determinants of FDI have faced identification problems, though researchers have managed to provide good insights on the issue (Shatz 1997b). The theoretical literature also highlights the impact of FDI on the development of the host country through technological spillovers and the increased availability of new inputs to both the multinational firm and to other local firms (Rodríguez-Clare 1996).

Case studies are not as common in the literature, mainly due to data constraints. Available case studies, however, do provide evidence of the positive effects of FDI on the host economy, either through systematic analysis or by providing anecdotal, non-systematic evidence (Ranis and Schive 1985; Meyanathan 1994; Lim and Fong 1991). Country-level studies have emphasized the macroeconomic impact, using aggregate data of FDI on country-level aggregate variables (Galenson 1985).

This chapter studies the impact on the Costa Rican economy of Intel's decision to move into that country in 1997. We use indicators of both direct effects and selected fiscal and macroeconomic effects as evidence; sometimes, however, these indicators are more qualitative than quantitative, due to the shortage of systematically collected data. We also examine training externalities, as well as the "signaling" effect that Intel has had on other firms' decision to invest in Costa Rica, thus making Intel itself into a factor of attraction. Weaknesses that the Costa Rican economy has had to overcome in terms of FDI attraction are an important part of the discussion that follows, as is the fact that large FDI firms like Intel may help bring about needed institutional reforms by influencing the political balance through a new arrangement of stakeholders.

The chapter starts by examining the rationale behind Intel's decision to move to Costa Rica, and the main obstacles it faced. The next section reviews the literature on the determinants of FDI and its effects on the host economies. This is followed by a survey of the indicators that measure the effects of Intel's arrival on the economy. We first look at some partial equilibrium indicators—gross income generated, not at shadow prices—and then discuss potential general equilibrium consequences, such as the pressure on prices in the inputs market. For this purpose, we detail the findings of a short survey we carried out in Costa Rica. We then describe a number of potential training ex-

---

3. A classical work is Dunning's OLI model (Dunning 1977), focused on three factors: ownership, location-specific, and internalization (the way in which technology is transferred).

ternalities and linkages, also showing data from a survey to Intel suppliers. The chapter closes with some general conclusions based on our findings.

THE DECISION PROCESS AND ITS RATIONALE: INTEL CHOOSES COSTA RICA

A firm invests abroad either to exploit a foreign market (as have several companies that invested in Ireland to gain better access to the European Union) or to secure better access to certain inputs, especially cheap labor. This second motive is typical of FDI in small and poor countries, and certainly influenced Intel's decision to invest in a microprocessor plant in Costa Rica in 1997.

But why Costa Rica? Spar (1998), after analyzing Intel's decision process, concluded that Costa Rica was chosen because it offered important location-specific advantages. Among these, the most important ones were the already existing tax exemptions for any firms satisfying certain conditions under the free zone scheme, the high educational level of the labor force, a stable political scenario, and a relatively corruption-free environment.

Intel's Decision Making

During the process to select the location, the company carefully looked at six countries in addition to Costa Rica: Indonesia, Thailand, Brazil, Argentina, Chile, and Mexico. Some basic data about these countries are contained in Table 6-1. In the final stage, the short list included Mexico (State of Jalisco) and Costa Rica. Mexico seemed to have a better location in terms of transport costs to the North American market and the Pacific Basin, and it is also a much larger country. The relatively small size of Costa Rica to receive an investment of the dimension of Intel's (US$300 million or equivalent to 2.1 percent of Costa Rican GDP) over two years, with a total committed investment of about US$600 million, made Bob Perlman, one of Intel's vice presidents, declare that bringing his company to Costa Rica was like "putting a whale in a swimming pool" (Spar 1998). As discussed below, Intel would later recognize some bottlenecks, especially in the realm of infrastructure, whose elimination required a good deal of political and financial effort. There has been a consensus, however, that Costa Rica's political institutions and educated labor force, combined with the free-zone regime benefits, more than offset the potential weaknesses that its small size imposes on investors.[4] Executives of the com-

---

4. A summary of the fiscal benefits offered to companies under the Costa Rican free-zone scheme is provided in Appendix I.

Table 6-1.   *Human Development Indicators*

Indicator	Indonesia	Thailand	Brazil	Argentina	Chile	Mexico	Costa Rica
IDH	105	67	79	39	34	50	45
GNP (US$ billions) 1997	221.5	165.8	784.0	319.3	70.5	348.6	9.3
GNP annual growth rate (%) 1975-95	7.1	7.8	3.5	1.4	5.5	2.8	3.7
Average annual rate of inflation (%)							
1985-1996	8.6	4.8	569.8	162.9	16.0	40.7	17.8
1996	8.5	4.0	17.2	1.9	2.9	28.7	16.2
Real GDP per capita (PPP$ 1997)	1,110	2,740	4,790	8,950	4,820	3,700	2,680
Adult Literacy rate (%)	85.0	94.7	84.0	96.5	95.2	90.1	95.1
Combined first, second and third level gross enrollment ratio (%)	64	59	80	79	77	70	66
Life expectancy at birth (years)	65.1	68.8	66.8	72.9	74.9	72.2	76.0
Human Poverty Index (HPI-1 rank)	46	29	19	-	6	13	4

Source: Human Development Report. UNDP (1999).

pany seem to have valued the fact that Intel's bargaining power would be greater in a smaller country, as opposed to a larger one like Mexico. They also felt that Mexico, with both Federal and state governments, represented a double risk of policy changes.

The process of making Intel executives aware of the advantages that Costa Rica represented for the company was neither easy nor cheap in financial terms, though its cost-effectiveness soon became evident. Intel's decision process took more than one year, and involved four phases: prequalification, site research, contingent announcement and delivery, and start-up. Seven institutions were directly involved in the process on the side of the Costa Rican government, all under the direction of the Presidency and the Ministry of Foreign Trade, and with the coordination and support of CINDE (Coalición Costarricense de Iniciativas para el Desarrollo), a USAID-funded institution whose main responsibility is investment promotion. The institutions involved included the Ministry of Education and the Costa Rican Technology Institute. This would later become an "Intel Associate," a status that allows its faculty and students to engage in educational exchange activities, share curricula with other Intel associates like the California Institute of Technology, and seek funding for technology development programs carried out by its own researchers.[5]

Strengths and Weaknesses

A study carried out in 1999 confirmed that other foreign investors' perceptions of Costa Rica coincided with Intel's assessment to a large extent (ARC 1999). The 61 foreign investors interviewed ranked "political stability" and "well-educated labor force" as the top strengths of Costa Rica's business environment (evaluated at above 8 on a scale from 1 to 10).[6] These companies cited "globalization and competition" as the most important force that was driving them to look for new locations to invest in. "Going abroad is often a defensive decision," they affirmed (ARC 1999, 11). The top ten strengths included "good governance" and "effective legal system" (with grades between 7 and 8 using the same scale as above). At the bottom of the list were "geographical proximity to markets" and "size of the domestic market" (between 4 and 6 in the scale). A very important piece of information to come out of the survey was that 72 percent of the respondents claimed that they had heard,

---

5. Intel provides an annual amount of money from which Intel associates can withdraw funds on a competitive basis in order to carry out research and development activities.

6. Among the companies that participated, 36 were in the electronics industry, 13 in medical devices manufacturing, 3 in business services, and 9 in other sectors.

seen, and read more about Costa Rica as an investment prospect after Intel's decision to set up a plant in that country. This reinforces the belief that investment decisions like Intel's have an important "signaling" effect on other potential investors. Within the "awareness" section of the interview, the recent information about Costa Rica included, as the top five characteristics its political stability, "relationship with the US," "democratic government," "educated labor force," and "good governance" (ARC 1999, 30). Among Costa Rica's strengths, respondents also mentioned the bilingual education and the "good quality of life."

Shortcomings in infrastructure services, especially roads, ports, and the airport, are mentioned throughout the survey as major drawbacks of Costa Rica. To a lesser extent, shortcomings were noted in power generation and distribution, and telecommunications infrastructure. The small size of the domestic market was also considered a weakness

It is important to mention that Intel executives changed their perception of two factors after investing in Costa Rica. These were the quality and education of the labor force, and the quality of infrastructure services.[7] The former has been seen ex-post as one of the top strengths of Costa Rica as a location for production, and the latter as an important weakness whose correction requires a decisive effort on the side of the government. Training its workers, the so-called "intelization" of its labor force, proved relatively successful in terms of cost and time, due to the high absorption capacity of the employees. However, Intel was reconsidering some investments after potential bottlenecks were discovered in the telecommunications and electricity services. Intel executives were hoping for structural reforms in those sectors to ameliorate potential problems and allow them to launch ambitious expansion plans. An internal document circulated by an Intel executive in July 1998 stated "It is clear from the outset that ICE (Instituto Costarricense de Electricidad) does not have a 'customer service' philosophy and is not used to dealing directly with a private firm."[8]

The explicit plan to promote investment in the country under a coordinated effort did pay off in the case of Costa Rica. The survey of potential investors and personal interviews with Intel executives reveal that search costs are considerably reduced when credible information is provided, and especially when there exists a well-coordinated effort to match the investor's needs. As Spar (1998) and the ARC (1999) survey suggest, two important factors explain Intel's decision to move into Costa Rica: the specific advantages the country offered—tax exemptions, good governance and institutional

---

7. This discussion is based on private interviews with an Intel executive in Costa Rica, in August 1999.

8. ICE is the state monopoly that controls the electricity and telecommunications sectors.

strength, and a highly educated labor force, among the top ones—and the explicit and coordinated effort by the Costa Rican government to convince Intel that going to that country was the right decision. A fundamental point, also emphasized in Spar (1998), is that the Costa Rican government did not promise Intel any special benefits, fiscal or other; rather, it offered existing advantages that any other foreign investment under similar conditions could obtain. The latter is a key factor in making FDI policy credible and reducing the perceived risk of policy change.

The Impact of FDI on the Host Economy: Some Theoretical Considerations

The impact of FDI in the host economy can be divided into four main areas:

- the direct effects caused by the investment and subsequent operation of the company, including the impact on workers and on local suppliers of inputs;
- macroeconomic effects, such as the impact on exports and imports, on GDP, on unemployment, on wages, and on prices of other inputs;
- fiscal effects related to extra fiscal income generated by the multinational firm, its suppliers and employees; and
- the impact on productivity of the whole economy or at least the sector most related to the foreign investment, through externalities generated to other firms, including "forward" or "backward" linkages, technological spillovers, and employee training that is not firm-specific.

The first three effects do not require explanation. Thus, the rest of this subsection focuses on the fourth effect. An important potential effect of FDI on host countries has to do with the impact on aggregate productivity, which happens through the externalities generated to other firms. This type of externalities is divided here into three main groups: i) knowledge and technological spillovers; ii) backward and forward linkages, which make available to domestic firms new or higher quality inputs that were not available before; and iii) training externalities.

Knowledge Spillovers

The discussion on the existence of knowledge spillovers, or a primitive version of it, can be traced back to the 1970s, when emphasis was placed on improving business practices and the business "atmosphere" (Findlay 1978). More important externalities, however, may take place at the level of technological sophistication that is transferred to other sectors by the technicians and engineers of foreign firms in the form of tacit knowledge. This can be transmitted even informally, for example by the interaction of workers of different firms.[9] These externalities are very difficult to measure. Some indirect measures, however, have shown their positive impact on aggregate productivity in Kenyan and Philippine manufacturing (Pack 1987).

Rodríguez-Clare (1996) has shown that FDI may have important positive effects by changing the environment so that it becomes profitable to invest in some activities that were not profitable before the arrival of the multinational corporation. In this way, multinationals can lead to the local availability of inputs that were previously not obtainable in the host economy, or to improvements in the quality of existing inputs. This important externality rests on the fact that those new products or services are made available not only to the multinational corporation, but also to other firms, both foreign and domestic. Moreover, because the inputs satisfy international quality standards, the competitiveness of the economy at the aggregate level is enhanced. These could be called "backward-forward" linkages.[10]

Reform and Training Externalities

There is one type of "backward-forward" linkage that is not discussed in the literature but becomes especially important in economies where opposition to structural reforms, such as privatization, is strong. Consider a case where there is opposition to private participation in some type of essential infrastructure, like electricity generation and distribution. Suppose that the strength of the opposition forces, measured by the number of supporters, is a function of the quality of the service provided by the existing monopoly and/or the demand-supply gap or relative scarcity of the service. The arrival of the multinational corporation, and its demand for the service, in terms of both quantity and quality, may become an important force to weaken opposition to the reforms, by making evident the insufficiency of the existing service and the incapacity of the government to invest the required amounts to satisfy demand. Opening such infrastructure sectors to private participation may increase the quantity and quality of the supply of the input, and thereby raise the productivity of both foreign and domestic firms. Multinationals

---

9. An interesting discussion of this informal way of diffusing knowledge is in Arrow (1999).

10. As shown in Rodríguez-Clare (1996), the positive effect of FDI is maximized if the input used by the multinational firms—and potentially made available to other firms—is less tradable, if the multinationals use few employees relative to the use of inputs, and if the transmission of information between the headquarters and the branch is more costly.

would in this indirect way play an important political role in pushing for the required structural reforms.

Training externalities are an obvious benefit from FDI. From a theoretical perspective, this could be seen as another way to make a better input available not only to the multinational firm itself, but eventually to other firms, provided that the training involves some general, non-firm-specific skills.

INTEL IN COSTA RICA: A WHALE IN A SWIMMING POOL?

After the above theoretical considerations, there remains the important question of whether the effects of Intel's investment have been positive or negative for the Costa Rican economy as a whole. The next two sections provide evidence that Intel's investment has been positive for the Costa Rican economy in the short run and is likely to continue being so in the future. In this section we explore the direct effects of Intel; then, we discuss the macroeconomic effects.

Wages and Employment

The amount paid as wages and benefits (which includes contributions by both employees and employer to social security, the national training program and mandatory savings, among others) to Intel employees between September 1997 and September 1998 was US$5.5 million, and US$25.29 for the same period one year later (see Table 6-2). This last amount is equivalent to 0.2 percent of Costa Rica's 1999 GDP.[11]

The number of employees increased from 441 between September 1997 and September 1998, to 2,217 over the next 12 months, with an important component of professional employees (see Table 6-3). The total work force in Costa Rica was 1,383,452 in 1999.

As can be seen in Table 6-4, the average wage per employee is higher at Intel than the corresponding figure for the total manufacturing sector in Costa Rica. We lack the data required to tell how much of this difference is due to the fact that Intel hires better-qualified workers, and how much to the fact that Intel pays higher wages than other companies to retain workers after they have been trained or "Intelized."

---

11. Of course, this is only mentioned for the sake of comparison. The actual value generated should be measured at the shadow price of labor.

Table 6-2.   *Intel Wages Sept. 97 to Sept. 99 (millions of dollars)*

	Sept 97 Sept 98	Sept 98 Sept 99
Wages	3.73	16.35
Benefits	1.77	9.24
Total	**5.50**	**25.59**

Source: PROCOMER. Annual Report of Intel Operation.

Domestic Purchases

Table 6-3.   *Intel Emploment Sept. 97 to Sept. 99*

	Sept 97 Sept 98	Sept 98 Sept 99
Professional Employees	359	562
Technicians	80	554
Operators and Others	2	**1101**
Total Employees	**441**	**2,217**

Source: PROCOMER. Annual Report of Intel Operation.

Another indicator of the direct effect of a company like Intel on the host economy is its domestic purchases. Intel's confidentiality policies did not allow access to the whole range of links with domestic suppliers, especially those that provide more sophisticated inputs. However, using data from nonspecialized providers of goods and services in 1998 allows us to set the lower bound on domestic purchases at US$19 million. The latter only includes providers of goods and services that are not related to the production process itself, but are related to construction, safety, office appliances, etc. As a company benefiting from the "free-zone" arrangement, Intel has to disclose information on purchases "imported" into the zone, i.e., purchases from suppliers outside this scheme. Information is not available, however, on purchases from other electronic companies or more sophisticated suppliers that are also within the free-zone scheme. As an example, if Intel had bought inputs from, let us say, Protek—a company within the free-zone plan that pro-

Table 6-4. *Manufacturing Sector (dollars per month)*

Wage per employee	Sept-98	Sept-99
Intel	562	615
Total for the Sector	389	406

Source: Own estimates with data from PROCOMER.

duces high tolerance electronic components—that would not be reported in Table 6-5 below.

Investment

The amount invested by Intel to December 1999 was close to 390 million dollars (equivalent to 2.6 percent of GDP), which is more than the US$300 million they originally planned to invest. The extra investment occurred in 1999, when Intel decided to start production of the Pentium III processor. Around 65 percent of the total investment consisted of machinery (Table 6-5). To understand the importance of this investment, notice that total FDI into Costa Rica in 1998 was $612 million.

Total FDI as a share of GDP was 2.5 percent in 1991 and 3.2 percent in 1997. That share represented 4.4 percent and 3.9 percent of GDP in 1998 and 1999, respectively, according to the levels of investment committed by Intel and other companies, which places Costa Rica among the top countries in the world in that respect. Among countries in South-East Asia, the FDI contribution is, on average, 6 percent of GDP (Central Bank of Costa Rica 1997).

Table 6-5. *Intel, Lower Bound on Domestic Purchase 1998-1999*

(million dollars)

	1998	1999
Services	14.5	17.5
Others	4.9	5.7
Total Purchases	**19.4**	**23.2**

Source: Own estimates with data from PROCOMER.

Macroeconomic Effects of Intel

Overall Growth

The growth rate of the Costa Rican economy went from an average 4.9 percent between 1990 and 1996 to an average 7.3 percent between 1997 and 1999. More importantly, the growth rate in Costa Rica in the two years after Intel started operations—8 percent in both 1998 and 1999—was the highest in Latin America; taking the two years combined, it has been the highest in the last three decades for Costa Rica. Considering that Intel started operations on November 1997, this appears to confirm that Intel had a large impact on the growth rate of GDP. This is shown more clearly in Figure 6-1, where one should take into account that although Intel started operations only on November 1997, the investment took place throughout the year.[12]

The increase in the growth rate during 1997 and the high growth rates of 1998 and 1999 could also be explained by the fact that Costa Rica was coming out of a recession in 1996. On that year, GDP grew by a mere 0.3 percent. Thus, to confirm that Intel was key in these very high growth rates, we must turn to Central Bank data that decomposes the growth rate with and without Intel (see graph 6-2).

The impact is clearer for 1999, when Intel accounted for 5 points out of the 8 percent growth rate. On that year, Intel accounted for $330 million of value added, approximately 7 percent of GDP at domestic real prices. In addition to its contribution to GDP, Intel also had important macroeconomic effects through its impact on international trade figures. In terms of the trade balance, the data shows Intel's net exports of about $205 million and $1496 million dollars for the years 1998 and 1999, respectively (Table 6-6). Those amounts represent around 1.5 percent and 9.8 percent of GDP in the respective years.

Foreign Trade

Intel's gross exports represented 17.8 percent of the total amount of exports of the Costa Rican economy in 1998, and 38.7 percent in 1999. This contributed to an increase in the ratio of exports to GDP, which went from 33.2 to 43.5 in the 1997– 99 period. Moreover, the ratio of external-debt service to exports fell from 4.1 percent to 3 percent in the same years (without Intel exports, this ratio would have been 4.9 percent in 1999).

---

12. The monthly Index of Economic Activity measures the real variation on monthly production. Figure 6-1 represents the 12-month average rate of change.

Table 6-6. *Intel Investment 1997–1999 (millions of dollars)*

	1997	1998	1999
Land	16.4	5.8	1.4
Buildings	36.5	50.6	15.1
Machinery	20.3	156.7	72.1
Transportation	0.0	0.0	0.0
Equipment	1.3	4.3	2.5
Total Investment	**74.5**	**217.4**	**91.0**

Source: Own estimates with data from PROCOMER.

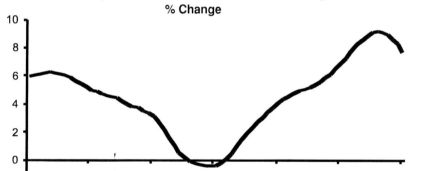

Monthly Index of Economic Activity

Figure 6-1.
Source: Central Bank of Costa Rica.

The openness ratio, that is exports plus imports over GDP, increased from 70 percent to 83 percent between1997 and 1999. It was already growing before then, but, as Figure 6-3 shows, this trend accelerated in 1997.

Intel's most dramatic impact has been on the trade balance, which went from a deficit of $497.6 million in 1997 to a surplus of $632.1 million in 1999.[13] This was Costa Rica's first surplus in 50 years. Most of the impact is

---

13. This happened at the same time that the real exchange rate remained relatively stable.

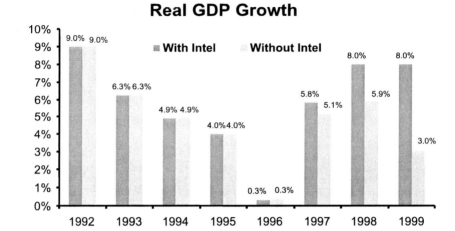

Real GDP Growth

Figure 6-2.
Source: Central Bank of Costa Rica.

Table 6-7. INTEL, Trade Balance 1998–1999 (millions of dollars)

Year	Exports	Imports				Balance
		Total	Inputs	Capital Goods	Other	
1998	987.2	781.7	616.8	158.2	6.7	205.5
1999	2,558.6	1,062.6	983.8	73.0	5.8	1,496.0

Source: PROCOMER.

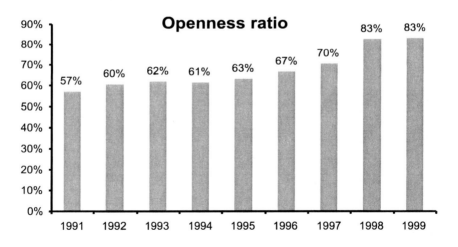

Figure 6-3.

purely an accounting matter, however, since Intel's surplus is then repatriated as profits, and this shows as a strong deficit in the "rents" component in the current account. This component went from a deficit of $254.5 million in 1997 to a deficit of $1,67 billion in 1999. What is the net effect? In 1999, Intel's net exports were $1.5 billion, and it repatriated profits for $1.2 billion so the net effect on the current account was almost $300 million. Appendix II has the complete balance of payments for the years 1996 through 1999.

Moreover, Intel helped to strengthen the diversification of Costa Rican trade patterns, increasing the number of countries with which that nation trades as well as the types of goods that are traded. The share of exported goods from the primary sector fell from 42.4 percent to only 23.8 percent in the 1997–1999 period, while the participation of goods manufactured within the free zones in total exports went from 21 percent to 54 percent in the same period. As Figure 6-4 shows, the share of exported goods from the primary sector was already declining before Intel arrived, but the tendency clearly accelerated after 1997.

Intel has a very diversified trade pattern in terms of the countries to which the production is exported. Its imports are more concentrated, as can be seen in Tables 6-8 through 6-10.

It is worth noticing the amount exported to Malaysia (although this falls significantly in 1999) and, in general, the important commercial links Intel has developed with major South East Asian economies and Japan.

The company also has a positive trade balance with European countries, as observed in Table 6-10. The strongest links are with the United Kingdom and Germany. That has helped Costa Rica strengthen commercial links with the

Figure 6-4.
Source: Central Bank of Costa Rica.
*Includes industrial and free-zone exports.

Table 6-8. INTEL Exports and Imports 1998–1999, American Countries (millions of dollars)

Country	1998			1999		
	Exports	Imports	Balance	Exports	Imports	Balance
Brazil	1.8	0.1	1.7	4.5	0.0	4.5
Mexico	14.2	1.3	12.9	60.4	1.6	58.8
United States	409.2	718.8	-309.6	1,391.2	988.6	402.7
Canada	1.1	0.7	0.4	5.7	0.0	5.7

Source: PROCOMER.

Table 6-9. INTEL Exports and Imports 1998–1999, Asian Countries (millions of dollars)

Country	1998			1999		
	Exports	Imports	Balance	Exports	Imports	Balance
China	0.4	0.0	0.4	0.6	0.0	0.6
Korea	22.2	0.0	22.2	35.0	0.0	35.0
Japon	32.9	30.3	2.6	104.2	49.7	54.5
Malaysia	114.5	5.5	109.1	62.8	6.0	56.8
Hong Kong	31.4	0.1	31.4	28.3	9.9	18.4
Philippines	5.8	8.4	-2.6	30.5	0.0	30.5

Source: PROCOMER.

Table 6-10. INTEL Exports and Imports 1998–1999, European Countries (millions of dollars)

Country	1998			1999		
	Exports	Imports	Balance	Exports	Imports	Balance
Germany	37.0	0.5	36.5	1.0	0.1	0.9
Switzerland	0.4	0.0	0.4	0.0	0.8	-0.8
United Kindom	100.4	0.7	99.7	320.1	0.0	320.1
Ireland	11.7	0.0	11.7	36.7	0.1	36.6
Italy	16.1	0.7	15.4	0.0	0.0	0.0

Source: PROCOMER.

European Union, which has historically been a difficult market for manufactured exports from developing countries. In this respect, although the externalities are discussed below, one can think of Costa Rican executives "learning" about doing business in markets otherwise closed, and becoming potentially important assets for other companies interested in having access to those foreign markets. In terms of regional diversification, the most important change Intel introduced in the country's historical patterns was an increase in the trade flows with Asian countries (exports to Asian countries almost tripled between 1997 and 1999, increasing from $148.1 million to $434 million). Intel has important investments in Malaysia, the Philippines, and more recently, China (Spar 1998). Table 6-11 shows the important role of Intel in strengthening Costa Rica's trade relations with Asia and Europe.

Fiscal Effects

There is a now a discussion in Costa Rica about the "dual economy" arrangement that exempts firms in the Export Processing Zones (EPZs) from paying taxes. This imposes a burden on the rest of the economy and is made all the more problematic by the fact that the firms in the EPZs constitute the most dynamic sector of the economy. Thus, unless other measures are taken, tax revenue as a share of GDP will fall progressively in the years ahead, leading to either higher taxes for domestic firms, higher deficits and the associated macroeconomic problems, or imposing the need of an expenditure cut.

If there is unemployment, so that no opportunity cost is associated with the workers hired by the Export Processing Zone companies, then all the profits generated by the EPZ companies are additional profits; that is, they do not reduce the profits generated by the domestic economy. In other words, in the presence of unemployment, there is no fiscal cost attributable to the EPZ

Table 6-11.   *Composition of Costa Rica's Exports 1999*

	% of total exports	
	Without Intel	*With Intel*
USA	49	51
México	2	2
Canada	1	1
Rest of America	26	16
European Union	18	21
Rest of Europe	1	1
Asia	2	6
Others	1	1
Total	**100**	**100**

Source: PROCOMER

companies. But, of course, even if there is aggregate unemployment, the kind of workers hired by EPZ companies in general, and Intel in particular, have a high probability of getting alternative job opportunities. The latter implies the existence of a positive fiscal cost. To put it simply, if Intel had not come to Costa Rica, the domestic economy would be larger, as it would have more highly qualified workers at its disposal, and thus it would generate more tax revenue for the Government.

One hypothesis is that the fiscal cost changes over time. In the short run, it is likely that FDI in EPZs generates extra employment, and thus the fiscal cost is low. In the medium run, the fiscal cost increases, because of the argument laid out above. Then, in the longer run, the fiscal cost disappears, since the EPZ entails a tax holiday of 12 years, after which the company loses its EPZ status and starts paying taxes like domestic firms. This is reinforced by the possible reaction of supply to increased labor demand. For example, the supply of electrical engineers will surely increase greatly as a consequence of demand from Intel, so it is unlikely that any other firm will suffer a shortage of electrical engineers because of Intel in the long run.

Presumably, the "gamble" with the EPZ scheme is that the revenue lost is minimal for two reasons: first, because unemployment exists, there is little displacement of labor from domestic firms, and second, domestic firms will not go to the EPZs due to the requirements of the scheme. Moreover, whatever displacement there is, the resulting reduction in tax revenue is more than justified (and compensated for or even reversed in the long run) by the positive effects of FDI through other channels. Certainly, this topic needs further empirical work to be clarified.

Externalities

In order to have some indicators of the general equilibrium effects Intel has had on the economy, a survey was carried out on twenty firms that were considered potential competitors of Intel in the market for inputs. Special emphasis was placed on determining the effect on wages, because of the obvious theoretical implications and also because of comments made in the newspapers about the so-called "Intel effect." Firms in the electronics industry claimed that Intel had put pressure on the wages for skilled labor (*La Nación* 1997). The survey asked respondents about the effect Intel's arrival had had on the prices of certain inputs and their general perception of the fact that Intel had become a local competitor in the inputs market.[14]

The survey also asked several questions to determine whether these "com-

---

14. Eleven firms responded to the request for information.

petitor" firms perceived some positive effects on their productivity as a consequence of Intel's operations. The firms surveyed, on average, export more than 60 percent of their production but also sell an important fraction in the internal market (around 30 percent). The composition of their work force was 20 percent engineers, less than 15 percent administrative employees, and the rest relatively unskilled labor, the equivalent of what Intel calls "technicians." The firms were selected from the pool of firms registered at CINDE. The fact that the firms that we chose to survey are involved with CINDE may indeed have introduced a selection bias. The survey firms perhaps showed a special interest in CINDE because they may have benefited more from Intel's arrival to the country. The results of the survey are summarized below.

Effect on the Labor Market and Other Input Prices

The average effect of Intel on the labor market—measured by the pressure on overall wages—was estimated as a 4.5, measured on a scale from 1 (no effect) to 7 (a very large effect).[15] When specifically asked about wage increases and changes in the benefits to employees, seven firms said they had increased wages after Intel's arrival, but five of those increased wages only to engineers. Increases were, on average, 10 percent to 12 percent in nominal terms over and above the hypothetical contractual increase those employees would have received in the absence of any pressure in the labor market. All of those who granted increases, however, declared that those increases did not affect their competitive position in the market over the medium term.[16]

Also, 80 percent of them perceived the increase in real wages as temporary, especially given the new programs established by the Costa Rican Technology Institute and the University of Costa Rica, and the expected increase in the supply of engineers and technicians in the future.[17]

At the time of the survey, only three firms said that they had hired personnel previously employed at Intel, and all of them perceived performance of these employees as above the average or average. Eight firms said they had hired graduates of the "Electronics Diploma," a one-year program aimed at preparing potential employees in electronics firms at the level of technicians. This program was specifically created after Intel's arrival in Costa Rica, under

---

15. In most of these questions the scale chosen was from 1 to 7, 1 being always the "best" outcome, and 7 being the "worst" outcome. Values closer to one are thus "better."

16. Moreover, most of these companies are foreign-owned, so the increase in wages was a net benefit to Costa Rica, since the owners of capital who lost as a consequence were foreigners.

17. According to the data, enrollment in the engineering schools at the Universities almost doubled after 1997 (interview with officials of the Costa Rican Technology Institute, August 1999).

an agreement with the Technology Institute. Those firms that hired people from such program believed that they had significantly benefited from its creation. All the firms interviewed, with the exception of one, declared that Intel's arrival was good for the formation of human capital in the country and the training of labor. Only two firms admitted to having changed their training policies—including expenditures devoted to training—as a result of Intel's competitive pressure on the labor market.

From the answers of the firms surveyed it is possible to conclude that Intel did indeed have an effect on the price of labor, especially skilled labor. The "Intel Effect" was thus a reality. This effect, however, may well be temporary. Intel's arrival in Costa Rica apparently increased not only the demand for labor with specific skills, but also its supply, through the agreements with the educational institutes and the creation of specific programs to train potential workers in the electronics industry.

The survey included questions regarding the prices of inputs, other labor, and changes in their prices as a result of Intel's pressure on the market. On a scale from 1 (a decrease in prices) to 7 (an increase in prices), the declared effect was, on average, 4.5, that is, practically no change. The firms did notice an increase (5.5 on average) in the price of certain services but that increase might not be linked to Intel's pressure on the market, according to the survey.

Training and the Intel Associate Status

The survey had questions designed to shed some light on the training externalities, potential spillovers, and linkages derived from Intel's arrival. In terms of training externalities, some answers were already discussed above, for instance, the fact that firms were hiring people graduated from the new program created at the Technology Institute, as well as the fact that the enrollment in engineering fields in the two most important higher education institutions of the country almost doubled in two years. At the Technology Institute, for instance, the number of students enrolled in engineering fields grew from 577 in the first quarter of 1997 to 874 in the year 2000, that is, from 9.5 percent to 12.5 percent of the total number of students enrolled. More details on this issue are worth mentioning.

In 1999, faculty members of the Costa Rican Technology Institute visited Cal Tech with the objective of redesigning the curriculum of the local programs in Costa Rica and opening new exchange possibilities for students and faculty. On the other hand, as mentioned earlier, these "Intel Associates" can apply for Intel-provided funds devoted to specific research and development programs, competing on an equal basis against other Intel Associate institutions around the world. An estimate of the funds Intel channels through this mechanism every year is about US$300 million.

The strongest link was created by Intel and the Costa Rican Technology Institute (ITCR). The "Intel Associate" status also involved: i) the creation of an additional one-year "certificate" program for technical high school or academic high school graduates to update their technical skills; ii) the creation of a one-year "associate degree" program for qualified applicants and graduates of the one-year "certificate program" focused on manufacturing semiconductors and iii) a program of language training that ITCR would provide to foreigners arriving in Costa Rica (Spanish) and Intel employees hired in Costa Rica (English). All this required the approval and supervision of the Ministry of Education.

Informal Transmission of Knowledge Spillovers

Even though it is difficult to measure the spillovers properly in terms of know-how and technological capacity, questions were asked about the interaction of technicians and engineers of different companies—including Intel—and potential gains from such interaction. Concretely, firms were asked whether they had formal channels of interaction between their employees and people working at Intel. Only two of them mentioned some type of formal interaction at the level of skilled labor, but none at the level of unskilled labor. To the question of whether such interaction took place in the academic world, in professional organizations, or some other way, the answer was that there had been only informal contacts with Intel personnel. No firm had evidence that their employees benefited from informal or formal contact with Intel employees.

It is important to mention here that companies like Intel have very strict confidentiality policies due to the competitive pressure in the market. These policies notwithstanding, Intel agreed to allow us to carry out a survey to the suppliers. The results are described in the next section.[18]

LINKAGES: BACK TO SUPPLIERS

The attraction by Intel of other, more sophisticated suppliers is another important effect of Intel's operations in Costa Rica. In 1998, for example, the

---

18. A total of 43 suppliers of goods and 37 suppliers of services answered the questionnaire.

American company Photocircuits announced a $40 million investment in Costa Rica, and projected a work force of 700 employees.

The Different Suppliers and Their Reactions

According to available information, there are more than 200 Intel suppliers locally, ranging from very small service providers to larger companies especially created to supply a specific input to Intel. Intel declared that the most important suppliers of inputs were 63 firms and more than 100 were providing services. The areas in which these suppliers are involved include:

Group 1, Services. Cafeteria service, computer services, document translation, garbage disposal, janitorial, pest control, security, training services (including language courses), hotel services, transport, consulting.

Group 2, Manufactured goods. Computer equipment, office equipment, packaging material, office supplies, spare parts, construction material, security equipment.

The assessment of the economic effect generated through the suppliers, including indicators of linkages and technological spillovers, would require a detailed analysis of Intel's purchases, training programs with suppliers, etc. We would have liked more specific information from some companies that had set up in Costa Rica specifically to supply Intel, such as RVSI, NTK, Phillips, Magnéticos Toroid de Costa Rica, Tiros, Alphasem Corp., Delta Design S.A. and Esec USA, Inc. The data obtained through the survey, however, allowed us to give some insights of the Intel effect.[19]

---

19. Ideally, a "linkage index" could be created and compared for different FDI firms to measure potential technological externalities. This index is based upon the idea of the spillover effect of FDI and is an imperfect way to approximate the ideal linkage index as discussed in Rodríguez-Clare (1996), which links the labor input requirements by the FDI and supplier firms.

The index could be of the following, rather rough, form:

$$LI = \frac{\sum_i VHI_i}{TE} \, ii$$

where LI is the linkage index, VHI_i is the value of the total amount of high technology input i purchased locally, and TE is the number of employees at the lowest level of skills (técnicos u operarios). Inputs will be classified as technologically more or less demanding. The rationale is that some firms could indeed be demanding a large amount of local inputs per employee, but those inputs could be technologically not demanding, which reduces the scope of potential technological externalities of that firm.

Among providers of goods and services to Intel, the arrival of Intel to Costa Rica was perceived as "very positive" for the economy (60 percent of the firms). Tables 6-12 shows the composition of the activities in which suppliers are involved.

In terms of training externalities, 35 percent of the providers of services declared to have received training from Intel (around 80 percent of the training took place at Intel´s plant). Among providers of inputs, 17 percent of the firms declared to have engaged in some kind of training by Intel. It is important to mention that 40 percent of the providers of inputs carry out more than 60 percent of the production process inside Costa Rica. Around 18 percent of the providers of goods stated that they had changed their organizational practices due to their activities with Intel. Around 8 percent of the providers of goods and 9 percent of the providers of services reported some changes in their product variety due to Intel, which is very important in terms of the backward-forward linkages discussed above.

Only two years after Intel had been established in Costa Rica by the time of the survey—around 10 percent of the firms surveyed were selling more than 50 percent of their total output to Intel. Another 8 percent were selling between 10 and 50 percent. The latter, along with the reported changes in lines

Table 6-12.   *Intel Suppliers in the Survey by Activity*

	Frequency	Percentage	Cumulative percentage
Lithographic products	9	20.9	34.9
Packing	4	9.3	9.3
Aluminum	4	4.7	14
Products and reparation of metal-mechanical parts	5	11.6	46.5
Furniture	3	7	53.5
Gas bottling	2	4.7	58.1
Computing Products (software, hardware)	2	4.7	62.8
Architecture	2	4.7	67.4
Office appliances	3	7	74.4
Electronic equipment	2	4.7	79.1
Products for industrial maintenance	2	4.7	83.7
Painting and construction	2	4.7	88.4
Plastic	1	2.3	90.7
Uniforms	1	2.3	93.0
Other appliances	1	2.3	95.3
Optics	1	2.3	97.7
Security	1	2.3	100.
Total	43.0	100.0	

Source: Authors' calculation from survey results.

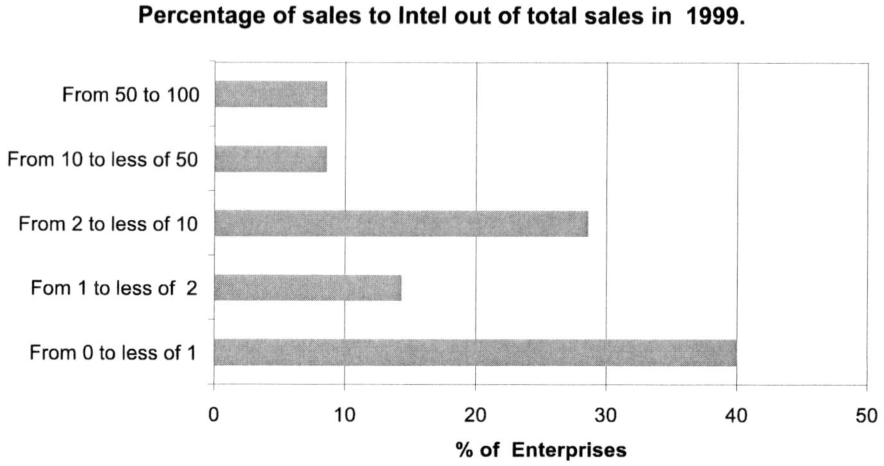

Percentage of sales to Intel out of total sales in 1999.

Figure 6-5.

of products and organizational forms in only two years, leads us to believe that the backward-forward externalities –making available newer and better goods and services to firms other than Intel—could indeed be taking place.

In terms of joint ventures with foreign partners, 12 percent of goods providers reported to be associated with a foreign firm. Among those, 80 percent have received training by the foreign partner, both in Costa Rica and abroad. Training externalities and forms of technology transfers were thus already showing up after a short period of time.

A first glance at the aggregate results of the survey, considering the fact that Intel had been in Costa Rica for only two years at the time the questionnaire was sent to them, allows us to say that the effects discussed in the theoretical literature seem to be already taking place. Important gains are showing not only at the macro, but also at the microeconomic level.

Supporting the Development of Suppliers

A program initiated by the government to develop and support suppliers of firms in the free-zones has shown important results, especially since 1997. Again, this program is not a specific policy to support suppliers of Intel, but to help any firm whose intention is to supply inputs to exporting firms under the free-zone agreement. Of course, given the high proportion of the total demand for inputs generated by Intel, since 1997 this firm has become a fundamental player in the program.

A fundamental characteristic of the inputs that Intel requires is that they have to satisfy international standards of quality. In addition, they must satisfy norms of environmental safety.[20] Quality and environmental safety have indeed been the two most important areas of advisory work with suppliers. The idea of the program to support Intel suppliers was supported by the United Nations and the Inter-American Development Bank (IDB) from 1997, and the program itself was formulated in 1998. It is finally being implemented in 2000, with IDB support. The three main sectors in which firms have developed are machinery and parts, plastics, and packaging (including the materials for shipping at the ports). Successful examples are companies that provide freight transportation services to firms in the free-zones, as well as one that produces high-electric-resistance packaging materials for Intel. There are also several small firms that now provide services to Intel's machinery and manufacture parts for repairing sophisticated equipment at Intel. Again, all the inputs and services under this program are made available not only to Intel or to firms in the free-zone, but also to all firms in the economy.

The survey of Intel competitors in the inputs market, already discussed above, also allowed us to obtain some indicators of Intel effects. The arrival of FDI firms such as Intel have made available inputs that did not exist before. These new inputs can be used, as mentioned, not only by the FDI firm, but also by all firms in the economy, thereby enhancing aggregate competitiveness. Eight firms maintained that some supplier of inputs had improved their quality after Intel's arrival, and specifically mentioned a certain type of service. As an example, packaging was mentioned as an input that had become more sophisticated in some specific firm, directly or indirectly due to Intel demand for similar services. The firms surveyed did not observe a reduction in prices of inputs after 1997, though they claimed that more specialized input providers had started businesses in Costa Rica, which could potentially benefit their firms. They did not mention any specific example of inputs under this category. Summarizing, only two years after Intel's arrival in Costa Rica, similar firms were seeing some evidence of backward-forward linkage effects through new or better input providers.

Two questions were asked regarding the general perception or assessment of the Intel effect: first, the perception of the effect on the specific firm being surveyed, and second, the perception of the overall effect in the economy.[21] Firms ranked Intel's effect on their own companies at 2.5, within a scale rang-

---

20. These international standards are under the classification ISO-9000 (quality) and ISO-4000 (environmental norms).

21. Specifically, these questions were: "In general, for your company, Intel's arrival has been . . .", and "In your opinion, the effect of Intel investment on the Costa Rican economy has been . . . ?"

ing from 1 (very positive) to 7 (very negative). The impact on the overall economy was estimated as highly positive as well (between 1 and 2). These rankings thus turned out surprisingly positive, even among firms that could be seen as competitors of Intel in certain input markets in Costa Rica.

Institutional Reforms and the Signaling Effect

An important component of the effect of FDI in host countries, as discussed throughout, consists of the so-called backward-forward linkages. In this respect, by 1999 Intel had started to play an important role in the political discussion about the reform of the power and telecommunications sectors in Costa Rica. Intel has very clearly avoided any intervention in the political debate about opening up telecommunications, but it has been used by the proponents of reform as an element in favor of opening up the market. The opponents also use it, saying that a firm such as Intel decided to come to Costa Rica despite the supposedly bad telecommunication services. The political balance among stakeholders in this realm seems to have changed after Intel's arrival, and the reforms are more likely to take place, benefiting not only Intel, but also all other companies in the Costa Rican economy, and even the consumers themselves. This development could be seen as a clear effect of the backward-forward linkage type, in which an institutional reform was required.

A very important externality that arises from Intel's decision to move into Costa Rica is the "signaling" or informational externality to other firms that could potentially invest in the country. As mentioned above, the survey carried out with multinational firms reflected that those firms had heard more about Costa Rica after 1997, the year in which Intel moved into Costa Rica (ARC 1999). If we consider the research costs that firms have to undergo when deciding where to invest abroad as a fixed entry cost, relatively small firms might decide not to enter because of their inability to cover such costs. The signaling effect by Intel could trigger entry decisions by smaller firms under such conditions. A second possibility in this respect is that large firms which could financially afford those entry costs, would anyway "free-ride" on Intel's location-search investment, and thereby reduce part of their costs of going into the country. This is especially the case considering that Intel did not get any legal or fiscal firm-specific benefits, but only the same type of arrangement any other firm could get in the same conditions. The fact that potential entrants into foreign markets benefit from previous entrants, who already incurred the research costs and developed commercial linkages has been explored by Aitken et al. (1997) from a theoretical perspective.

Conclusions

Though the decision of Intel to move into Costa Rica in 1997 came as a surprise in some academic and policy circles, this paper strongly suggests that the conditions of the country could clearly justify this decision from a theoretical and practical perspective. Previous research and interviews with Intel executives confirmed that the most important factors attracting Intel to Costa Rica were its political stability, highly educated labor force, relatively corruption-free environment, and the credibility of the legal institutions. Some weaknesses were also found: the small size of the country and its poorly developed and maintained infrastructure services, especially its roads, ports, and airports, and to a lesser extent electricity and telecommunications. The process of attracting Intel required a well-coordinated effort that involved ministries, independent agencies, and institutions of higher education. The fiscal benefits under the Costa Rican free-zone regime for FDI companies was also a key determinant in Intel's decision process.

The gross income generated by Intel in terms of net exports, investment, wages and benefits, and local purchases is very important for the Costa Rican economy. Net exports, and the economy as a whole have been growing at a significantly higher rate since 1997. Also, the composition of Costa Rica's exports has shown a decline in the share of natural resource-related exports and an increase in manufactures.

There were some worries, however, regarding the potential negative effects of Intel's arrival from a general equilibrium perspective. Concretely, it was believed that the increase in demand for certain inputs would raise their price, affecting other sectors negatively. The survey carried out with Intel competitors in the inputs market showed that such negative effects have indeed been felt, especially in terms of an increase in wages for skilled labor. Most firms, however, saw the effect as temporary and foresaw an increase in the supply of skilled labor through the creation of new programs in higher education institutions and the higher enrollment in existing engineering programs. A majority of them saw Intel's arrival in Costa Rica as good for themselves and the Costa Rican economy.

Available information supports the existence of positive externalities generated by Intel in the Costa Rican economy. Specifically, Intel has helped to create new training programs in higher education institutions, and these institutions have become "Intel Associates," which allows them to exchange curricula, faculty, and students with Intel Associates around the world, and to obtain substantial research funds. New investors and potential investors in Costa Rica claimed to have heard more about Costa Rica after Intel's decision, showing that the investment by Intel does play a signaling role to other multinationals. Moreover, new suppliers of Intel have arrived in Costa Rica. In terms of informal communication among employees, especially at the engineering level, the survey gave some (but not much) evidence of knowledge spillovers. A survey of Intel local suppliers was initially thwarted by Intel's strict confidentiality policies, which do not allow Intel executives to disclose the names of their suppliers and prevent those suppliers from giving any information regarding their commercial relation with the company. Later on, the authors were allowed to carry out such a survey in order to answer some research questions in more detail. The results strongly suggest the existence of positive Intel effects on local suppliers and on other companies using inputs from Intel suppliers, just as predicated by the theoretical literature.

The overall effect of Intel moving into Costa Rica appears to be unambiguously positive. Though the data shown in this chapter has shortcomings, the evidence points in the direction of a positive net effect, especially when the medium- and long-term effects are considered. Intel has increased the export capacity of the country, has diversified exports, has helped or might help attract other companies into the country, has established important links with the education community to develop human resources for the benefit of the whole economy, and has changed the balance among stakeholders in the public discussion regarding important institutional reforms. Moreover, the development of local suppliers has been fast and ambitious, thanks to a coordinated effort by the government. Even though the free-zone regime implies a substantial fiscal sacrifice in terms of tax collection, the figures shown above suggest that those foregone revenues could be money well spent, if they help establish an industrial base that becomes the engine of Costa Rica's future economic growth.

REFERENCES

Aitken, B., H. H. Gordon, and A. E. Harrison. 1997. "Spillovers, Foreign Investment, and Export Behavior." *Journal of International Economics* 43:

ARC (Applied Research and Consulting). 1999. Foreign Investment in Costa Rica and Other Developing Countries. Coalición Costarricense de Iniciativas para el Desarrollo (CINDE). Mimeographed. San José.

Arrow, K. 1999. "Knowledge as a Factor of Production." *Paper Presented at the ABCDE 1999 Conference.* Washington, D.C.: World Bank.

Blomstrom, M. 1989. Foreign Investment and Spillovers: A Study Of Technology Transfer To Mexico. London: Routledge.

———. 1997. "The Effects of Foreign Direct Investment in Host Countries."

Blomstrom, M. and A. Kokko. 1997. "How Foreign Investment Affects Host Countries." *Policy Research Working Paper No. 1745.* Washington, D.C.: World Bank International Economics Department, International Trade Division.

Buffie, E. 1993. "Direct Foreign Investment, Crowding Out, and Underemployment in the Dualistic Economy." *Oxford Economic Papers* 45: 639-667.

Caves, R. 1971. "International Corporations: The Industrial Economics of Foreign Investment," *Econometrica* 38:149.

———. 1976. *Multinational Enterprise and Economic Analysis.* London: Cambridge University Press.

Central Bank of Costa Rica 1997. Indicadores Económicos. San José.

Dunning, J.H. 1977. "Trade, Location of Economic Activity, and the MNE: A Search for An Eclectic Approach." In *The International Allocation of Economic Activity,* edited by B. Phlin, P.O. Hesselborn, and P.M. Wijkman. London: Macmillan.

Haddad, M. and A. Harrison. 1993. "Are there Positive Spillovers from Direct Foreign Investment? Evidence from Panel Data for Morocco." *Journal of Development Economics* 43: 51-74.

Hymer, S. H. 1976. The International Operations of National Firms: A Study of Direct Foreign Investment. Cambridge, MA: MIT Press.

La Nación. 1997. "Falta Mano de Obra Calificada." October 3.

Lim, L.Y.C. and P. E. Fong. 1991. *Foreign Direct Investment and Industrialization in Malaysia, Singapore, Taiwan, and Thailand.* Paris: Organization for Economic Cooperation and Development (OECD).

Meyanathan, S. D. 1994. Industrial Structures and the Development of Small and Medium Enterprise Linkages. Washington D.C: World Bank

Pack, H. and L. E. Westphal. 1986. "Industrial Strategy and Technological Change: theory vs. Reality." *Journal of Development Economics* 22: 87-128.

Pack, H. and A. Rodríguez-Clare.1998. "A Firm-Level Analysis of the Effect of FDI: A Case Study of Intel Costa Rica." Mimeographed. San José.

Phlin, B., P.O. Hesselborn, and P.M. Wijkman, eds. 1977. *The International Allocation of Economic Activity.* London: Macmillan.

Ranis, G. and C. Schive (1985); "Direct Foreign Investment in Taiwan's Development." In, *Foreign Trade and Investment: Economic Development in the Newly Industrializing Asian Countries,* edited by Walter Galenson. Madison, WI: University of Wisconsin Press.

Rodríguez-Clare, A. (1996); "Multinationals, Linkages, and Economic Development." *American Economic Review* 86:852-73.

Rugman, A. M. 1980. "Internalization as a General Theory of Foreign Direct Investment: A Critique." *Weltwirtschaftliches Archiv* 116.

———. 1985. "Internalization is Still a General Theory of Foreign Direct Investment." *Weltwirtschaftliches Archiv* 121.

————. 1986. "New Theories of the Multinational Enterprise: An Assessment of the Internalization Theory." *Bulletin of Economic Research* 38.

Saito, M. 1998. "The Determinants of FDI: Theoretical Overview and Implications for the Baltics." Washington, D.C.: International Monetary Fund (IMF). Mimeographed.

Shatz, H. 1997. "What does the Theoretical Literature on Foreign Direct Investment Tell Us About Location?" Cambridge, MA: HIID, Harvard University. Mimeographed.

————. 1997. "What Attracts FDI?" *The Global Competitiveness Report 1997.* Geneva: World Economic Forum.

Spar, D. 1998. "Attracting High Technology Investment: Intel's Costa Rican Plant." *Foreign Investment Advisory Service Occasional Paper 11.* Washington. D.C.: World Bank.

Stewart, J.C. 1976. "Linkages and Foreign Direct Investment." *Regional Studies* 10 (2).

Todo, Y. 1999. Foreign Direct Investment, Licensing, and Technology Transfer. Stanford University, Stanford, CA. Mimeographed.

UNDP 1999. Human Development Report. United Nations.

Vernon, R. 1966. "International Investment and International Trade in the Product Cycles." *Quarterly Journal of Economics* 80.

Appendix I: Summary of Benefits Under Costa Rica's Free-Zone Incentive Package

The following are the benefits program under which 190 companies had come to Costa Rica as of June 1997. These firms are distributed in eight different industrial parks. Intel is geographically located in a different area but receives the benefits as though it were in one of such parks.

i) 100 percent exemption on import duties on raw materials and capital goods.

ii) 100 percent exemption on taxes on profits for eight years, and 50 percent for the following four years.

iii) 100 percent exemption on export taxes, local sales, and excise taxes, as well as taxes on repatriation of profits.

iv) 100 percent exemption on municipal and capital taxes.

v) No restrictions on repatriation of profits or foreign currency management.

vi) Fully expedited on-site customs clearance.

vii) Possibility of selling products to local exporters.

viii) Possibility of selling up to 40 percent of the production locally, exempt from sales tax.

Intel also received the benefits offered to firms located in the Puntarenas free trade zone:

i) Longer exemption from taxes on profits: 100 percent for twelve years and 50 percent for the following six years.

ii) Every year, for five years, the government repays the investors a percentage of its payroll in the chosen base year (15 percent the first year, 13 percent the second, 11 percent the third, 9 percent the fourth, and 7 percent the fifth year).

iii) Subsidized training programs in a way that practically results in three months of free labor for the firm, provided workers receive on-site training.

Source: Spar (1998).

APPENDIX II: BALANCE OF PAYMENTS

		1996	1997	1998	1999*
I.	Current account (A+B+C+D)	−264.1	−480.9	−520.7	−583.7
	A. Goods	−249.2	−497.6	−399.0	632.1
	Exports FOB	3,774.1	4,220.6	5,538.3	6,616.0
	Imports FOB	−4,023.3	−4,718.2	−5,937.3	−5,983.9
	B. Services	20.3	140.2	233.6	357.9
	Transportations	−250.8	−189.1	−213.6	−183.3
	Travels	374.0	394.3	504.6	583.2
	Others Services	−102.9	−65.1	−57.4	−42.0
	C. Income	−184.6	−249.0	−468.5	−1,685.2
	Compensation of employees	1.9	5.5	−7.1	−7.0
	Investment income	−186.5	−254.5	−461.4	−1,678.2
	D. Current Transfers	149.5	125.5	113.2	111.5
	General Government	45.7	37.5	39.8	39.5
	Other Sectors	103.8	88.0	73.4	72.0
II.	Capital and Financial Account (A+B)	67.5	508.5	547.7	1,063.7
	A. Capital Account	28.1	0.0	0.0	0.0
	Capital transfers	28.1	0.0	0.0	0.0
	Non–produced non–financial assets	0.0	0.0	0.0	0.0
	B. Financial Account	39.4	508.5	547.7	1,063.7
	Direct Investment Abroad	421.3	402.5	606.9	578.3
	Portfolio Investment	−21.5	74.4	−85.6	232.5
	Other Investment	−360.3	31.6	26.5	252.9
III.	NET ERRORS AND OMISSIONS	142.0	189.1	−176.6	−
IV.	Reserve Assets	54.5	−216.7	149.6	−480.0
V.	Total Balance of Payments (I+II+III+IV)	0.0	0.0	0.0	0.0

Net errors and omissions" for 1999 include "Other Investment" from B. Financial Account.
Source: Central Bank of Costa Rica.

7

Export Processing Zones in Central America

MAURICIO JENKINS, GERARDO ESQUIVEL, AND
FELIPE LARRAÍN B.[1]

Introduction

In the hope of emulating the path of development of the newly industrialized countries of East Asia (Hong Kong, Singapore, Taiwan, and Korea), many developing countries have moved from a strategy of development based on import substitution to one based on export promotion.[2] As one of the measures taken to support the switch in strategy, many of these countries have established export processing zones (EPZs). These zones have been seen as a quick and efficient way of generating employment, earning much-needed foreign exchange, attracting foreign direct investment (FDI) and transferring technology.[3]

The first EPZ was established in 1959 in Ireland, near Shannon Airport. The zone was developed by the Irish authorities as a response to the advent of

1. The authors thank all people and institutions that contributed their time and provided valuable insights and data. Particularly helpful were Procomer in Costa Rica, FIDE in Honduras, the Ministry of Economy in Guatemala, the Ministry of Economy in El Salvador, and the Corporación de Zonas Francas in Nicaragua. The authors wish to thank Roberto Artavia, Arnoldo Camacho, Lucia Marshall, John Marshall, and Amina Tirana for their helpful comments, as well as Ellie Stewart and Porfirio Guevara for excellent assistance.

2. The issue of whether export promotion and outward orientation cause higher rates of economic growth, or whether the causation runs the other way around, has not been unambiguously determined in empirical studies. Linneman (1996), contains a brief but good review of the recent literature on this topic, and offers some potential explanations for the ambiguous results.

3. See Basile and Germidis (1984), Rondinelli (1987), and World Bank (1992).

the jet airliner, which, in contrast to its predecessors, did not need to refuel at Shannon on the transoceanic flight. The area surrounding the airport was then transformed into the first modern EPZ, with the intention of attracting export-oriented foreign firms and thereby replacing jobs expected to be lost through the decline in the airport's activities.[4]

Fueled by the Irish success at Shannon as well as their own interest in promoting exports and attracting FDI, several countries in East Asia and Latin America adopted the EPZ concept during the 1960s. By the end of the decade there were about eight zones located in Korea, Taiwan, India, the Dominican Republic, Colombia, and Mexico.[5] Beginning in the early 1970s and throughout the next 25 years, the number of countries with EPZs and the number of zones themselves increased rapidly. According to some authors, the number of zones grew from 79 to 176 between 1975 and 1986, while the number of developing countries with zones grew from 25 to 47 during the same period.[6] More recent surveys conclude that by the mid-1990s there were over 200 EPZs located in more than 65 nations.[7]

Given the number of zones already in place and the rate at which a growing number of less-developed countries have been adopting the EPZ concept, it is extremely important for policymakers throughout the developing world to understand the benefits and limitations of EPZs.

The purpose of this paper is threefold. First, it looks at EPZs from a worldwide perspective and attempts to draw useful lessons from the experience accumulated in several countries. Second, it examines the development and economic significance of the zones in Central America. The paper ends with a set of conclusions and policy proposals for EPZ development in the Central American region.

THE EPZ CONCEPT

Unfortunately, there is no universally accepted definition of what constitutes an EPZ. The lack of consensus and the plethora of terms that have been used in the literature to refer to the zones,[8] create numerous problems for the

---

4. For more details about the Irish experience see Roberts (1992), Burns (1995), and ILO/UNCTC (1988).

5. UNCTAD (1993).

6. Kreye, Heinrichs, and Fröbel (1987).

7. See UNCTAD (1993) and UNIDO (1995).

8. For example, Burns (1995) uses the term Free-Trade Zones, which includes zones dedicated primarily to commerce and trading with almost no manufacturing process involved. The World Bank (1992) limits their study to what they call "fenced-in" EPZs. Grubel's (1982) definition of Free Economic Zones encompasses a wide range of activities and regimes.

analysis of zone activity. For the purpose of this research, EPZs are understood as geographic zones (not necessarily industrial parks) established outside the customs territory of a particular country, where products can be stored, processed and manufactured without the payment of import duties, and with the intention of exporting most of the output. The fact that our definition limits EPZs to geographical areas within a country implies that Singapore and Hong Kong, where the entire territory is fundamentally an EPZ, are excluded. Furthermore, our definition limits the primary purpose of the zone as manufacturing for export. This requirement implies that the more than 200 free-trade zones that exist in the United Sates (Burns 1995),[9] and zones like Manaus in Brazil—more of an "import processing zone" than an EPZ (ILO/UNCTC 1988)—are also excluded.

Although the specific laws governing the operation of zone enterprises vary from country to country, in most cases EPZ legislation contains regulations along the following four dimensions.

Location of EPZ Firms

With regard to the specific location of zone enterprises within the host nation, two different types of arrangements exist. In some countries (e.g., Taiwan, Korea), EPZ firms can only locate within the boundaries of industrial parks specifically developed for that purpose. In other countries (e.g., El Salvador, Honduras, Mexico, Mauritius), the zone legislation allows EPZ firms to locate anywhere within the country. Thus, these countries allow the operation of what has been called "single-factory" or "one-firm" EPZs. It is also noteworthy that in many nations (e.g., Costa Rica, El Salvador, and Honduras) both of the options described above are available to EPZ investors.

Duties and Customs Procedures

EPZs invariably have unrestricted access to imported raw materials, intermediate inputs, equipment, and machinery free of any import duties, as long as these are used in the production of goods and services that are eventually exported. Exported goods and services are also exempt from all export or sales taxes.

A distinctive characteristic of EPZ regimes is the existence of special and

---

9. Manufacturing activities performed in these zones are mainly in the auto, appliance, and electronics industries. The United States market is the primary destination for these products (USITC 1988), and the share of domestic value added in exports is unusually high (two-thirds according to USITC 1988). The objective of many of the firms that establish operations in these zones is simply to defer the payment of import duties on parts and intermediate inputs (Crystal 1993).

streamlined customs procedures for zone enterprises. EPZ firms can frequently complete formalities for import and export transactions within a matter of hours, bypassing much of the red tape affecting non-EPZ enterprises. Frequently, customs clearance and related procedures are performed at the firm's own location, with the intention of speeding up import and export activities as much as possible.

Income Tax Holidays and Other Fiscal Incentives

With a few exceptions (e.g., the Philippines), firms with EPZ status are normally granted a tax holiday that exempts them from paying income tax for a number of years. The length of holiday varies greatly among nations. In Jamaica and Honduras, the legislation does not specify an expiration date, which means that the holidays never expire. In most nations, the holiday extends between 5 and 15 years.

EPZ firms are also exempted from the payment of other taxes such as property, municipal, or excise taxes, normally for the same period of time for which the income tax holiday applies. Likewise, EPZ firms are not subject to normal withholding taxes on royalties, dividends, or repatriation of capital. In almost all cases, EPZ enterprises are allowed complete freedom to manage their foreign-exchange transactions.

Other incentives offered less frequently include a tax deduction for training local personnel, provision of public services (e.g., water and electricity) or factory space at subsidized prices, and access to local financing at preferential interest rates.

Domestic Sales

Given the fiscal and other privileges that EPZ firms enjoy, sales of their products in the domestic economy are almost always regulated. The proportion of domestic sales allowed, in any case permitted only after payment of the corresponding import duties and upon the approval of the local authorities, usually ranges between zero (e.g., India) to 40 percent (e.g., Costa Rica) of total output. In some very unique cases (e.g., El Salvador) EPZ firms are allowed to sell 100 percent of their output in the domestic market.

A GLOBAL OVERVIEW OF EPZs

International comparisons of EPZs are difficult because comprehensive data for several countries are very hard to compile. As a consequence, empirical studies of EPZs that make comparisons among nations are rare. Notwithstanding these limitations, published works do reveal a number of empirical regularities about the operation of EPZs in many nations. The most important of these regularities are summarized in the following sections.

Economic Importance

Given numerous problems with data on production, investment and exports, the economic significance of EPZ regimes in individual nations has been traditionally gauged using the share of EPZ employment in total manufacturing employment (e.g., ILO/UNCTC 1988). Table 7-1 estimates these shares for nations for which EPZ and manufacturing employment data were available during the early 1990s.

According to the figures in Table 7-1, the median share of EPZ employment in total manufacturing employment for all the countries depicted was just 2.80 percent.[10] The share does, however, vary substantially both across geographical regions and individual countries. For example, for the twelve Latin American countries for which the share could be estimated, the median share was 6.1 percent, while in the nine countries of the Asia/Pacific region it was just 0.9 percent. In Africa and Europe, the median shares were 5.6 percent and 2.7 percent respectively. Thus, the economic relevance of EPZ regimes is significantly larger in Latin America and Africa than in Asia or in the less-developed parts of Europe.

Regarding individual nations, EPZs seem to account for a relatively small share of total manufacturing employment in larger economies (e.g. India, Thailand, Korea, Venezuela, Colombia) and for a larger share in smaller economies (e.g. Fiji, Mauritius, the Dominican Republic, Barbados).[11] In fact, in some of the latter nations the shares are strikingly large.

Geographical Distribution

As Table 7-1 reveals, EPZ activity is primarily a phenomenon of the developing world. Indeed, 35 out of the 39 nations identified as having established EPZs in their territories can be classified as developing nations—i.e.,

---

10. The median share is used instead of the average share, given that the latter is greatly skewed by the large shares observed in some small countries.

11. A simple OLS regression between the share of EPZ employment against the size of the country measured by population or total GDP reveals a negative and statistically significant relationship at the 5 percent level between these variables.

Table 7-1. *Share of EPZ Employment in Manufacturing Employment (Early 1990s)*

Country	Manufacturing Employment		EPZ Employment		EPZ Share (%)
	Year	Jobs	Year	Jobs	
Latin America					
Barbados	1990	10,000	1992	6,200	62.0
Belize	1993	7,165	1990/1	600	8.4
Chile	1990	716,200	1990/1	8,500	1.2
Colombia	1990	1,030,900	1990/1	8,500	0.8
Dominican Republic	1990	200,000	1990	112,000	56.0
Grenada	NA	NA	1990/1	500	NA
Jamaica	1990	136,100	1990/1	5,300	3.9
Mexico	1991	4,806,000	1990/1	487,000	10.1
Netherlands Antilles	1990	4,725	1990/1	800	16.9
Panama	1991	69,400	1990/1	6,500	9.4
Peru	1991	453,000	1990/1	600	0.1
St. Lucia	NA	NA	1990/1	1,500	NA
Trinidad and Tobago	1990	37,200	1990/1	400	1.1
Venezuela	1990	994,580	1990/1	300	0.0
Europe					
Turkey	1992	317,500	1992	9,000	2.8
Ireland	1992	226,700	1992	6,000	2.6
Asia/Pacific					
Bangladesh	NA	NA	1990/1	10,000	NA
Fiji	1992	21,180	1992	10,000	47.2
India	1989	6,245,000	1990/1	30,000	0.5
Indonesia	1990	7,693,300	1990/1	50,000	0.6
Korea	1990	4,911,000	1990/1	22,000	0.4
Malaysia	1990	1,332,800	1990/1	99,000	7.4
Pakistan	1992	3,813,000	1992	4,500	0.1
Philippines	1992	2,546,000	1992	54,000	2.1
Sri Lanka	1992	672,200	1992	104,000	15.5
Taiwan	NA	NA	1990/1	72,000	NA
Thailand	1990	3,132,500	1990/1	28,000	0.9
United Arab Emirates	NA	NA	1990/1	5,000	NA
Africa					
Botswana	1992	25,500	1992	1,700	6.7
Cameroon	NA	NA	1992	600	NA
Egypt	1990	1,867,800	1990/1	25,000	1.3
Ghana	1990	28,700	1990/1	2,600	9.1
Kenya	1991	188,900	1992	1,000	0.5
Madagascar	1991	93,100	1992	4,200	4.5
Mauritius	1992	110,630	1992	90,000	81.4
Morocco	1991	1,012,700	1990/1	3,100	0.3
Senegal	NA	NA	1990/1	500	NA
Togo	1991	6,096	1990/1	1,000	16.4
Tunisia	NA	NA	1992	109,000	NA

NA: Not available
Sources: Elaborated from data published by the International Labor Office (several issues), and UNIDO (1995).

they have either lower-middle or low-income economies according to World Bank (1996).[12]

Another interesting fact regarding EPZs is that zone activity is largely concentrated in East Asian and Latin American nations. As the data in Table 7-1 indicate, in the early 1990s, about 75 percent of total EPZ employment was located in these two regions of the world. Data on the number of zones themselves are equally revealing. According to UNCTAD (1993), about half of the existing 200 EPZs were then located in Asia, while another 80 were in Latin America.

Industry Composition

The industries that are more likely to be found in EPZs are labor-intensive lightweight manufactures. The most common industries are textiles and apparel, electric and electronic components, food processing, metal products and machinery, optical instruments, and sporting goods and toys.[13] Unfortunately, detailed data regarding the sectoral composition of EPZ activity in terms of the value of investment or production is extremely scanty. To our knowledge, data on EPZ production by sector for several countries has been published only by UNIDO (1995), while data on value of EPZ investment are provided solely in a handful of country-specific studies.

Table 7-2 reproduces the industry breakdown of EPZ output from UNIDO (1995), supplemented with data for the Dominican Republic and Malaysia compiled from other sources. Unfortunately, the industry groupings used by UNIDO (1995) are broad and offer limited detail on the sectoral composition of EPZ output. Nonetheless, the data in Table 7-2 reveal an important fact regarding the industry composition of EPZ activity—namely, that the bulk of it is concentrated in the textile/garments (hereafter, textiles for short) and electric/electronic (hereafter, electronics for short) industries. Together, the textiles and electronics sectors account for more than 50 percent of total EPZ activity in 9 of the 20 countries depicted, and are the largest sectors in at least 11 (probably 15) nations.

Employment data, which have traditionally been used to examine the composition of EPZ activity by sector, tend to confirm this result. Table 7-3 reproduces data gathered from several of the studies that used employment data to analyze the industry composition of EPZ activity. As the table shows, in terms

---

12. The proportion of developing nations with EPZs that these numbers imply is actually underestimated. There are several countries, mostly developing economies (e.g., Jordan, Haiti, Lesotho, Nigeria, Burundi, Liberia, Vietnam), that had established zones but are not included in Table 1 because data on EPZ employment were not available.

13. See ILO/UNCTC (1988), Rondinelli (1987), and Kreye, Heinrichs, and Fröbel (1987).

Table 7-2. *Sectoral Composition of EPZ Output in Selected Countries in the Early 1990s (Percentages)*

Country	Textiles and Garments	Electric and Electronic	Data Processing	Other
Barbados	17	5	27	41
Costa Rica	42	7	0	51
Dominican Republic	39	6	0	55
Jamaica	77	0	0	23
Mexico	5	45	0	50
Venezuela	65	0	0	35
Fiji	20	0	0	80
India	9	12	8	71
Jordan	76	0	0	24
Korea	5	70	0	25
Malaysia [1]	22	43	0	35
Philippines	36	30	0	34
Sri Lanka	57	0	0	43
Botswana	20	0	0	80
Cameroon	0	0	0	100
Madagascar	91	0	0	9
Mauritius	83	2	0	15
Morocco	68	4	0	28
Senegal	44	0	0	56
Tunisia	58	21	0	21

Notes: (1) By investment
Sources: UNIDO (1995), Sivalingam (1994), and Mortimore, Duthoo, and Guerrero (1995)

Table 7-3. *EPZ Employment Breakdown by Sector in Selected Countries (Percentages)*

Country	Year of Data	Textiles and Garments	Electric and Electronic	Footwear and Leather	Sporting Articles and Toys	Metal Products and Machinery	Other
Colombia[1]	1985	46.0	10.0	3.0	0.0	23.0	18.0
Dominican Republic	1993	73.0	5.0	8.0	3.0	0.0	11.0
Jamaica	1985	89.0	0.0	0.0	0.0	0.0	11.0
Mexico	1990	9.1	37.1	1.6	NA	21.3	30.9
Bangladesh	1986	81.0	1.0	0.0	0.0	15.0	3.0
Korea	1986	10.0	50.0	5.0	NA	NA	35.0
Malaysia	1990	11.0	64.8	NA	NA	2.0	22.2
Philippines[1]	1980	43.0	13.9	8.2	NA	10.2	24.7
Sri Lanka	1981	89.9	2.0	NA	NA	NA	8.1
Taiwan	1983	17.0	54.0	4.0	0.0	6.0	19.0
Egypt	1980	54.0	NA	NA	NA	3.8	42.2
Mauritius	1991	89.5	0.5	1.5	NA	NA	8.5

NA: Not Available
Notes: (1) Data for only one zone (Bataan in The Philippines, and Barranquilla in Colombia)

of employment, a single industry seems to dominate EPZ activity in most nations, this single industry being in all the cases either textiles or electronics. In fact, in 8 out of the 12 countries depicted, one of these two industries accounts for 50 percent or more of total EPZ employment, while in 10 nations the dominant industry (i.e., textiles or electronics) is at least three times larger than the second most important one. These results indicate that EPZ activity is concentrated in the textiles and electronics sectors, and suggest, as Roberts (1992) argues, that once a particular industry begins to dominate EPZ activity in a particular nation, it tends to become overwhelmingly dominant.

Ownership in EPZs

Since EPZ regimes contain a series of incentives specially targeted to attract foreign firms, some researchers have erroneously maintained or implicitly assumed that FDI is by far the most important source of capital in EPZs.[14] In fact, several studies have pointed out that investment by local entrepreneurs represents a significant proportion of total investment in the EPZs of many nations.[15]

Table 7-4 shows the ownership distribution of EPZ firms in 22 developing nations for which these data were available. In half the nations depicted, foreign firms do outnumber domestically owned firms, but in the other half domestically owned firms are more numerous than foreign firms. A simple manipulation of the data in Table 7-4 shows that 45 percent of the more than 6,300 EPZ enterprises are domestically owned, while only 31 percent are foreign owned. Thus, at least in terms of the number of firms in the zones, it is clear that domestic participation in zone activity represents a very important proportion of the total. It is worth mentioning that the ownership data in Table 7-4 also reveal that joint ventures are an important form of investment in quite a few nations.

Unfortunately, data on the nationality of investment is not available for several nations; but the same general pattern indicating a significant proportion of local participation in EPZs can be discerned from the few country-specific studies that have reported these data. For example, ILO/UNCTC (1988) reports that during the early 1980s, 75 percent of EPZ investment in Indonesia, and 85 percent in Thailand was of domestic origin. In Sri Lanka, nearly 48 percent of investment in the zones up until 1992 was of domestic origin.[16] For Malaysia, Sivalingam (1994) reports that more than 14 percent

---

14. See, for example, Warr (1990) and Wei (1993).
15. See, among others, ILO/UNCTC (1988), UNCTAD (1993), and UNIDO (1995).
16. Abeywardene, et al. (1994).

Table 7-4. Ownership of EPZ Enterprises (Early 1990s)

Country	Number of Firms	Foreign Owned (%)	Domestically Owned (%)	Joint Venture (%)
Barbados	124	29.0	47.6	23.4
Colombia	70	27.1	58.6	14.3
Dominican Republic	357	80.4	19.6	0.0
Guatemala	12	0.0	100.0	0.0
Jamaica	14	92.9	7.1	0.0
Mexico	2634	32.4	43.2	24.4
Venezuela	13	0.0	38.5	61.5
Jordan	15	33.3	60.0	6.7
Fiji	119	30.3	53.8	16.0
India	102	2.0	79.0	19.0
Korea	91	37.4	33.0	29.7
Philippines	187	53.9	17.5	28.6
Sri Lanka	139	42.4	3.6	54.0
Cyprus	11	54.5	45.5	0.0
Turkey	297	7.7	62.6	29.6
Botswana	17	64.7	11.8	23.5
Cameroon	8	25.0	12.5	62.5
Madagascar	19	10.5	0.0	89.5
Mauritius	586	11.4	60.1	28.5
Morocco	36	94.4	0.0	5.6
Senegal	9	44.4	11.1	44.4
Tunisia	1458	25.2	49.7	25.1

Source: UNIDO (1995).

of investment in the zones came from local sources, a much smaller but still significant share.

Employment and Labor Conditions

According to Kreye et al. (1987) the vast majority of workers in EPZ firms are young women aged 16–25 years. The proportion of women in the labor force is inversely related to the age of the zone, and depends on the industrial composition of the firms in it.[17] In fact, ILO/UNCTC (1988) contends that the large proportion of women in the labor force of EPZs is more a reflection of the industrial composition of the firms (fundamentally electronics and garments) than anything else.

Several researchers have also argued that working conditions in the zones

---

17. In the Masan Zone in Korea, the proportion of women in the area decreased from over 90 percent in 1971 to 75 percent in 1979 (Rabbani 1980). In Mauritius, the proportion of men working in the zones grew from 20 percent in 1984 to over 33 percent in 1989 (Roberts 1992). In Malaysia, it grew from 13 percent in 1972 to 28 percent in 1976 (Basile and Germidis 1984).

are as good as, or even better than, outside them (e.g., Willmore 1995). For example, ILO/UNCTC (1988) reports that working hours in EPZs in Mexico, Malaysia, Mauritius, and Sri Lanka were not very different from working hours in other manufacturing industries, especially in the textile and electronics industries. Also, wages in EPZ firms tend to be roughly similar to those prevailing in the local manufacturing sector (ILO/UNCTC 1988; Basile and Germidis 1984). Safety and health conditions have also been found to be better in EPZ firms than in comparable domestic enterprises (World Bank 1992).

Since EPZ activity in developing nations is largely concentrated in East Asia and Latin America, it is interesting to contrast the development of the zones in these two geographical regions. Likewise, given that a very high proportion of EPZ activity around the world is concentrated in the textile and electronics industries, it is also interesting to examine the differences that may exist in EPZ activity across these industrial sectors. The next two sections examine the special characteristics of EPZs along these two dimensions.

Contrasting the EPZs of East Asia and Latin America[18]

Many of the most successful EPZs are located in East Asia, especially in Taiwan and Korea. Initially, the zones in these two countries attracted labor-intensive industries with relatively unsophisticated technologies (i.e., garments and electronics) that required large numbers of unskilled workers. However, both countries were successful in diversifying away from the low-skill labor-intensive industries that sprang up in EPZs in their first years of operation, and in promoting 'linkages between local industries and the firms in the zones. In the Masan Zone of Korea, for example, the zone administration gave technical assistance to local suppliers and sub-contractors. In Taiwan, under government guidance, personnel from firms in the zones were placed at potential suppliers' factories to offer advice in production methods and quality control. As a result of this effort, the domestic value added of the Masan zone in Korea increased from 27.8 percent to 52.2 percent between 1971 and 1979. In Taiwan, local supplies increased from 8 percent of total imports to 46 percent between 1969 and 1979.

Contrary to popular belief, EPZs in Latin America are not a new phenomenon. The first EPZs in the region were inaugurated in Colombia (the

18. For further details of EPZs in East Asia see Rabbani (1980), Gil Van (1980), Basile and Germidis (1984), Balasubramanyam (1988), World Bank (1992), and Willmore (1995). For further details of EPZs in Latin America see Teutli (1980), ILO/UNCTC (1988), Grunwald (1991), Kaplinsky (1993), Burns (1995), Mata (1995), Mortimore, Duthoo, and Guerrero (1995), and Willmore (1995).

Barranquilla zone in 1964) and the Dominican Republic (La Romana in 1965).[19] Other countries quickly followed. The maquiladora program in Mexico began in the mid-1960s, when the government created the Border Industrialization Plan. Guatemala, Honduras, and El Salvador inaugurated their first EPZs in the early 1970s. A few years later, Nicaragua (1976), Jamaica (1976), and Costa Rica (1981) inaugurated theirs. Except in the Dominican Republic, the first zones in Latin American countries were developed and administered by the public sector with the objective of achieving regional development.

EPZ activity in Latin America is highly concentrated in two countries: Mexico and the Dominican Republic. In 1994, *maquiladoras* in Mexico employed more than 600,000 workers. Initially a high share of the *maquiladoras* produced garments and electronic products. Later, a more diverse group of industries emerged under the program. Backward linkages, however, never really formed.[20] This is the more paradoxical given Mexico's large and well-diversified industrial sector. The Mexican case shows that the development of these linkages may not occur without the proper incentives.

In the Dominican Republic there are currently more than 19 EPZs that employ about 141,000 workers. The importance of the zones for the country's economy cannot be overemphasized. EPZ firms account for a very high share of exports, especially manufactured exports, and employment. Moreover, some of the zones in the Dominican Republic are among the largest EPZs in the world; the Santiago and the San Pedro de Macoris zones employ about 35,000 workers each. As in Mexico, backward linkages with the domestic economy have been difficult to achieve.

In all, there seem to be several important differences between EPZs in East Asia and Latin America. First, East Asian governments have been much more successful in actively promoting backward linkages between EPZ firms and the rest of the domestic economy. As a consequence, the share of locally purchased inputs in East Asian EPZs steadily increased after the first few years of zone operations. In the Latin American case, governments seem to have used EPZs mostly as instruments to generate employment and foreign exchange, and backward linkages have been rare. Second, EPZs in East Asia are larger and more evenly distributed across countries than in Latin America. Among zones with five or more years of operation, the median zone in Asian countries has 10,500 employees, while in Latin America the median zone has just over 3,500 employees.[21] In addition, while the three largest EPZ countries in East Asia account for about 57 percent of total activity (measured by employ-

---

19. A distinctive characteristic of this zone was that it was developed by the private sector, specifically by the Gulf and Western Corporation.

20. Raw material purchases from domestic firms represent just about 2 percent of the total (Grunwald 1991).

21. Estimated from data in World Bank (1992).

ment), in Latin America the two largest account for over 93 percent. Lastly, as noted above, the economic relevance of the EPZ regimes in Latin American seems to be much greater than in East Asia.

Contrasting EPZs in the Textile and Electronics Industries

An important difference between EPZ activity in textiles and electronics is that the number of countries that have specialized in the former sector is much larger. The industry breakdown of EPZ activity in several nations depicted in Tables 7-2 and 7-3 confirms this. In particular, at least between nine and twelve countries (out of 20) have specialized in textiles (i.e., have textiles as the largest sector), while only two have specialized in electronics. In terms of employment, the data in Table 7-3 shows that eight nations, out of twelve for which data is available, have specialized in textiles, while only four have specialized in electronics.

Regarding the characteristics of the nations that tend to specialize in textiles or electronics, the only study that has touched on the issue (ILO/UNCTC 1988) claimed that country specialization is in large part the result of random factors. The evidence suggests though, that the size of the manufacturing sector in the host nation is somehow related to specialization in either textiles or electronics. Figure 7-1 depicts the degree of country specialization of EPZ output in the textile industry (taken from Table 7-2) against the country's value added in manufacturing in 1992 (taken from World Bank 1996). A pat-

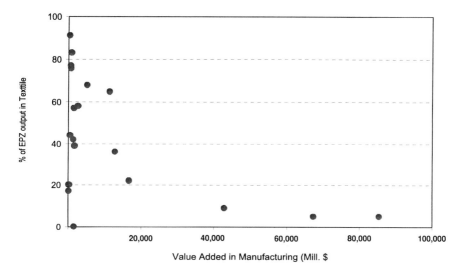

Figure 7-1.   Specialization in Textiles versus Value Added in Manufacturing in 1992
Source: Table 7-2 and World Bank.

tern showing a negative relationship is clearly evident, indicating that the greater the overall size of a nation's manufacturing sector, the smaller the share of EPZ output in textiles. Unfortunately, the paucity of data precludes comprehensive statistical tests,[22] but the figure casts strong doubts in the argument given in ILO/UNCTC (1988).

With respect to the potential of the textile and electronics industries to generate linkages in the host economy, different researchers, many of whom offer little or no evidence to back up their claims, have held conflicting positions. For example, Warr (1990) argues that garments and footwear manufacture use a much higher proportion of local raw materials than electronics assembly. In contrast, Dunning (1993) asserts that the nature of the production process in the electronics industry has led to more inter-firm linkages than those generated by low-technology garment and footwear assembly. A similar position is maintained by Battat, Frank, and Shen (1996) who argue that the electric/electronics industry is more likely to form backward linkages than the textile industry.

By looking at the accumulated experience in some nations, one may be inclined to support the view that the electric/electronics sector tends to generate more linkages. For example, Roberts (1992) showed that in Mauritius, where EPZs are highly specialized in textiles, domestic value added (as a percentage of exports) remained low and even declined during the 1980s. According to Kaplinsky (1993), exactly the same happened in the Dominican Republic, another country where the textile industry dominates EPZ activity. Evidence from imports into the U.S. under the HTS 9802.00.80 category (former provision 807) also shows a tendency for a smaller domestic value added in the offshore processing of garments over time.[23] On the other hand, some of the countries whose EPZs specialized in electronics (including Korea, Taiwan, Malaysia and India) have increased the share of domestic value in total output with time.[24] The Santa Cruz Electronics Export Processing Zone in India, for example, has achieved domestic value added of over 50 percent (Makhija 1980).

While suggestive, all this cannot be taken as unequivocal proof that firms in the electronic subsectors are more likely to form backward linkages than other types of firms. Empirical testing that controls for the size and development of the industrial sector in the host nation is needed to disentangle the

---

22. A simple regression analysis revealed a negative and statistically significant coefficient (at 1 percent) with an adjusted R-squared of nearly 0.24.

23. For example, the data of U.S. textile imports under that provision reveal that foreign value added decreased between 1989 and 1992 in six out of nine countries sampled in Mortimore et al. (1995).

24. See Healey (1990), Rabbani (1980), and Basile and Germidis (1984).

effect of both industry and country-specific variables.[25] This research, however, is beyond the scope of this chapter.

Another significant difference between textile and electronics firms in EPZs is their relative capital intensity. Investment in the electronics subsector is much more capital intensive. For example, in Taiwan, from 1969 to 1979 average investment per employee in electronics firms was $17,145, while in textile firms it was just $1,794. In the Dominican Republic between 1989 and 1993, investment per employee in electronics firms was $16,209 while in textile firms it was just $3,575.[26] The difference in capital intensity is noteworthy because it is plausible that more capital intensive firms have less flexibility to move from one place to another when economic conditions change. Thus, capital intensity may correlate inversely with "footlessness" of EPZ firms, a fact that has been a source of concern in the EPZ literature. This is of course another hypothesis that needs empirical testing.

THE EMPIRICAL EVALUATION OF EPZs

Given that EPZs do create numerous streams of benefits as well as costs in the domestic economy, perhaps the best way to net out the aggregate contribution of the zones in host nations is to carry out a cost/benefit analysis. This analysis tries to measure the net benefit derived from the presence of the zone as opposed to what the net gain would have been if the domestic resources committed to it had been employed somewhere else. Its crux resides in accurately estimating the different streams of benefits and costs in several years, as well as their opportunity costs (i.e., their shadow prices). The analysis also requires the calculation of a social discount rate, which itself is the subject of much discussion and controversy in the economics literature. Peter Warr has pioneered this line of research for EPZs. In particular, Warr carried out four cost/benefit analyses for zones in Indonesia, Korea, the Philippines, and Malaysia.

The main streams of benefits considered by Warr were foreign exchange

---

25. Regarding this issue, ILO/UNCTC (1988) contends that a higher share of domestic value added in total output from EPZs seems to be more a function of the industrial development of the host nation than of the specific industry in which the EPZs specialize.

26. Data are from Rabbani (1980) and Mortimore, Duthoo, and Guerrero (1995). Mortimore (1995) finds many other interesting differences between electronics and garment firms in the EPZs of the Dominican Republic, among them, that electronics firms are more dynamic and aggressive, are more technologically sophisticated, have a higher proportion of foreign ownership, and are more interested in increasing their international market shares than simply in reducing production costs.

revenues, wages paid to zone workers, revenues obtained from renting or sell-ing factory space, earnings from domestic products purchased by EPZ firms, and taxes raised by host governments.[27] Among the main sources of costs were expenses associated with the building of infrastructure, the provision of public services, access to local financing at artificially low rates, and EPZ ad-ministrative costs.

According to Warr's exercises, the generation of foreign exchange and the creation of employment tended to be the most important benefits for the host economy. These components represented between 75 percent and 90 percent of gross benefits in three of the four cases analyzed (Korea, Malaysia, and the Philippines). In Indonesia, strikingly, the main source of benefit turned out to be noncompulsory commissions (presumably bribes) paid to local authori-ties by EPZ enterprises, which represented over 70 percent of gross benefits. Purchases of local supplies and raw materials constituted between 2 and 16 percent of total gross benefits (Warr 1990). In general, tax collections tended to be very small, even in the Philippines where EPZ firms do not enjoy in-come tax holidays.

On the cost side, the expenses associated with managing and building up the zone (including the construction of factory space) tended to be the largest component, ranging from 48 percent of total costs in Malaysia to 94 percent in Indonesia. The next most important component of cost was the provision of public services (especially electricity), except in the case of the Philippines, where local borrowing at artificially low rates turned out to be the next most important cost for the host nation.

After estimating the main streams of costs and benefits, Warr estimates the social rate of return obtained by the host nation. Of the four zones he exam-ined, three of them (Malaysia, Indonesia, and Korea) achieved social rates of return of over 15 percent measured in constant U.S. dollars. The zone in the Philippines achieved a negative return of -3 percent, attributable in large part to the very high infrastructure costs and the availability of local financing for EPZ investment at preferential rates.

Although the determination of the net effect of EPZs in host nations using a cost/benefit approach has strong appeal, the analysis requires several assump-tions and rough estimates. In particular, with a few exceptions, the calculation of the social value of all the streams of benefits and costs requires the estima-

---

27. Warr (1987) identifies two additional sources of benefits: sales in the domestic market and firms' profits. In the case of local sales, he assumes that prices paid by consumers in the do-mestic market reflect the marginal value given to these items, and hence there are no social net gains or costs associated with them. In the case of firms' profits, he assumes that all EPZ indus-tries are foreign-owned, and therefore that their profits or losses are irrelevant from the host nation's perspective.

tion of shadow prices. Given the numerous regulations in trade, labor, and financial markets prevalent in most developing nations, this is not straightforward. Despite these limitations, the analysis indicates the relative importance of different sources of benefits and costs, and uncovers key issues that host governments should take into account when setting up EPZs. In particular, given that EPZs tend to generate relatively significant amounts of foreign exchange and employment, the social value of foreign currency and wages compared to their prevailing values in the domestic market, has great impact in determining whether the host nation obtains a positive social return from EPZ investments. Also, when the exchange rate is overvalued and/or when the host nation suffers from high unemployment rates, EPZ nations are more likely to obtain a positive social return from zone operations. Conversely, in those cases where there are significant costs associated with building EPZ infrastructure and/or services are provided at artificially low rates, the chances of obtaining a positive social return on EPZ investment are greatly reduced.

What Have We Learned About EPZs?

EPZs in Theory

In this chapter we will not describe in detail the current theoretical debate about the possible benefits and/or costs that are associated with the presence of EPZs in any economy. In this regard, Jenkins, Esquivel and Larraín (1998) present a brief summary of the recent contributions to this debate. In general, theoretical treatments of EPZ formation teach us that EPZs can be a second-best policy under some circumstances. The literature has identified two fundamental ways in which this can happen. First, EPZs can serve to counteract the welfare-decreasing impact of a distortion in the host economy. This is the case when the domestic economy suffers from unemployment and/or higher prices thanks to import tariffs. In such circumstances, setting up EPZs can reduce the losses associated with these distortions.[28] Second, EPZs can stimulate production in the domestic economy, increasing economic activity and, thereby, national income through backward linkages.[29]

EPZs in Practice

EPZs are becoming increasingly popular throughout the developing world. Nowadays more than 65 nations have established about 200 EPZs in their do-

---

28. See, for instance, Miyagiwa (1986), and Young and Miyagiwa (1987).
29. See, among others, Din (1994).

mestic territories. This proliferation is partly due to increasing levels of off-shore manufacturing by multinational enterprises that find in these zones an ideal place to locate their overseas operations.

The economic importance of EPZs varies greatly among countries. The available data suggest that the EPZs' economic weight is inversely related to the size of the host nation. In several small nations, the economic importance of EPZs is strikingly large. EPZs are fundamentally concentrated in East Asia and Latin America, which account for about 75 percent of EPZ employment and 90 percent of zones worldwide. EPZs in Asia are larger and more widely spread across countries than those in Latin America. However, Asian EPZs account for a smaller share of manufacturing employment than their Latin American counterparts. On the other hand, Asian governments have been successful in promoting linkages between EPZ firms and the rest of the domestic economy, while in Latin America these linkages have remained very small.

A striking feature of EPZs around the world is that they always seem to be specialized in either the textile/garment or electric/electronics industries. The number of countries that have specialized in the textile/garment subsector is much larger than the number of countries that have specialized in electronics. Whether a particular country's EPZs become specialized in textiles or electronics seems to be related to the degree of industrial development of the host nation.

Contrary to what is commonly believed, in the EPZs of many nations, local participation is very significant. In fact, in many nations domestic firms in the zones outnumber foreign firms. Joint ventures between domestic and foreign investors are also an important form of investment in some nations.

In general, employment and labor conditions in the zones are reported to be at least as good as those that prevail in the surrounding economy. The vast majority of workers in the zones are relatively young women aged 16–25 years. The proportion of women in the labor force depends upon the age of the zone and upon the industrial composition of the activities in it.

The empirical evaluations (i.e., Warr's cost/benefit analysis) show that the generation of employment and foreign exchange are frequently the main source of benefit for the host economy. These studies have also shown that the benefit from selling intermediate inputs to EPZ firms varies greatly between countries, although in most cases it tends to be comparatively small.

Theoretical work on EPZs shows that the establishment of zones is more likely to improve the host nation's welfare when two conditions exist: 1) when there are relatively large levels of unemployment; and 2) when EPZ firms form strong backward linkages with intermediate-producing local firms.

In developing nations with relatively high levels of unemployment, EPZs might represent an efficient mechanism for reducing the economic and social burden of large pools of unemployed people. In this case, as Warr's cost/benefit calculations also showed, EPZs can have significant net positive effects on the host economy, since wages paid to people employed in EPZ firms tend to be much higher than their opportunity cost.

With regard to backward linkages, the experience with EPZs has shown that those countries (mostly in East Asia) that made a special effort to create those linkages seem to have benefited more from the creation of the zones. The experience in countries like Mexico also demonstrates that these linkages are not easily developed and that a relatively large and well-diversified industrial sector does not alone guarantee their formation.

The creation of these linkages may be also desirable in light of dynamic considerations, an issue stressed in the development literature (Caves 1996). Both backward and forward linkages created by foreign firms may generate enough demand for (or supply of) intermediate goods and services such that entire subsectors of industries that otherwise would not exist become viable. Thus, under these circumstances investment in EPZs may be directly linked to higher levels of economic activity and growth.[30] In addition, foreign firms often provide training in quality control and technical assistance while working with local suppliers. This improves the host nation's labor and managerial skills, and constitutes another dynamic consideration that makes linkages between EPZs and local firms highly desirable.

An important lesson derived from EPZs in several nations is that host economies have limited possibilities to benefit from taxation of EPZ activity. The current income tax provisions, coupled with the prevailing tariff schedule in many developed nations, gives multinational enterprises (MNEs) strong incentives to operate their export-oriented affiliates as cost centers. For example, in the United States, parent companies may claim an income tax credit for taxes paid by a foreign affiliate that completely offsets their income tax liability in the U.S. Thus, in the absence of import tariffs, the U.S. MNEs should be indifferent to a price transfer scheme that shifts profits from one location to another, since the firm will end up paying the same amount on income taxes.[31] If, however, the parent firm buys products from its foreign affiliate, and these products are subject to import duties when entering the U.S. customs territory, then the MNE has an incentive to declare the lowest price

---

30. For example, Lin (1993) showed that the presence and growth of an export-processing sector exerted a positive influence on aggregate economic growth using data for 23 developing nations.

31. This is the argument that some authors give to explain why income tax holidays offered by the host nations should not matter for the location of outward FDI by U.S. multinationals.

possible for these goods in order to minimize import duty payments. This creates a strong incentive for MNEs to operate their export-oriented affiliates abroad as cost centers, and probably explains why many foreign firms in EPZs operate with no profits, or even with losses, for many years.

Lastly, it is widely recognized that EPZs are useful but transitory policy instruments for economic development during the first phases of industrialization and implementation of export-led growth strategies (e.g., World Bank 1992; Rondinelli 1987). As countries achieve higher levels of economic development and income, the relative significance of EPZs in economic terms should be expected to decline. Thus, developing nations embarked on export-led growth strategies cannot rely solely on EPZs to achieve higher levels of income and economic growth in the long term. They should acknowledge the transitional aspect of EPZs, and manage wisely the opportunities they may bring to upgrade labor and managerial skills, and to acquire superior technology and access foreign markets. For the same reason, EPZs should not replace economy-wide trade and financial reforms required to support a long-term outward-oriented commitment. Rather, they should be part of a more extensive package of policies aimed at improving the international competitiveness of the host nation.

EPZs in Central America

The remaining parts of this paper examine the development, relevance, and other economic characteristics of EPZs in Costa Rica, El Salvador, Guatemala, Honduras and Nicaragua. A warning note is indispensable here. Comprehensive and reliable data for EPZ activities in Central America are very hard to compile. In some countries, statistics are available for some EPZ firms, but not for others. For example, at the time of writing, data for EPZ firms in Guatemala were unavailable and therefore we had to rely on data for export-oriented textile firms (commonly termed maquila firms) as well as on data for other export-oriented enterprises compiled from different sources. Countries also differ on how they collect data on EPZ activities. For example, Costa Rica, El Salvador and Nicaragua register gross exports from EPZ firms, whereas Honduras and Guatemala only record their domestic value added (i.e., their contribution to the balance of payments). In all, we believe the data we were able to gather provide a good indication of the EPZ dimensions we wanted to study in each nation. However, given the limitations just mentioned, comparisons among countries have to be made with great caution.

Legislation and Development

All Central American nations have special laws that allow the establishment of EPZs within their domestic territories. Table 7-5 contains a comparison of the most relevant aspects of EPZ laws in the region. A brief discussion of the special provisions in the legislation and of the development of EPZs in each individual nation follows.

Costa Rica

Legislation. In 1998 EPZ firms in Costa Rica operate under the EPZ Law promulgated in 1981. The original Law has been reformed several times (i.e., in 1984, 1990, 1992, 1996, and more recently in 1998). This Law gives EPZ firms several fiscal and other incentives. In particular, the Law gives an income tax holiday for 12 years, plus 50 percent exemption for four additional ones for EPZ enterprises located in developed regions. For firms in backward regions, the 50 percent holiday after the first twelve years lasts for six additional ones instead of four (see Table 7-5). All EPZ firms enjoy exemption from import duties on raw materials and equipment, sales and other taxes, as well as streamlined import/export procedures. Firms are also exempt for ten years from municipal and net worth taxes. Upon payment of the corresponding import duties the Costa Rican EPZ Law allows manufacturing firms to sell up to 25 percent of their output in the local market, while service firms can sell up to 50 percent of theirs locally. EPZ firms are not subject to withholding taxes on repatriated capital or profits, and can manage foreign exchange freely.

Development. The first two EPZ zones in Costa Rica were established in the early 1980s in Puntarenas and Limon, the two most important port cities in the country. As with zones in other nations that have been established in economically depressed areas and managed by local authorities, the performance of these two EPZs has been very disappointing. Only a small number of firms have located there and the zones have had recurrent legal and infrastructure problems.

Private zones in Costa Rica on the other hand have been much more successful. The first privately developed zone began operations in 1985 in Cartago and quickly attracted many export-oriented companies. Activity in EPZs accelerated with the award of seven concessions to develop private EPZs between 1988 and 1990. All these zones were established near urban centers in Alajuela and Heredia, not far from the capital San José. Currently there are eight privately developed EPZs in Costa Rica, and at least two under construction.

Table 7-5. *Comparison of EPZ Laws in Central America*

Items	Costa Rica	Honduras	Nicaragua	El Salvador	Guatemala
Import duties on machinery, equipment and raw materials	- Exempt 100%	- Exempt 100%	- Exempt 100%	- Exempt 100%	- Exempt 100%
Income tax	a) Developed regions 100% exempt for 12 first years 50% exempt for next 4 years b) Backward regions 100% exempt for first 12 years 50% exempt for next 6 years	- Exempt 100%	- Exempt 100% for 10 years and 60% thereafter.	- Exempt 100% for 10 years although renewable upon request	- Exempt 100% for 12 years
Sales or value added taxes	- Exempt 100%	- Exempt 100%	- Exempt 100%	- Exempt 100% for 10 years although renewable upon request	- Exempt 100%
Municipal, net worth, and other taxes.	- Exempt 100% for the first 10 years	- Exempt 100%	- Exempt 100%	- Exempt 100% for 10 years although renewable upon request	- Exempt 100%

Table 7-5. (Continued)

Import procedures	- Streamline procedures - At the EPZ location	- Streamline procedures - At the EPZ location	- Streamline procedures - At the EPZ location	- Streamline procedures - At the EPZ location	- Streamline procedures - At the EPZ location
Local Sales	- Up to 25% of output for manufacturing firms, 50% for service companies and 0% for commercial enterprises - Must pay corresponding import duties.	- Only 5% of production for industrial users. - Up to 50% for commercial users - Requires authorization by the Ministry of Economy - Must pay corresponding import duties.	- Between 20-40% depending upon type of firm. - Requires authorization by the Ministry of Economy. - Must pay corresponding import duties.	- Up to 100% of production - Must pay corresponding import duties.	- Up to 20% for industrial enterprises only. - Must pay corresponding import duties.
Foreign Exchange	- Free management	- Free management	- Free management	- Free management	- Free management
Repatriation of profits and capital	- Tax exempt	- Tax exempt	- Tax exempt	- Tax exempt	- Tax exempt

Sources: Costa Rica—Decrees 7830 and 7210; Honduras—Decrees 37-87, 80-92, and 131-98; Nicaragua—Decree 46-91; El Salvador—Decree 405; Guatemala—Decrees 65-89 and 41-98.

By the end of the 1990s, Costa Rican export processing industrial parks have about 155 operating enterprises. Additionally, there were about 50 firms outside industrial parks with EPZ status (permitted by the 1990 modification of the law). EPZ firms inside and outside industrial parks employed about 29,700 workers by 1998.

Honduras

Legislation.   There are two different laws under which EPZ industries may operate in Honduras: 1) The Free Zone (FZ) Law, approved by the Honduran government in the early 1970s but reformed in 1998; and 2) The Export Processing Zone (EPZ) Law enacted in 1987.[32]

The FZ law gives export-oriented companies the usual benefits associated with EPZs: exemption from import duties for equipment and raw materials, streamlined import procedures, income and other tax exemptions, freedom to manage foreign exchange, etc. (see Table 7-5). The income tax holiday never expires and manufacturing firms must export at least 95 percent of their annual production. The Ministry of Economy must approve any sales in the local market.

Up until 1998, the FZ Law made entire geographical areas (i.e., municipalities) Free Zones, where export-oriented firms could locate and be eligible for EPZ benefits upon the approval of the Honduran Government. These FZs were not the typical fenced industrial parks commonly associated with EPZs, but a collection of firms located within a municipality that operated under the legislative umbrella of the FZ regime. Originally only six municipalities were given FZ status, i.e., Puerto Cortés, Amapala, Tela, Choloma, Omoa and La Ceiba. In 1998, however, the Law was reformed to allow the location of export-oriented firms anywhere within the country. Thus, an export-oriented firm can now locate anywhere within Honduran territory and still apply for EPZ status and benefits.

The EPZ Law of 1987 opened the way for private development of zones in Honduras of the type most commonly associated with the concept of EPZs (i.e., fenced industrial parks). The benefits for firms operating under this regime are fundamentally the same as those granted under the FZ Law (see Table 7-5 for details), but the EPZ law provides additional fiscal benefits for the zone developer. These companies may import materials and all inputs free of duties as long as they are used to develop the zone. In addition, developing

---

32. Since the FZ and EPZ Laws give almost the same benefits to export-oriented firms, they are grouped under one heading in Table 7-3.

companies are exempt from income taxes for 20 years. One interesting requirement of the EPZ Law for park developers is that they have to guarantee that in five years the zone will generate at least 5,000 jobs.

Development. The first export-processing zone in Honduras was established in Puerto Cortes in the early 1970s under the FZ Law.[33] The government established this first zone with the objective of improving the depressed economy of the country's northwestern region.

Until the passage of the Export Processing Law in 1987, no other zones were developed in Honduras. In 1988, the first privately developed EPZ was approved in La Lima, near San Pedro Sula, the second largest city in Honduras and the industrial capital of the nation. In 1989, two additional zones were inaugurated under this law, also located near San Pedro Sula. In the 1990s, EPZ activity boomed in Honduras. Between 1990 and 1993, about ten additional EPZs were inaugurated. Overall, in 1999 there were nearly twenty EPZs in operation, and there were plans to build more than 10 new zones (Economist Intelligence Unit 1999).

By the end of 1990s, EPZs developed by private investors hosted about 150 firms that employed almost 79,000 workers, whereas the 40 or so FZ firms throughout the country employed only a little more than 19,000 workers.

Nicaragua

Legislation. EPZ firms in Nicaragua operate under the provisions of the Export Processing Zone (EPZ) Law promulgated at the end of 1991. EPZ firms enjoy the usual benefits of exemption from import duties on materials, machinery, and equipment, as well as from municipal and other taxes. They have total income tax exemption for 10 years, and 60 percent permanent exemption thereafter (see Table 7-5). EPZ firms have free management of foreign exchange, and pay no withholding taxes on repatriated capital or profits. The Nicaraguan legislation distinguishes three different categories of EPZ firms. The categorization is based on the number of jobs created and the percentage of locally purchased inputs, and is used to determine the percentage of output that EPZ firms may sell in the local market. Lastly, Nicaraguan Law also allows firms outside industrial parks to apply and get EPZ status.

---

33. In order to differentiate firms that operate in industrial parks under the EPZ Law and those that operate independently in Free Zones, herein we will refer to them as EPZ and FZ firms respectively.

Development. The first EPZ in Nicaragua, Las Mercedes, was created in 1976. In 1979, after the Sandinista revolution, most of the firms in the zone left the country. The zone was then converted into a warehouse for the Sandinista army and, later, into a prison. After the 1991 EPZ Law, the zone was transformed back into an industrial park for export-oriented activities. By 1999, 14 companies operated in Las Mercedes and they employed more than 15,000 people. Since the promulgation of the EPZ Law in 1991, the government has granted more than six concessions to develop private EPZs. Only two zones (i.e., Index and Opinsa Siglo XXI), however, have initiated operations. By 1999, EPZ Index operated three firms, while Opinsa had only one. Another 12 firms outside industrial parks also enjoyed EPZ status. In total, by 1999 there were 30 firms with EPZ status in Nicaragua, employing almost 17,000 workers.

El Salvador

Legislation. In El Salvador, EPZ industries may operate under the umbrella of the Industrial and Commercial Free Zone Law, promulgated in September 1998. This law reformed the EPZ and Bonded Area Law of 1990, which was the regime previously used by most export-oriented operations in the country. The new Free Zone Law provides the legal framework for the establishment of industrial parks where export-oriented industries can locate their operations. It also allows for the location of export-oriented firms anywhere within the domestic territory (i.e., outside industrial parks). These firms are eligible for the same benefits as industrial-park firms.

EPZ firms enjoy exemption from income and other taxes for 10 years, exemption from import duties for materials, machinery and equipment used in their production process, simplified import/export procedures, free management of foreign exchange, and free repatriation of profits and capital (see Table 7-5). Income and other tax holidays are renewable upon request. A very distinctive feature of the Salvadorian EPZ legislation is that, upon payment of the corresponding import duties, EPZ firms operating under this regime may sell up to 100 percent of their output in the domestic market.

Development. The first EPZ in El Salvador, the San Bartolo zone, was established by a special law in the early 1970s (World Bank 1992). Until the promulgation of the EPZ and Bonded Areas Law in 1990, no more EPZs were developed in El Salvador.

At the beginning of the 1990s, the first privately developed zone, El Progresso, was inaugurated in Santa Tecla, not far from the capital, San Salvador. Between 1992 and 1993 three more privately developed zones were inaugurated: San Marcos, Export Salva, and El Pedregal. American Park, another privately developed EPZ, began operations in 1996. By the end of the 1990s, there were six EPZs in El Salvador which hosted about 50 EPZ firms, and about 300 firms that operated under the FZ Law outside industrial parks. In all, the 350 of these so-called FZ firms in El Salvador employed about 86,000 workers by 1998.

Guatemala

Legislation. The EPZ Law, promulgated in 1989 by the Guatemalan parliament, provides the legal framework and incentives for EPZ firms in Guatemala.[34] According to the provisions of this Law, EPZ firms have to be located within the boundaries of an approved industrial park. They enjoy exemption of import duties for all equipment, machinery, raw materials and intermediate inputs needed in their production process (see Table 7-5). EPZ enterprises enjoy 12 years of tax holiday, are exempted from added value and other taxes, and have streamlined import procedures at the EPZ location. Only manufacturing enterprises in the zones are allowed to sell part of their production in the local market. In particular, manufacturing EPZ firms may sell up to 20 percent of their output in the domestic Guatemalan market, upon authorization and payment of the corresponding import duties. EPZ firms in Guatemala have free management of foreign exchange and are not subject to any withholding tax on repatriated profits or capital.

A recent reform to the EPZ Law in Guatemala (Decree 131-98) allows for the establishment of EPZ firms anywhere within the Guatemalan territory with the same tax and other benefits that industrial-park firms enjoy under the EPZ Law of 1989 (Economist Intelligence Unit 1999).

Development. The development of traditional EPZs in Guatemala has been relatively modest when compared to the rest of the Central American nations. Since the promulgation of the EPZ Law in 1989, about ten EPZ projects have been approved, but only two or three have attracted export-oriented firms. The first EPZ in Guatemala, and the only one in operation until very recently, began operations in 1991. This zone, developed by the same group that developed three zones in Costa Rica, is located in Amatitlan, some

---

34. The Guatemalan Congress also created the Santo Tomas de Castilla Free Zone in 1973. Export-oriented firms may locate there, but today the zone is more an import-processing zone than an EPZ. The zone currently has more than 30 firms, but only three or so are industrial enterprises with some level of exports. Following our definition of EPZs above, this zone is not included in this analysis.

30 kilometers from the capital, Guatemala City. Currently the zone has less than ten companies that employ a little more than 1,000 workers. Another zone with some level of activity is located in Tecun Uman, near the Guatemala-Mexico border. Only one firm, owned by the EPZ developers, was operating there until very recently. In total, traditional EPZs in Guatemala had only about ten firms and employed about 1,500 workers in 1997.

Most export oriented activity in Guatemala operates under the umbrella of the Export Activity and Maquila (EA&M) Promotion and Development Law approved in 1989. This Law provides the legal framework for several categories of exporting enterprises and resembles in some ways the provisions of the Regime of Temporary Admission (RTA) that exist in many other nations. Interestingly, firms that operate under the EA&M Law do not have to be primarily export-oriented and must follow ordinary import/export procedures. In all, more than 660 exporting firms in Guatemala have been granted one of the five statuses that the EA&M law confers. Unfortunately, employment figures for these firms are very sketchy. A study of the firms operating under this regime in 1995 found that only 39 percent of them reported employment figures to the Guatemalan Institute of Social Security, as required by the law.[35]

Several factors contributed to the slow development of traditional EPZs in Guatemala. First, the EA&M Law (Decree 29-89) gives export-oriented firms similar benefits to those offered under the EPZ Law (Decree 65-89). Second, until a couple of years ago, only one EPZ had been developed in Guatemala, resulting in a limited supply of factory space under this regime. Furthermore, the geographical region where this EPZ is located has been characterized by numerous and even violent labor conflicts that undoubtedly hindered its growth.

Economic Significance

Even though there are numerous problems with statistics on EPZ activity in almost every country in Central America, two important conclusions can be drawn from the data that are available. First, the economic importance of EPZ activities has increased very rapidly in recent years in all Central American countries. Second, as a result of their rapid growth, EPZ regimes currently account for a very large share of both manufacturing employment and exports in the region. Following is a brief discussion of how the economic weight of the EPZ regimes evolved in each individual Central American nation during the 1990s.

---

35. See Ministerio de Economía de Guatemala (1995 and 1997).

Table 7-6. *Economic Importance of EPZ Firms in Costa Rica*

(employment in thousands, exports in US$ millions)

	No. of Firms[1]	EPZ Employment[1]	Manufacturing Employment[2]	% of Total	EPZ Gross Exports[1]	Exports of Goods[3]	% of Total
1990	56	7.0	183.0	3.8	94.0	1,346.0	7.0
1991	88	11.2	188.7	6.0	145.0	1,490.0	9.7
1992	119	13.6	197.2	6.9	234.1	1,729.0	13.5
1993	131	18.6	196.8	9.4	273.6	1,874.0	14.6
1994	149	21.5	203.5	10.6	343.4	2,869.4	12.0
1995	177	25.4	192.8	13.2	434.2	3,453.0	12.6
1996	188	25.5	188.9	13.5	643.0	3,730.0	17.2
1997	195	25.7	191.0	13.5	891.4	4,334.7	20.6
1998	205	29.7	NA	NA	1847.4	5,528.1	33.4

Sources: (1) Data provided by Procomer; (2) International Labor Office (several issues); (3) Banco Central de Costa Rica (1999)

Costa Rica

EPZ activity in Costa Rica has increased rapidly since 1990. Between 1991 and 1998, the number of EPZ firms in Costa Rica increased on average more than 17 percent per year, while employment increased almost 20 percent per year (see Table 7-6). The growth experienced in gross EPZ exports has been more dramatic. Gross EZP exports have increased on average more than 45 percent per year since 1990. The growth in activity has resulted in an increasing share of export-oriented firms in manufacturing employment. In 1997, these firms accounted for 13.5 percent of manufacturing employment in the country, up from 3.8 percent in 1990. The participation of EPZs in total exports of goods has also increased. In 1998, gross exports from EPZ firms represented about 33.4 percent of total exports of goods, up from 7 percent in 1990.[36]

Honduras

As in Costa Rica, activity in the EPZs and FZs of Honduras expanded rapidly in the 1990s. The number of firms that operate under both the EPZ and FZ regimes increased on average more than 33 percent per year between 1990 and 1998, while employment in the zones increased more than 37 percent per

---

36. The doubling of EPZ exports in 1998 is largely explained by the beginning of export activities of Intel's $500 million microprocessor plant. Currently, Intel is the largest single exporting firm in the country.

Table 7-7.   *Economic Importance of EPZ and FZ Firms in Honduras*

(employment figures in thousands, export figures in US$ millions)

	No. of Firms[1]	EPZ and FZ Employment[1]	Manufacturing Employment[3]	% of Total	EPZ and FZ Net Exports[1]	Exports of Goods[2]	% of Total
1990	24	9.0	137.6	6.6	14.2	895.2	1.6
1991	53	20.1	222.4	9.0	33.9	840.6	4.0
1992	72	27.2	250.5	10.9	61.8	839.3	7.4
1993	88	33.3	NA	NA	81.6	999.6	8.2
1994	114	42.5	NA	NA	96.7	1,101.5	8.8
1995	135	55.0	325.7	16.9	132.9	1,377.2	9.7
1996	151	66.0	352.4	18.7	172.3	1,638.4	10.5
1997	203	83.5	361.7	23.1	258.1	1,856.5	13.9
1998	238	NA	NA	NA	NA	NA	NA

NA: Not available
Sources: (1) Torres (1997) and Banco Central de Honduras (1996 and 1998); (2) International Labor Office (several issues); (3) International Monetary Fund (1999)

year between 1990 and 1997. Net EPZ and FZ exports increased more than 51 percent per year between 1990 and 1997.[37] In 1997, EPZs and FZs accounted for a significant 23.1 percent of manufacturing employment in Honduras (see Table 7-7). In 1997, net exports from these zones represented almost 14 percent of all Honduran exports of goods, up from 1.6 percent at the beginning of the decade (see Table 7-7).

Nicaragua

Just as in Costa Rica and Honduras, EPZ activity grew rapidly in Nicaragua during the 1990s. The number of EPZ firms tripled, while EPZ employment increased by more than fourteen times between 1992 and 1998 (see Table 7-8). EPZ employment accounted for almost 28 percent of industrial employment in 1997, while gross EPZ exports represented almost 32 percent of total exports of goods in 1998.

El Salvador

Overall activity in the Free Zones (FZ) of El Salvador has also increased very rapidly during the 1990s. The number of FZ firms increased on average almost 13 percent per year between 1993 and 1998 (see Table 7-9), while FZ employment more than doubled during the same period. Gross exports from

---

37. Net exports are the total amount of domestic expenditures that EPZ and FZ firms made in the Honduran economy in a particular year. These data had to be employed here since, unfortunately, the Honduran authorities do not keep records of gross exports for EPZ and FZ enterprises.

Table 7-8. *Economic Importance of EPZ Firms in Nicaragua*

(employment figures in thousands, export figures in US$ million)

	No. of Firms[1]	EPZ Employment[1]	Manufacturing Employment[2]	% of Total	EPZ Gross Exports[1]	Exports of Goods[3]	% of Total
1992	8	1.1	33.4	3.4	2.8	223	1.3
1993	9	2.0	33.7	5.8	7.2	267	2.7
1994	14	5.4	31.9	16.8	27.3	351	7.8
1995	18	7.9	32.9	24.0	66.0	526	12.6
1996	18	10.2	36.8	27.7	126.3	671	18.8
1997	19	12.8	NA	NA	164.0	704	23.3
1998	24	16.8	NA	NA	181.8	573	31.7

NA: Not available
Sources: (1) Data provided by Corporación de Zonas Francas; (2) Wilkie, Aleman, and Ortega (1999); (3)Banco Central de Nicaragua (1999)

FZ firms have increased on average almost 69 percent per year since 1990, and almost 33 percent since 1993. As a result of this growth, the share of manufacturing employment and exports accounted for by FZ firms has become very significant in El Salvador. In 1998, FZ firms accounted for a little more than 19.1 percent of manufacturing employment in the nation and more than 48.6 percent of total exports of goods.

Guatemala

Since activity under the EPZ regime in Guatemala has remained relatively very small, to have a better idea of how important export-oriented activity really is in that country, data for export-oriented textile firms is going to be employed. The vast majority of these firms operate under the EA&M Law of

Table 7-9. *Economic Importance of FZ Firms in El Salvador*

(employment figures in thousands, export figures in US$ million)

	No. of Firms[1]	FZ Employment[1]	Manufacturing Employment[1]	% of Total	FZ Gross Exports[1]	Exports of Goods[1]	% of Total
1990	NA	NA	NA	NA	18.0	600.3	3.0
1991	NA	NA	308.8	NA	20.4	608.4	3.4
1992	NA	NA	302.8	NA	42.1	597.5	7.0
1993	185	38.3	331.2	11.6	290.1	1,032.1	28.1
1994	222	45.7	382.7	11.9	430.4	1,249.3	34.5
1995	260	54.4	380.7	14.3	646.6	1,652.0	39.1
1996	287	61.1	370.6	16.5	764.1	1,788.4	42.7
1997	311	69.8	332.9	21.0	1,056.8	2,415.9	43.7
1998	339	79.5	415.6	19.1	1,189.0	2,446.1	48.6

NA: Not available
Sources: Data provided by the Ministry of Economy

Table 7-10.   *Economic Importance of Maquila Firms in Guatemala*

(employment figures in thousands, export figures in US$ million)

	No. of Firms[1]	Maquila Employment[1]	Manufacturing Employment[2]	% of Total	Maquila Net Exports[3]	Exports of Goods[4]	% of Total
1990	NA	NA	103.3	NA	39	1,212	3.2
1991	NA	NA	118.8	NA	68	1,230	5.6
1992	NA	NA	130.7	NA	96	1,284	7.5
1993	NA	80.0	136.7	58.5	106	1,363	7.7
1994	NA	70.0	152.8	45.8	136	1,550	8.8
1995	NA	54.0	142.5	37.9	167	1,989	8.4
1996	220	61.8	NA	NA	184	2,031	9.0

NA: Not available
Sources: (1) Gitli (1997); (2) International Labor Office (1996) and Gitli (1997); (3) Gitli (1997) and Banco Central de Guatemala (1995); (4)Actualidad Economica (1997)

1989. Table 7-10 summarizes the available data on export-oriented textile firms in Guatemala. Even though the share of EPZ employment decreased between 1993 and 1996, export-oriented textile firms account for a significant share of manufacturing employment in Guatemala. The table also shows that net exports of textile firms increased on average almost 30 percent per year between 1990 and 1996. In 1996 those exports represented 9 percent of total exports of goods.

After examining how the economic importance of EPZ activity in each individual nation in Central America changed in the 1990s, it is interesting to compare it across countries. The comparison has to be based on employment data since the available data on exports are not directly comparable.[38] Figure 7-2 summarizes how the share of EPZ employment in total manufacturing employment evolved in all Central American nations in the 1990s. The figure clearly indicates that EPZ regimes in Central America have been a very significant source of manufacturing employment in recent years. In particular, Figure 7-2 evidences the significant growth of employment in manufacturing activities of EPZ regimes in Costa Rica, Honduras, Nicaragua, and El Salvador in the 1990s. By 1998, the share in manufacturing employment varied from a low of almost 14 percent in Costa Rica to a high of more than 38 percent in Guatemala. The simple average of these shares reveals that by 1998 roughly one of every four workers in manufacturing activities in Central America is employed by firms in EPZ regimes. This is undoubtedly a large share when compared with average shares for other nations. For example, according to

---

38. Recall that some counties (i.e., Guatemala and Honduras) report net exports while others (i.e., Costa Rica, Nicaragua, and El Salvador) report gross exports from EPZ firms.

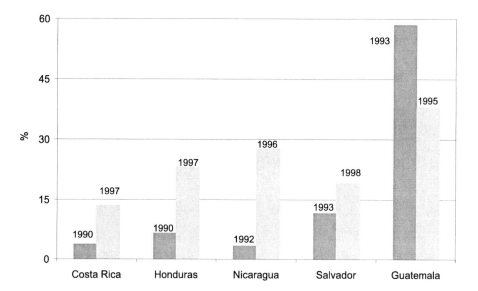

Figure 7-2.   EPZ Share in Manufacturing Employment

the data in Table 7-1, the unweighted average EPZ employment share of the twelve Latin American nations is less than 16 percent, while the average (unweighted) share for all the countries with data in the table is a little less than 12 percent.

Industry and Ownership Distributions

Industry and ownership distributions can be constructed according to several criteria, including the number of firms, employment figures, investment, or the level of production. For most of the five countries studied, the number of firms and employment data are the only available statistics at the firm level. We thus use these two criteria to construct the distributions that appear in Tables 7-11 to 7-15.

Since data are not available for all EPZ firms in all countries, we sometimes construct industry and/or ownership distributions from data for a subset of all the firms. In consequence, the number of firms or total EPZ employment figures in Panels A and B, as well as the ones in Tables 7-6 through 7-10, may not coincide.

Table 7-11.   *Industry and Ownership Distribution of EPZ Firms in Costa Rica (1999)*

	No. of Firms	% of Total	Employment	% of Total
Panel A: Industry distribution of EPZ firms				
Textile	33	23	11,971	40
Electronics	30	21	7,107	24
Footwear/Leather	7	5	1,578	5
Machinery/Metal	9	6	1,646	5
Pharmaceutical/Medical	4	3	1,688	6
Other Manufacturing	40	28	4,334	15
Services and Commercial	22	15	1,485	5
Total	145	100	29,809	100
Panel B: Ownership distribution of EPZ firms				
U.S.	90	62	24,417	82
Costa Rica	22	15	1,924	6
Europe	11	8	1,008	3
Korea	2	1	548	2
Other	20	14	1,912	6
Total	145	100	29,809	100

Source: Elaborated from data provided by Procomer

Costa Rica

In Costa Rica, textile/garment firms represent the largest industrial sector, accounting for 23 percent of all firms and more than 40 percent of employment (see Table 7-11, Panel A). The electronics industry is the second largest

Table 7-12.   *Industry and Ownership Distribution of EPZ and FZ Firms in Honduras (1999)*

	No. of Firms	% of Total	Employment	% of Total
Panel A: Industry distribution of EPZ and FZ firms				
Textile	166	88	95,540	97
Electronics	6	3	1,614	2
Other Manufacturing	7	4	827	1
Commercial/service	9	5	139	0
Total	188	100	98,120	100
Panel B: Ownership distribution of EPZ and FZ firms				
U.S.	96	51	52,716	54
Honduras	32	17	15,761	16
Korea	22	12	12,988	13
Taiwan	6	3	3,244	3
Hong Kong	6	3	3,343	3
Other Asian	8	4	2,338	2
Other	17	9	7,344	8
Total	187	100	97,734	100

Source: Elaborated from data provided by FIDE

Table 7-13. *Industry and Ownership Distribution of EPZ Firms in Nicaragua (1999)*

	No. of Firms	% of Total	Employment	% of Total
Panel A: Industry distribution of EPZ firms				
Textile	21	70	18,497	97
Cigars	5	17	232	1
Footwear/Leather	2	7	365	2
Other	2	7	NA	0
Total	30	100	19,094	100
Panel B: Ownership distribution of EPZ firms				
U.S.	10	33	4,537	24
Nicaragua	5	17	1,551	8
Taiwan	6	20	10,152	53
Other	9	30	2,854	15
Total	30	100	19,094	100

Source: Elaborated from data provided by Corporación de Zonas Francas

sector, accounting for about 21 percent of firms and 24 percent of employment. Many of these electronics firms are relatively new investments, with at least 15 of the 30 firms having been established in or after 1995. Machinery/Metal and Pharmaceutical/Medical products are the next largest manufacturing sectors, accounting for about 5 percent or 6 percent of firms and employment. The rest of the manufacturing activities correspond to a large variety of industries, including jewelry, footwear/leather products, instruments, and sporting goods. Interestingly, about 15 percent of firms, which account for 5 percent of employment in the Costa Rican EPZs, are service and

Table 7-14. *Industry and Ownership Distribution of FZ Firms in El Salvador (1999)*

	No. of Firms	% of Total	Employment	% of Total
Panel A: Industry distribution of FZ firms				
Textile	260	73	78,754	92
Electronics	2	1	206	0
Footwear/Leather	6	2	1,214	1
Commercial	23	6	1,738	2
Other	64	18	4,110	5
Total	355	100	86,022	100
Panel B: Ownership distribution of FZ firms				
U.S.	46	13	23,363	27
El Salvador	223	63	35,830	42
Korea	25	7	13,350	16
Taiwan	20	6	7,016	8
Guatemala	4	1	199	0
Other	37	10	6,264	7
Total	355	100	86,022	100

Source: Data provided by the Ministry of Economy

Table 7-15. *Industry and Ownership Distribution of Export-oriented Firms in Guatemala (1995/1996) (Number of firms for 1996, employment for 1995)*

	No. of Firms	% of Total	Employment	% of Total
Panel A: Industry distribution of EA&M				
Manufacturing firms	263	56	25829	63
Electronics	2	1	267	1
Footwear/Leather	11	2	303	1
Machinery/Metal	25	5	1369	3
Food	24	5	1030	2
Fish and Marine Products	25	5	1726	4
Other	118	25	10595	25
Total	468	100	41119	100
Panel B: Ownership distribution of maquila firms (1996)				
U.S.	20	9	NA	NA
Guatemala	95	43	NA	NA
Korea	96	44	NA	NA
Other	9	4	NA	NA
Total	220	100.0	NA	NA

Sources: Elaborated from firm data provided by the Ministry of Economy, employment data from Ministerio de Economia de Guatemala (1995), and data in Gitli (1997).

commercial enterprises. Even though the textile/garments industry is the largest one in Costa Rica's EPZs (as in all other Central American nations), the Costa Rican regime is the most diversified in terms of the economic sectors represented in the zones.

Panel B of Table 7-11 shows the nationality of the EPZ firms in Costa Rica. About 62 percent of firms, which account for 82 percent of employment, are U.S. subsidiaries. Domestic Costa Rican firms account for 15 percent and 6 percent of firms and employment, respectively. European firms represent 8 percent of firms and 3 percent of employment, while firms of Asian origin account for just 1 percent and 2 percent of firms and employment respectively. The small presence of Asian investment in the EPZs of Costa Rica is certainly unique in the Central American region.

Honduras

In Honduras, EPZ and FZ activity is highly concentrated in the textile industry. About 88 percent of the firms, employing more than 97 percent of the work force in the zones, are textile enterprises (see Table 7-12, Panel A). Furthermore, there are only about six electronic firms that account for 3 percent of the firms and 2 percent of employment in the zones. Other manufacturing activities, which include wood products, machinery, and plastics, account for

4 percent of the firms and just over 1 percent of total employment. Commercial and services enterprises represent 5 percent of the firms and an insignificant share of employment.

Regarding ownership, about 51 percent of Honduran EPZ and FZ firms are subsidiaries of U.S. companies. These firms account for 54 percent of zone employment in Honduras (see Table 7-12, Panel B). After Costa Rica, Honduras is the Central American nation with the second largest presence of U.S. investment in the zones. Asian firms, many of which are Korean, account for 22 percent of the firms and 21 percent of employment. Local Honduran companies represent just over 17 percent of the firms and 16 percent of employment in the zones.

Nicaragua

In Nicaragua, as in Honduras, EPZ activity is highly concentrated in the textile industry (see Table 7-13, Panel A). These enterprises account for over 70 percent of the firms in the zones and for more than 97 percent of employment. Cigar companies in Nicaragua account for 17 percent of EPZ firms and 1 percent of employment. The remaining firms, which include a couple of footwear/leather companies, represent together about 14 percent of the firms and over 2 percent of employment.

Regarding ownership, about a third of EPZ firms in Nicaragua, which account for about a quarter of employment, are U.S. subsidiaries. Taiwanese firms account for almost 20 percent of firms and over 53 percent of employment, a relatively high share when compared to the Costa Rican and Honduran cases.

El Salvador

In El Salvador, as shown in Table 7-14, Panel A, export-oriented activity is also highly concentrated in the textile industry. Textile firms account for 73 percent of total FZ firms and for about 92 percent of employment in the zones. The second most important group of firms is commercial enterprises, which represent 6 percent of the firms and 2 percent of employment. Footwear/leather companies, which account for 2 percent and 1 percent of firms and employment, respectively, form the next most important sector. Electronics firms have a very small share of total activity. The "other" category consists of firms from a diverse group of industries including toy repairs, and the manufacture of jewel cases, plastic items, and paper products.

Regarding the ownership of enterprises, interestingly, Salvadorian companies are the most important group. These enterprises represent 63 of the firms and 42 percent of employment in the zones. Another 13 percent of FZ firms are U.S. affiliates. These account for 27 percent of FZ employment (see Table 7-14, Panel B). The third largest group of investors in the Salvadorian FZs is of Asian origin (mostly from Korea and Taiwan); these account for 13 percent of firms and 24 percent of employment.

Guatemala

Since most export-oriented companies in Guatemala operate under the EA&M Law, industry and ownership distributions are constructed with data from firms that operate under this regime. This law, however, does not limit the amount of domestic sales and therefore the degree of export-orientation of EA&M firms is not known. As a consequence, the data may include firms that export just a small fraction of their output (i.e., firms that do not comply with the definition of an EPZ firm given above). Nevertheless, lacking other sources of information, we were compelled to use these data to construct the industry distribution that appears in Table 7-15, Panel A. For the ownership distribution we used the data for export-oriented textile firms published by Gitli (1997).

The industry distribution of Table 7-15, Panel A shows that, as in all other Central American nations, the textile/garment sector accounts for the largest share of export-oriented activity in Guatemala. More specifically, these firms account for about 56 percent of firms and 63 percent of employment.[39] Next in importance are Machinery and Metal Products, Fish and other Marine Products and Food items, each of which represents around 5 percent of the number of firms and between 2 percent and 4 percent of employment. Electronics industries account for a very small share of activity in Guatemala.

Regarding ownership, Table 7-15, Panel B shows that 44 percent of export-oriented textile firms in Guatemala are Korean, 43 percent are locally owned, and just 9 percent are U.S. owned. The low share of U.S. investment in the Guatemalan export sector is very distinctive in the Central American region.

After discussing the industry and ownership distributions of EPZ activity in each individual nation, it is interesting to compare them across nations. Figures 7-3 and 7-4 show simplified industry and ownership distribution according to the number of firms for all Central American nations.

---

39. It is also important to mention that in 1995 textile firms accounted for more than 93 percent of total exports by all firms operating under the EA&M Law (Ministerio de Economía de Guatemala 1995). This suggests that the other industrial sectors may be over-represented in Table 13 as a consequence of not being able to segregate export-oriented firms from this data set. In fact, based on that information, one can argue that export-oriented activity in Guatemala is highly specialized in the textile industry.

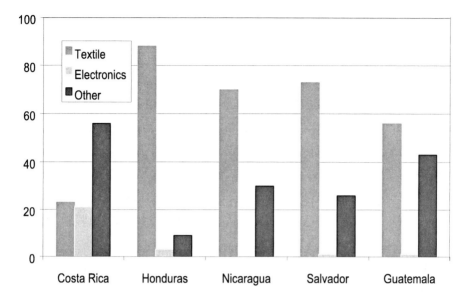

Figure 7-3.   Industry Distribution of EPZ Activity

Figure 7-3 clearly shows that Costa Rica has attracted a wider diversity of industries to its EPZs. The other Central American nations remain fundamentally specialized in the textile sector. It is particularly interesting to note that Costa Rica is the only nation in the region that has been able to attract

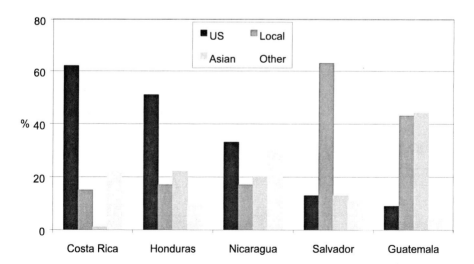

Figure 7-4.   Ownership Distribution of EPZ Activity

quite a few electronics firms to its zones. At the other extreme, export-oriented activity in Honduras, El Salvador, and Nicaragua is highly specialized in textiles.

Regarding ownership, Figure 7-4 reveals the relatively large presence of Asian investment in Guatemala, as well as the large share of domestic investments in both El Salvador and Guatemala. It is also interesting to note the relatively high presence of U.S. firms in Costa Rica and Honduras, as well as the very small Asian presence in Costa Rica.

Real Wages

Unfortunately, reliable time-series data on EPZ wages are available only for Costa Rica and Honduras. The other Central American nations do not have reliable statistics on wages paid by EPZ firms.

Table 7-16 constructs a real EPZ wage index for Costa Rican EPZ firms based on data provided by Procomer. As can be seen, real wages in the Costa Rican EPZs remained without much variation between 1993 and 1997.

In contrast, real wages in EPZ activities in Honduras increased significantly during the 1990s as a consequence of the rapid growth in EPZ and FZ activity. Table 7-17 constructs a real wage index for EPZ and FZ firms in Honduras. Between 1990 and 1997, real EPZ wages increased at an average rate of 9.5 percent per year in Honduras.

Labor Conditions

Labor conditions in EPZ firms throughout the region vary greatly. At one extreme are companies with very good standards with regards to labor conditions. In general, these firms tend to locate their operations in industrial parks and many of them are well-known MNEs with internationally recognized

Table 7-16. *Real Wages in Costa Rican EPZ Firms*

	EPZ Monthly Wage[1]	Average Exchange Rate[2]	Average Monthly Wage (in colones)	Consumer Price Index[3] (1990 = 100)	EPZ Real Wage (in colones of 1990)	EPZ Real Wage Index
1993	308	139.76	43,046	172	25,012	100
1994	336	155.59	52,278	195	26,754	107
1995	345	178.43	61,558	241	25,575	102
1996	350	206.52	72,282	283	25,550	102
1997	333	231.82	77,196	320	24,101	96

Notes: (1) Data in US$ provided by Procomer; (2) The June exchange rate for each year was taken from Banco Central de Costa Rica (several issues); (3) International Monetary Fund (1999)

Table 7-17. *Real Wages in Honduran EPZ & FZ Firms*

	EPZ and FZ Yearly Wage[1]	EPZ and FZ Workers	Average Yearly Wage[1]	Consumer Price Index	EPZ and FZ Real Wage	EPZ and FZ Real Wage Index (1990 = 100)
1990	31.1	9,030	3,444	100	3,444	100
1991	116.5	20,121	5,790	134	4,321	125
1992	205.6	27,217	7,554	146	5,185	151
1993	316.4	33,331	9,493	161	5,881	171
1994	432.5	42,541	10,167	196	5,177	150
1995	758.2	54,995	13,787	254	5,421	157
1996	1282.5	65,950	19,447	315	6,175	179
1997	2058.5	83,464	24,663	379	6,516	189

Notes: In local currency from Banco Central de Honduras (1998)

brand names (e.g., Hanes, Levi's, Fruit of the Loom, Conair). Working conditions in these firms tend to be at least as good as, and generally better than, those prevailing in comparable manufacturing operations in the same country. Employees in these firms work in a clean, well-ventilated (or air-conditioned) environment, and have access to medical attention, subsidized meals, and transportation.

At the other extreme, we find firms whose only objective seem to be to set up manufacturing operations at the lowest cost possible in Central America, often just to take advantage of textile quotas. In general, these firms are located outside industrial parks where rent costs tend to be lower.[40] Working conditions in these firms tend to be very different from those discussed above. Employees do not have access to medical attention, their workplace is not clean, and working hours are often stretched to the limit. Violation of workers' rights and the domestic labor legislation is not uncommon among these firms.

A striking feature in all five countries is the high rate of personnel turnover in EPZ firms. Most of these companies have turnover rates that range between 2 percent and 5 percent per month, but rates as high as 8 percent are some times reported. Many firms are experimenting with new incentive mechanisms and systems of production to cut absenteeism and turnover.[41]

---

40. This does not imply that every firm outside an industrial park is from this second group. Many firms outside industrial parks offer excellent working conditions.

41. For example, the so called 4x4 system, where employees work 12-hour shifts for four days and then rest for four days, has been introduced in several firms in Honduras. Also, in Honduras attendance bonuses are regularly offered. In Costa Rica attendance and other bonuses related to the number of years that the worker stays with the company are being offered.

Table 7-18.   *Share of Domestic Raw Materials and Supplies in Total Output*

(in percentages)

	Costa Rican EPZ Firms[1]	Guatemalan Maquila Firms[2]	Salvadorian Maquila Firms[2]
1993	8.9	NA	NA
1994	7.5	6.9	NA
1995	5.5	8.4	3.8
1996	5.7	3.5	5.7
1997	3.4	NA	NA

Sources: (1) Data provided by Procomer; (2) Gitli (1997)

Backward Linkages

Measuring backward linkages created by EPZ firms is not straightforward. There are numerous problems with the definition and statistics relating backward linkages. Most empirical studies on backward linkages have employed either the share of domestic expenditures in total output or the share of raw materials and supplies in total purchases to examine linkages at the firm level.[42] In the Central American case, only a few data on domestically procured raw materials and supplies were available for Costa Rica, El Salvador, and Guatemala, as shown in Table 7-18.

In Costa Rica, the percentage of locally purchased inputs has steadily decreased since 1993. Also, in any year, the percentage of locally procured inputs is relatively small. Both, the public and private sectors in Costa Rica have recognized this. There are now at least three initiatives aimed at increasing the share of locally purchased raw materials and supplies in export-oriented activities.[43] The little data available for Guatemala and El Salvador indicates that in both countries the share of locally purchased raw materials in production has remained also very small. Hence, the available data suggests that in Central American nations, as in other Latin American countries relatively few linkages have been formed between EPZ firms and the rest of the domestic economy.

POLICY RECOMMENDATIONS

The analysis in this paper has some important implications for policymakers. In particular, there are three distinct areas where Central American

---

42. See, for example, McAleese and McDonald (1978), and Smith and Barkley (1991).

43. These are the so called Programa Mil sponsored by the Ministry of Science and Technology, the Subcontracting Program sponsored by the Costa Rican Chamber of Industries, and the PROFOVE program sponsored by the Ministry of Foreign Trade.

governments can improve their export-oriented regimes. They are as follows: a) diversification of industry composition; b) development of linkages within the host economy; and c) improvement and harmonization of export-oriented legislation.

Diversification of Industry Composition

Most nations in the region need to make a determined effort to diversify the industry composition of EPZ activity. In some Central American countries, these activities are almost exclusively specialized in textiles, a sensitive sector for developed nations where the threat of limiting quotas and other trade barriers abroad is always present. Diversification into electronics and certain types of services (e.g., data processing) seems particularly desirable. Casual observation suggests that electronics firms are less "footloose" and more likely to be the source of new skills for the Central American economies than are garment firms. On the other hand, the increasing importance of international service industries like data processing, software production, and back-office support, offer an interesting opportunity for the EPZs of Central America.

In order to diversify the industry composition of export-oriented activity, Central American governments may need promotional programs targeted to specific industries. The Costa Rican effort is noteworthy in this regard. Costa Rican authorities targeted foreign firms in specific subsectors of the electronics industry that were considered willing to start operations in Central America. Several market studies and promotional campaigns were developed with the very specific objective of attracting those firms to Costa Rica.[44] The results have been impressive. Of the 30 EPZ electronics firms currently operating in Costa Rica, about half initiated operations in or after 1995. Similar programs and campaigns have been successfully implemented in other countries, too. In the mid-1980s, Ireland targeted financial services and established a specialized EPZ for that purpose near Dublin. Today, the zone employs thousands of people, most of them with university degrees (UNIDO 1995). Jamaica, the Dominican Republic, and India are also examples of nations that developed specific promotional programs for particular industries (i.e., data processing and electronics).

When targeting specific export-oriented activities, it is important to recognize that different industries require different types of facilities. For relatively sophisticated electronics firms and pharmaceutical companies, a factory layout that includes a lower density of buildings with higher standards of landscape and appearance is necessary. In contrast, garment firms may require a

---

44. The Costa Rican Investment and Trade Development Board (CINDE) financed most of those studies.

higher density of buildings and lower appearance standards. For data processing, back-office support and similar services, good international telecommunications are crucial. Thus, to diversify the industry composition of export-oriented regimes, Central American authorities should also consider the development of specialized zones, built specifically to accommodate the types of industries and companies that are being targeted.

Pharmaceutical, electronic, and certain service industries require some skilled personnel, not abundant in much of Central America. Therefore, diversification of industries will also require the active participation of local universities and technical institutions to develop the skills that these industries will demand. The case of Intel in Costa Rica is particularly revealing of the kind of collaboration needed from educational institutions to attract more technologically advanced companies to export-oriented regimes.[45]

Development of Backward Linkages

Central American governments need to direct their attention to the development of stronger backward linkages between EPZ firms and the rest of their local economies. These linkages have remained relatively weak in the region. Empirical observation and theoretical developments have showed that strong linkages may be a significant source of benefit for the host economy from the operation of EPZs. Export-oriented firms cannot be held responsible for not developing backward linkages. This is not their raison d'être. Experience has demonstrated that linkages do not arise automatically and that appropriate government policies are required to create them.[46]

Several countries have been able to successfully promote the formation of EPZ linkages, most notably Korea, Taiwan and Ireland. Programs to foster linkages in these countries have had three elements in common. First, at some point in the development of EPZ activity, the local authorities established a clear and explicit objective of integrating EPZ firms into their respective economies. They regarded this regime as an integral part of their export-led strategy. Unfortunately, this has not been the case in many host

---

45. Several universities and technical institutions signed agreements to assure Intel that workers with the proper skills would be available to staff the plant recently built in Costa Rica. For a more detailed analysis of the economic impact of Intel in Costa Rica see Chapter 6 in this volume.

46. For example, Keesing (1990) argues that countries need to develop what he calls "superior policies" in order to bolster backward linkages. McAleese and McDonald (1978) argue that governmental intervention is often helpful and sometimes even essential in creating linkages. UNIDO (1993) maintains that linkages "do not take place automatically; they must be planned and encouraged with appropriate policies, institutions and regulations."

nations. The need to create linkages within the host economy has generally been regarded as an issue of secondary importance by local authorities.[47]

EPZ regimes in Central America have been seen mostly as mechanisms to create employment and generate foreign exchange, but not as drivers of an export-led growth strategy. Consequently, the creation of linkages has not been a priority in the policy agenda in most of the region. Therefore, governments in the region need to make the creation of linkages a priority, and to think about export-oriented regimes as drivers of an export-led growth strategy, not as mere sources of unskilled employment, generators of foreign exchange, or instruments for regional development.

This view of the role of EPZ regimes has an important implication for the location of export-oriented activity. EPZs should not be encouraged to locate in rural areas to promote regional development. Even if some firms are attracted to such locations, linkages will be much harder to develop because of the lack of an industrial base in those areas.

A second common element that fostered linkages in Taiwan, Korea, and Ireland is that the authorities of all these countries were especially efficient in granting potential local producers of intermediate goods quick access to inputs at competitive prices. In Taiwan, for example, domestic producers got a rebate for taxes paid on inputs that went into products eventually sold to EPZ firms. In practice, the rebate was given to EPZ firms directly, which had the alternative to pass it on to the local producer. Potential producers were identified in advance, and both the EPZ firm and the local producers were co-responsible for the proper use of the tax rebates. In Korea, an efficient "drawback" system was instituted in which indirect exporters (i.e., those providing inputs to export-oriented firms) were able to recover duties paid on materials and other items embedded in the products sold to EPZ firms. Irish producers of intermediate goods also had duty-free access to inputs if their products were eventually incorporated into exports. Central American firms need the same access to inputs as their Taiwanese, Korean, and Irish counterparts in order to become suppliers of EPZ firms. To give Central American producers access to inputs under competitive conditions, we propose a modification of the existing Regime of Temporary Admission (RTA), plus a rebate system like that used in Taiwan for firms that do not qualify for RTA status. The drawback scheme is not recommended here, given the difficulty and cost of administering such a system and the lack of confidence of domestic investors in recuperating paid duties and taxes.

---

47. For example ILO/UNCTC (1988) argues that in many cases the incentives in place for the local authorities make them "a rather inadequate instrument for promoting technological development per se, or even for fostering linkages. . . . " UNIDO (1993) states that "Backward linkages and technology transfer are often neglected."

The third and final common element that helped foster linkages in Taiwan, Korea, and Ireland is the role that local authorities played in promoting personnel exchanges, supporting training efforts, and providing technical assistance to potential suppliers. For example, the Irish program to increase linkages included the active participation of technical departments of local universities. The program also encouraged purchasing managers of EPZ firms to work with local suppliers (sometimes for long periods) to help them achieve the quality standards and delivery times required. Moreover, the Irish program also had the particularity that the president of a local technological university was appointed Director of the Zone Authority, in order to raise the level of technology and research in the zone, and to assist in the development of local suppliers.

In Taiwan and Korea, the zone authorities provided technical assistance to potential EPZ suppliers, and they actively encouraged personnel exchanges between EPZs and domestic firms. It is worth mentioning that the most common reason given by export-oriented firms for not buying a larger proportion of their inputs in the host economy is that local products and services do not fulfill the quality standards and delivery times they demand. Central America is no exception. EPZ firms there have stated that low quality and unreliable delivery prevent them from buying a larger portion of their inputs locally. It is clear, then, that a program to offer technical assistance and training for local producers of intermediate goods is required in Central America to foster the creation of backward linkages.[48]

Upgrading Export-Oriented Legislation

It is important for Central American nations to upgrade and harmonize the legislation that supports their respective export-oriented regimes. Following are some of the most important aspects to consider:

- *The Zone Authority:* Given the importance, recent growth, and relative size of EPZ regimes in Central America, it is important for governments in the region to have a strong and independent Zone Authority to manage, overlook, and monitor the EPZ regimes in their respective economies. The only countries in the region that currently have such an agency are Costa Rica and Nicaragua (Procomer and Corporación de Zonas Francas, respectively). This should be a government agency with a highly qualified Board of Directors and General Manager. The agency should be responsible for managing the regimes, approving new applications, monitoring the activities of EPZ firms, collecting statistical data on their activities, overseeing customs procedures, making sure that

---

48. More on this in the next sub-section.

EPZ firms comply with labor, environmental and other regulations, and promoting the formation of linkages with local suppliers.

- *Types of Export-Oriented Regimes:* Export-oriented firms operate under several regimes in most Central American nations. This causes confusion among potential investors and can be the source of unfair advantages in some cases. Therefore, the first step in upgrading the legislation is to reduce the number of available regimes to two in each nation. It is our belief that the traditional EPZ regime and the Regime of Temporary Admission (RTA), both of which already exist in most nations, are the two regimes that should be maintained and made uniform across the region. The main differences between the two regimes should be as follows:

  —1) *The EPZ Regime.* This regime would be primarily destined for manufacturing firms that export outside the Central American region. EPZ firms would enjoy income and other tax holidays, as well as the benefit of importing equipment and raw materials duty free. The possibility of selling within the Central American region for EPZ firms would be limited, say, up to five percent of their total output (firms wanting to sell a higher proportion would have to apply for RTA status).

  —2) *The RTA Regime.* This regime would be for firms that export both within and outside the region, but would not have the benefit of tax holidays. RTA firms would be allowed to sell their products in the Central American region free of duties as long as those products are eventually incorporated into exports outside the region. RTA firms would be allowed to sell their products in the domestic market without any restriction upon the payment of the corresponding import duties (i.e., should pay duties for the full amount of the value of the finished product).

- *Income Tax Holiday:* Many developing countries offer 10 years of income tax holiday for export-oriented activities. This has been considered adequate in most circumstances (UNIDO 1995). In Central America there is great disparity among nations regarding this benefit. It is important for countries in the region to establish a uniform schedule of benefits under each regime to prevent harmful competition among the countries to attract foreign direct investment. We consider that a uniform tax holiday limited to, say, 5 or 10 years, is an adequate incentive. A permanent tax exemption reduces the possibilities of integration of export-oriented firms into the domestic economy in the long run. The legislation might extend the holiday based on objective reinvestment and/or domestic value added indicators. For example, the legislation might stipulate an additional 3 to 5 years of tax holiday if domestic value added by a firm exceeds 40 percent of the value of exports and/or if the company reinvests 50 percent or more of its initial investment before the original tax holiday expires. The latter incentive should be available only for firms whose original investment exceeds a certain minimum.

- *Customs Administration:* A particularly common complaint of firms participating in EPZ regimes relates to customs administration. Since one of the most appreciated benefits of the regime has to do precisely with the streamlining of customs procedures and the absence of red tape for import/export operations, improvement of these procedures is critical for the long-run success of the regimes. Several countries have experimented with different organizational customs arrangements. In Taiwan and Korea, the zone authority has a supervisory role over customs at the zone location. In Sri Lanka and the Philippines, the zone authority has joint responsibility for customs procedures. The Dominican Republic created a special department under the regular customs administration to oversee customs operations at zone locations. We believe that the zone authority in each nation should be given full responsibility for the operation, control, and management of the EPZ and RTA regimes, and consequently over customs. That is, specially trained customs personnel for export-oriented operations should be put under the supervision of the zone authority and given responsibility for monitoring customs procedures at EPZ locations.

- *Domestic Suppliers*: As explained in the previous section, to foster backward linkages, potential suppliers of EPZ firms should be given access to inputs at competitive prices. This can be accomplished through the proposed modification of the RTA regime plus the implementation of the system of tax rebates mentioned earlier (i.e., much like the system in Taiwan) for those firms that do not qualify for RTA status. Under this scheme, potential suppliers of EPZ firms in different countries may be allowed to qualify as local even if they sell their intermediate inputs to an EPZ firm in a different Central American nation. This will strengthen backward linkages throughout the region. This is important at this stage of development of EPZ activity in Central America because of economies of scale in the production of intermediate goods, and because there are several companies (mostly textile firms) that currently have operations in more than one Central American nation.

- *"Single-Factory" EPZs*: The current EPZ legislation in all Central American nations allows EPZ firms to locate anywhere in the country and still be eligible for EPZ status and benefits. This creates numerous problems for the authorities in charge of managing the EPZ regime. For example, it makes the smuggling of products, inputs, and/or equipment into the domestic economy relatively easy for unscrupulous firms. As a result of the lack of controls, firms scattered singly outside the zones are often the ones that violate labor, environmental and other regulations, and give a bad reputation to all EPZ firms in the country. The legislation that supports EPZ regimes in Central America should be modified so that single-factory EPZs may be authorized only in very special cases (i.e., when the size, technology, or other particularity of the project justifies it, but never for unsophisticated, low-skill assembly operations).

Conclusion

We have showed in this paper that EPZ activity in Central America grew very rapidly in the 1990s. By the end of the decade, EPZs accounted for a large share of manufacturing employment and exports in all the countries in the region. The development of EPZ activities in Central America, however, has not been uniform across countries. There are numerous and striking differences in legislation and industry/ownership distributions. The specific characteristics of the EPZ regime also vary greatly from country to country. With respect to industry and ownership distributions, Guatemala represents a unique case, since U.S.-owned companies in that country represent just a small fraction of the total. Costa Rica is also a special case: the share of electronics firms in its EPZs is much larger there than in any other nation in the region.

In this chapter, we have also proposed important policy recommendations for the further development of EPZ regimes in the Central American region. First, most nations in the region should make a determined effort to diversify the industry composition of EPZ activity. In some Central American nations, EPZ industry is highly concentrated in the textile industry, a sector that is very sensitive to trade restrictions abroad. Diversification into electronics and some types of services (e.g., data processing) is particularly desirable and plausible.

Second, Central American governments need to encourage the development of more and stronger backward linkages between export-oriented firms and the rest of their local economies. The little data that we have been able to gather indicates that backward linkages between EPZ firms and the rest of the domestic economies in Central America remain very small. The experience in other developing nations has demonstrated that these linkages do not develop automatically and that active government involvement is needed to create them. In this regard, it is desirable that Central American authorities follow the successful steps of countries such as Ireland, Korea, and Taiwan. In particular, it seems that most potential suppliers in Central America require technical assistance and duty-free access to inputs and equipment in order to achieve the quality and price that EPZ firms demand.

Third, Central American nations should upgrade their export-oriented legislation. We propose that they focus on the following six aspects:

1. Establish a Zone Authority in each country to manage, overlook, and monitor EPZ regimes.
2. Reduce the number of export-oriented regimes throughout the region. We believe that the EPZ and the RTA regimes should be maintained and unified.
3. Establish a uniform schedule of benefits under each regime to prevent harmful competition amongst host countries, especially in regards to the income tax holiday. We propose a uniform 5- to 10-year income tax holiday, which may be extended based on reinvestment and/or domestic value added indicators.

4. Improve customs administration. We believe that the Zone Authority in each nation should be given full responsibility over custom procedures.

5. To foster backward linkages it is necessary that potential suppliers of export-oriented firms in different countries may be allowed to qualify as of local origin even if they sell their intermediate inputs to an export-oriented firm in a different Central American nation.

6. Modify export-oriented legislation to preclude the designation "single-factory EPZ," unless the size, technology, or other particularity of the project justifies it.

To conclude, one final warning is in order here. The establishment of EPZ regimes should not serve to retard other economy-wide reforms in Central America. These nations cannot expect EPZs to attract foreign investment and become engines of industrialization and growth in the absence of an appropriate economic environment. In particular, experience has demonstrated that countries that have accompanied the establishment of especial export-oriented regimes (e.g., EPZs) with economic policies consistent with an outward orientation, have benefited more from the operation of these regimes than countries that kept an inward-looking mentality in the rest of their economies.

In any event, it must be clear that the promotion and strengthening of EPZ regimes throughout Central America is already a very important first step in providing insurance and transparency to foreign investors. In a sense, the establishment of EPZs is a proof of the commitment of the governments of the region to respect property and maintain a stable legal environment. Therefore, EPZ regimes in the region should not be seen only as mechanisms to generate employment and foreign exchange; they may also be one of the most important components of an integral export-based development strategy that depends heavily on foreign investment and transfer of technology.

References

Abeywardene, J., R. de Alwis, A. Jayasena, S. Jayaweera and T. Sanmugam . 1994. *Export Processing Zones in Sri Lanka: Economic Impact and Social Issues.* International Labor Organization Working Paper No. 69. Geneva: International Labor Organization.

Actualidad Económica. 1997. "America Central en Cifras," *Actualidad Económica,* (11): 26-108.

Balasubramanyam, V. N. 1988. "Export Processing Zones in Developing Countries:

Theory and Empirical Evidence." In *Economic Development and International Trade*, edited by David Greenaway. New York: St. Martin's Press.

Banco Central de Costa Rica (several issues). *Libro Negro*. San José, Costa Rica.

Banco Central de Costa Rica. 1999. *Indicadores Economicos: Sector Externo* (online). Available at *http//www.websiec.bccr.fi.cr/indicadores* (09/16/1999).

Banco Central de Guatemala. 1995. *Estudio Económico y Memoria de Labores 1995*. Guatemala: Guatemala City.

Banco Central de Honduras. 1996. Comportamiento de la Actividad Maquiladora Durante 1995 y Perspectivas para 1996. Honduras: Tegucigalpa.

Banco Central de Honduras. 1998. *Actividad Maquiladora en las Zonas Francas de Honduras, 1990-1997*. Honduras: Tegucigalpa.

Banco Central de Nicaragua. 1999. *Indicadores Economicos* (online). Available at *http//www.bnc.ni/economia/inidicad* (09/16/1999).

Basile, A. and D. Germidis. 1984. *Investing in Export Processing Zones*. Paris: Organization for Economic Cooperation and Development.

Battat, J. , Frank, I., and X. Shen (1996). *Suppliers to Multinationals*. Occasional Paper 6. Washington D.C.: Foreign Investment Advisory Service.

Burns, J. G. 1995. "Free Trade Zones: Global Overview and Future Prospects." *Industry Trade and Technology Review*. United States International Trade Commission. September: 35-47.

Caves, R. E. 1996. *Multinational Enterprises and Economic Development*. New York: Cambridge University Press.

Crystal, C. 1993. "Cheap Imports." *International Business* 6 (3): 98-100.

Din, M. 1994. "Export Processing Zones and Backward Linkages." *Journal of Development Economics* 43: 369-85.

Dunning, J. 1993. *Multinational Enterprises and the Global Economy*. Great Britain: Addison-Wesley.

Economist Intelligence Unit. 1999. *Investing, Licensing and Trading in Central America*. New York: The Economist Intelligence Unit.

Gil Van, B. 1980. "Economic and Social Impacts of the Masan Free Export Zone in the Republic of Korea." In *Economic and Social Impacts of Export Processing Zones in Asia*, edited by F. A. Rabbani. Tokyo: Asian Productivity Organization.

Gitli, E. 1997. *La Industria Maquiladora en Centroamerica*. Report prepared for the International Labor Organization Desk for Central America and Panama. San Jose, Costa Rica: Oficina Internacional del Trabajo.

Grubel, H. 1982. "Towards a Theory of Free Economic Zones." *Weltwirtschafttliches Archiv* 118: 39-61.

Grunwald, J. 1991. "Opportunity Missed: Mexico and Maquiladoras." *Brookings Review* 9 (1):44-48.

Healey, D. 1990. "The Underlying Conditions for the Successful Generation of

EPZ-local Linkages: The Experience of the Republic of Korea," *Journal of the Flagstaff Institute*, XIV (1), 43-88.

International Labor Organization. *Yearbook of Labor Statistics.*(several issues). Geneva: International Labor Organization.

International Monetary Fund. 1999. *International Financial Statistics*. Washington D.C.: International Monetary Fund.

ILO/UNCTC. 1988. Economic and Social Effects of Multinational Enterprises in Export Processing Zones. Geneva: International Labor Organization.

Kaplinsky, R. 1993. "Export Processing Zones in the Dominican Republic: Transforming Manufactures into Commodities." *World Development* 21 (11):1851-65.

Keesing, Donald B. 1990. "Which Export Processing Zones Make Most Sense in Light of the Spillover Benefits and Practical Needs of Manufactured Exports?" *Journal of the Flagstaff Institute* 14 (1): 29-42.

Kreye, O., Heinrichs J., and F. Fröbel. 1987. *Export Processing Zones in Developing Countries: Results from a New Survey*. International Labor Organization Working Paper No. 43. Geneva: International Labor Organization.

Larraín, Felipe, Luis Felipe Lopéz-Calva, and Andres Rodríguez. 2000. "Intel: A Case Study of Foreign Direct Investment in Costa Rica." Chapter 6 in this volume.

Lin. S. A. Y. 1993. "Multinationals' Intra-Firm trade and Technology Transfer's Effects on LDCs' Growth." In *Transnational Corporations and International Trade and Payments*, edited by H. P. Gray. London: Routledge.

Linneman, H. 1996. "On Trade and Growth." *Economist-Leiden*144 (2): 325-332.

Makhija, N. 1980. "Santacruz Elecronics Export Processing Zone," in Rabbani, F.A. (ed.) *Economic and Social Impacts of Export Processing Zones in Asia*. Tokyo: Asian Productivity Organization.

Mata, R. 1995. "Nafta Update: Steady U.S. Bilateral Trade Growth with Mexico Faces Mixed Prospects in 1995." *Industry, Trade, and Technology Review*. United States International Trade Commission (March): 1-4.

McAleese, D., and D. McDonald. 1978. "Employment Growth and the Development of Linkages in Foreign-Owned and Domestic Manufacturing Enterprises." *Oxford Bulletin of Economics and Statistics* 40: 321-39.

Ministerio de Economía de Guatemala. 1995. Situación de las Empresas Calificadas al Amparo de la Ley de Fomento y Desarrollo de la Actividad Exportadora y de Maquila, Decreto 29-89 del Congreso de la Republica. Guatemala City, Guatemala: Ministerio de Economía de Guatemala.

———. 1997. Situación del Control de las Empresas Acogidas a la Ley de Fomento y Desarrollo de la Actividad Exportadora y de Maquila, Decreto 29-89. Guatemala City, Guatemala: Ministerio de Economía de Guatemala.

Miyagiwa, K. 1986. "A Reconsideration of the Welfare Economics of a Free-Trade Zone." *Journal of International Economics* 21: 337-50.

Mortimore, M., Duthoo, H., and J. A. Guerrero. 1995. *Informe sobre la*

Competitividad Internacional en las Zonas Francas en la República Dominicana. Santiago de Chile: Comisión Económica para América Latina.

Rabbani, F.A., ed. 1980. *Economic and Social Impacts of Export Processing Zones in Asia.* Tokyo: Asian Productivity Organization.

Roberts, M. 1992. Export Processing Zones in Jamaica and Mauritius: Evolution of an Export-Oriented Development Model. San Francisco: Mellen Research University Press.

Rodríguez, C. 1976. "A Note on the Economics of the Duty Free Zone." *Journal of International Economics* 6: 385-88.

Rondinelli, D. 1987. "Export Processing Zones and Economic Development in Asia: A Review and Reassessment of a Means of Promoting Growth and Jobs." *American Journal of Economics and Sociology* 46 (1): 89-105.

Sivalingam, G. 1994. *The Economic and Social Impact of Export Processing Zones: The Case of Malaysia.* International Labor Organization Working Paper No. 66. Geneva: International Labor Organization.

Smith, Stephen M., and David L. Barkley. 1991. "Local Input Linkages of Rural High-Technology Manufacturers." *Land Economics* 67 (4): 472-83.

Teutli, G. 1980. "Maquiladoras in Mexico." In *Economic and Social Impacts of Export Processing Zones in Asia,* edited by F. A. Rabbani. Tokyo: Asian Productivity Organization.

Torres, O. 1997. *Honduras: La Industria Maquiladora.* Mexico: Comisión Económica para América Latina.

UNCTAD. 1993. *Export Processing Zones: Role of Foreign Direct Investment and Development Impact.* Geneva: United Nations Conference on Trade and Development.

UNCTC. 1985. Export Processing Free Zones in Developing Countries: Implications for Trade and Industrialization Policies. Geneva: United Nations Conference on Trade and Development.

UNIDO. 1995. *Export Processing Zones: Principles and Practices.* Vienna: United Nations Industrial Development Organization.

USITC. 1988. The Implications of Foreign-Trade Zones for U.S. Industries and for Competitive Conditions between U.S. and Foreign Firm. Washington, D.C.: United States International Trade Commission.

Warr, P. 1987. "Export Promotion via Industrial Enclaves: The Philippines' Bataan Export Processing Zone." *The Journal of Development Studies* 23(2): 220-41.

————.1990. "Export Processing Zones." In *Export Promotion Strategies: Evidence from Developing Countries,* edited by Chris Milner. New York, NY: New York University Press.

Wei, Ge. 1993. Export Processing Zones, Multinational Firms, and Economic System Transformation. Ph.D. Dissertation in Regional Science, University of Pennsylvania.

Wilkie, J. W., Aleman, E., and J. G. Ortega. 1999. *Statistical Abstract of Latin America.* Vol.35: 35. Los Angeles, CA: UCLA Latin American Center Publication.

Willmore, L. 1995. "Export Processing Zones in the Dominican Republic: A Comment on Kaplinsky." *World Development* 23 (3): 529-35.

World Bank.1992. *Export Processing Zones.* Washington, D.C.: World Bank.

———. 1993. *The East Asian Miracle: Economic Growth and Public Policy.* New York, NY: Oxford University Press.

———. 1996. *World Development Report 1996.* Washington, D.C.: World Bank.

Young, L. 1987. "Intermediate Goods and the Formation of Duty-Free Zones." *Journal of Development Economics* 25: 369-84.

Young, L., and K.F. Miyagiwa . 1987. "Unemployment and the Formation of Duty-Free Zones." *Journal of Development Economics* 26: 397-405.

8

The External-Debt Problem in Central America: Honduras, Nicaragua, and the HIPC Initiative

GERARDO ESQUIVEL, FELIPE LARRAÍN B., AND
JEFFREY D. SACHS[1]

Over the past several years, Central America has gone through a substantial process of adjustment and modernization. After years of social unrest, the entire region is finally at peace and has begun to establish conditions for rapid and sustainable economic growth. However, despite the fact that all the countries in the region have made important structural reforms in recent years, not all of them have yet started to reap the benefits of these economic policies.

Between 1990 and 1998, Costa Rica, El Salvador and Guatemala achieved important gains in per capita output, while Honduras and Nicaragua remained practically stagnant (see Figure 8-1). Because the latter two countries are also the poorest in the region, this trend has entailed a worrisome increase of inequality within Central America. Furthermore, since Honduras and Nicaragua have the largest external-debt burden in the region, it is quite likely that this factor has had a negative effect on their capacity to grow in recent years, and that it will continue to do so in the near future. This might become an impediment to the promotion of economic convergence within the region.

---

1. The first version of this work was written in early 1998, before Honduras and Nicaragua had signed ESAF agreements with the IMF, and well before the mid-1999 review of the HIPC initiative. The authors wish to thank the excellent assistance of José Acevedo and Ximena Clark and the useful comments of Amina Tirana.

It must be stressed that the challenge faced by Honduras and Nicaragua is tremendous. To get an idea of the magnitude of this challenge, consider the following: the per capita income of Nicaragua and Honduras is less than one-fourth that of Costa Rica, the richest country in the region, whose income is in turn about one-fourth that of the United States. Assuming a conservative population growth rate of 2.5 percent per year, the GDP in Honduras and Nicaragua will have to grow at a constant rate of about 6 percent per year during the next forty years simply to reach the income per capita that Costa Rica has today. It is therefore clear that any obstacle to economic growth in these two countries has to be removed if they are to satisfy the growing demands of their population.

Krugman (1988) and Sachs (1989a) have argued that an excessive debt burden acts as a high marginal tax rate that discourages investment and economic adjustment. This occurs because a large foreign debt imposes severe constraints on the development of debtor countries and limits their ability to service foreign obligations. The argument implies that it may be in the best interest of both creditors and debtors to agree on a debt reduction. Achieving deep debt reduction may then be a prerequisite to start a sustained process of economic growth in highly indebted economies. In this chapter we explore this possibility for the cases of Honduras and Nicaragua.

This chapter begins with a brief review of the foreign-debt burden in Central America, with special emphasis on the cases of Honduras and Nicaragua. This chapter continues with a review of the existing debt-relief mechanisms, with special emphasis on the new initiative aimed at reducing the debt burden of the highly indebted poor countries (the HIPC Initiative). Then the chapter goes on to discuss the prospects of Honduras and Nicaragua to qualify for the new initiative. The last section presents our conclusions. Finally, a statistical appendix shows the historical external debt data for Honduras and Nicaragua.

External Debt and Growth in Central America

The Burden of Foreign Debt

The Central American countries, like most of the rest of the developing world, have made extensive use of some form of external savings to finance their domestic investments. However, as a result of the combination of inadequate infrastructure, low levels of human capital, inward-oriented policies, political instability, and a strong comparative advantage in certain agricultural products (mainly coffee and bananas), the region has been relatively unsuccessful in attracting foreign direct investment into areas other than agriculture.[2] Because of this, Central American countries have had to resort to external debt as an important means of financing development.

All Central American countries have used foreign resources to fill their savings-investment gaps. Yet they have attained very different levels of foreign indebtedness. Table 8-1 shows some of the key indicators of the foreign-debt burden in each of the five Central American countries at the end of 1997.

Table 8-1 shows the seriousness of the foreign-debt problem in Honduras and Nicaragua. The first three rows of the table show that the magnitude of Nicaragua's stock of external debt at the end of 1997 was excessive—more than three times its GNP and more than five times its total exports. The burden of foreign debt in Honduras is above 100 percent of GNP. Although this figure is lower than that for Nicaragua, it is also excessive. The external debt of Costa Rica, El Salvador, and Guatemala, which is between 26 percent and 40 percent of their annual GNP, is more moderate and appears manageable with sound budgeting and macroeconomic policies.

The middle of Table 8-1 shows some indicators of the magnitude of the resources used by Central American countries to serve their external obligations. Not surprisingly, the service costs are much higher in Honduras and Nicaragua than in the rest of the region. For example, whereas the other countries in the region devote between 2.3 percent and 6.2 percent of their annual GNP to serve their external obligations, Honduras and Nicaragua have to forego 12.1 percent and 19.4 percent of their GNP, respectively. It is unlikely that any country can achieve sustainable economic growth while devoting so many resources to the service of their external debt.

The previous conclusion is also supported by the World Bank classification, which is listed in the last two rows of the table. According to these criteria, both Honduras and Nicaragua are classified as severely indebted low-income countries, whereas Costa Rica, El Salvador, and Guatemala are classified as lower-middle income countries with a relatively low level of indebtedness. Based on these results, the next section will focus mainly on the external debt of Honduras and Nicaragua.

---

2. This trend, however, is changing with the recent adoption of export processing zone regimes throughout Central America. For further details see Jenkins, Esquivel, and Larraín in Chapter 7 of this volume. A successful nonagricultural foreign direct investment in the region is the case of Intel in Costa Rica. Larraín, López-Calva and Rodríguez-Clare analyze this case in detail in Chapter 6 of this volume.

Table 8-1. Key Indebtedness Ratios in Central America (1997)

	Costa Rica	El Salvador	Guatemala	Honduras	Nicaragua
Total External Debt (percent of GNP)	39	32	26	113	336
Present Value of External Debt (percent of GNP)	36	27	23	91	268
Present Value of External Debt (percent of exports of goods and services)	76	80	108	181	510
Total External-Debt Service (percent of GNP)	6.2	2.7	2.3	12.1	19.4
Total External-Debt Service (percent of exports of goods and services)	13	8	11	24	37
Interest Payments (percent of GNP)	2.4	1.4	1.1	4.5	8.4
Interest Payments (percent of exports of goods and services)	5	4	5	9	16
Classification by Income	Lower-Middle	Lower-Middle	Lower-Middle	Low	Low
Classification by Indebtedness	Less-Indebted	Less-Indebted	Less-Indebted	Severely Indebted	Severely Indebted

Source: World Bank (1999a)

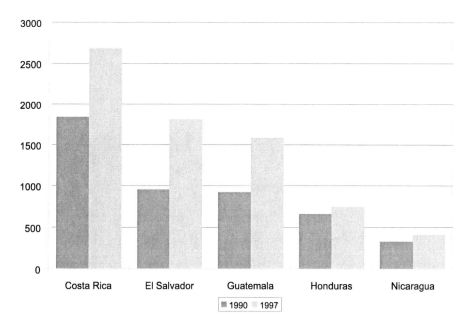

Figure 8-1.   Per Capita Income (U.S. dollars)
Source: The World Bank (1999b)

Growth in Central America

Figure 8-1 shows the per capita GNP in U.S. dollars for the five Central American countries in 1990 and 1997. This figure illustrates a worrisome feature of the recent pattern of growth in the region: the poorest countries in the area have remained practically stagnant during the 1990s while the relatively wealthier countries achieved important income per capita gains. These trends imply that regional inequalities have increased in the recent past and that there must be a divergent trend among the countries of the region.

To investigate whether this divergent trend is a recent phenomenon or whether it has been occurring for a long period, the dispersion of per capita income in Central America since 1970 was computed. Figure 8-2 shows the standard deviation of the log of per capita income for two groups of Central American countries for the 1970–97 period. The first group consists of the three less-indebted countries of the region: Costa Rica, El Salvador, and Guatemala. The second group includes all five nations; that is, it adds Honduras and Nicaragua to the first group.

As the figure shows, there has been no major variation in the dispersion of per capita income among the three less-indebted Central American countries for the past 27 years. The dispersion of per capita income across the whole re-

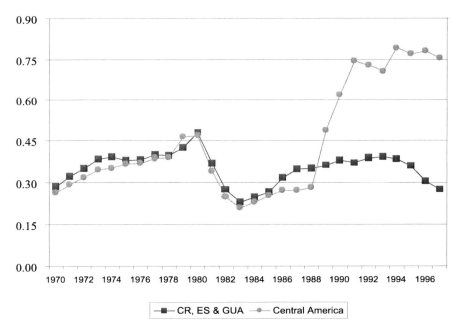

Figure 8-2. *Dispersion of Per Capita Income*
Source: Calculations based on data from The World Bank (1999b)

gion, however, has increased dramatically since 1988. A simple comparison of the two lines in Figure 8-2 suggests that the increase in the variability of the region's per capita income can then be mainly attributed to the presence of Honduras and Nicaragua in the larger sample.

Although there is no obvious causal link between debt burden and growth, it is certainly suggestive that the two most indebted countries in Central America, Honduras and Nicaragua, are also the countries that are lagging behind within the region.[3] Moreover, it must be pointed out that the beginning of the divergent process in the region coincided with the moment when Nicaragua began to make substantial payments to the international financial community in order to reestablish negotiations with its main creditors, and when positive net transfers to Honduras stopped.

There are certainly other factors (i.e., political instability, economic distor-

---

3. Such a trend is even more intriguing since Honduras and Nicaragua, like the rest of the region, have achieved important progress in their structural reform, mainly in trade and financial liberalization. Nicaragua has also made progress in tax reform and has even experienced an incipient process of privatization (Inter-American Development Bank 1996 and 1997; Chapters 13 and 14 in Volume II).

tions, and a lack of infrastructure) that may explain the relatively slow pace of economic growth in Honduras and Nicaragua. However, these factors do not adequately account for the divergent trend just described. These problems are not particular to Honduras and Nicaragua; instead they pervade most of the region. Therefore, these factors, although important, may explain a negative effect on the growth rate of the region and not just on that of specific countries. The elements just described, as well as evidence drawn from other experiences (i.e., sub-Saharan Africa), supports the idea that slower growth in Honduras and Nicaragua is in some way related to the large external-debt burden that afflicts them, and that foreign indebtedness may be hindering their achievement of sustained economic growth.

A Brief Look at the Foreign-Debt Evolution of Honduras and Nicaragua

Honduras

At the end of 1997, Honduras' foreign debt reached US\$4,698 million, of which almost 89 percent was long-term obligations and 83 percent was public or publicly guaranteed obligations. Figure 8-3 shows the most important features of the external debt of Honduras, as well as its main components. Public or publicly guaranteed debt has steadily increased over the past 27 years. From 1970 to 1997, Honduras' total foreign debt grew in nominal dollars at a

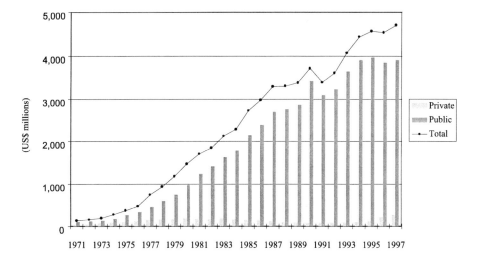

Figure 8-3. Honduras: Total Foreign Debt Stocks

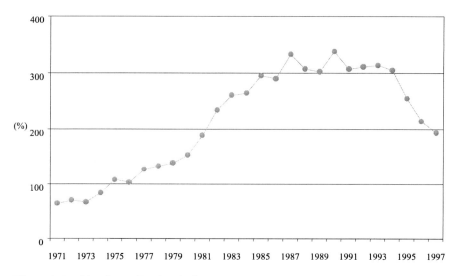

Figure 8-4.   Honduras: Foreign Debt to Exports

compounded rate of 14.9 percent per year, mostly due to long-term net flows from official creditors.

Conventional measures of the degree of indebtedness of a nation are given by the debt-to-exports and debt-to-output ratios. By the end of 1997, the ratio of foreign debt-to-exports of goods and services in Honduras was 194 percent, while the ratio of foreign debt-to-GNP was 103 percent.[4] These ratios compare unfavorably with the same indicators for all the developing countries in 1997 (129 percent and 35 percent, respectively).

Figures 8-4 and 8-5 present the historical trend of the two standard stock-of-debt ratios for Honduras during the 1970–97 period. Both figures show a well-defined rising trend during most of the period, and interestingly, both ratios continued to rise even during the most critical part of the 1980s debt crisis. Of course, this pattern is related to the geopolitical importance of Honduras during those years. This element also explains why, for example, bilateral debt as a percent of total debt increased from 20 to 40 percent between 1980 and 1990.

---

4. The nominal value of the debt is used in this section, whereas in other sections of this chapter the net present-value equivalent is used. This is in part due to the lack of historical information for the variable in present-value terms. The World Bank started to compute this variable as recently as 1991. The debt in present-value terms is usually lower than the nominal value since the former takes into account the concessional component of the debt.

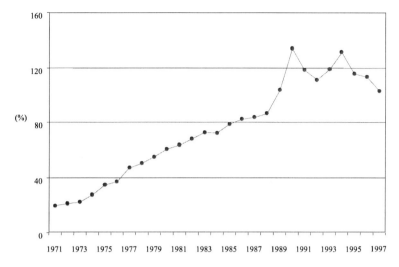

Figure 8-5.   Honduras: Foreign Debt to GNP

By 1990, the two debt indicators seemed to have reached a peak. Starting in 1994, immediately following both the opening of the economy and the first stabilization attempts of the Honduran economy, the two debt ratios began to show a remarkable downward trend.

In terms of flows, standard debt-burden measures are the ratios of debt service-to-output and debt service-to-exports. They indicate the annual effort that a country has to make to cover its foreign obligations. Honduras' total debt service paid in 1997 was $505 million, which represented about 21 percent of its exports of goods and services and 11 percent of its GNP. Figures 8-6 and 8-7 show the 27-year trend in these two indicators. The debt service-to-GNP ratio has been consistently above 10 percent during the last eight years, whereas debt service has averaged around 30 percent of the exports of goods and services during the same period. By comparison, the same indicators for all the countries classified by the World Bank as "severely-indebted low-income countries" are about 4 percent and 16 percent, respectively. These figures already indicate the magnitude of the economic and fiscal efforts that Honduras has undertaken in the past few years to cover its foreign debt service. Interest on external debt alone has consumed an average of about 12 percent of total exports and 5 percent of GNP during the 1990s.

Net resource-transfers, defined as net flows minus interest payments, give an alternative indicator of the contribution of external savings to the domestic economy. Figure 8-8 plots this variable over the last 27 years and shows the reversal that has occurred in recent years in the trend of this contribution to

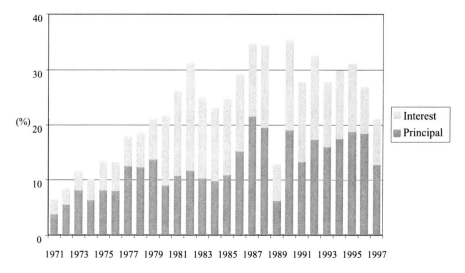

Figure 8-6. Honduras: Debt Service to Exports

the Honduran economy. This variable, with its ups and downs, has been mostly negative since 1986.

Nicaragua

At the end of 1997, Nicaragua's foreign debt reached $5,677 million, of which 85 percent was long-term publicly guaranteed obligations. Short-term

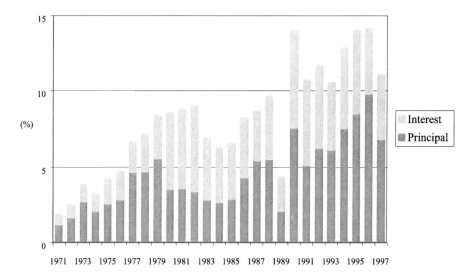

Figure 8-7. Honduras: Debt Service to GNP

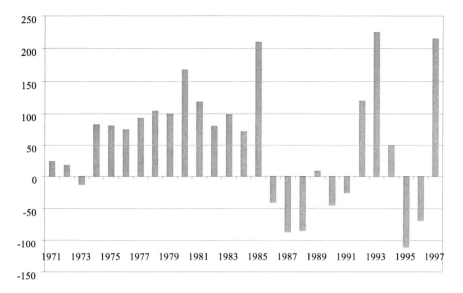

Figure 8-8.   Honduras: Net Transfer

debt comprised mainly interest arrears on long-term debt. Accumulation of principal and interest arrears accounted for 37 percent—on average—of total foreign debt stocks between 1988 and 1997.

Figure 8-9 shows the evolution of Nicaragua's nominal foreign debt between 1971 and 1997. During this period, the country's debt grew at an average compounded annual rate of 12.8 percent in nominal dollars. However,

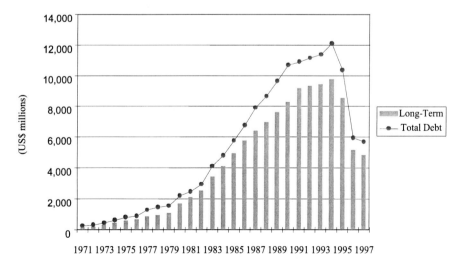

Figure 8-9.   Nicaragua: Total Foreign Debt Stocks

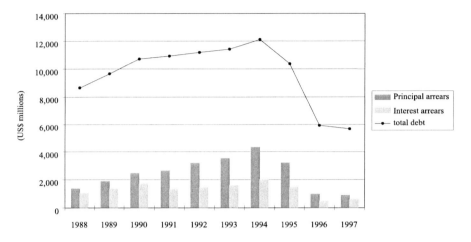

Figure 8-10.   Nicaragua: Total Debt and Arrears

the rapid accumulation in Nicaragua's foreign debt really occurred mainly in two sub-periods: first, between 1971 and 1979, when foreign debt increased fourfold (25 percent annual average growth rate); second, between 1979 and 1989, when it multiplied by a factor of six (20 percent of annual average growth rate). Part of the debt increase in the latter period was due to non-voluntary long-term net flows from official creditors (as principal arrears rose sharply in the late 1980s) and to the rapid accumulation of interest arrears. Figure 8-10 plots both total debt stock and external-debt arrears between

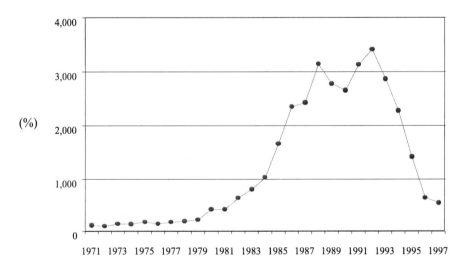

Figure 8-11.   Nicaragua: Foreign Debt to Exports

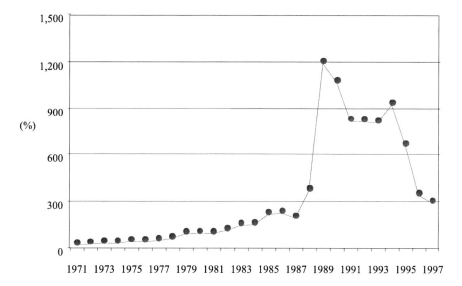

Figure 8-12. Nicaragua: Foreign Debt to GNP

1988 and 1997. This figure shows that arrears are one of the most important factors in explaining the rapid accumulation of foreign debt in Nicaragua that occurred in the late 1980s and early 1990s.

The ratio of foreign debt-to-exports of goods and services in Nicaragua at the end of 1997 was 552 percent, while foreign debt represented 305 percent of GNP. Both ratios are depicted in Figures 8-11 and 8-12, from 1971 to 1997. These two figures, together with Figure 8-9, illustrate the rapid increase in foreign debt that took place in Nicaragua during the years of the Sandinista regime (1979–89). Governments sympathetic to the new regime (mainly the former Soviet Union) supplied most of the foreign-debt flows that took place in this period. Only five years after the Sandinistas had taken power, the ratios of debt-to-exports and debt-to-GNP had already reached 1,000 and 200 percent, respectively. These ratios were by then among the highest in the world. Measured by the conventional debt-to-GNP ratio displayed in Figure 8-11, Nicaragua had the doubtful honor of being the most indebted economy in the world between 1989 and 1995.[5]

Between 1987 and 1989, Nicaragua's debt-to-GNP ratio increased enormously as a result of the combination of two elements. First, total foreign debt went from 7 billion to 10 billion dollars in this period—an important in-

---

5. By 1996, the most indebted countries in the world were São Tomé and Mozambique. See World Bank (1999a).

crease. Second, a huge fall of real output accompanied the hyperinflation that afflicted Nicaragua in the final years of the Sandinista regime.[6]

Figures 8-11 and 8-12 also show the remarkable decline that has occurred in both ratios since 1990. This decline reflects the combination of three elements: first, the relative success of the export-oriented policies implemented by the democratic governments that succeeded the Sandinistas after the 1989 elections; second, the removal of the U.S. embargo that accompanied the fall of the Sandinista regime; and, third, the successful debt-reduction agreements reached by the Nicaraguan government with several of its most important creditors. In fact, by the end of 1998, total foreign-debt stocks in Nicaragua amounted to almost $6 billion, 40 percent lower in nominal terms than its external debt at the end of 1993. This decrease was mainly due to debt-relief agreements reached with Russia, Mexico, the Paris Club, and the Commercial Bank.[7]

Figures 8-13 and 8-14 display the two conventional foreign debt-service indicators for Nicaragua. These figures show that Nicaragua substantially reduced the service of its external obligations during most of the 1980s in spite of having an increasing external debt. This behavior partially explains the rapid accumulations of the external debt that occurred in this period. Figure 8-13 also shows how, starting in 1991, Nicaragua increased substantially the service of its external debt in an attempt to normalize its relations with the international financial community. By then, however, the magnitude of the foreign debt had reached unsustainable levels and Nicaragua was unable to service it in full (see Figure 8-10).

Figures 8-13 and 8-14 also provide an idea of the effort that Nicaragua has made to cover its external obligations in recent years. During 1997, Nicaragua devoted 32 percent of its total exports of goods and services and 18 percent of its national output to service its foreign debt. It is likely that the divergent pattern in Central America described above is related to the tremendous effort that both Honduras and Nicaragua have made in the last eight years to continue servicing as much of their foreign-debt obligations as possible.

Net resource-transfers confirm the trends just described. Figure 8-15 shows the large transfers that Nicaragua received during most of the 1980s as well as their sudden decline since 1990. Data from the most recent years indicate that Nicaragua is no longer benefiting from access to fresh resources from the international financial community. It is important to stress that be-

---

6. Ocampo (1991) contains a very precise description of Nicaragua's macroeconomic conditions during this period.

7. A detailed account of Nicaragua's debt negotiations during the 1990–96 period is provided in Ministerio de Cooperación Externa (1997).

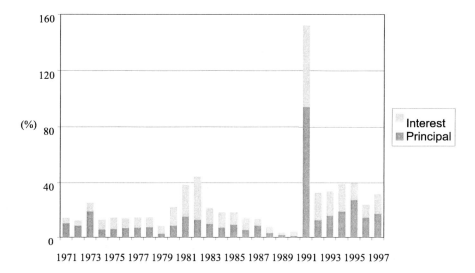

Figure 8-13.   Nicaragua: Debt Service to Exports

tween 1991 and 1997 Nicaragua did not received positive net transfers from abroad (on average), in spite of having carried out very important economic reforms. This trend is puzzling, since it is clear that the medium- and long-run viability of the economic reforms in Nicaragua need the support of

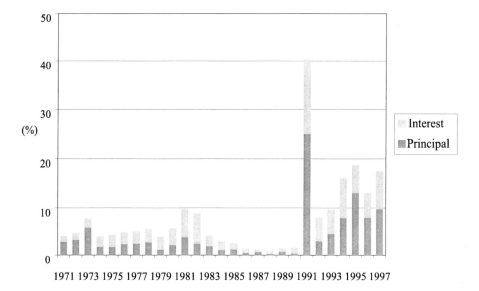

Figure 8-14.   Nicaragua: Debt Service to GNP

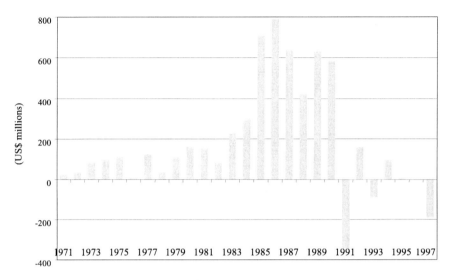

Figure 8-15. Nicaragua: Net Transfers

external financing that may help to deepen and strengthen the economic policy changes already adopted.

By the end of 1998, the composition of Nicaragua's external debt was as
follows: 27 percent was due to multilateral institutions (11 percent to the
Inter-American Development Bank, 7 percent to the Central American Bank
for Economic Integration, 7 percent to the World Bank, 2 percent others).
Twenty-seven percent was due to Paris Club governments (Russia and Germany 6 percent each, Spain 4 percent, Italy, France, and Japan 2 percent each).
Forty-two percent was due to non–Paris Club governments (Costa Rica 8 percent, Guatemala 7 percent, Bulgaria 4 percent, Libya 4 percent, Brazil, Venezuela, and Taiwan 3 percent each).

DEBT-RELIEF MECHANISMS AND THE HIPC INITIATIVE

Over the past two decades the international financial community has developed several mechanisms to alleviate the problems that poor countries
have faced in fulfilling their external obligations. During most of the 1980s,
official and Paris Club creditors[8] saw the debt problem as one of liquidity.

---

8. Paris Club refers to the group of government creditors (mainly OECD countries) that
meet with debtor countries under the auspices of the French government. Recently, Russia has
been accepted as a member of the Paris Club.

Consequently, the typical approach to debt relief was to refinance or reschedule arrears and payments that were due during a period in which the debtor had an IMF-supported adjustment program. The result of this approach, however, was a steady increase in both the stock of outstanding debt and in the debt-burden ratios of many of the poorest countries.[9]

In 1988, after the G-7 summit in Toronto, the debt problem in the poorest countries was widely perceived as one of solvency rather than liquidity. Consequently, Paris Club members agreed to provide up to one-third of debt relief to the poorest rescheduling countries by either forgiving part of the debt or by granting concessional interest rates. These terms, known as the *Toronto terms*, were later modified in the 1991 G-7 summit in London, where creditor countries agreed to provide maximum relief of up to 50 percent on the net present value of the stock of debt (the *London terms*). In 1994, the Paris Club creditors agreed to raise the maximum amount of debt relief to two-thirds of the eligible stock of rescheduling debt for those countries that had a three-year track record of successful macroeconomic management. The new conditions became known as the *Naples terms*; they are described in more detail in Box 8-1.

Recently, as a result of rising concerns about the service capacity of some severely indebted poor countries, the World Bank and the IMF launched a new initiative. The objective was to look for a "comprehensive solution" to the unsustainable debt of some of these countries. First proposed at the April 1996 meetings of the IMF and the World Bank, the *Heavily Indebted Poor Countries Debt Initiative* (hereafter referred as "the HIPC initiative") was rapidly endorsed and supported by a large number of countries around the world.

The HIPC Initiative

This most recent debt-relief mechanism was officially approved in September 1996 by the boards of the World Bank and the International Monetary Fund. The HIPC initiative represents a commitment by the international financial community to act together to alleviate the external-debt situation of the neediest countries.[10] At the outset, the HIPC initiative identified forty-one countries as potentially eligible for debt relief. [11]

The HIPC initiative is oriented toward providing debt relief for those

---

9. See Sachs (1989b) for a critical review of this approach.

10. For more details about the origins and goals of the HIPC initiative see Boote and Thugge (1999).

11. The original list included Nigeria. Subsequently, Nigeria was eliminated, and Malawi was added, keeping the list at 41.

Box 8-1.

Paris Club Naples Terms

(Replaced the Toronto and London Terms)

Eligibility: Determined by creditors on a case-by-case basis according to a country's income and level of indebtedness. Countries that previously received relief under Toronto or London terms become automatically eligible.

Concessionality: Most countries receive a reduction in eligible non-ODA (official development assistance) debt of 67 percent in net present-value terms. Some countries with per capita income of more than $500 and a ratio of debt-to-exports of less than 350 percent in present-value terms may receive 50 percent net present-value reduction, which would be determined on a case-by-case basis.

Coverage: Coverage of non-ODA pre–cutoff-date debt is determined case by case in light of balance-of-payments need. Debt previously rescheduled on concessional terms may be subject to further rescheduling to top-up the amount of concessionality granted. Under the top-up, the net present-value reduction is increased from the original level given under Toronto or London terms to the level agreed under the Naples terms.

Choice of Options: Creditors have a choice of two concessional options for achieving a 67 percent (or 50 percent) reduction in net present-value (NPV) terms: the debt-reduction option, under which repayment is made over twenty-three years with a six-year grace period, or the debt-service-reduction option, under which the NPV reduction is achieved by concessional interest rates with repayment in less than 33 years. There is also a commercial, long-maturity option that provides for no NPV reduction and repayment over 40 years with a 20-year grace period. Creditors choosing this option make their best efforts to change to a concessional option at a later date when feasible. The long-maturity option provides for repayment over 25 years with a 16-year grace period.*

ODA: Pre-cutoff-date credits are rescheduled on interest rates at least as concessional as the original interest rates over 40 years with a 16-year grace period (30-years maturity with a 12-year grace period for 50 percent NPV reduction). Creditors can also choose an option reducing the NPV of ODA debt by 67 percent (or 50 percent).

Flow Rescheduling: Service on eligible debt falling due during the consolidation period, generally in line with the period of the IMF arrangement, can be rescheduled. There is no grace period for this operation.

Stock-of-Debt Operations: The term in which the entire stock of eligible pre–cutoff-date debt is rescheduled concessionally is reserved for countries with a satisfactory three-year record of both payments under rescheduling agreements and good performance under IMF arrangements. Creditors must be confident that the country will be able to respect the debt agreement as an exit rescheduling (with no further rescheduling required). The grace period for this operation is three years.

---

* In addition, there is an option to capitalize interest due, which also achieves the NPV reduction by a lower interest rate over the same repayment (and grace) periods as the debt-service-reduction option.

countries that have demonstrated strong policy performance and that, after taking full advantage of the traditional debt-relief mechanisms, are still considered to have unsustainable debt levels (as defined by the IMF and the World Bank). The traditional debt-relief approach usually consists of the following steps on the part of the debtor country:

1. Adopt an economic reform program supported by concessional loans from the IMF and the World Bank.
2. Obtain a flow-rescheduling agreement with Paris Club creditors (on concessional terms) in support of the economic program. If the debtor country maintains a good track record with the IMF and follows the rescheduling agreement, the country may obtain a stock-of-debt reduction operation after a three-year period.
3. Commit to seek at least comparable terms on debt owed to private and other non–Paris Club bilateral creditors.
4. Seek bilateral forgiveness of official development assistance (ODA) debt by some creditors.
5. Obtain new financing on appropriate concessional terms.

According to the terms of the HIPC initiative (see Box 8-2), if a country reaches sustainable debt levels after obtaining a stock-of-debt reduction with other creditors, it is not eligible to benefit from the initiative. If, however, the debt reduction is not enough to bring the debtor country back to sustainable

Box 8-2.
How Does the HIPC Initiative Work?*

FIRST STAGE

Paris Club creditors reschedule debt flows under Naples Terms (up to 67 percent reduction of the NPV of eligible debt) along with comparable action by other bilateral and commercial creditors. Multilateral institutions provide support under adjustment programs. Countries establish their first three-year track record of good performance. At the end of this stage the "decision point" is reached.

Decision Point

At the end of the first stage, generally three years, the IMF, World Bank, and country authorities carry out a debt-sustainability analysis. There are three possible outcomes:

1) If strong policies and a Paris Club stock-of-debt operation in Naples Terms are sufficient to put the country in a sustainable external-debt position within three additional years, the country could request a stock-of-debt operation and would not be eligible for assistance under the HIPC initiative.
2) If the assessment indicates that a country's overall debt burden will not be sustainable at the end of the second three-year period, it will be deemed eligible for support under the HIPC initiative.
3) In borderline situations, the country may defer the stock-of-debt operation and request a further flow-rescheduling under Naples terms. The country would also be assured of additional action at the end of the second three-year period.

At this point, commitments are made and countries that are deemed eligible for support under the initiative move to the second stage.

SECOND STAGE

The Paris Club and other creditors reschedule flows on more concessional terms involving an NPV reduction of up to 80 percent for eligible debt. The country must establish a further three-year track record of good performance under the adjustment programs supported by the IMF and the World Bank. Part of the exceptional assistance could be granted during this period.

Completion Point

The completion point comes at the end of the second stage. The Paris Club provides a stock-of-debt reduction of up to 80 percent in present-value terms on eligible debt. Multilateral institutions take additional measures for the country to reach a sustainable debt situation.

---

* This box describes the terms of the official HIPC initiative as of July 1999. As stated in the text, representatives of G-8 countries meeting in Cologne proposed several modifications to these terms, which were later endorsed by the boards of both the IMF and the World Bank.

debt levels, then both the Paris Club and the multilateral organizations commit themselves to grant further relief until the debtor country achieves debt sustainability.

Under the original HIPC initiative, the Paris Club creditor countries agreed to provide debt relief of up to 80 percent in net present-value (NPV) terms on a case-by-case basis. Similarly, multilateral creditors committed to reduce the present value of their claims so as to guarantee a sustainable debt level, also defined on a case-by-case basis. Generally, a sustainable debt-to-exports ratio lay in the 200 percent to 250 percent range (in present-value terms) and 20 percent to 25 percent for the debt service-to-exports ratio. Specific targets were identified for each country, depending on the concentration and variability of exports and on the fiscal burden of the debt service.

On April 24, 1997, the boards of the World Bank and the IMF agreed to modify the interpretation of the HIPC initiative for the case of highly open economies. The boards of the multilateral organizations considered that the previously specified debt-to-exports ratio (200 percent to 250 percent) might not lead to debt sustainability for very open economies. In consequence, they reduced the debt-to-exports target (in net present-value terms) below 200 percent for those economies satisfying the following criteria: first, a ratio of fiscal revenues-to-GDP above 20 percent, and second, a ratio of exports-to-GDP of at least 40 percent (hereafter, these two conditions will be referred as the fiscal-and-openness criteria). For countries satisfying both criteria, the NPV debt-to-exports target is set at a level that achieves a 280 percent ratio of the NPV debt-to-fiscal revenue at the completion point.

In June 1999, the G-8 (the G-7 plus Russia) leaders met in Cologne to discuss, among other issues, a revision of the original HIPC initiative. At the end of the meeting, the G-8 leaders issued a statement suggesting several modifications. This statement is now known as the Cologne Debt Initiative[12] and the boards of the IMF and The World Bank approved it in August 1999. The main changes to the HIPC initiative are as follows:

- The Paris Club will provide debt relief of up to 90 percent, and more in individual cases if needed (up from the 80 percent limit in the original HIPC initiative).
- Debt is now considered sustainable if the net present value of debt is lower than 150 percent of total exports of goods and services (down from a 200 percent to 250 percent range in the original HIPC initiative).
- For highly open economies, there is a new sustainability criterion and lower thresholds for the ratios of exports-to-GDP and fiscal revenues-to-GDP. Now, countries may qualify for the HIPC initiative if they have a ratio of exports-to-GDP above 30 percent (compared to 40 percent) *and* a ratio of fiscal revenues-to-GDP above 15 percent (compared to 20 percent). The new sustainability criterion is a net present value of debt below 250 percent of fiscal revenues (down from 280 percent).
- There are also several changes to the initiative's implementation timetable. The G-8 leaders suggested a considerable shortening of the second stage of the initiative. They also suggested that "the amount of debt reduction should be determined at the 'decision point'" rather than at the completion point. The G-8 leaders also suggested that "interim relief" by the International Financial Institutions should be provided before the completion point. In general, these proposals intend to provide faster debt relief to qualifying countries.

First Results of the HIPC Initiative

By April 2000, nine low-income countries had reached debt-reduction agreements with the Paris Club: Uganda (February 1995), Bolivia (December 1995), Mali (May 1996), Guyana (May 1996), Burkina Faso (June 1996), Benin (October 1996), Senegal (June 1998), and Mozambique (June 1999). All these countries were considered to have successfully completed the first stage of the HIPC initiative and had reached the decision point. In addition to this group, other countries belonging to the list of 41 potentially eligible countries that had completed a three-year track record of good policy performance on an IMF-supported program had also reached the decision point.

As of May 2000, resolutions under the HIPC initiative were reached for eleven countries. Nine countries were deemed eligible to benefit from the initiative: Uganda (April 1997), Bolivia (September 1997), Burkina Faso (September 1997), Guyana (December 1997), Cote d'Ivoire (March 1998), Mozambique (April 1998), Mali (September 1998), Mauritania (February 2000) and

---

12. See Sachs et al. (1999) for a critical evaluation of the Cologne Debt Initiative.

Tanzania (April 2000). Two countries, Benin and Senegal, were considered able to achieve sustainable debt levels through traditional debt-relief mechanisms and therefore were not eligible to benefit from the HIPC initiative.[13]

Table 8-2 summarizes the benefits obtained by each of the nine qualifying countries. It shows both decision and completion points, as well as the preliminary results of a debt sustainability analysis carried out by the World Bank in early 1997. Table 8-2 also shows that the net present value of the debt reduction granted under the enhanced HIPC Initiative (that is, in addition to the traditional debt-relief mechanisms) ranges from 6 percent in the case of Cote d'Ivoire, to 72 percent for Mozambique.

Guyana, Côte d'Ivoire, and Mauritania were the first three countries to benefit from the fiscal-and-openness criteria introduced in April 1997. This explains the low debt-to-exports target ratios set for these three countries (107, 141, and 137, respectively), which compare favorably with previous ratios established under the initiative.

Prospects of Honduras and Nicaragua to Qualify for the HIPC Initiative

Eligibility

According to the terms of the HIPC initiative, 41 countries, including both Honduras and Nicaragua, were deemed potentially eligible for benefits. Although a further restriction of the initiative was that only countries eligible for IDA (International Development Assistance) could apply to the HIPC initiative, both Honduras and Nicaragua satisfy this criterion as well.

Preliminary Debt Sustainability Analysis

A preliminary assessment carried out by the World Bank in 1997 concluded that Nicaragua's foreign-debt level was unsustainable, whereas that of Honduras was deemed to be sustainable (World Bank 1997). The latter result seems to imply that Honduras may not qualify for the HIPC initiative because its foreign debt could reach sustainable levels after a stock-of-debt operation with the Paris Club. The results of the preliminary debt-sustainability analysis, however, should not be considered definitive. For example, the preliminary analysis of Burkina Faso's debt, which has already benefited from the initiative, concluded that it was sustainable. Similarly, debt-sustainability

---

13. These countries, however, are eligible for a reassessment under the 1999 enhanced HIPC framework.

Table 8-2. *Debt Relief under the HIPC Initiative*

Country	Decision Point [1]	Completion Point [1]	Preliminary Assessment[2]	NPV Debt-to-Exports Target[1]	NPV Debt Reduction[1][3] (in percent)
Uganda	Apr. 1997	Apr. 1998	Possibly Stressed	202	20
	Feb. 2000	Apr. 2000		150	40
Bolivia	Sept. 1997	Sept. 1998	Possibly Stressed	225	13
	Feb. 2000	Floating		150	30
Burkina Faso	Sept. 1997	Apr. 2000	Sustainable	205	14
Guyana	Dec. 1997	May 1999	Possibly Stressed	107	24
Cote d'Ivoire	Mar. 1998	Mar. 2001	Possibly Stressed	141	6
Mozambique	Apr. 1998	June 1999	Unsustainable	200	63
	Apr 2000	Floating		150	72
Mali	Sept. 1998	Mar. 2000	Unsustainable	200	10
Mauritania	Feb. 2000	Floating		137	50
Tanzania	April 2000	Floating		150	54

Notes: (1) Whenever two dates are given, the first one refers to the original terms of the HIPC Initiative, and the second one to the enhanced terms of the Cologne Revision. (2) Based on a preliminary evaluation by the World Bank at the outset of the HIPC Initiative (World Bank 1997). (3) Sources: IMF/World Bank (1999) and World Bank (2000b)

analyses for three other countries that have already benefited from the initiative (Bolivia, Uganda, and Guyana) originally showed the countries to be "possibly stressed" (see Table 8-2). Therefore, while the results of a preliminary debt-sustainability analysis confirm that Nicaragua has very good prospects for qualifying for the HIPC initiative, Honduras will require an additional effort to convince the IMF and the World Bank that it needs additional debt relief from the multilateral organizations.

Comparison with Other Highly Indebted Poor Countries

In this section, the first three countries that benefited from the HIPC initiative (Uganda, Bolivia, and Burkina Faso, hereafter referred as the three HIPCs)[14] are used as a benchmark to evaluate the viability of Honduras and Nicaragua to qualify for the initiative. Some of the key indebtedness indicators for these five countries are compared. Comparisons are made using the latest available data for Honduras and Nicaragua (1997), and value averages of the 1994–96 period for the three HIPCs in order to capture their situation at the moment at which they qualified for the initiative.

---

14. We restrict ourselves to these three countries for two reasons: (i) they were the first three countries that qualified for the initiative; and (ii) limiting the number to three keeps our comparisons manageable.

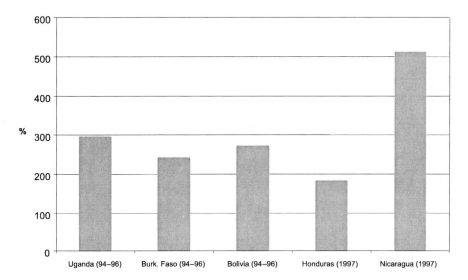

Figure 8-16. Present Value of Debt (as percentage of exports of goods and services)

Figures 8-16 and 8-17 show the ratios of NPV debt-to-exports and debt service-to-exports for the five highly indebted countries mentioned above. These figures show that Nicaragua has the highest debt and debt-service ratios among the five countries in the graph. This confirms that Nicaragua has a

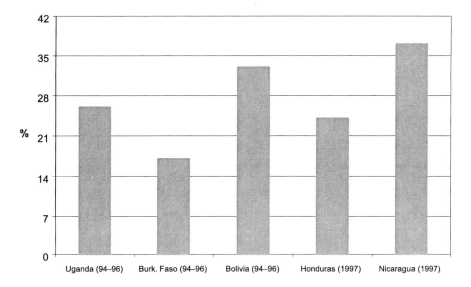

Figure 8-17. Total Debt Service (as a percentage of exports of goods and services)

very high probability of qualifying for the HIPC initiative, once it fulfills the other requirements. The results for Honduras are less definitive. Figure 8-16, for example, shows that Honduras has a ratio of NPV debt-to-exports lower than that for any of the three HIPCs. Similarly, Figure 8-17 shows that Honduras' ratio of debt service-to-exports is lower than that of Uganda and Bolivia. These graphs, however, should not lead us to conclude that Honduras' debt is more sustainable than that of the three HIPCs. Instead, a different and more definite picture emerges if we use alternative indicators of indebtedness.

Figures 8-18 and 8-19 show the ratios (in net present-value terms) of external debt-to-GNP and external debt service-to-GNP, respectively, for the same group of highly indebted poor countries. These ratios are calculated considering the debt burden with respect to the economies' income, not just on the basis of their generation of foreign exchange, as in the debt-to-exports ratios. Ultimately, it can be argued that using exports as a measure of a country's capacity to pay is misleading because export proceeds do not belong to the governments. Figures 8-18 and 8-19 clearly show that debt-to-output ratios are much higher for Honduras and Nicaragua than for any of the three HIPCs. These two graphs suggest that if the relevant debt ratios are those related to the country's capacity to generate output, and not just exports, then Honduras is in a much more vulnerable and difficult situation than some of the countries that have already qualified for the HIPC initiative.

The debt problem in Honduras and Nicaragua is all the more difficult be-

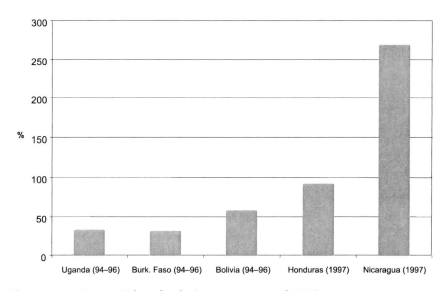

Figure 8-18. Present Value of Debt (as a percentage of GNP)

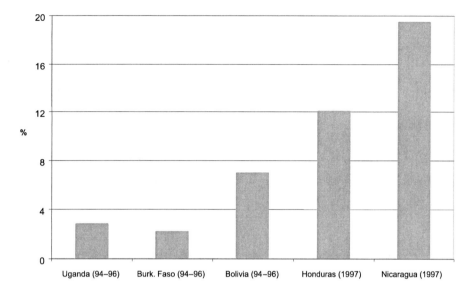

Figure 8-19.   Total Debt Service (as a percentage of GNP)

cause foreign debt service in these countries involves a substantial drain of re-sources from the public sector. This fact is shown in Figure 8-20, which plots the public-sector debt service *due* in 1996 as a percentage of total government expenditures. The difference in this indicator between Honduras and Nicara-gua, and the first three beneficiaries of the HIPC initiative (Bolivia, Burkina Faso, and Uganda) is striking. While service due on the public-sector external debt of the latter countries was equivalent to around 15 percent of their gov-ernment expenditures in 1996, the corresponding figures for Honduras and Nicaragua were close to 60 percent and 100 percent, respectively. Not surpris-ingly, the latter countries have been unable to service all their external obliga-tions in the last several years.

Figure 8-20 also reveals an issue that has been widely discussed in the liter-ature on debt and solvency—namely, that the standard criteria applied to de-cide whether or not a country is solvent are not necessarily correct. There are situations in which the governments themselves are insolvent.[15] In cases like this, the external-debt problem of some countries should be viewed from a fiscal perspective. When discussing the sustainability of Honduras' and Nica-ragua's foreign debts, this is certainly the right approach.

---

15. See Agenor and Montiel (1996) for a summary of the different approaches to the debt problem.

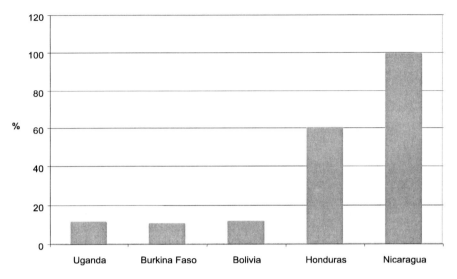

Figure 8-20.   Public-Sector External Service Due in 1996 (as a percentage of government expenditure)
Source: Boote and Thugge (1999).

Why are such radically different conclusions about Honduras' debt sustainability obtained when using alternative indebtedness indicators? In part, the answer lies in Honduras' level of exports. Honduras is a small open economy with a relatively high ratio of exports-to-GNP. In particular, it is a much more open economy than the three HIPCs used above as a benchmark. In consequence, Honduras has a higher foreign exchange-generating capacity and, by this standard alone, it is deemed to have a more sustainable debt level than other economies, despite the fact that it has a much higher debt burden relative to its total income-generating capacity. A similar argument applies to Nicaragua: it can also be considered a highly open economy and is therefore subject to the same bias as Honduras.

Thus, it seems crucial for both Honduras and Nicaragua to qualify for the HIPC initiative under the special treatment given to highly open economies. As mentioned earlier, the IMF and the World Bank agreed to special targets for economies that satisfy the openness-and-fiscal criteria at the decision point. However, before analyzing the usefulness of this alternative for these two countries, let us look in more detail at some of the implications of these criteria.

The Fiscal-and-Openness Criteria

One of the most recent modifications to the HIPC initiative is the introduction of fiscal-and-openness criteria to determine alternative levels of debt sustainability. This modification is relevant here because Honduras and Nicaragua seem to satisfy both criteria; in consequence, they may obtain additional benefits if they qualify for the HIPC initiative under these modified terms.[16] As shown below, this modification fails to correctly address the debt-sustainability concerns of highly indebted open economies. Furthermore, the strict application of the criteria creates a moral hazard problem in terms of the fiscal effort undertaken by potentially qualifying countries. It is therefore clear that if the HIPC initiative aims to provide substantial debt relief to these countries, then the fiscal-and-openness criteria should be modified accordingly.

As mentioned above, the fiscal-and-openness criteria were introduced in response to growing concerns about the debt sustainability of highly open economies. The basic idea underlying this change was that establishing sustainability thresholds based on debt-to-exports ratios could seriously overestimate the paying capacity of very open economies. These economies could therefore end up with relatively high debt-to-GDP ratios in spite of having a "sustainable" debt-to-exports ratio. On the other hand, the fiscal criterion was introduced "to avoid moral hazard" problems in fiscal revenue collection and to ensure that potentially qualifying countries had a good record of fiscal performance (International Monetary Fund/World Bank 1999). To eliminate the problem of using a debt-to-exports target, this modification establishes that the targeted net present value of debt would be the lower of 250 percent of fiscal revenues or 150 percent of exports.

To analyze the debt-alleviation implications of the fiscal-and-openness criteria, it may be convenient to translate them into easily comparable measures of the debt burden. Thus, we obtain estimates of the debt-to-exports and debt-to-output ratios implicit in different combinations of the fiscal-and-openness criteria. The implicit debt ratios are obtained as follows. Let us define D as the net present value of total external debt, X as total exports of goods and services, T as fiscal revenues, and Y as output. The Cologne fiscal-and-openness criteria require a share of exports in total output (X/Y) higher than 0.3 and a ratio of fiscal revenues-to-output (T/Y) higher than 0.15. Now, consider the following identity:

---

16. As discussed in the working paper upon which this chapter is based, Honduras was in a borderline situation under the original terms of the highly open economy status (Esquivel, Larraín, and Sachs 1998). As a result of the modifications suggested in the Cologne Debt Initiative, it is clear now that Honduras satisfies both criteria.

$$\frac{D}{X} \equiv \frac{D}{T} \cdot \frac{T}{Y} \cdot \frac{Y}{X}$$

where D/X is the debt-to-exports ratio (in net present-value terms) and D/T is the debt-to-fiscal revenues ratio. For qualifying countries, the modification to the HIPC initiative sets a D/T ratio of 250 percent. Therefore, the implicit debt-to-exports ratio for qualifying countries is given by

$$\left(\frac{\hat{D}}{X}\right) = 2.5 \cdot \frac{T/Y}{X/Y}$$

The implicit debt-to-output ratio is given by

$$\left(\frac{\hat{D}}{Y}\right) = \frac{D}{T} \cdot \frac{T}{Y} = 2.5 \cdot \frac{T}{Y}$$

Therefore, we can obtain the two implicit debt ratios simply by using different combinations of the fiscal-and-openness criteria. Table 8-3 shows the debt ratios that are compatible with alternative values of the fiscal-and-openness criteria.[17] This table presents several interesting results. For example, it shows that the introduction of the fiscal-and-openness criteria imply that an economy that exactly matches both criteria will be set to target (in net present-value terms) debt-to-output ratios and debt-to-exports ratios of 37.5 and 125, respectively, at the completion point. The latter represents an additional 20 percent debt reduction over the most advantageous agreement possible that could have been obtained under the original terms of the HIPC initiative (a debt-to-exports ratio of 150).

Also, as expected, Table 8-3 shows that the implicit debt-to-exports ratio decreases with the level of openness, whereas the implicit debt-to-output ratio does not depend on the share of exports on total output. Interestingly, both debt ratios increase with the level of fiscal effort. In fact, there are some combinations of fiscal effort and openness that do not render any additional benefit in terms of debt reduction when compared to the standard classification of debt sustainability. The shaded area in Table 8-3 shows the combinations of debt and fiscal ratios that would lead to an implicit debt-to-exports ratio above 150 percent. Since this is exactly the debt-to-exports target under the standard version of the HIPC initiative, these fiscal-and-openness combinations do not lead to any further debt relief.

This result clearly contradicts the spirit of the modification to the HIPC initiative. It shows that a simple application of the new fiscal-and-openness criteria tends to penalize those economies that are currently making a sub-

---

17. The working paper upon which this chapter is based shows the equivalent to Table 8-3 using the original fiscal-and-openness threshold values (20 percent and 40 percent) and a debt-to-fiscal revenues target of 280 percent (see Esquivel, Larraín, and Sachs 1998).

Table 8-3. Implicit Debt Ratios for Highly Open Economies under the HIPC

Tax Revenues-To-Output Ratio	**Implicit Debt-to-Exports Ratio** Exports-to-Output Ratio											**Implicit Debt-to-Output Ratio**
	30	32	34	36	38	40	42	43	45	47	49	
15	125	117	110	104	99	94	89	87	83	80	77	37.5
17	142	133	125	118	112	106	101	99	94	90	87	42.5
19	158	148	140	132	125	119	113	110	106	101	97	47.5
21	175	164	154	146	138	131	125	122	117	112	107	52.5
23	192	180	169	160	151	144	137	134	128	122	117	57.5
25	208	195	184	174	164	156	149	145	139	133	128	62.5
27	225	211	199	188	178	169	161	157	150	144	138	67.5
29	242	227	213	201	191	181	173	169	161	154	148	72.5
31	258	242	228	215	204	194	185	180	172	165	158	77.5
33	275	258	243	229	217	206	196	192	183	176	168	82.5
35	292	273	257	243	230	219	208	203	194	186	179	87.5

Note: Shaded area indicates combinations that do not yield extra benefits under the highly open economy status.

stantial fiscal effort by imposing relatively large debt ratios on them. In other words, there is an obvious moral hazard problem in revenue collection, since some countries would obtain a much larger debt reduction if they had a ratio of fiscal revenues-to-output just slightly above the required threshold.

A numerical example illustrates the inequity of applying the new criteria. Consider two highly indebted and very open economies, each with a 40 percent share of exports on total output. Now, let us assume that country A has implemented and enforced a structural fiscal reform that allows the government to collect taxes equivalent to 31 percent of total output. Country B has just made minor improvements to its fiscal policy, so that these changes have led to fiscal revenues equivalent to 15 percent of total output. Applying the sustainability criterion of the HIPC initiative for open economies, foreign debt for these countries would be considered sustainable at a debt-to-exports ratio of 150 and 94 for country A and B, respectively.[18] Thus, whereas the high fiscal-effort country does not receive additional benefits from the initiative, the low fiscal-effort country receives an extra 30 percent reduction in its total external debt compared to what it would have received under the standard sustainability criterion. In terms of the ratio of debt-to-output, country A would end up with a ratio of 60, while country B's ratio would be only 37.5. That is, country B would be saving 22.5 percent of its total output by not incurring a high fiscal effort!

Now compare the results just described with those that would be obtained by a highly indebted but relatively closed economy, with fiscal revenues and exports that represent only 10 percent of its total output. By assumption, this economy satisfies none of the fiscal-and-openness criteria. In consequence, it would not qualify to receive "additional" benefits from the HIPC initiative. If this country were to receive the standard HIPC treatment, its external debt would be set at a ratio of debt-to-exports of 150 percent. It is easy to see that this debt target implies a debt-to-output ratio of 15 percent, which is much lower than the 37.5 ratio that would have been obtained in the best scenario by an economy that satisfies the fiscal-and-openness criteria!

In terms of the debt-to-fiscal revenues ratio, our hypothetical closed economy would end up with a 150 percent ratio, which is also much lower than the 250 percent ratio that applies for open economies with a relatively high fiscal effort. Therefore, our simple numerical example sheds light on the fact that as the fiscal-and-openness criteria stand right now, they tend to provide the wrong incentives. Furthermore, these criteria still discriminate against very open economies as compared with relatively closed economies.

---

18. Note that the assumed combination of values for country A lie on the shaded area of Table 8-2, and therefore the standard sustainability criterion was used.

Alternative Debt-Reduction Scenarios for Honduras and Nicaragua

The net present value of debt-to-export ratios for Honduras and Nicaragua at the end of 1997 was 181 percent and 510 percent, respectively (see Table 8-1). IMF preliminary estimates show that the net present value of debt-to-exports ratios at the completion point, after having taken full advantage of traditional debt-relief mechanisms, would be 158 for Honduras and 447 for Nicaragua (IMF/World Bank 1999). These ratios imply a debt reduction of around 13 percent for each country.

However, because the debt-to-exports ratios would still exceed the 150 percent ratio considered as sustainable by the HIPC initiative, both countries would qualify to receive additional debt relief through the initiative. Thus, under the standard terms of the initiative, Honduras would receive an additional 5 percent of debt relief whereas Nicaragua would be entitled to receive an extra 66 percent debt reduction. These additional debt cancellations would bring the debt-to-exports ratios of these countries to the 150 percent level considered to be sustainable by the initiative. However, IMF/World Bank estimates show that both Honduras and Nicaragua satisfy the fiscal-and-openness criteria established in the mid-1999 modification of the HIPC initiative. More specifically, Honduras' exports and fiscal revenues represent 47 percent and 18 percent of its total output, respectively. The corresponding ratios for Nicaragua are 43 and 25. Therefore, these countries could be entitled to receive additional debt relief based on the fiscal-and-openness criteria.

Using the exports and fiscal revenue ratios for Honduras mentioned above, together with the results in Table 8-3, we obtain a debt-to-exports target of 96 percent for this country. Nicaragua, on the other hand, would be set a 145 percent debt-to-exports ratio. Hence, the highly open economy status would represent an additional 36 percent and 3 percent debt reduction for Honduras and Nicaragua, respectively, as compared with the standard application of the HIPC initiative. The small amount of the debt relief that Nicaragua would obtain in these circumstances calls into question the usefulness of the new fiscal-and-openness criteria, since they tend to penalize countries that are undertaking substantial fiscal efforts to comply with their external obligations. To see this more clearly, note that the debt-to-output ratios that would be set for Honduras and Nicaragua would be 45 percent and 62 percent, respectively. These ratios compare very unfavorably with the hypothetical example of a highly indebted closed economy discussed above—which ends with a 15 percent debt-to-output ratio.

As another possible scenario, consider what would happen if both Honduras and Nicaragua choose to reduce their fiscal-revenues collection to exactly 15 percent of their total output. This is the lowest fiscal-revenue level that would still allow them to qualify to the HIPC initiative with a highly open economy status. In this scenario, Honduras would have a debt-to-exports target of 80 percent, whereas Nicaragua would be set an 87 percent debt-to-exports ratio. These ratios represent a 17 percent and 40 percent additional debt reduction for Honduras and Nicaragua, respectively, as compared to what they would receive if they had opted to keep their current level of fiscal effort unchanged.

Table 8-4 summarizes the alternative scenarios and shows the total debt reduction that would be achieved under each scenario. For example, we can see that Honduras could get a 56 percent reduction in its best-case scenario. Nicaragua, on the other hand, would receive up to 83 percent of total debt cancellation in its most advantageous situation. A strict application of the current terms of the HIPC initiative, however, would imply a debt cancellation of 47 percent and 72 percent for Honduras and Nicaragua, respectively.

This example clearly illustrates the moral hazard problems implicit in the current definition of the fiscal-and-openness criteria. Right now, eligible countries are penalized for any additional fiscal revenue effort beyond the "bliss point" of 15 percent of total output. This result contradicts the spirit of the criteria and must be modified in the near future.

Good Record of Macroeconomic Performance

According to the terms of the HIPC initiative, qualifying countries must acquire three years of satisfactory macroeconomic performance under the supervision of the IMF before they may actually become eligible to benefit from the initiative. Let us quickly review the stance of Honduras and Nicaragua in this regard.

Honduras

This country signed letters of intent with the IMF in 1992 and 1995. In both cases, however, Honduras failed to meet some of the specified targets, and the IMF regarded Honduras as "off track" in 1993 and 1996. In early 1997, Honduras agreed to follow a program monitored by the staff of the IMF and established new macroeconomic targets. During 1997, Honduras made significant efforts to comply with the new program and also made several attempts to sign a third letter of intent with the IMF. Despite progress shown in the monitored program, Honduras was unable to fulfill the last part of the agreement with the IMF.

In early 1998, a new government took office in Honduras and immediately attempted to reach an agreement with the IMF. In October of that year, how-

Table 8-4. Alternative Scenarios of Debt Reduction for Honduras and Nicaragua

	Honduras			Nicaragua		
	NPV of debt-to-exports ratio	Percentage in NPV Debt Reduction		NPV of debt-to-exports ratio	Percentage in NPV Debt Reduction	
		w/respect to previous scenario	w/ respect to initial debt level		w/respect to previous scenario	w/ respect to initial debt level
Initial situation (end of 1997)	181			510		
Situation after having taken full advantage of traditional debt relief mechanisms	158	12.7	12.7	447	12.4	12.4
Situation after standard HIPC initiative treatment	150	5.1	17.1	150	66.4	70.6
Situation under highly open economy status (assuming unchanged values at decision point)	96	36.0	47.0	145	3.3	71.6
Situation under highly open economy status (assuming a 15 percent fiscal revenues-to-output ratio)	80	16.7	55.8	86	40.7	83.1

ever, Hurricane Mitch hit Honduras (as well as other parts of Central America The magnitude of the damage made the provision of food, medicine, and shelter for the thousands of homeless and displaced persons a national priority. As part of the recovery efforts, Honduras and the IMF signed an initial letter of intent in November 1998. This initial agreement was later ratified and extended in March 1999, when the IMF approved a three-year Enhanced Stability Adjustment Facility (ESAF) arrangement with the government of Honduras. If Honduras meets the first-year targets of the new ESAF agreement, it can then make a case for a substantial reduction in its probation period. If this is the case, Honduras may receive a considerable shortening of the period needed to reach the decision point under the HIPC initiative. In fact, Honduras may reach this point by the end of the year 2000.

Nicaragua

Throughout the 1990s, Nicaragua made an extensive set of structural macroeconomic reforms. Trade- and exchange-rate systems were liberalized, inflation was brought under control, and an incipient process of privatization began. Most of these reforms were carried out under the supervision of the IMF—a Stand-By arrangement in 1991–92 and an Enhanced Structural Adjustment Facility arrangement (ESAF) in 1994–97. In general, Nicaragua complied with both arrangements at least until mid-1995. During 1996 and 1997, Nicaragua had several problems in fulfilling the objectives of the ESAF arrangement.

In March 1998, Nicaragua signed a second ESAF Program with the IMF. Later in that year, Hurricane Mitch hit Central America and the Paris Club granted Nicaragua a debt-service moratorium until February 2001. As per the agreement reached with the IMF, it seems clear that it will take Nicaragua at most two years of compliance with the ESAF before obtaining access to a stock-of-debt reduction agreement with the Paris Club (Gobierno de Nicaragua 1998a and 1998b). Therefore, Nicaragua could reach the decision point by the end of the year 2000. If this occurs, the completion point could be reached as early as 2001. Otherwise, Nicaragua's completion point could be delayed until 2002 or 2003. The latter schedule is not recommended because any delay in the reduction of Nicaragua's debt could endanger many of the structural reforms that have been implemented in the last decade. Furthermore, the relatively good economic performance of Nicaragua in the last years (modest economic growth together with low inflation rates and relative macroeconomic stability) suggests that it should receive partial credit for some of the previous years of sound economic management.

CONCLUSIONS

Honduras and Nicaragua have a serious debt overhang. Several indicators suggest that foreign debt has reached an excessive level and has become a serious impediment to economic growth in both nations. Honduras and Nicaragua, the poorest countries of Central America, have lagged behind the rest of the region, leading to an increase in regional inequality during the 1990s. for these reasons, both Honduras and Nicaragua require alleviation of their foreign debt as a prerequisite for sustained growth. If the burden of the debt remains at current levels, it is unlikely that these countries will be able to grow at the rates necessary to increase the standards of living of their populations in the next decades (6 percent per year at a minimum). Success in achieving deep debt reduction hinges on a set of macroeconomic criteria, a solid record of macroeconomic reforms, and the credibility of the indebted country's government.

Honduras and Nicaragua have favorable prospects of qualifying for the multilateral initiative aimed at assisting highly indebted poor countries (the HIPC initiative). In general, both countries meet most of the eligibility criteria; and in a comparison with three countries that have already qualified for HIPC treatment, it is clear that Honduras and Nicaragua face a higher foreign-debt burden. The main obstacle for both countries is demonstration of a successful macroeconomic performance under the supervision of the IMF.

In addition to fulfilling the good macroeconomic performance requirement, Nicaragua should negotiate a shorter period of evaluation (possibly one year instead of the usual three years) on the basis that it has implemented a consistent structural-reform policy since 1990. Such special treatment is allowed by the HIPC initiative and has already been granted to Uganda and Guyana. Nicaragua should also attempt to qualify for the HIPC initiative with a highly open economy status, but should forcefully make the case that it should not be punished because it has been fiscally responsible. In fact, as a matter of fairness, Nicaragua should have an NPV debt-to-exports target similar to the one that would be set if it only had a ratio of fiscal revenues-to-output of 15 percent. That is, Nicaragua's foreign debt should be reduced by as much as 83 percent.

On the other hand, Honduras should comply with its agreement with the IMF and make a strong economic case to prove that its foreign debt level is clearly unsustainable. It is very important for Honduras to put special emphasis on the fact that the right approach is to analyze the burden of its external debt from a fiscal perspective. It is clear that servicing the external debt imposes a tremendous pressure on its public finances and severely limits resources available for social expenditure.

Finally, we believe that it is necessary to consider the debt burden of the poorest countries from a truly fiscal perspective. As shown in this paper, the fiscal-and-openness criteria recently introduced in the HIPC initiative do not grant additional benefits to countries that have made substantial efforts to increase their fiscal revenues as a share of GDP. Instead, such criteria discriminate against countries with relatively high fiscal revenues by setting higher debt-to-exports targets than if they had moderate fiscal revenues. Therefore, it is necessary to reformulate the HIPC initiative in such a way as to guarantee greater benefits for those countries that are making serious fiscal efforts and for which the fiscal burden of the debt has reached unsustainable levels. Both Honduras and Nicaragua undoubtedly fit into this category.

References

Agenor, P., and P. Montiel. 1996. *Development Macroeconomics*. Princeton, NJ: Princeton University Press.

Banco Central de Nicaragua. 1997. *Informe Annual, 1996*. Managua, Nicaragua: Banco Central de Nicaragua.

Boote, Anthony R., and K. Thugge. 1999. *Debt Relief for Low-Income Countries and the HIPC Initiative*. Pamphlet No. 51, revised version. Washington, D.C.: International Monetary Fund.

Esquivel, G., F. Larraín and J. D. Sachs. 1998. "The External Debt Problem in Central America: Honduras, Nicaragua and the HIPC Initiative." *HIID Development Discussion Paper 645*. Central America Project Series (August). Cambridge, MA: Harvard Institute for International Development.

Gobierno de Nicaragua. 1998a. "Carta de Intención y Memorandum de Políticas Económicas sometidos al Fondo Monetario Internacional bajo el Servicio Reforzado de Ajuste Estructural ESAF." Gobierno de Nicaragua. Mimeographed (January).

———. 1998b. "Aspectos Fundamentales de la Política Económica: Programa de Saneamiento y Crecimiento Económico." Gobierno de Nicaragua. Mimeographed (January).

Inter-American Development Bank. 1996. "Making Social Services Work." In *Economic and Social Progress in Latin America Report*. Washington D.C.: Inter-American Development Bank.

———. 1997. "Latin America after a Decade of Reforms." In *Economic and Social Progress in Latin America Report*. Washington D.C.: Inter-American Development Bank.

International Monetary Fund/World Bank. 1999. "Modifications to the Heavily Indebted Poor Countries (HIPC) Initiative." Prepared by the staffs of the IMF and World Bank, July 23. *http://www.imf.org/external/np/hipc/modify/hipc.htm.*

Jenkins, M., G. Esquivel, and F. Larraín. 2000. "Export Processing Zones in Central America." Chapter 7 in this volume.

Krugman, P. 1988. "Financing vs. Forgiving a Debt Overhang." *Journal of Development Economics* 29: 253–68.

Larraín, F., L. F. López-Calva and A. Rodríguez. 2000. "Intel: A Case Study of Foreign Direct Investment in Central America." Chapter 6 in this volume.

Ministerio de Cooperación Externa. 1997. *Historia de la Deuda Externa de Nicaragua, 1990–96.* Managua, Nicaragua: Ministerio de Cooperación Externa.

Ocampo, J.A.. 1991. "Collapse and (Incomplete) Stabilization of the Nicaraguan Economy." In *The Macroeconomics of Populism in Latin America,* edited by Rudiger Dornbusch and Sebastian Edwards. Chicago and London: University of Chicago Press.

Sachs, J. D. 1989a. "The Debt Overhang of Developing Countries." In *Debt, Stabilization, and Development,* edited by G. Calvo, R. Findlay, P. Kouri, and J. Braga de Macedo. Oxford: Basil Blackwell.

———. 1989b. "Conditionality, Debt Relief, and the Developing Country Debt Crisis." In *Developing Country Debt and the World Economy,* edited by J. Sachs. Chicago, IL: University of Chicago Press/National Bureau of Economic Research.

Sachs, J. D., K. Botchwey, M. Cuchra, and S. Sievers. 1999. "Implementing Debt Relief for the HIPCs." *Policy Paper No. 2* (August). Cambridge, MA: Center for International Development.

World Bank. 1997. *Global Development Finance Report, 1997.* Washington, D.C.: World Bank.

———. 1999a. *Global Development Finance Report, 1999.* Washington, D.C.: World Bank.

———. 1999b. *World Development Indicators, 1999.* Washington, D.C.: World Bank.

Table A-1. Honduras: External-Debt Stocks

(US$ millions)	1970	1980	1988	1989	1990	1991	1992	1993	1994	1995	1966
Total external debt stocks	—	**1,473**	**3,308**	**3,386**	**3,724**	**3,396**	**3,614**	**4,077**	**4,436**	**4,570**	**4,453**
Long-term	111	1,168	2,859	2,951	3,492	3,171	3,322	3,740	4,002	4,096	3,981
Public and publicly guaranteed	91	976	2,758	2,867	3,426	3,096	3,232	3,651	3,902	3,982	3,855
Official creditors	88	697	2,269	2,403	2,982	2,746	2,965	3,259	3,533	3,618	3,529
Multilateral	63	459	1,361	1,484	1,581	1,658	1,801	1,952	2,062	2,163	2,118
Bilateral	24	238	908	919	1,401	1,089	1,163	1,307	1,470	1,455	1,411
Private creditors	4	280	489	464	443	349	267	392	369	365	327
Memo: Concessional debt	54	321	1,168	1,199	1,393	1,102	1,356	1,611	1,868	2,013	2,194
Memo: Nonconcessional debt	37	655	1,590	1,668	2,033	1,994	1,876	2,040	2,034	1,969	1,661
Private nonguaranteed debt	19	191	101	84	66	75	90	88	100	114	126
Short-term debt	—	272	412	400	199	192	180	219	325	375	414
of which interest arrears	—	0	137	172	89	75	55	92	68	56	55
Use of IMF credit	0	33	37	35	32	34	55	118	109	99	58
Memo: principal arrears	—	3	341	354	190	138	109	167	150	142	130

Table A-2. Honduras: Change in Debt Stocks

(US$ millions)	1970	1980	1988	1989	1990	1991	1992	1993	1994	1995	1996
Total change in debt stocks	—	**287**	**9**	**78**	**338**	**(328)**	**218**	**463**	**360**	**133**	**(117)**
Net flows on debt	—	287	73	81	133	134	294	375	228	105	24
Net change in interest arrears	—	(0)	24	35	(83)	(14)	(20)	37	(24)	(12)	(1)
Interest rescheduled	—	0	0	10	140	23	34	32	14	8	21
Net interest capitalized	—	(0)	24	45	57	9	14	69	(10)	(4)	20
Debt forgiveness or reduction	—	0	(10)	(57)	(51)	(490)	(29)	(3)	(20)	(10)	(2)
Cross-currency valuation	—	0	0	(37)	91	8	(63)	14	113	30	(122)
Residual	—	1	(103)	46	108	12	2	8	49	12	(38)

Table A-3. Honduras: Debt Service

(US$ millions)	1970	1980	1988	1989	1990	1991	1992	1993	1994	1995	1996
Total debt service	—	**208**	**369**	**142**	**389**	**307**	**377**	**361**	**433**	**553**	**564**
Principal repayments	6	87	211	70	211	147	203	210	254	336	391
Interest payments	—	120	158	72	178	160	174	151	178	217	173

Table A-4. *Honduras: Net Flows on Debt*

(US$ millions)	1970	1980	1988	1989	1990	1991	1992	1993	1994	1995	1996
Net flows on debt	**39**	**287**	**73**	**81**	**133**	**134**	**294**	**375**	**228**	**105**	**24**
Long-term debt	32	258	135	129	256	126	205	367	114	56	23
Public and publicly guaranteed	26	225	143	117	274	117	189	369	102	42	10
Official creditors	27	128	147	83	223	121	221	218	101	41	33
Multilateral	20	92	63	43	53	58	171	151	37	60	20
Bilateral	7	35	84	41	170	63	50	67	64	(19)	13
Private creditors	(1)	97	(4)	34	50	(4)	(32)	151	2	2	(23)
Bonds	0	0	0	0	0	0	0	152	0	(13)	(13)
Commercial banks	0	45	(4)	3	19	(6)	(25)	2	(9)	20	(2)
Other	(1)	52	0	32	32	2	(7)	(3)	11	(4)	(8)
Private nonguaranteed	7	33	(9)	12	(18)	9	15	(2)	12	14	13
Bonds	0	0	0	0	0	0	0	0	0	0	0
Commercial banks	7	33	(9)	12	(18)	9	15	(2)	12	14	13
Short-term	—	—	(25)	(48)	(117)	7	8	2	130	62	39
IMF	6	29	(36)	(0)	(6)	1	81	7	(16)	(13)	(38)

Table A-5. *Honduras: Net Transfer on Debt*

(US$ millions)	1970	1980	1988	1989	1990	1991	1992	1993	1994	1995	1996
Disbursements	45	374	309	199	461	274	489	584	352	379	375
plus:											
net short-term inflows	—	—	(25)	(48)	(117)	7	8	2	130	62	39
minus:											
principal repayments	6	87	211	70	211	147	203	210	254	336	391
Net flows on debt	39	287	73	81	133	134	294	375	228	105	24
minus:											
interest payments	—	120	158	72	178	160	174	151	178	217	173
Net transfers on debt	—	**167**	**(85)**	**9**	**(45)**	**(26)**	**120**	**225**	**50**	**(112)**	**(150)**

Table A-6. *Honduras: Debt Rescheduled*

(US$ millions)	1970	1980	1988	1989	1990	1991	1992	1993	1994	1995	1996
Total debt rescheduled	**0**	**0**	**0**	**101**	**310**	**88**	**133**	**83**	**45**	**25**	**66**
Principal	0	0	0	13	153	64	99	50	29	17	45
Interest	0	0	0	10	140	23	34	32	14	8	21
Debt forgiven	—	—	0	0	10	442	8	3	20	10	2
Memo: interest forgiven	—	—	0	6	11	0	2	1	0	0	2
Debt stock reduction	0	0	10	57	41	48	20	0	0	0	0
of which debt buyback	0	0	0	0	0	0	0	0	0	0	0

Table A-7. *Nicaragua: External-Debt Stocks*

(US$ millions)	1970	1980	1988	1989	1990	1991	1992	1993	1994	1995	1996
Total external debt stocks	—	**2,189**	**8,741**	**9,650**	**10,707**	**10,912**	**11,177**	**11,408**	**12,103**	**10,359**	**5,929**
Long-term	147	1,668	7,020	7,589	8,280	9,153	9,311	9,440	9,761	8,541	5,122
Public and publicly guaranteed	147	1,668	7,020	7,589	8,280	9,153	9,311	9,440	9,761	8,541	5,122
Official creditors	101	863	5,616	6,080	6,735	7,032	7,218	7,362	7,682	7,531	4,665
Multilateral	48	421	918	882	930	942	1,077	1,112	1,317	1,457	1,551
Bilateral	53	442	4,698	5,198	5,805	6,091	6,141	6,250	6,365	6,074	3,115
Private creditors	45	805	1,404	1,509	1,545	2,120	2,093	2,078	2,079	1,010	457
Memo: Concessional debt	60	468	2,487	2,866	3,270	3,552	3,689	3,708	3,924	3,856	2,152
Memo: Nonconcessional debt	87	1,200	4,533	4,723	5,010	5,601	5,622	5,732	5,837	4,685	2,970
Private nonguaranteed debt	0	0	0	0	0	0	0	0	0	0	0
Short-term debt	0	472	1,721	2,061	2,427	1,735	1,843	1,945	2,292	1,779	77
of which interest arrears	0	12	1,056	1,343	1,688	1,301	1,427	1,582	1,996	1,469	47
Use of IMF credit	8	49	0	0	0	24	23	23	51	39	2
Memo: principal arrears	0	32	1,393	1,874	2,452	2,635	3,186	3,527	4,337	3,212	97

Table A-8. *Nicaragua: Change in Debt Stocks*

(US$ millions)	1970	1980	1988	1989	1990	1991	1992	1993	1994	1995	1996
Total change in debt stocks	—	**655**	**765**	**997**	**1,057**	**205**	**266**	**231**	**695**	**(1,745)**	**(4,430)**
Net flows on debt	—	230	438	636	593	(140)	223	(16)	198	88	85
Net change in interest arrears	—	—	0	305	345	(387)	126	155	413	(526)	(995)
Interest rescheduled	—	—	178	54	30	470	33	28	3	94	203
Net interest capitalized	—	—	178	359	375	83	159	183	416	(432)	(792)
Debt forgiveness or reduction	—	—	0	0	0	(228)	(6)	(1)	(16)	(1,641)	(3,088)
Cross-currency valuation	—	—	0	6	107	(44)	(90)	(71)	77	79	(92)
Residual	—	425	(29)	(3)	(18)	534	(20)	136	20	161	(543)

Table A-9. *Nicaragua: Debt Service*

(US$ millions)	1970	1980	1988	1989	1990	1991	1992	1993	1994	1995	1996
Total debt service	—	**115**	**20**	**11**	**16**	**530**	**104**	**134**	**207**	**288**	**221**
Principal repayments	30	46	9	7	4	329	42	65	103	203	134
Interest payments	—	69	12	5	11	201	65	69	104	86	88

Table A-10. *Nicaragua: Net Flows on Debt*

(US$ millions)	1970	1980	1988	1989	1990	1991	1992	1993	1994	1995	1996
Net flows on debt	**24**	**230**	**438**	**636**	**593**	**(140)**	**223**	**(16)**	**198**	**88**	**85**
Long-term debt	28	231	418	583	572	(19)	241	37	239	87	101
Public and publicly guaranteed	28	231	418	583	572	(19)	241	37	239	87	101
Official creditors	28	257	416	572	552	(16)	243	42	245	169	105
Multilateral	9	76	9	4	6	(2)	130	32	180	130	99
Bilateral	20	181	406	569	546	(14)	113	10	65	39	6
Private creditors	(1)	(26)	3	11	21	(3)	(2)	(5)	(6)	(81)	(4)
Bonds	0	0	0	0	0	0	0	0	0	0	(8)
Commercial banks	1	(20)	3	(1)	0	0	2	1	0	(77)	9
Other	(2)	(6)	0	12	21	(3)	(4)	(5)	(7)	(4)	(4)
Private nonguaranteed	0	0	0	0	0	0	0	0	0	0	0
Bonds	0	0	0	0	0	0	0	0	0	0	0
Commercial banks	0	0	0	0	0	0	0	0	0	0	0
Short-term	—	—	20	53	21	(144)	(18)	(53)	(67)	14	(7)
IMF	(3)	(1)	0	0	0	23	0	0	26	(13)	(9)

Table A-11. *Nicaragua: Net Transfer on Debt*

(US$ millions)	1970	1980	1988	1989	1990	1991	1992	1993	1994	1995	1996
Disbursements	54	276	427	590	577	332	283	102	368	277	226
plus:											
net short-term inflows	—	—	20	53	21	(144)	(18)	(53)	(67)	14	(7)
minus:											
principal repayments	30	46	9	7	4	329	42	65	103	203	134
Net flows on debt	24	230	438	636	593	(140)	223	(16)	198	88	85
minus:											
interest payments	—	69	12	5	11	201	65	69	104	86	88
Net transfers on debt	—	**161**	**427**	**632**	**582**	**(341)**	**158**	**(85)**	**94**	**3**	**(2)**

Table A-12. *Nicaragua: Debt Rescheduled*

(US$ millions)	1970	1980	1988	1989	1990	1991	1992	1993	1994	1995	1996
Total debt rescheduled	**0**	—	**500**	**54**	**30**	**2,065**	**73**	**55**	**6**	**263**	**761**
Principal	0	—	121	0	0	474	53	62	4	249	303
Interest	0	—	178	54	30	470	33	28	3	94	203
Debt forgiven	—	—	0	0	0	228	6	1	7	530	23
Memo: interest forgiven	—	—	0	0	0	205	1	0	0	762	923
Debt stock reduction	0	—	0	0	0	159	0	0	9	1,200	3,065
of which debt buyback	0	—	0	0	0	159	0	0	0	89	0

9

Exchange Rate Regimes: Assessing Central America's Options

CRISTINA GARCÍA-LÓPEZ, FELIPE LARRAÍN B., AND
JOSÉ TAVARES

The creation of the European Monetary Union in 1999 and the recent currency crises in East Asia, Russia, and Brazil have focused attention anew on the operations of exchange rate arrangements within the international monetary system. Throughout most of the twentieth century, Central America lived under monetary arrangements characterized by their stability—namely, nominal exchange rates fixed to the U.S. dollar. This scenario was abruptly interrupted in the 1980s as countries in the region successively abandoned the dollar peg. Given the small size of the Central American economies, their high degree of openness to international trade, and the fragility of their financial systems, the choice of an exchange rate regime is clearly an important decision for the countries of the region. Some analysts have argued for dollarization in Central America.[1] Several other observers have strongly advocated dollarization as an option for Argentina and other countries in Latin America.[2]

An alternative policy option would be the adoption of a common currency in Central America. This possibility was originally raised in Young (1965) and Triffin (1968), the first of which sketched a program for regional monetary unification. On the other hand, Kafka (1973) argued against a currency area in the region, given the poor development of financial institutions and the

---

1. IMF Survey (1999) summarizes Frankel's position in a recent debate on dollarization held at the IMF, where he suggested that dollarization probably is a good idea for some countries in Latin America, especially those that are quite small and open like Central America.

2. Within this, the term LatinAmerica excludes Central America.

need to further stabilize fiscal policy.[3] The Central American Common Market (CACM) has made little progress in the area of monetary integration. Although the CACM established a reference regional unit of account, the Peso Centroamericano (equivalent to one U.S. dollar) is merely a unit of account.

This chapter reviews the recent evolution of the Central American exchange rate regimes in Central America and then evaluates the applicability of two possible monetary arrangements to the region. The first arrangement is a Central American common currency area. We assess how close the region is to being an optimum currency area in comparison to other possible integration areas—namely Europe, Latin America, and Asia. The second one is official dollarization, that is, adopting the U.S. dollar as the currency in the region. We evaluate the appropriateness of this option by assessing the degree of economic integration between the Central America and the United States. Our analysis reviews the criteria for an optimal currency, provides quantitative indices comparable across countries and regions, and then uses these criteria to measure directly the determinants of real exchange.

The historical evolution of the exchange rate regimes of the five Central American countries is summarized in the Appendix at the end of this chapter.

EXCHANGE ARRANGEMENTS IN THE REGION

In recent years, the number of countries espousing fixed exchange rate regimes has declined sharply. As Table 9-1 shows, between 1987 and 1997 the number of countries fixing the parity of their currency has decreased from 93 to 66 in spite of an increase in the absolute number of countries in the world as a result of the disintegration of the Soviet bloc. The trend toward flexible exchange rates has been present throughout the last 30 years. The high levels of inflation and large external shocks of the 1980s, as well as the volatile capital movements of the 1990s, have been regarded as responsible for most of the switches from fixed to flexible exchange rate regimes.

Central American countries maintained a fixed exchange rate system for a longer period than most countries. All five countries in the region—Costa Rica, El Salvador, Guatemala, Honduras, and Nicaragua—embraced fixed exchange rates in the 1920s after a period of instability and currency reforms

---

3. Kafka stated that "Latin America is obviously not an optimum currency area either now or for the foreseeable future. The same is true of its subdivisions, like the Latin American Free Trade Agreement (LAFTA) and, it seems, even the Central American Common Market (CACM). In fact, many Latin American countries are only gradually acquiring the characteristics of optimum currency areas."

Table 9-1. *Evolution of World's Exchange Rate Regimes*

Type of Regime (Number of countries)	Fixed	Limited Flexibility	Floating	Total
1969	116	0	1	117
1987	93	11	47	151
1997	66	17	101	184

Source: IMF. Several years. "Exchange Rate Arrangements and Restrictions."

that followed the collapse of the gold standard.[4] The Central American countries chose to peg their currencies to that of the United States, their main trading partner, and managed to keep unchanged parities and monetary stability until very recently. Honduras maintained the same parity for the longest period, from 1918 to 1990, followed by Guatemala (1925 to 1986), and El Salvador (1935 to 1986). Costa Rica and Nicaragua undertook periodic currency readjustments and abandoned their pegs in 1981 and 1985, respectively. Most readjustments took place in the early 1920s and 1930s, a period of monetary instability in the world due to the Great Depression in the United States.

A feature common to all countries in Central America was that a complex and diverse systems of exchange rate controls, parallel markets, and multiple-exchange rate systems coexisted with the official fixed exchange rate system.[5] These controls emerged and intensified in periods of monetary trouble (the early 1970s and the early 1980s); they acted both as an implicit devaluation and as a mechanism to ration scarce reserves. The controls have been progressively eliminated, often as part of country agreements with the International Monetary Fund (IMF). By 1987, the IMF's "Exchange Arrangements and Restrictions" classified all Central America as pegged to the U.S. dollar, except for Costa Rica, which was listed as "other managed floating." In December 1997, all were classified as flexible regimes: Guatemala as "independent floating," and the other four Central American countries as "managed floating." Nevertheless, the actual degree of flexibility varies across countries. El Salvador still keeps a de facto fixed nominal exchange rate with the U.S. dollar, while Costa Rica follows a depreciation rule that has kept its real exchange rate relatively constant. Nicaragua has a crawling peg, and Honduras has kept a nearly constant parity in the last years. Guatemala has allowed its currency to move more freely.

---

4. See Bulmer-Thomas (1987) and Young (1925; 1965) for an account of the exchange rate regimes in this early period.

5. Gaba (1990) analyzes the currency gap between the parallel and black markets and the official market from 1980 to 1987.

Central America's revealed preference for fixed exchange rates fits within one of the general prescriptions for exchange rate regimes—i.e., fixed rates are best for small, open economies. The regional economies are characterized foremost as small, open economies whose main trading partner is the United States.[6] At the same time, these economies are subject to large terms-of-trade shocks due to an export structure that is based on a few agricultural commodities, most prominently coffee and bananas. In theory, a flexible exchange rate generates a faster response to this type of shock. However, given the demand and supply elasticities for Central America's export products, presumably quite low, the adjustment would require a substantial depreciation, which would have a significant short-term economic cost.

In the early 1970s, all Central American countries experienced internal tensions. These were due both to the military conflicts in the region and to the first oil shock.[7] With the exception of Costa Rica, however, all countries were able to keep their parity with the U.S. dollar. The second oil shock had more serious consequences. It occurred simultaneously with, or right after, serious political turmoil in Nicaragua, El Salvador, and Guatemala, and was followed by an increase in world interest rates in the 1980s, leading to a debt crisis.[8] These circumstances led to the abandonment of the fixed system in all five countries over the next fifteen years.

According to the IMF (1997), "all countries that shifted to 'independent floating' between 1985 and 1992 did so in response to severe balance-of-payments difficulties and most did so as a prior action or performance criterion in the context of an IMF program." Eichengreen and Masson (1998) analyze exits from pegs between 1977 and 1995. They find that countries typically exited under pressure, with declining reserves, and slow output growth. In most cases, there was an abrupt fall in the value of the currency, real exchange rate volatility increased for an extended period of time after exit, and output remained depressed for an extended period of time. This was indeed the case for Central American countries.[9] The recessions that followed the currency devaluations, however, were shorter and milder than those Eichengreen and Masson (1998) found for the average peg exit, with the exception of Costa Rica in 1981 and Nicaragua. These are the two countries where inflation was

---

6. The average share of exports that went to the United States between 1980 and 1995 were: 43 percent for Costa Rica, 35 percent for El Salvador, 34 percent for Guatemala, 54 percent for Honduras, and 22 percent for Nicaragua. With respect to imports, the relationship of the Central American countries with the United States is even more intense.

7. In 1969, there was a war between El Salvador and Honduras, which led to withdrawal of Honduras from the Central American Common Market.

8. Chapter 3 in this volume reviews the impact of the debt crisis in Central America.

9. For a description of their currency crises and the underlying factors, see Chapter 10 in this volume.

highest: 90 percent in 1982 in Costa Rica, and above 10,000 percent in Nicaragua in 1988, at the peak of the hyperinflation period.[10] High inflation was one of the consequences of the crises. This was especially true in Costa Rica and Honduras, which still have very high inflation rates, whereas Nicaragua, after the 1990 stabilization plan, has been able to achieve relatively low inflation. Inflation remains in double digits for three of the five countries. The evolution of the exchange arrangements in each country is examined in the Appendix to this chapter.

FIXED VERSUS FLEXIBLE EXCHANGE RATE REGIMES: THE DEBATE

The historical debate over the relative benefits of fixed versus flexible exchange rate regimes has recently reemerged. Prevailing opinion seems to be that there is no regime that is best for all countries or for a country in all circumstances, so that the specifics of each situation need to be taken into account. Moreover, sound economic policies are a precondition for any exchange rate system to work effectively.

Aghevli et al. (1991) review the main criteria for selecting one system over another. At the same time, these authors emphasize that the question of optimality of a particular system has to be considered with reference to the authorities' objectives. The early literature suggests that a flexible exchange rate system is preferable for countries experiencing mostly external shocks (nominal or real) or real domestic shocks, whereas a fixed exchange rate system is superior when the main shocks are domestic and nominal. A fall in export prices or a decrease in external demand for goods can be partially accommodated through depreciation. A negative shock to the domestic demand for goods also might be counteracted with a depreciation that would increase foreign demand. An increase in money demand, in a fixed exchange regime, would imply a corresponding increase in the money supply and in international reserves, leaving interest rates and the parity unchanged. These prescriptions assume that the goal of the authorities is to minimize the variance of real output in the face of transitory shocks, and that there are nominal rigidities that make the exchange rate a superior tool for nominal adjustment.

Other country characteristics, such as openness, may not provide such a clear answer. It is often argued that a small, open economy should peg its exchange rate to that of its main trading partner.[11] Eichengreen and Masson (1998) state that "small countries that trade extensively with large neighbors

---

10. For a description of the different stabilization attempts in Nicaragua see Gibson (1991; 1993) and Ocampo (1991)

11. See IMF (1997).

and/or have large tourism receipts benefit little from an independent monetary policy." The argument goes back to McKinnon (1963) and the optimal currency area theory: major trading partners should keep fixed exchange rates, given that continuous parity adjustments are costly and lead to inefficiencies. The loss of an independent monetary policy may be the main cost of adopting a fixed exchange rate system. Since monetary policy is less effective the more open the economy, advising fixed parities to open economies is desirable. On the other hand, the more open the country is, the more vulnerable it is to external shocks, so that flexible nominal exchange rates may be required to facilitate real adjustment. Devarajan and Rodrik (1992) analyze the benefits of a fixed exchange rate for countries with large terms-of-trade shocks and conclude that the benefits from lower inflation do not outweigh the cost in lost output.[12]

For developing countries, which often lack credible monetary and fiscal institutions, fixed exchange rates can facilitate the control of domestic inflation by providing the needed discipline.[13] Some authors have argued that the decrease in country risk associated with fixed nominal rates can lead to beneficial effects through lower interest rates, higher levels of investment, and higher inflows of capital. Another traditional argument in favor of fixed exchange rate regimes for developing countries is the lack of developed financial markets, which could lead to a very high short-run exchange rate volatility. This was the view prevalent in the IMF in the 1970s, which has since been revised in the wake of successful experiences with the operation of flexible regimes in developing countries.[14]

Performance evaluations of both exchange rate regimes have so far failed to produce conclusive results. Collins (1996) finds some evidence that currency misalignment would make a flexible system preferable, since it is easier to hide small adjustments; but Collins also warns against drawing conclusions about growth performance under each system, since the choice of the exchange rate system itself is endogenous. IMF (1997) is also inconclusive regarding the inflation and growth performance of both systems. More recently, Hausmann et al. (1999) conclude that flexible exchange rates in Latin America have prevented a more stabilizing monetary policy. They also find that these countries have made little use of their exchange rate flexibility.

Frankel et al. (1991) suggest three reasons for choosing one exchange rate regime over the other: monetary credibility, structural characteristics as suggested above, and other commitments to regional integration. Trade agree-

---

12. Their analysis assumes that policymakers would have used the exchange rate to respond appropriately to terms-of-trade shocks.

13. However, Velasco and Tornell (1999) have argued that flexible exchange rate regimes may, in some circumstances, provide a higher degree of macroeconomic discipline.

14. See Quirk (1994) and Collins (1996).

ments have led to fixed exchange rate arrangements in the case of the European Common Market, with exchange bands around a central parity, leading eventually to a complete monetary union. Higher trade volumes and common political institutions have increased the cost of allowing for diverging exchange rates. The monetary credibility argument was developed in the 1980s. It is based on the idea that a fixed exchange rate provides a nominal anchor that helps agents to consolidate noninflationary expectations, not least because it creates a cost for a government that wants to change the monetary regime. Underlying the credibility argument is the idea that the government will be more disciplined on the fiscal and monetary fronts under fixed exchange rates rather than under flexible ones.[15] Tornell and Velasco (1999), however, recently have argued that fixed exchange rate systems also impose costs in terms of credibility, the only difference being that the costs are delayed into the future. The conclusion that fixed exchange rates provide more fiscal discipline is not clear cut; instead, it depends on how the government values the present versus the future: a government that is overly focused on the short term may indeed derive less fiscal discipline from a fixed exchange rate regime. Westbrook and Willet (1999) also criticize the credibility argument on two different grounds. First, traditional pegs would not provide sufficient credibility, so that more credible institutional arrangements would be necessary. Second, pegging to a currency that does not fulfill the optimum currency area criteria would not be a credible move in itself.[16]

Eichengreen and Masson (1998) provide an updated list of factors that influence the choice of a fixed exchange rate regime: inflation levels, the amount of reserves, labor mobility and nominal flexibility, the degree of production and export diversification, fiscal flexibility, trade, symmetry of shocks and, last but not least, political integration and other noneconomic criteria. We turn now to a brief review of their argument. Inflation levels must converge for a stable peg to be sustainable: permanent differentials would lead to overvaluation and the need to readjust the exchange rate. In order to keep a fixed exchange rate, the monetary authority needs to have sufficient reserves, and high capital mobility increases the level of reserves needed. High labor mobility between regions or countries and/or high levels of wage and price flexibility make asymmetric shocks less of an issue.[17] A diversified production and export structure translates into less vulnerability to terms of trade shocks, and therefore less need for exchange rate flexibility. Under fixed exchange rates, monetary policy is lost as a policy instrument, and fiscal policy becomes the

---

15. For an exposition of the argument see Aghevli et al. (1991) and Edwards (1995; 1996).

16. See the description of the optimal currency area criteria, below. These criteria include a high degree of trade integration and factor mobility between the countries.

17. Openness in itself may lead to more flexible prices and wages. See McKinnon (1963).

main instrument to respond to shocks. To cushion asymmetric shocks, fiscal transfers between members would therefore have to become more common. A higher degree of trade integration would result in greater benefits from a fixed exchange rate, since the volume of trade affected by lower transaction costs and reduced uncertainty is larger. As explained above, extremely asymmetric shocks are not compatible with a combination of fixed exchange rate, low factor mobility, and low nominal flexibility. Real shocks would require a flexible exchange rate, whereas nominal domestic shocks are better handled with a fixed exchange rate.

The recent currency crises in Asia and Latin America have highlighted the vulnerability of intermediate exchange rate systems to high capital mobility. The high levels of international mobility of capital have refocused the debate on the issue of whether intermediate exchange rate regimes are actually a realistic choice. Obstfeld and Rogoff (1995) had already illustrated the difficulties for fixed exchange regimes in a world of high capital mobility, namely the unlikelihood that central banks would ignore the effects on the economy of defending a peg under a speculative attack. Eichengreen and Masson (1998), in their review of the options between pure fixed and pure float, suggest that only very hard pegs and managed floats are likely to survive high levels of capital mobility. The authors argue in favor of more exchange rate flexibility in developing countries, and discuss how to move toward that goal with minimum disruption. Larraín and Velasco (1999), reviewing the recent debate, argue against currency boards or full-scale dollarization for developing countries. They show that it is possible for small, developed economies with exchange rate flexibility to have inflation performance similar to that of currency-board countries.

A Monetary Union for Central America?

The possibility of instituting a Central America currency area is worth considering. The high degree of trade transactions between the countries in the region, and their similar exposure to external shocks as exporters highly dependent on a few commodities, suggest the reasonableness of the currency area option. The small economic size also supports instituting a common currency, whose wider use would favor the deepening of the local financial systems.[18]

Indeed, the region has functioned with a common currency in the past. Central American countries shared a variety of coins under the Spanish do-

---

18. See Chapter 20 in Volume II for an analysis of the financial systems in the region and the reforms needed.

minion, during the brief life of *La República Centro-Americana*, and the early years of each country's independence. National currencies developed only late in the nineteenth century. The initial dispositions of the Central American Common Market treaty in the 1960s included, among the monetary agreements, the establishment of fixed rates among Central American currencies and a commitment not to change rates without prior agreement. They also called for the establishment of a clearing house and a common unit of account, the Central American peso, to facilitate inter-regional trade. A Central American peso is equivalent to one U.S. dollar. In 1968, Robert Triffin presented a project before the Consejo Monetario Centroamericano, describing the steps toward a monetary union.

Eichengreen (1998) proposes four prerequisites for a monetary union to function smoothly: an independent central bank, wage and price flexibility, a strong financial sector, and significant barriers to exit the union. With an independent central bank for the region, countries will not be tempted to issue debt in the hope that the central bank will eventually provide an inflationary bailout whose cost would be borne by all member countries. This argument highlights the importance of institution building in Central America as a prerequisite for a viable currency union.[19] Exit costs may be increased, with the concomitant increase in the credibility of the currency union, if additional economic, social, and political agreements are associated with the monetary arrangement. Partly for this reason, monetary unions tend to be instituted between neighboring countries or countries with significant economic and political ties. This precondition is substantially met by the Central American countries: they share the same language, as well as deep cultural and historical ties. Regional integration, revived in the 1990s, corresponds to the interests of the Central American countries, given the importance of intraregional trade.

Optimal Currency Areas

Mundell (1961) made the first substantial and enduring contribution to the theory of optimal currency areas. The key insight was that in an optimum currency area, shocks should affect the different countries or regions within a country symmetrically. If different countries (or regions) are subject to different exogenous shocks, then the levels of intercountry labor and capital mobility should be high enough to ensure that pockets of unemployment do not persist at the country level. If the different countries in a currency area face similar shocks, and increases in unemployment can be overcome through

---

19. Being able to establish and manage such an institution, on the other hand, could give a tremendous boost to the region's image and international credibility.

wage or price flexibility, relinquishing the ability to change the nominal exchange rate does not impose a significant cost.[20] In terms of adjustment, nominal exchange rate movements, nominal wage or price changes, and labor mobility between regions are substitutes.

Several criteria have been presented as prerequisites for a functioning currency area. The asymmetry of output shocks is looked at most often. The idea is that if two countries have output shocks that move closely together, there will be less need to use the exchange rate as a tool to affect their relative outputs. This means that they will be interested in similar exchange rate policies. Consequently, the real exchange rate of countries for which output shocks are correlated will vary less than for countries with different output shocks and vice versa, i.e., countries with more asymmetric shocks should have larger exchange rate volatility.

As for trade intensity, the consensus is that the more two countries trade among themselves, the more they will value exchange rate stability. One would expect a negative correlation between trade intensity and exchange rate variability. Nonetheless, differences in the production structure and the composition of exports between countries make it more likely that they will be subject to different external shocks and, thus, will need to rely on nominal exchange rate adjustments.[21] Also, the more diverse a country's production base, the less likely that a sectoral shock will require intercountry adjustment and, thus, the better the country is as a candidate for a currency area.[22]

Small countries may benefit more than larger countries from a reduction in transaction costs brought about by a more a stable currency. The thinness of local exchange markets may lead these countries to pursue exchange rate stability in order to avoid the costs associated with substantial fluctuations. As a result, there should also be a positive correlation between transaction costs and exchange rate volatility.

An obvious benefit from a currency area is the elimination of transaction costs associated with the exchange of currencies to finance flows of goods and capital. A more substantial benefit is the greater attractiveness of the region for foreign investment, which comes from its being treated as a larger, integrated market. The costs are associated with the loss of an independent monetary policy by each of the countries involved. These costs, however, may be negligible if the output shocks the countries face are similar, so that most conflicts between alternative policies can be avoided. Given their specialization in

---

20. Aizenman and Flood (1992) argue that Mundell's classic argument relates to demand shocks only, adding that the benefits of currency areas are stronger when supply shocks are considered.

21. Kenen (1969) emphasizes this point.

22. See Bofinger (1994).

similar products, this is likely to be the case with Central American countries. Whether the net benefits of a monetary union are positive or negative is an empirical matter. Below, we evaluate the potential benefits of a Central American monetary union by comparing how well the region fares in the criteria for an optimal currency area when compared with the European Union.

There is evidence that currency unions also have dynamic effects, the very creation of a currency union may change the economic relationship between its members. Fatás (1997) has argued that a currency union may have two distinct effects on business cycles among the countries considered: on the one hand, increased regional specialization may make cycles more pronounced and less synchronous among them; on the other hand, increased intercountry demand linkages and intra-industry trade can lead to greater synchronism of country cycles. Frankel and Rose (1996b) have shown that trade integration and the correlation of country business cycles are mutually reinforcing. As to exchange rate variability, Bayoumi and Eichengreen (1998) present evidence that more trade integration leads to lower exchange rate variability. Marsden (1992) argues that regional integration, and the parallel product market integration, decreases the market power of firms, so that labor markets become more responsive to short-term conditions.[23] In sum, the case for a currency area may be stronger ex-post than ex-ante, because its institution increases trade flows and makes output cycles more synchronous between its members. For Central America, these dynamic effects may be important, especially as far as trade volume is concerned. The countries in the region have experienced more intense trade relations in the past. The institution of a currency area could make Central America regain those higher levels of trade integration.

Is Central America an Optimal Currency Area?

In this section, we evaluate the degree to which Central America is an optimal currency area by relying on some of the criteria mentioned above. We present a measure of bilateral real exchange rate volatility, as well as measures of trade integration, trade dissimilarity and output-shock correlation for Central American economies in the 1970s, 1980s, and 1990s. These variables are constructed in a way similar to Bayoumi and Eichengreen (1997a). To obtain a comparative perspective, we present results for other geographical ar-

---

23. The idea is that firms with no market power cannot cushion short-term fluctuations in profitability so that wages have to adjust immediately; this means that labor markets respond more directly to economic shocks.

eas, namely Europe, Asia, and Latin America.[24] Our sample excludes the extremely volatile post-1997 Asian currencies; their inclusion would most probably have changed the indicators of volatility with respect to the U.S. dollar.

We measure real exchange rate volatility as the standard deviation, over a period of time, of the yearly change in the log of the bilateral real exchange rate. The real exchange rate is constructed using consumer price indices and nominal exchange rate data from the IFS. The asymmetry of output shocks is computed as the standard deviation, over a period of time, of the difference in the shocks for every pair of countries; where the output shocks for each country are calculated as annual change in the log of real GDP. The source for real GDP data is the IFS series of GDP (missing values were completed with national sources or the World Development Indicators from the World Bank). Trade dissimilarity is measured as the mean of the absolute value of the differences for every two countries in yearly export shares for different export sectors. Export shares by SITC are calculated using a combined data set obtained from the merge of the Feenstra, Lipsey, Bowen data set (1970–92) and the Statistics of Canada data set (1980–96).[25] Trade intensity is measured as the average bilateral export-to-GDP ratio for each pair of countries. Bilateral export data come from the trade data set previously described, while the GDP data come from World Development Indicators 1998 (GDP in current dollars). Country size, a variable that we also include in our regressions, is calculated as the mean over time of the average of the log of the absolute GDP of the two trading partners, in constant dollars.

Tables 9-2 to 9-5 present the average value of real exchange rate volatility, asymmetry of output shocks, trade dissimilarity, and bilateral trade intensity for different geographic areas and time periods. The upper halves of these tables present the average of the variable for within-region-group pairs,

---

24. The composition of these geographic areas is: *Europe*—Belgium-Luxembourg, Denmark, France, Germany, Greece, Ireland, Italy, Netherlands, Portugal, Spain, and the U.K.; *Industrialized*—the countries in Europe, Canada, Japan, and the U.S.; *Asia*—Hong Kong, Indonesia, Korea, Japan, Malaysia, Philippines, Singapore, and Thailand; *Latin America*—Argentina, Bolivia, Brazil, Chile, Colombia, Ecuador, Mexico, Peru, Paraguay, Uruguay, and Venezuela; *Central America*—Costa Rica, El Salvador, Guatemala, Honduras, and Nicaragua. Nicaragua, however, is excluded from most calculations due to its hyperinflation of the late 1980s and early 1990s, which unduly influences the results.

25. Bayoumi and Eichengreen (1997a) use the sum of the differences in three export sectors: agriculture, manufacture, and services. Our measure of trade dissimilarity is based on a finer export sector classification, namely the one-digit SITC codes. Code 9, "not elsewhere classified, gold and military equipment," was removed from total exports, as it may lead to errors in many cases because of the size of the "not elsewhere classified" items.

Table 9-2.   *Real Exchange Rate Volatility*

	1970s	1980s	1990s	1970–97
Whole sample	0.122	0.180	0.115	0.151
Intraregional				
Europe	0.056	0.056	0.052	0.057
Industrialized	0.066	0.081	0.075	0.076
Asia	0.109	0.099	0.058	0.094
Latin America	0.202	0.257	0.147	0.218
Central America* (w/o Nicaragua)	0.041	0.203	0.131	0.148
Crossregional				
Europe/Rest	0.114	0.189	0.124	0.153
Industrialized/Rest	0.118	0.190	0.120	0.155
Asia/Rest	0.122	0.159	0.105	0.137
Latin America/Rest	0.149	0.217	0.127	0.181
Central America/Rest (w/o Nicaragua)	0.095	0.213	0.150	0.170

Variable definition: *Real exchange rate volatility* is the standard deviation of the yearly change in the log of the bilateral real exchange rate, over a period of time
*When Nicaragua is included: 0.048, 0.071, 0.178, and 0.435.

Table 9-3.   *Asymmetry of Output Shocks*

	1970s	1980s	1990s	1970–97
Whole sample	0.033	0.044	0.030	0.040
Intraregional				
Europe	0.026	0.019	0.015	0.023
Industrialized	0.026	0.021	0.018	0.023
Asia	0.030	0.042	0.023	0.035
Latin America	0.042	0.061	0.043	0.053
Central America* (w/o Nicaragua)	0.030	0.037	0.022	0.034
Crossregional				
Europe/Rest	0.032	0.041	0.029	0.037
Industrialized/Rest	0.032	0.043	0.030	0.039
Asia/Rest	0.032	0.046	0.029	0.040
Latin America/Rest	0.037	0.053	0.035	0.046
Central America/Rest (w/o Nicaragua)	0.032	0.043	0.031	0.040

Variable definition: *Asymmetry of output shocks* is computed as the standard deviation over a period of time of the difference between two countries in the log of yearly real GDP
*When Nicaragua is included: 0.0656, 0.0526, 0.0271, and 0.0543

whereas the lower halves present the variable's average value among countries in the group and countries outside the group.[26]

As Table 9-2 shows, Central America was the region with the lowest level of intraregional exchange rate volatility in the 1970s. Since then, its relative position has changed: in the 1980s the volatility of the real exchange rate between Central American countries increased by a factor of five. Even though it has declined in the 1990s, real exchange rate volatility in the region is still the second highest of the regions discussed, and its level remains very close to Latin America's. By contrast, Europe and Asia have progressively reduced their intraregional real exchange rate volatility: Europe remained the least volatile region throughout, while Asian volatility declined sharply, placing it very close to European levels. Between 1970 and 1997, Asian volatility went from being twice as high a that in Central America, to being less than half as high.

As to the comparison between intraregional volatility and crossregional volatility, note how the former is usually lower, as could be expected. Latin America is the only exception, with real exchange rates within the region being more volatile than between the countries in the region and countries outside, for every period.

Central America has lower intraregional volatility than crossregional volatility, but the two measures have increased over time and approached each other at higher levels. Intraregional volatility was half the level of outside volatility in the 1970s.

Table 9-3 presents summary statistics for the asymmetry of output shocks across countries. A higher number denotes more asymmetric shocks. Europe and the industrialized countries are the groupings with the lowest intraregional asymmetry of output shocks. Over time, these countries have reduced output asymmetry even further. Central America, together with Asia and Latin America, experienced substantial increases in asymmetry in the 1980s, followed by a decline in the 1990s. But, whereas for Latin America the measure is now higher than in the 1970s, for Central America and Asia the asymmetry of output shocks between countries today is actually lower than the European level was in the 1970s.

Most countries have their output cycle less in tune with countries outside the region than with countries within the same region, the only exception being Latin America.

We now turn to trade dissimilarity, that is, the degree to which any two countries (or group of countries) export different products. Table 9-4 shows

---

26. That is, in computing this latter average, we do not include the within-group observations. For example, the bilateral real exchange rate variability between Costa Rica and Guatemala is not included in the row "Central America* " in Table 9-2.

Table 9-4. Trade Dissimilarity

	1970s	1980s	1990s	1970–97
Whole sample	11.64	11.48	10.44	11.27
Intraregional				
Europe	6.69	6.28	5.94	6.34
Industrialized	6.94	6.75	6.33	6.71
Asia	13.12	11.56	8.27	11.29
Latin America	11.90	12.11	11.00	11.74
Central America* (w/o Nicaragua)	4.25	3.99	4.33	4.17
Crossregional				
Europe/Rest	12.08	11.49	10.16	11.36
Industrialized/Rest	12.92	12.28	10.83	12.14
Asia/Rest	12.45	11.79	10.68	11.75
Latin America/Rest	12.58	12.96	12.13	12.61
Central America/Rest (w/o Nicaragua)	11.98	13.08	12.66	12.56

Variable definition: *Trade dissimilarity* is measured as the mean, over a period of time, of the absolute value of the differences in yearly export shares for different export sectors
*When Nicaragua is included: 4.78, 4.48, 4.54, and 4.61

that the Central American countries are the most similar as a group of exporters, a reflection of their heavy dependency for exports on a few agricultural products.[27] Europe, the industrialized countries, and especially Asia have all become more alike over time as far as goods exported go, but they have greater differences among themselves than do the countries of Central America.

In Table 9-5 we present results for trade integration. Now, the higher the value presented, the more integrated any pair of countries is. We can see that Central America in the 1970s was as integrated as Europe, but its index has decreased to less than half the European level in the 1990s, which is higher than in the 1970s. That is, the average two European countries trade twice as much relative to their gross domestic products as do the average two Central American countries. All other regions have seen trade integration rise with time.

As far as trade intensity with countries outside the region is concerned, Central America's degree of integration has remained at similar levels throughout.

In conclusion, while most areas are more integrated in the 1990s than they were in the 1970s, that does not seem to be the case with Central America. Real exchange rates within the region are more volatile today than in the 1970s, the countries are less alike as far as their export structure is concerned,

---

27. See Chapter 5 in this volume for documentation and a comment on the issue of diversification.

Table 9-5. *Bilateral Trade Integration*

	1970s	1980s	1990s	1970–97
Whole sample	0.52	0.61	0.66	0.59
Intraregional				
Europe	1.38	1.80	1.91	1.67
Industrialized	1.09	1.42	1.51	1.32
Asia	1.97	2.41	2.76	2.34
Latin America	0.27	0.34	0.37	0.32
Central America* (w/o Nicaragua)	1.24	0.99	0.83	1.04
Crossregional				
Europe/Rest	0.28	0.28	0.30	0.28
Industrialized/Rest	0.57	0.61	0.63	0.60
Asia/Rest	0.33	0.41	0.46	0.39
Latin America/Rest	0.21	0.22	0.23	0.22
Central America/Rest (w/o Nicaragua)	0.27	0.24	0.23	0.25

Variable definition: *Trade intensity* is the average bilateral-export-to-GDP ratios for each pair of countries, over a period of time.
*When Nicaragua is included: 1.32, 0.82, 0.81, and 1.00.

and they trade relatively less among themselves. The only measure where Central America seems to be more integrated today than in the 1970s is in the asymmetry of output shocks. Europe and Asia, and especially the latter, have become more integrated. Latin America, which seems to be by the far the least regionally integrated group of countries, has had a more mixed evolution.

In Table 9-6 we present a simple summary index that captures the degree of integration enjoyed by countries within a region compared to countries outside that region. As we will see, here and in the section on dollarization, the ranking that emerges with this simple index is in tune with what would be expected. The table also includes the ratio of intraregional values to crossregional values for the four variables from Tables 9-2 to 9-5, for the 1990s. We construct the index as sum of those three ratios for the determinants of real exchange rate volatility, that is, relative output-shock asymmetry, trade dissimilarity, and trade integration. A lower value of any of these indicators implies that countries in a particular region are more similar among themselves than relative to countries that do not belong to that region.[28] In the top part of the table, we make comparisons across regions; in the bottom half, however, we present values for four individual Central American countries, comparing their integration with the rest of Central

---

28. The trade-intensity variable is measured as the ratio of the average trade intensity with all countries divided by trade intensity with countries in the same region; that is, a lower number indicates higher regional integration.

Table 9-6.   *Currency Area Criteria 1990s*

	Relative Output Asymmetry (1)	Relative Trade Dissimilarity (2)	Relative Trade Intensity (3)	Index (1)+(2)+(3)	Relative Real Exch.Rate Volatility
Region					
Europe	0.527	0.584	0.155	1.27	0.419
Asia	0.796	0.774	0.168	1.74	0.552
Latin America	1.233	0.907	0.621	2.76	1.156
Central America	0.716	0.342	0.275	1.33	0.876
Central America (w/o Nicaragua)	0.872	0.356	0.286	1.51	1.198
(Country/Region) / (Country/Rest)					
Costa Rica	0.637	0.283	0.534	1.45	1.492
Guatemala	0.910	0.292	0.137	1.34	0.835
Honduras	0.754	0.350	0.618	1.72	0.699
El Salvador	0.619	0.453	0.090	1.16	0.824

American countries versus their integration with non-Central American countries in the sample.

Note first how countries within a region are more integrated among themselves than with outside countries. This is highlighted by the fact that most values in the table are lower than 1. The exception is Latin America, whose output-shock asymmetry and real exchange rate volatility are higher within the region than between countries within and outside the region. This reflects the sharp and erratic fluctuations in macroeconomic conditions in Latin America. The overall index shows that Europe is the most natural candidate for a currency area, as expected, followed by Central America, Asia, and Latin America.[29] The only criterion for which Europe does not have the lower value is in trade dissimilarity; here, Central American countries are the best candidates for integration since they are very similar to one another in the products they export and very different from countries outside the region in this respect.

As for the four individual Central American countries, it turns out that, according our index, El Salvador and Guatemala lead as candidates for regional integration, followed by Costa Rica and Honduras.

We now turn to the econometric analysis.

Determining whether a certain region constitutes an optimal currency area is not an easy task since the criteria are usually relative rather than absolute.

---

29. Note that these results have to be interpreted with caution, specially given Asia's high absolute levels of trade integration and low values of output-shock asymmetry with all countries in the sample.

Many of the existing studies on whether a given group of countries might appropriately become a currency area have focused on a regional grouping.[30] In the wake of Bayoumi and Eichengreen (1997a), we use a methodology that relies on the idea that, if the Optimal Currency Area criteria are correct, then the variables suggested by this literature should be important determinants of exchange rate volatility, i.e. their coefficients in a regression should be significant and display a particular sign. For instance, the asymmetry of shocks and trade dissimilarity should come out with a positive coefficient and trade intensity with a negative coefficient. The basic regression is

$$\text{RER Volatility}_i = \alpha + \beta_1 * \text{Output Asymmetry}_i + \beta_2 * \text{Trade Dissimilarity}_i + \beta_3 * \text{Trade Intensity}_i + \beta_4 * \text{Size} + u_i$$

where the definitions for the variables are those mentioned earlier in this section and u_i is a white noise error term, assumed uncorrelated across observations. We estimate this model by OLS, for different periods and samples, and with and without regional dummies, which take the value 1 when both countries are in the same region and 0 otherwise. An important issue is the possible endogeneity of the trade intensity variable.[31] The idea is that lower real exchange rate volatility leads to more bilateral trade and thus the sign of the coefficient may capture the impact of volatility on trade and not the opposite. However, Eichengreen (1998) addresses this problem and finds that the results do not differ substantially when he uses an instrument for that variable.

Tables 9-7 and 9-8 present the results from the econometric analysis for two different samples and the four different periods considered, 1970–79, 1980–89, 1990–97, and 1970–97.[32] They also include the results from the estimation of the model as a panel with time dummies. The regressions in Table 9-7 use the whole sample of countries. The coefficients on the explanatory variables come out with the expected signs and are significant except for country size in the 1980s, which is negative and nonsignificant. Regional dummies for Central America and Asia are nonsignificant only in the 1970s; the signs of the coefficients indicate a lower volatility than average for Central America and the reverse for Asia. In the 1980s and 1990s, when the coefficients are significant, the opposite statement holds true. For Latin America,

---

30. See Bayoumi and Eichengreen (1996b; 1997a; 1997b) and Eichengreen (1998).

31. This issue is raised in Frankel and Rose (1996a; 1996b; 1996c).

32. In the case of the trade dissimilarity, trade intensity, and country size variables, the last two periods are actually 1990-96 and 1970-96. Changes in these variables in the year 1996-97 are likely to be small enough not to affect the average for the period, since they mostly reflect structural factors that evolve very slowly over time.

Table 9-7. *Assessing Real Exchange Rate Volatility*

Sample: All countries, i.e. Central America*, Industrialized countries, Latin America, and Asia

	1970–79				1980–89				1990–97			
Output Shock	3.1357	15.24	2.9150	13.66	1.5585	10.76	1.4429	10.54	2.1947	13.81	2.1560	13.06
Trade Dissimilarity	0.0009	1.07	0.0008	0.95	0.0044	5.92	0.0050	6.75	0.0021	3.53	0.0024	4.13
Bilateral Trade	-0.0084	-5.41	-0.0086	-5.66	-0.0103	-6.83	-0.0086	-5.14	-0.0052	-4.2	-0.0044	-3.08
Size	0.0077	2.99	0.0095	3.51	-0.0042	-1.76	-0.0011	-0.45	0.0057	3.27	0.0076	3.99
Central America*			-0.0328	-1.6			0.0738	2.38			0.0672	4.66
Latin America			0.0662	4.11			0.0487	4.07			0.0081	0.95
Asia			0.0122	1.28			-0.0598	-5.91			-0.0317	-5.35
R^2	0.24		0.28		0.33		0.38		0.33		0.36	
N	630		630		630		630		630		630	

	1970–97				Panel Estimates: 1970–97			
Output Shock	2.6387	13.25	2.4351	12.47	2.1843	21.07	2.0409	19.71
Trade Dissimilarity	0.0022	3.63	0.0027	4.28	0.0024	5.31	0.0027	5.9
Bilateral Trade	-0.0075	-6.72	-0.0067	-5.53	-0.0078	-7.95	-0.0071	-6.73
Size	0.0021	1.2	0.0041	2.14	0.0031	2.33	0.0053	3.69
Central America*			0.0461	2.49			0.0352	2.01
Latin America			0.0369	3.75			0.0409	5.33
Asia			-0.0318	-4.89			-0.0276	-4.68
R^2	0.41		0.44		0.82		0.83	
N	630		630		1890		1890	

*Nicaragua excluded.

Note: The numbers next to the coefficients are robust t-statistics

315

Table 9-8. *Assessing Real Exchange Rate Volatility*

Sample: Industrialized countries and Central America*

	1970–79				1980–89				1990–97			
Output Shock	0.0943	0.64	0.0921	0.63	4.0274	8.68	3.9065	8.37	2.1386	4.19	2.04	4.16
Trade Dissimilarity	0.0013	3.96	0.0014	3.46	0.0051	3.63	0.0064	4.5	0.0057	4.43	0.01	5.62
Bilateral Trade	-0.0057	-7.94	-0.0057	-7.86	-0.0061	-2.42	-0.0061	-2.43	-0.0056	-2.81	-0.01	-2.87
Size	0.0058	5.86	0.0060	4.66	-0.0060	-1.6	-0.0022	-0.59	-0.0005	-0.16	0.01	1.66
Central America*			0.0021	0.31			0.0519	1.44			0.07	3.75
R²	0.36		0.36		0.57		0.58		0.46		0.49	
N	153		153		153		153		153		153	

	1970–97				Panel Estimates: 1970–97			
Output Shock	1.6155	4.2	1.4451	3.48	2.3904	8.64	2.3216	8.36
Trade Dissimilarity	0.0047	5.93	0.0064	7.6	0.0039	5.45	0.0050	6.83
Bilateral Trade	-0.0055	-4.64	-0.0057	-5.28	-0.0058	-4.85	-0.0059	-4.97
Size	-0.0044	-1.68	0.0005	0.21	-0.0007	-0.4	0.0029	1.53
Central America*			0.0642	3.35			0.0455	2.82
R²	0.56		0.60		0.85		0.85	
N	153		153		459		459	

*Nicaragua excluded.

Note: The numbers next to the coefficients are robust t-statistics

on the other hand, there is evidence of higher volatility than average in all periods, though its dummy for the 1990s is not significant.

Table 9-8 repeats the exercise of Table 9-7 for a different sample; the 14 industrialized countries[33] with the four Central American ones.[34] This allows us to estimate whether exchange rate volatility is higher for Central American countries as a group than for a group of countries that has not experienced major macroeconomic instability in the past decades. All variables have the expected signs, except the size variable, which has a negative sign in some periods but is not significant in these cases. The coefficient for the asymmetric output-shocks variable is not significant in the 1970s, but has the correct sign. It is the coefficient that changes most noticeably in the 1980s and 1990s (it becomes larger). The dummy for Central American countries is not significant in 1970s and 1980s, in this case, but is highly significant in the 1990s. The results confirm that Central America's exchange rate volatility is higher than for the industrialized countries, and that it increased in the 1980s and 1990s.

Table 9-9 shows the prediction errors of exchange rate volatility for each pair of Central American countries, corresponding to the 1990s and using the regression with the Central American dummy in Table 9-8.

The model over-predicts the volatility of Costa Rica, El Salvador, and Guatemala, countries that also have low real exchange rate volatility among them, and under-predicts the volatility of Nicaragua with the other four countries.[35] As the raw index in Table 9-6 shows, Costa Rica, Guatemala, and El Salvador as a group are much closer to being an optimal currency area according to the three criteria considered. Table 9-10 confirms that these three countries have lower asymmetry of output shocks and lower trade dissimilarity and their trade intensity is higher, i.e. they are more integrated. In spite of this, they still have considerably higher real exchange rate volatility than the European countries.

In addition to the criteria examined above, we should also analyze the degree of intracountry and intercountry factor mobility in Central America. The higher the mobility of labor and capital within and between countries, the stronger the case for a currency area. As mentioned above, this is because exogenous shocks can be handled with minimal unemployment and disruption of production, making it easier for factors of production to pursue their best employment. Certainly the argument can be made that the more syn-

---

33. That is, the European countries in our sample plus Canada, Japan, and the United States.

34. As explained before, Nicaragua was excluded from the regressions due to its high volatility, which makes it very influential.

35. Note that for Nicaragua the predicted value results from an out-of-sample prediction, since the observations including Nicaragua were not considered for the estimates.

Table 9-9. *Actual and Predicted Real Exchange Rate Volatility in the 1990s*

	Real Exch. Rate Volatility	Predicted	Error
Costa Rica–El Salvador	0.0807	0.1126	−0.0319
Guatemala–El Salvador	0.0865	0.1067	−0.0203
Costa Rica–Guatemala	0.1102	0.1158	−0.0056
Guatemala–Honduras	0.1382	0.1396	−0.0015
Honduras–El Salvador	0.1608	0.1644	−0.0037
Costa Rica–Nicaragua	0.1696	0.1676	0.0020
Costa Rica–Honduras	0.2108	0.1480	0.0628
Guatemala–Nicaragua	0.2310	0.1375	0.0934
Nicaragua–El Salvador	0.2390	0.1775	0.0615
Honduras–Nicaragua	0.3561	0.1505	0.2056

chronous the shocks between countries, the less they need to rely on intercountry factor mobility to respond to them. In this case the whole region can adjust its nominal exchange rate versus the outside world and no intercountry adjustments in the nominal exchange rates will be needed. As we have seen above, the level of trade dissimilarity among Central American countries is the lowest among all other regions we have examined, which reduces the probability of having asymmetric shocks from an external source.

As presented in Chapter 10 of Volume II, the level of financial deepening in

Table 9-10. *Alternative Central American Currency Areas*

	Real Exch. Rate Volatility	Output Shock	Trade Dissimilarity	Bilateral Trade
1970s				
Central America	0.048	0.066	4.78	1.32
Central America w/o Nicaragua	0.041	0.030	4.25	1.24
Costa Rica, El Salvador, and Guatemala	0.045	0.021	3.88	2.01
Europe	0.056	0.026	6.69	1.38
1980s				
Central America	0.714	0.053	4.48	0.82
Central America w/o Nicaragua	0.203	0.037	3.99	0.99
Costa Rica, El Salvador, and Guatemala	0.228	0.042	3.30	1.55
Europe	0.056	0.019	6.28	1.80
1990s				
Central America	0.178	0.027	4.54	0.81
Central America w/o Nicaragua	0.131	0.022	4.33	0.83
Costa Rica, El Salvador, and Guatemala	0.093	0.017	3.46	1.21
Europe	0.052	0.015	5.94	1.91

Central America is very low, even by Latin American standards. The lack of sophistication and regional integration of financial markets is thus a potential obstacle to the constitution of a currency area in the region. On the other hand, improvements in capital mobility may be easier to implement after the currency area is established. Movements of capital are not as likely to draw political opposition as movements of laborers.[36]

As regards labor mobility, Central America is characterized by widely different population densities across countries, with El Salvador at the high end and Nicaragua and Honduras at the low end.[37] Population movements from El Salvador to Honduras have ignited interstate conflicts in the past. In the 1980s, however, the opposite occurred: internal conflicts in Guatemala, El Salvador, and Nicaragua led substantial fractions of the population to move across borders as refugees. IIDH (1992) estimates the Central American refugees from other Central American countries at 160,000 just in the 1980–84 period.[38] This figure is for legally registered movements alone. The number of undocumented refugees from Central America, according to the same source, may have amounted to another 140,000 in 1990. Internal displacement runs at much higher numbers, from 180,000 and 300,000 for Guatemala and Nicaragua to 500,000 for El Salvador.[39] The number of Nicaraguans in Costa Rica has been recently estimated at around 700,000, that is, almost 20 percent of the population. This is probably one of the highest, if not the highest, percentage of foreign workers in a country. A substantial fraction of the displaced will not return to their place of origin. For better or for worse, the Central American instability of the 1980s has created a large pool of individuals willing to move for better opportunities.

The existence of a large pool of Central Americans abroad may contribute to future labor mobility in response to real shocks. This is particularly relevant with respect to the United States. Campbell and Gibson (1999), using data from the U.S. Bureau of the Census, show a striking increase in the number of Central American nationals living in the United States. From 1970 to 1990, immigrants to the United States from El Salvador went from 15,000 to 465,000. For Guatemala, they increased from 17,000 to 226,000; for Nicaragua, from 16,000 to 168,000; for Honduras, from 19,000 to 108,000; and for Costa Rica, from 16,000 to 43,000. According to the U. S. Bureau of the Cen-

---

36. The experience of the European Union seems to confirm this.

37. See Chapter 2 in this volume for a characterization of general population and population density patterns.

38. See IIDH (1992, 31). Refugees from the region to Mexico were 175,000.

39. See IIDH (1992, 163). Crosby (1990) puts the figures of displaced persons in the 1980s at 460,000 for El Salvador and 487,000 for Nicaragua.

sus (1997), there were 607,000 persons from El Salvador as of March 1997, of which only 110,000 were U.S. citizens.

Central America also can rely on two additional characteristics of its labor market to encourage labor mobility: its low level of female participation in the labor force and the still high percentage of agricultural workers. Together, these ensure that there is a large pool of labor market participants whose decisions can respond to local shocks.

In light of these findings, we believe that the option of a common currency is worth serious consideration.

The Dollarization Option

Central American countries have long had a special relationship with the United States, and so have naturally been eager to avoid substantial fluctuations in the value of the U.S. dollar in relation to their local currencies. Since the early twentieth century, the United States has been Central America's most important commercial partner. All five countries in the region have kept a fixed nominal parity with the U.S. dollar for a substantial period. The bilateral exchange rates with the U.S. dollar often have been more stable than between Central American countries. It is thus appropriate to evaluate dollarization as an option for Central America.

A number of proposals for full dollarization, that is, the adoption of the U.S. dollar as national currency and legal tender, have been made in the past year. Hanke and Schuler (1999) put forward a dollarization proposal for Argentina, which the Argentinean government is evaluating. Calvo (1999) defends a monetary treaty between Argentina and the United States that would allow Argentina to receive part of the benefits from seignorage derived from full dollarization. Hausmann et al. (1999) have highlighted the potential benefits of dollarization for Latin American countries. Paul Krugman (1999), on the other hand, has argued against dollarization.

Hildebrand (1987) considers dollarization in Central America.[40] At that time the concerns were not so much instability and the financial contagion generated by capital flows, but the generation of trade and economic growth. Drawing on the experience of Panama, Hildebrand envisioned dollarization

---

40. The proposal was inspired by the experiences with dollarization of other small developing countries: Panama from 1904 till today; Liberia, which switched from the pound sterling to the U.S. dollar after World War II until today (although the US dollar is still the official currency, the military conflict in the 1980s gave rise to a parallel market with discounted Liberian notes), and the Dominican Republic between 1905 and 1947.

in Central America as a way to further economic integration with the United States. He mentioned as benefits those of a common currency: lower exchange rate uncertainty and the elimination of transaction costs from exchange rate conversion. In addition, the use of the dollar would eliminate speculative currency crises and thus facilitate foreign direct investment by U.S. companies. An agreement to share the revenues from seignorage and mitigate the problem of loss of sovereignty was also considered.

The American administration typically has been lukewarm about dollarization proposals. Larry Summers and Alan Greenspan have warned of the seriousness of the decision, and have suggested that the Federal Reserve is not ready to act as lender of last resort for other countries. On the other hand, *The Economist* (1999) hinted that, although it is unlikely that the Federal Reserve would act as lender of last resort for any individual country, it might just do so if the crisis were to affect a larger area and threaten the health of American banks.

The Benefits and Costs of Dollarization

In regions with a record of macroeconomic instability, such as Latin America and Central America, the use of the dollar as an unofficial currency is relatively widespread.[41] The stable value of the dollar as a unit of account is reinforced by its use as a reserve value and means of transaction. Dollarization occurs when the U.S. dollar to some extent displaces the domestic currency as the means to make payments, hold savings or liabilities, or price goods. Official dollarization is the monetary regime in which a country relinquishes the issue of domestic notes and coins and adopts the U.S. dollar as the national currency.

The main benefits of dollarization[42] are the convergence between domestic inflation and U.S. inflation rates, the downward pull on local interest rates due to the disappearance of currency risk,[43] and greater exposure to competition from international financial markets.

On the other hand, dollarization has its costs: the abandonment of an independent monetary policy, the lack of a lender of last resort, the loss of seigniorage revenues, and a diminished sovereignty. Dollarization makes it difficult to absorb real shocks: if export prices decline and/or capital flows dry

---

41. Baliño et al. (1999) estimate that in 18 countries, foreign currency deposits exceeded 30 percent of broad money while in 34 others these deposits were significant, at an average of 16 percent. A study by Porter and Judson (1996) for the Federal Reserve estimates that 55 percent to 70 percent of the dollars issued are held by foreigners, mostly in Latin America and Russia.

42. See Larraín and Velasco (1999) for a survey, on which this section draws.

43. Since there is a level of country risk that remains, interest rates will certainly not converge fully to the U.S. level.

up, the adjustment may require a real depreciation of the currency. Since this cannot be achieved by changes in the nominal exchange rate, the result is a recession that, through domestic price declines, eventually leads to real depreciation and the restoration of competitiveness. The problem would be solved if the dollar were to depreciate in the international markets at the same time as the dollarized country suffered the external shock. But precisely the opposite tends to happen, as evidenced by the recent currency crises: the dollar appreciated as capital escaped the emerging markets to the safe haven of the United States. For regions as heavily dependent on commodity exports as Central America, this problem may be more extreme.

A second problem with dollarization is that by abolishing the currency-issuing function of its central bank, the country is left with no lender of last resort. The authorities thus become severely limited in providing liquidity to the banking system at times of financial crises.[44] It is, in fact, highly improbable that the United States would agree to undertake the official role of lender of last resort for foreign countries, and quite impossible to conceive that the United States would consider the effects on other countries when determining its monetary policy. This is much more so in the case of Central American economies, whose small size makes them relatively unimportant to the United States.

Countries entertaining the dollarization option also must consider that it amounts to ceding seignorage to the United States. For a developing economy under responsible monetary management, this can mean giving up between 1 percent and 2 percent of GDP from seignorage. Proposals to share the seignorage would require the critical acceptance of the United States, which as indicated above is rather unlikely. The political costs associated with both the loss of sovereignty and the loss of seignorage when an economy is officially dollarized, are not negligible. These may even surpass the strictly economic cost.

The exchange rate arrangement adopted by its neighbors and trading partners is not a matter of indifference for a country. For an economy with a hard peg to the dollar—resulting, say, from the official dollarization of the economy—it is uncomfortable to have partners operating under flexible exchange rate schemes that can confront adverse external shocks by allowing a depreciation of the currency as a way to adjust and restore competitiveness.[45] In the case of Central America, regional trade integration is a necessary condition

---

44. This inability to act to protect the local financial system in periods of crisis explains why the Argentine authorities have been approaching the U.S. Federal Reserve to explore the possibility of its acting as lender of last resort. So far, the response in the U.S. has been less than enthusiastic.

45. This has been the case, recently, with Brazil and Argentina when the former devalued. This dramatically altered the competitiveness of Argentinean exports to Brazil.

for producers and consumers to overcome the constraints of the small size of national markets. The dollarization of some of the economies in Central America and not others could delay regional integration substantially by making the movements of goods and capital within the region riskier.

Assessing the Dollarization Option

Table 9-11 presents results for the criteria from Tables 9-2 through 9-5 above, but now only between each region and the United States. In every period, Central American countries have a strikingly lower real exchange rate volatility with the U.S. dollar than among themselves. This is also true for Asia in the 1980s, and for Latin America in all periods. However, while other areas have reduced their volatility versus the dollar over time, Central American countries have experienced a three-fold increase between the 1970s and the1990s.

The asymmetry of output shocks for Central America with the United

Table 9-11. *Real Exchange Rate Volatility Against the U.S. Dollar and Its Determinants*

	1970s	*1980s*	*1990s*	*1970–97*
Real Exchange Rate Volatility				
US/All countries	0.088	0.135	0.089	0.115
US/Europe	0.064	0.135	0.099	0.104
US/Asia	0.092	0.070	0.062	0.080
US/Latin America	0.132	0.188	0.096	0.158
US/Central America (w/o Nicaragua)	0.032	0.140	0.107	0.116
Asymmetry of Output Shocks				
US/All countries	0.030	0.037	0.025	0.034
US/Europe	0.026	0.026	0.019	0.025
US/Asia	0.026	0.040	0.024	0.033
US/Latin America	0.038	0.052	0.033	0.046
US/Central America (w/o Nicaragua)	0.026	0.029	0.024	0.032
Trade dissimilarity				
US/All countries	10.64	10.27	9.06	10.09
US/Europe	6.64	6.35	3.87	6.27
US/Asia	11.58	9.61	6.70	9.56
US/Latin America	13.67	13.95	8.76	13.61
US/Central America (w/o Nicaragua)	12.71	13.54	11.16	13.22
Bilateral trade integration				
US/All countries	2.63	3.24	3.41	3.06
US/Europe	0.80	1.08	0.98	0.95
US/Asia	4.16	5.82	6.07	5.27
US/Latin America	2.08	2.43	2.77	2.39
US/Central America (w/o Nicaragua)	4.80	4.54	4.33	4.58

States is also lower than within the region itself, except for the 1990s, when interregional asymmetry declined. As regards exports, Central American countries and the United States have always been very dissimilar. Indeed, Central America is the area with the highest trade dissimilarity with the United States. For its part, trade intensity is much higher with the United States than among the four Central American countries, which is not surprising since the United States has been the main trading partner of these countries through most of the period. Over time, Asia and Latin America have increased their trade integration with the United States while Central America has reduced it. In the 1990s Asia had the highest trade integration with the United States and the lowest real exchange rate volatility with the U.S. dollar.

We now turn to regression estimates to evaluate whether the volatility between Central American currencies and the United States dollar is significantly different from the bilateral real exchange volatility between the typical country in the sample. Table 9-12 presents the regression results for the whole sample, while Table 9-13 is based on a smaller sample, only the industrialized countries and Central America. In both cases, we add a dummy for all Central American–United States observations to assess the regional currencies' volatility versus the dollar. The results with just a Central America dummy from Tables 9-7 and 9-8 are presented again for comparison purposes.

Table 9-12 presents a clear pattern: the real exchange rate volatility between Central America and the United States has increased over time. It is significantly lower than average in the 1970s and significantly higher than average in the 1990s, while the coefficient for the 1980s is positive but not significant. The results for the sample of industrialized countries in Table 9-13 show a similar pattern, but in this case the coefficient of the dummy is not significant in the 1990s.

Finally, in Table 9-14 we present our index of integration and the relative measures of real exchange rate volatility, output-shock asymmetry, trade dissimilarity, and trade integration between the United States dollar and Central American currencies.[46]

We compare these individual country indices for Central American countries with the indicators for European countries. The aim is to compare the degree of integration between Central American economies and the United States with a sample of benchmark countries that already belong to an existing and working monetary area. We have chosen the Deutsche mark (DM)

---

46. The relative indicators are constructed as the ratio of the indicator for each Central American-United States observation relative to the mean of all the other observations for that particular Central American country. Similarly, for the European countries and the Deutsche mark.

Table 9-12. Assessing Real Exchange Rate Volatility: Central American Countries Against the U.S. Dollar

Sample: All countries, i.e. Central America*, Industrialized countries, Latin America, and Asia

	1970–79				1980–89				1990–97			
Output Shock	2.9150	13.66	2.9120	13.65	1.4429	10.54	1.4381	10.51	2.1560	13.06	2.1525	13.02
Trade Dissimilarity	0.0008	0.95	0.0008	0.99	0.0050	6.75	0.0048	6.50	0.0024	4.13	0.0022	3.79
Bilateral Trade	−0.0086	−5.66	−0.0080	−5.19	−0.0086	−5.14	−0.0091	−5.42	−0.0044	−3.08	−0.0047	−3.25
Size	0.0095	3.51	0.0094	3.56	−0.0011	−0.45	−0.0018	−0.73	0.0076	3.99	0.0068	3.66
Central America*	−0.0328	−1.60			0.0738	2.38			0.0672	4.66		
US-Central America			−0.0364	−2.91			0.0469	1.81			0.0422	2.50
Latin America	0.0662	4.11	0.0660	4.11	0.0487	4.07	0.0483	4.04	0.0081	0.95	0.0076	0.88
Asia	0.0122	1.28	0.0108	1.13	−0.0598	−5.91	−0.0587	−5.74	−0.0317	−5.35	−0.0311	−5.17
R²	0.28		0.28		0.38		0.38		0.36		0.35	
N	630		630		630		630		630		630	

	1970–97				Panel Estimates: 1970–97			
Output Shock	2.4351	12.47	2.4292	12.43	2.0410	19.71	2.0370	19.68
Trade Dissimilarity	0.0027	4.28	0.0026	4.19	0.0027	5.90	0.0026	5.77
Bilateral Trade	−0.0067	−5.53	−0.0070	−5.59	−0.0071	−6.73	−0.0073	−6.78
Size	0.0041	2.14	0.0036	1.97	0.0053	3.69	0.0049	3.49
Central America*	0.0461	2.49			0.0352	2.01		
US-Central America			0.0285	1.98			0.0179	1.35
Latin America	0.0369	3.75	0.0367	3.73	0.0409	5.33	0.0406	5.29
Asia	−0.0318	−4.89	−0.0312	−4.73	−0.0276	−4.68	−0.0274	−4.63
R²	0.44		0.44		0.83		0.83	
N	630		630		1890		1890	

*Nicaragua excluded.
Note: The numbers next to the coefficients are robust t-statistics

Table 9-13. *Assessing Real Exchange Rate Volatility: Central American Countries Against the U.S. Dollar*

Sample: Industrialized countries and Central America*

	1970–79				1980–89				1990–97			
	Coef	t	Coef	t	Coef	t	Coef	t	Coef	t	Coef	t
Output Shock	0.1154	0.79	0.0921	0.63	3.9282	8.60	3.9065	8.37	2.1054	4.17	2.0439	4.16
Trade Dissimilarity	0.0012	3.55	0.0014	3.46	0.0054	3.76	0.0064	4.50	0.006	4.76	0.0075	5.62
Bilateral Trade	−0.0052	−8.16	−0.0057	−7.86	−0.0069	−3.13	−0.0061	−2.43	−0.0064	−3.11	−0.0054	−2.87
Size	0.0052	4.68	0.006	4.66	−0.0048	−1.31	−0.0022	−0.59	0.0014	0.46	0.0054	1.66
Central America*												
US-Central America	−0.0089	−1.97	0.0021	0.31	0.021	0.81	0.0519	1.44	0.0264	1.38	0.0724	3.75
R²	0.37		0.36		0.57		0.58		0.47		0.49	
N	153		153		153		153		153		153	

	1970–97				Panel Estimates: 1970–97			
	Coef	t	Coef	t	Coef	t	Coef	t
Output Shock	1.3982	3.33	1.4451	3.48	2.3392	8.50	2.3216	8.36
Trade Dissimilarity	0.0053	7.11	0.0064	7.60	0.0041	5.81	0.005	6.83
Bilateral Trade	−0.0069	−5.22	−0.0057	−5.28	−0.0065	−5.60	−0.0059	−4.97
Size	−0.0026	−1.09	0.0005	0.21	0.0005	0.27	0.0029	1.53
Central America*			0.0318	2.25			0.0175	1.49
US-Central America			0.0642	3.35			0.0455	2.82
R²	0.58		0.60		0.85		0.85	
N	153		153		459		459	

*Nicaragua excluded.

Note: The numbers next to the coefficients are robust t-statistics.

Table 9-14. *Relative Integration Index with the US dollar and the Deutsche mark in the 1990s*

	Relative Output Asymmetry (1)	Relative Trade Dissimilarity (2)	Relative Trade Intensity (3)	Index (1)+(2)+(3)	Relative Real Exch.Rate Volatility
(Country/US) / (Country/Rest)					
Guatemala	0.687	1.012	0.022	1.72	0.651
Costa Rica	0.792	1.054	0.023	1.87	0.492
Honduras	0.780	1.076	0.018	1.87	0.858
El Salvador	0.758	1.134	0.033	1.92	0.630
Nicaragua	0.588	1.107	0.039	1.73	1.025
(Country/Germany) / (Country/Rest)					
France	0.178	0.274	0.115	0.57	0.176
Belgium	0.214	0.501	0.036	0.75	0.147
Italy	0.322	0.405	0.109	0.84	0.683
Spain	0.379	0.362	0.126	0.87	0.482
Portugal	0.326	0.739	0.029	1.09	0.419
Netherlands	0.344	0.702	0.051	1.10	0.074
United Kingdom	0.657	0.197	0.247	1.10	0.842
Ireland	0.622	0.590	0.057	1.27	0.502
Denmark	0.460	0.808	0.032	1.30	0.208
Greece	0.431	1.178	0.030	1.64	0.322

and Germany as the points of reference, because they represent the strongest and most stable European currency associated with the largest European economy. A low value of the index signals that the countries under analysis are much more similar to the country of reference as far as output asymmetry, trade intensity, and trade dissimilarity are concerned than they are to the average country in the sample.

We conclude that it makes better sense for European countries to be linked to the Deutsche mark than for Central American countries to peg to the U.S. dollar. As far as the determinants of real exchange rate volatility go, European economies tend to be closer to the German economy than are the Central American economies to that of the United States. The European country for which it makes the least sense to be pegged to the DM, Greece, still has a lower index than any of the Central American countries. The variable that drives this result the most is trade dissimilarity. Its value is larger than 1 for all Central American countries, which means that their export structure is closer to the average country in the sample than to the United States. However, relative output shock asymmetry is also much higher for central American countries, which increases the value of the index. Although all the countries in the region share a similar value of the summary index, Guatemala is the country for which a hard peg to the U.S. dollar would come closest to making sense; Nicaragua would be the next.

In sum, both the statistical analysis and the index comparison of Central America's dollarization option with the European reality suggest that dollarization is not an obvious option for Central America. Volatility between the region and the United States has increased over time. The structure of exports and the timing of output shocks between the countries in the region and the United States are sufficiently distinct to overcome the fact that they have relatively high bilateral trade volumes with the United States, even when compared with intra-European standards. The substantial trade dissimilarity between the region and the United States suggests the two will frequently be subject to different external shocks. And the size of terms of trade shocks to which the region is subject has been substantial in the past.[47] If we add the fact that the small economic size of Central America makes it unlikely that U.S. monetary policy will consider local macroeconomic conditions, there is strong evidence against the dollarization option. The analysis of the country indices shows this result to be generalizable to the whole region, and not to a particular country.

Conclusions

Central American countries developed national currencies only in the late 19th century. In the early 20th century, monetary instability was curbed through monetary reforms that opened the way for a long period of stability based on fixed exchange rates vis-à-vis the U.S. dollar. The importance of the dollar in the region led to its adoption as legal tender, for short periods of time, in Guatemala and Honduras. The feasibility of a Central American monetary union came up for discussion during the early years of the Central American Common Market. The focus then was on the advantages of pooled reserves and reduced transaction costs.

In this chapter we have reexamined the case for a regional currency in light of recent empirical work on the determinants of real exchange rate volatility. It is an issue that clearly deserves attention, given the new realities faced by the Central American economies: the abandonment of the fixed exchange rate regimes, a world of high capital mobility and currency crises, and a renewed interest in integration in the region as a way to enhance trade and to attract foreign investment.

---

47. See Chapter 3 on the crisis of the 1980s and the recovery of the 1990s for a comment on how external shocks have impacted the region.

Our application of standard econometric methodology in the analysis of the determinants of real exchange rate volatility to a large sample of countries allows us to draw several conclusions. Central America is highly integrated, even when compared to other regions in the world. The countries in the region meet the optimal currency criteria: they have very similar export structures, they have a relatively high degree of bilateral trade integration, and their national business cycles show high intercountry correlation. However, Central America lags behind the countries of the European Union in all of the criteria except one: the degree of trade structure dissimilarity, which is lowest for Central America among all regions examined. Moreover, by all criteria Central America was closer to being an optimal currency area in the 1970s than it is now. When different groupings of Central American countries are examined, the smallest group of Costa Rica, Guatemala, and El Salvador shows a higher degree of regional integration, closer to European levels. This suggests the possibility of a two-tier monetary integration program, similar to that of the European Union, whereby some countries could accede to the regional grouping at a later stage. In addition, previous analyses suggest that Europe's progress in the direction of higher integration may be the result of three decades of common trade and monetary cooperation. Mediterranean countries that joined in the last 15 years have managed to reduce their inflation differentials and exchange rate variability. In light of this, a currency union is a valuable option for Central America as a means of deepening regional integration at all levels.

We have also evaluated the possibility of dollarization, following on recent suggestions favoring dollarization and currency boards for Latin America. The associated loss of seignorage, the lack of a lender of last resort in countries with fragile banking and financial systems, and the increased exchange rate volatility with countries other than the United States do not favor this option. Given the advantages for Central American countries of diversifying export markets, the latter may be a particularly serious consideration. These costs probably outweigh the benefits of an absolute peg to the U.S. dollar: lower interest rates and inflation rates, especially as the economies in the region have achieved considerable progress toward macroeconomic stabilization. Our analysis also shows that, in spite of Central America's high degree of integration with the United States, the countries in the region all display far lower levels of integration with the United States than European countries do relative to Germany.

The choice of an exchange rate regime for the countries in the region should thus consider those countries' extremely high degree of regional economic integration, close to European levels. As to the region's option of dollarization, the indices of Central American–United States bilateral integration are below those between European countries and Germany. Thus, though bilateral real exchange rate volatility is higher within the region than between countries in the region and the U.S. dollar, the similarity of export structures and the symmetry of output shocks make a regional monetary arrangement both feasible and advisable. The development of financial depth and of credible institutional arrangements that would ensure the smooth working of the union are the most critical elements not yet in place.

The high levels of bilateral trade would support the dollarization option. De facto dollarization is high in Nicaragua and Costa Rica, the two countries that suffered higher inflation rates, and moderate in El Salvador and Honduras. However, a full dollar-peg can become a hindrance if Central America truly aims to exploit its promising localization in order to develop higher trade volumes with Europe, Asia, and South America.

References

Aghlevi, Bijan B., Moshin S. Khan, and Peter J. Montiel. 1991. "Exchange Rate Policy in Developing Countries: Some Analytical Issues." Occasional Paper No. 78 (March). Washington, D.C.: International Monetary Fund.

Bayoumi, Tamim, and Barry Eichengreen. 1992. "Shocking Aspects of European Monetary Unification." Discussion Paper No. 643 (May). Centre for Economic Policy Research.

Bayoumi, Tamim, and Barry Eichengreen. 1996a. "Operationalizing the Theory of Optimum Currency Areas." Discussion Paper No. 1484 (October). Centre for Economic Policy Research.

Bayoumi, Tamim, and Barry Eichengreen. 1996b. "Is Asia an Optimum Currency Area? Can It Become One? Regional, Global, and Historical Perspectives on Asian Monetary Relations." Working Paper C96/081 (December). Berkeley: Center for International and Development Economics Research (CIDER).

Bayoumi, Tamim, and Barry Eichengreen. 1997a. "Ever Closer to Heaven? An Optimum-Currency-Area Index for European Countries." *European Economic Review* 41(3–5): 761–70.

Bayoumi, Tamim, and Barry Eichengreen. 1997b. "Optimum Currency Areas and Exchange Rate Volatility: Theory and Evidence Compared." In *International Trade and Finance: New Frontiers for Research: Essays in Honor of Peter B. Kenen*, edited by Benjamin Cohen. Cambridge: Cambridge University Press.

Bayoumi, Tamim, and Barry Eichengreen. 1998. "Exchange Rate Volatility and Intervention: Implications of the Theory Optimum Currency Areas." *Journal of International Economics* 45(2): 191–209.

Boughton, James M. 1993. "The Economics of the CFA Franc Zone." In *Policy Issues in the Operation of Currency Unions*, edited by Paul R. Masson and Mark P. Taylor. Cambridge: Cambridge University Press.

Bofinger, Peter. 1994. "Is Europe an Optimal Currency Area?" Discussion Paper No 915 (February). Centre for Economic Policy Research (CEPR).

Bulmer-Thomas, Victor. 1987. *The Political Economy of Central America since 1920.* Cambridge Latin American Studies Series, Volume 63. Cambridge: Cambridge University Press.

Bulmer-Thomas, Victor. 1998. "The Central American Common Market: From Closed to Open Regionalism." *World Development* 26(2): 313–22.

Calvo, Guillermo A. 1999. "Testimony on Full Dollarization." Presented before a Joint Hearing of the Subcommittees on Economic Policy and International Trade and Finance. Washington, D.C., 22 April 1999. Retrieved from *http://www.bsos.umd.edu/econ/ciecalvo.htm.*.

Campbell, J. Gibson, and Emily Lennon. 1999. "Historical Census Statistics on the Foreign-Born Population of the United States: 1850–1990." Population Division Working Paper No. 29 (February). Washington, D.C.: U.S. Bureau of the Census. Retrieved from *http://www.census.gov/population/www/documentation/twps0029/tab03.html.*

Collins, Susan M. 1996. "On Becoming More Flexible: Exchange Rate Regimes in Latin America and the Caribbean." *Journal of Development Economics* 51(1): 117–38.

Crosby, Benjamin L. 1990. "Central America." In *After the Wars: Reconstruction in Afghanistan, Indochina, Central America, Southern Africa, and the Horn of Africa*, edited by Anthony Lake. New Jersey: Overseas Development Council.

Devarajan, Shantayanan, and Dani Rodrik. 1992. "Do the Benefits of Fixed Exchange Rates Outweigh the Costs? The Franc Zone in Africa?" In *Open Economies: Structural Adjustment and Agriculture*, edited by Ian Goldin and Alan L. Winters. Cambridge: Cambridge University Press.

Economist, The. 1999. "Fix or Float?" (Global Finance Survey.) 30 January 1999.

Edwards, Sebastian. 1995. "Exchange Rates, Inflation, and Disinflation: Latin American Experiences." In *Capital Controls, Exchange Rates, and Monetary Policy in the World Economy*, edited by Sebastian Edwards. Cambridge: Cambridge University Press.

Edwards, Sebastian. 1996. "The Determinants of the Choice Between Fixed and Flexible Exchange-Rate Regimes." Working Paper No. 5756 (September). National Bureau of Economic Research (NBER).

Eichengreen, Barry. 1998. "Does Mercosur Need a Single Currency?" National Bureau of Economic Research (NBER) Working Paper No. 6821 (December).

Eichengreen, Barry, and Paul Masson. 1998. "Exit Strategies: Policy Options for Countries Seeking Greater Exchange Rate Flexibility." Occasional Paper No. 168. Washington, D.C.: International Monetary Fund.

Esquivel, Gerardo, and Felipe Larraín. 1999. "Currency Crises: Is Central America Different?" Mimeo (August).

Fatás, Antonio. 1997. "EMU: Countries or Regions? Lessons from the EMS Experience." *European Economic Review* 41(3–5): 743–51.

Frankel, Jeffrey A., and Andrew K. Rose. 1996a. "The Endogeneity of the Optimum Currency Area Criteria." Working Paper No. 5700 (August). National Bureau of Economic Research (NBER).

Frankel, Jeffrey A., and Andrew K. Rose. 1996b. "Economic Structure and the Decision to Adopt a Common Currency." Working Paper C96/073 (August). Berkeley: Center for International and Development Economics Research (CIDER).

Frankel, Jeffrey A., and Andrew K. Rose. 1996c. "Currency Crashes in Emerging Markets: An Empirical Treatment." *Journal of International Economics* 41: 351–368.

Frenkel, Goldstein, and Mason. 1991. "Characteristics of a Succesful Exchange Rate System." Occasional Paper No. 82 (July). Washington, D.C.: International Monetary Fund.

Gaba, Ernesto. 1990. *Criterios para Evaluar el Tipo de Cambio de las Economias Centroamericanas.* Mexico City: Centro de Estudios Monetarios Latinoamericanos.

Gibson, Bill. 1991. "The Inflation-Devaluation-Inflation Hypothesis in Nicaragua." *The Journal of Development Studies* 27(2): 23–55.

Gibson, Bill. 1993. "Nicaragua" In *The Rocky Road to Reform: Adjustment, Income Distribution, and Growth in the Developing World,* edited by Lance Taylor. Cambridge: The MIT Press.

Hanke, Steve, and K. Schuler. 1999. "A Dollarization Blueprint for Argentina." Mimeo.

Hausmann, R., M. Gavin, C. Pages-Serra, and E. Stein. 1999. "Financial Turmoil and the Choice of Exchange Rate Regime." Mimeo (March). Inter-American Development Bank.

Hildebrand, John R. 1987. *Monetary Integration: Key Currencies Contributing Equitably to Development.* Bristol: Wyndham Hall Press.

IMF. Various years. "Exchange Arrangements and Regulations." Washington, D.C.

IMF. 1997. "Exchange Rate Arrangements and Economic Performance in Developing Countries." World Economic Outlook (October).

IMF. 1998. "Costa Rica: Recent Developments." Country Staff Report. Washington, D.C.

IMF. 1998. "El Salvador: Recent Developments." Country Staff Report. Washington, D.C.

IMF. 1998. "Guatemala: Recent Developments." Country Staff Report. Washington, D.C.

IMF. 1998. "Honduras: Recent Developments." Country Staff Report. Washington, D.C.

IMF. 1998. "Nicaragua: Recent Developments." Country Staff Report. Washington, D.C.

IMF Economic Forum. 1998. "Dollarization: Fad or Future for Latin America." Washington, D.C. Retrieved from *http://www/imf.org/external/np/tr/1999/TR990624.htm*..

Instituto Interamericano de Derechos Humanos (IIDH). 1992. "La Migración por Violencia en Centro América" San Jose, Costa Rica.

Kafka, Alexandre. 1973. "Optimum Currency Areas and Latin America." In *The Economics of Common Currencies*, edited by Harry G. Johnson and Alexander K. Swoboda. Proceedings of the Madrid Conference on Optimum Currency Areas. Cambridge: Harvard University Press.

Kenen, Peter. 1969. "The Theory of Optimum Currency Areas: An Eclectic View." In *Exchange Rates and the Monetary System: Selected Essays of Peter B. Kenen*, edited by Peter B. Kenen. Economists of the Twentieth Century series. Aldershot, U.K.: Elgar. Distributed in the U.S. by Ashgate, Brookfield.

Larraín, Felipe, and Andrés Velasco. 1999. "Exchange Rate Policy for Emerging Markets: One Size Does Not Fit All." Mimeo (July).

Marsden, David. 1992. "European Integration and the Integration of European Labour Markets." *Labour* 6(1): 3–35.

McKinnon, Ronald. 1963. "Optimum Currency Areas." *American Economic Review* 53: 717–25.

Mundell, Robert A. 1961. "The Theory of Optimum Currency Areas." *American Economic Review* 51 (September).

Mundell, Robert A. 1973. "A Plan for a European Currency." In *The Economics of Common Currencies*, edited by Harry G. Johnson and Alexander K. Swoboda. Proceedings of the Madrid Conference on Optimum Currency Areas. Cambridge: Harvard University Press.

Obstfeld, Maurice, and Kenneth Rogoff. 1995. "The Mirage of Fixed Exchange Rates." *The Journal of Economic Perspectives* 9(4): 73–96.

Ocampo, Jose Antonio. 1991. "Collapse and (Incomplete) Stabilization of the Nicaraguan Economy." In *The Macroeconomics of Populism in Latin America*, edited by Rudiger Dornbusch and Sebastian Edwards. National Bureau of Economic Research (NBER) Conference Report. Chicago: University of Chicago Press.

Quirk, Peter J. 1994. "Recent Experiences with Floating Exchange Rates in Developing Countries." In *Approaches to Exchange Rate Policy: Choices for Developing and Transition Economies*, edited by Richard C. Barth and Chong-Huey Wong. Washington, D.C.: International Monetary Fund.

Porter, Richard, and Ruth Judson. 1996. "The Location of U.S. Currency: How Much Is Abroad?" *Federal Reserve Bulletin* 82(10).

Tornell, Aaron, and Andrés Velasco. 1999. "Fixed versus Flexible Exchange Rates:

Which Provides More Fiscal Discipline." Forthcoming. *Journal of Monetary Economics.*

Triffin, Robert. 1970. "Proyecto para un Fondo Centroamericano de Estabilización." *Revista del Banco Hipotecario de El Salvador* 5(2): 167–182. San Salvador.

United States Bureau of the Census. 1997. "Country of Origin and Year of Entry into the U.S. of the Foreign Born, by Citizenship Status: March 1997." *Current Population Survey.* March 1997. Retrieved from: *http://www.bls.census.gov/cps/pub/1997/for_born.htm*

Westbrook, Jilleen R., and Thomas D. Willet. 1999. "Exchange Rates as Nominal Anchors: An Overview of the Issues." In *Exchange-Rate Policies for Emerging Market Economies: Political Economy of Global Interdependence,* edited by Richard J. Sweeney and Clas G. Wihlborg.

Young, John Parke. 1925. *Central American Currency and Finance.* Princeton: Princeton University Press.

Young, John Parke. 1965. *Central American Monetary Union.* Guatemala. U.S. Dept. of State, Agency for International Development, Regional Office, Central American and Panama Affairs.

Appendix: Short Histories of National Exchange Rate Systems in Central America

Costa Rica

In 1981, Costa Rica became the first Central American country to abandon the fixed nominal exchange rate regime. It is also the country that readjusted its parity most often, a total of 14 times since 1920. Most of the readjustments took place in the 1920s and 1930s and went in both directions. There followed three major devaluations of the colon: in 1961 from 5.61 colones per dollar to 6.625, in May 1974 to 8.57, and in January 1981 to 13.27. The following months were marked by considerable instability, with continuous readjustments of the exchange rate. By September 1982, these had brought the colon to a level of 40 to the U.S. dollar. From then on, Costa Rica has successfully targeted the real exchange rate, in practice following a crawling peg without preannouncement.[48]

Costa Rica returned to a dual exchange rate market from 1971 to 1974, shortly after the unification of the previous dual system in 1969: imports lists; temporary prohibitions to operate in the so-called "free" market, which was heavily regulated; and a devalued rate in the "free" market were the norm. Alongside this "free" market, there was a black market that more closely reflected the actual value of the currency. The devaluation of 1974 set the new parity at the black market level and was accompanied by the elimination of the "free" market. A progressive effort to eliminate other restrictions followed. However, by 1980, both the dual market and the restrictions were re-established. From 1980 to 1983, there were multiple changes in the value of the currency and in the restrictions and regulations of foreign exchange transactions. In practice, a multiple exchange rate system prevailed. By the end of 1983, as the real exchange rate stabilized, the market was unified, and the elimination of restrictions regained force. Since 1985, there has been an effectively unified system, and since 1992 an officially "free negotiated rate." In 1995, several measures were taken to eliminate many of the remaining controls.

El Salvador

The value of the Salvadoran colon remained fixed at 2.5 C per U.S. dollar from 1935 till January 1986, when it was devalued to 5 C per U. S. dollar. This parity did not change until May 1990, when a new devaluation brought the colon to 6.9 C per U.S. dollar. Several readjustments throughout the year

---

48. According to the IMF Exchange Arrangements and Restrictions, a floating system with intervention to "stabilize large fluctuations" was introduced in March 1992.

brought the value down to 8.03 *C* in December. Since 1993, the colon has been kept virtually fixed at between 8.7 and 8.755 *C* to the dollar.

El Salvador allowed the currency to appreciate continually in real terms for a very long period, before it undertook the first devaluation. A similar development took place between 1986 and 1990. El Salvador is still the country that maintains the highest stability of its currency's nominal parity against the dollar. This has resulted in a continuous real appreciation of the colon up until 1997, when the slow-down in Salvadoran inflation helped stabilize the real rate versus the dollar. Workers' remittances from abroad played a substantial economic role over the entire last decade, surpassing merchandise exports revenues in importance since 1992. A side effect of these large flows of remittances has been a contribution to the real appreciation of the currency, which has harmed trade competitiveness.

Restrictions on the foreign exchange market in the early 1970s included taxes on exchange rate sales, deposit requirements on currency for travel, import licenses, and making imports above a certain amount subject to approval. These restrictions were partially relaxed between 1973 to 1978, only to be tightened again in 1979, when the civil war broke out. The restrictions became quite stringent over the following years. A parallel currency market functioned from 1982 to 1985. Long and changing lists of regulations determined the transactions going to each exchange rate market during this period. A preferential rate was established for transactions with Central American countries during 1984. In 1985, the Monetary Board got full control of the exchange rate policy. The gap between the parallel and the official market went from 52 in 1982 to almost 94 percent in December 1995, with an additional premium of 31 percent in the black market over the parallel market.[49] After the devaluation of 1986, the dual exchange rate market was unified, and the black market premium fell to levels closer to 10 percent, but other restrictions remained. By March 1990, a multiple exchange rate was in place; three months later, the exchange rate market was unified and a system weighting commercial banks and exchange houses was established. Exchange rate restrictions were mostly eliminated in 1992, the year that the peace accords were signed that ended the military conflict. The weighting system that determines the exchange rate changed in 1992, and in 1994, an electronic system was introduced.

Guatemala

Guatemala kept a parity of 1 quetzal per U.S. dollar from 1925 till June 1986, when it devalued to 2.5 quetzales per U.S. dollar. The new parity held

---

49. Gaba (1990).

for two more years, and was then readjusted to 2.705. After a series of small adjustments, the exchange rate was allowed to float in November 1989. A short-lived narrow band established in February 1990 led to a floating system in April of the same year. Two months later, an auction system was introduced; in the remainder of the year, three additional auction systems were tried. By September 1990 the quetzal had depreciated to 5.711 per U.S. dollar, but from that point on it has tended to appreciate in real terms. It is the Central American currency that has moved most freely in past years. Since March 1994, the exchange rate has been determined in the interbank market, with intervention by the Central Bank to prevent large fluctuations.

Guatemala has also had numerous restrictions and controls on foreign exchange transactions. Between 1971 and 1973, large transactions were subject to approval and a series of controls on capital movements were imposed in 1980. From 1984 to 1988, there was a multiple exchange rate system, and a tax on exchange rate transactions was imposed in 1985. The gap between the official and the black market, however, has been relatively small in Guatemala (below 10 percent), except for the period 1982–83.

Honduras

On March 1990, the lempira was devalued after 72 years of fixed parity with the U.S. dollar at 2 lempiras per dollar. The new rate was set at 4 lempiras per dollar, a nominal devaluation of 100 percent. The exchange rate was allowed to float within a narrow band of +/- 2.5 percent around the rate fixed by the Central Bank. The rate was modified a few more times during the year, and the band was eliminated in October. By December 1990, the lempira had depreciated to 5.3 lempiras per dollar. By 1992, the currency was allowed to float. The exchange rate market was further liberalized over this period: in 1994, an auction system was established, the rules were changed again in 1995 and in 1996, opening the exchange rate market to individuals and companies.[50] The currency continued to depreciate until September 1994 when it reached 9.11 lempiras to the dollar; from then on it has appreciated in real terms, due to Honduras' high rate of inflation and the Central Bank's policy of keeping a relatively constant nominal exchange rate, especially during 1997. The real exchange rate at the end of 1998 was nearly at the 1990 predevaluation level.

Despite the long run stability of the nominal exchange rate, Honduras is no exception to the tensions that affected Central American countries in the

---

50. For more details on functioning of the auction see the IMF (1998) Country Staff Report for Honduras.

1970s and early 1980s. In 1971, the Central Bank suspended transactions in currencies other than the dollar, and import controls were imposed. The period 1979–81 was marked by the imposition of controls on foreign exchange, to avoid capital flight and ration the available reserves among importers. Rates with Central America were set through a parallel market in 1985. Until 1990, there were regulations about the amount of export proceeds that had to be turned over to the Central Bank. The cumulative loss of reserves from 1982 to 1987 was partly compensated for by official transfers. The gap between the official market and the black market was very large for a long period of time. Restrictions have been progressively eliminated since 1990.

Nicaragua

Nicaragua has endured extremely high exchange rate instability over the past 20 years, due to its hyperinflation from 1985 to 1990. However, like its neighbors, it has managed to keep a fixed parity with the dollar for long periods of time: 1920–34, 1939–55, and 1955–79. In April 1979, the cordoba was devalued from 7 to 10 cordobas to the dollar. High inflation and a fixed parity translated into a large real appreciation under the Sandinista government that ended with a new major devaluation in February 1985, from 10 to 28 cordobas to the dollar. This proved insufficient. One year later, the rate was changed to 70 cordobas to the dollar. Inflation had gone from less than 5 percent in 1978 to double digits during the period 1979–84, to triple digits from 1985–87, and to hyperinflation in 1988—10,205 percent per year. The different attempts at stabilization were unsuccessful until 1991. A currency reform in February 1988 established the "new cordoba" equivalent to 1,000 old cordobas. The new currency was pegged to the dollar at a rate of 10 new cordobas per dollar. It had to be readjusted to 10.25 three days later, and by June it was automatically adjusted to follow the price level. The stabilization failed. By 1990, inflation was still more than 7,000 percent, and in 1991 it was still above 2,000 percent. In mid-1990, the "gold cordoba," equivalent to one dollar was introduced, and circulated along with the new cordoba until the following year. A large devaluation in March 1991, accompanied by a new currency reform and a series of measures (wage adjustment, backward indexation of term deposits, credit controls), finally stabilized inflation around 20 percent. In May 1991, the currency was devalued to 0.2 new cordobas per dollar or 5 million old cordobas per dollar. The new parity was kept fixed as part of the stabilization plan until January 1993; since then, it has followed a crawling peg aimed at stabilizing the real exchange rate.

Exchange rate restrictions have followed the familiar pattern described for the other countries, with additional restrictions and extensive use of the multiple exchange rate market during the Sandinista government. From 1970-74, there was a tax on exchange rate transactions; and in 1978 a multiple exchange rate system was reintroduced. In 1979, all commercial banks were nationalized, and exchange rate transactions were suspended temporarily in August. The parallel market operated discontinuously until 1990, when the exchange rate market was unified. In addition, there was a black market. The gap between the official rate and the parallel rate widened in the 1980s, especially since 1985. The gap with the black market was even wider. The restrictions on foreign exchange were progressively lifted during the years 1992–97.

10

Currency Crises in Central America

GERARDO ESQUIVEL AND FELIPE LARRAÍN B.

Introduction

During several decades, Central American countries had very stable exchange rates. In fact, some of them were able to keep the longest-lasting fixed exchange rate parities vis-à-vis the U.S. dollar in modern history (Edwards and Losada 1994). Nevertheless, especially during the 1980s and early 1990s, nations of Central America have also had to deal with episodes of exchange rate instability.

In this chapter we analyze the characteristics of some of the episodes of exchange rate instability that have occurred in the five countries of Central America (Costa Rica, El Salvador, Guatemala, Honduras and Nicaragua) since 1970. We also carry out a cross-country empirical analysis on the determinants of currency crises. The main objective of this exercise is to get a better understanding of the basic forces that underlie the collapse of the exchange rate, with a particular focus on Central America. The empirical framework that we use in this chapter was recently developed and implemented in an empirical study on the determinants of currency crises in a sample of 30 high-and middle-income countries (Esquivel and Larraín,1998). In that study, we found that high seignorage rates, large current account deficits, a real exchange rate misalignment, low foreign exchange reserves, negative terms-of-trade shocks, negative per capita income growth, and a regional contagion effect, were all highly significant in explaining the presence of the currency crises in our sample. These results were robust to changes in the specification, definition of variables, method of estimation, and country sample.

In this chapter, we extend our previous results by adding information relative to Central America. Our secondary objective is to study whether the small group of macroeconomic variables that we identified in our previous work is also useful in explaining the presence of exchange rate crises in Central American countries. Beyond the obvious domestic interest in the topic, we consider that there are at least three main reasons for studying the determinants of currency crises in this specific group of Central American countries.

First, these countries are poorer relative to the sample in our previous work. Thus, results based on our expanded sample may shed light on the validity of extrapolating our previous conclusions to other economies. Second, the Central American countries belong to a single geographical region and they tend to have strong commercial relationships with each other. In fact, these countries have a trade agreement that goes back to the 1960s (the Central American Common Market). This characteristic will allow us to put to a test our previous finding of a regional contagion effect. Third, as mentioned above, Central American currencies were kept fixed during relatively long periods. However, fixed official exchange rate parities often coincided with large premiums in the foreign exchange black market (Gaba 1990). The presence of a black market in this context may seriously undermine the explanatory and predictive power of any model that attempts to explain sudden changes in the nominal exchange rates. In this sense, we believe that this exercise provides one of the most challenging tests that we can impose on the whole approach of trying to explain currency crises based on the behavior of a small set of macroeconomic variables.

This chapter begins with a quick overview of the history of nominal and real exchange rates in Central America. A brief digression on the alternative models of currency crises that have been suggested in the theoretical literature is followed by a section in which we present our definition of currency crisis and establish the criteria that we use to identify these crises in our sample. We then go on to describe the data and the econometric methodology, before presenting the main empirical results. We test whether or not adding the Central American countries to our original sample changes our results and also evaluate the in-sample explanatory power of the estimated model, with special emphasis on Central America. We end with a discussion of our results.

EXCHANGE RATES IN CENTRAL AMERICA

Nominal Exchange Rates

Figure 10-1 shows the evolution of the nominal exchange rate for the Central American countries between 1950 and 1998. The exchange rate is in local

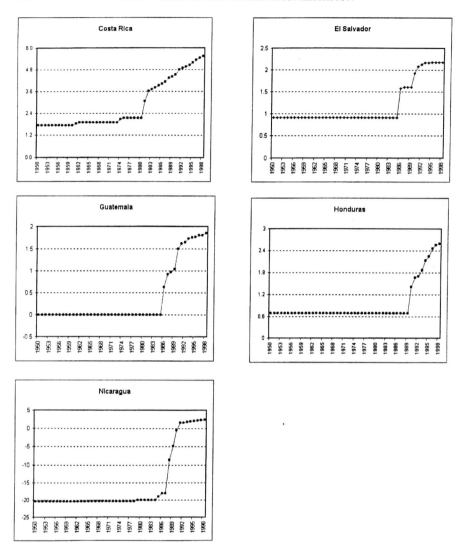

Figure 10-1.   *Annual Nominal Exchange Rates (in logs of local currency units per dollar)*
Source: International Financial Statistics, IMF

currency units per U.S. dollar and logs are used to illustrate proportional changes in the exchange rate. As can be seen in this figure, the nominal exchange rate history of Central American countries before 1980 differs markedly from the turbulent exchange rate history that characterized many other Latin American countries. Unlike these other countries, the small economies of Central America were able to keep a fixed exchange rate parity *vis-à-vis* the U.S. dollar for a very long period.[1]

The fixed parity of the Honduran currency had the longest duration among all the Central American currencies. The fixed exchange rate parity between the Honduran currency and the U.S. dollar lasted unchanged from 1918 until March 1990 (Edwards and Losada 1994), when the government was forced to devalue the lempira by 50 percent (the nominal exchange rate went from 2 to 4 lempiras per dollar). Since then, there has not been any significant unexpected variation in the Honduran nominal exchange rate.

El Salvador and Guatemala, on the other hand, were able to sustain a fixed parity only until the mid-eighties, when their currencies collapsed in the midst of internal civil conflicts and when the debt crisis in Latin America was at its worst. In January 1986, the Salvadoran government devalued its currency from 2.5 to 5 colones per dollar, and the official and the parallel market were unified. On March 1990, the Salvadoran colon was again devalued. This time the exchange rate was set at 6.9 per dollar. In Guatemala, the abandonment of the fixed exchange rate regime was defined by the implementation in 1984 of a three-tiered exchange rate system. The three types of exchange rates were as follows: an official rate (unchanged), a banking rate (freely determined) and an auction rate (determined by an auction process in which importers made their bids). Finally, in 1986 the Guatemalan government restructured the exchange rate system, which led to a de facto devaluation of the domestic currency.

Nicaragua, on the other hand, devalued its currency in early 1979, at a time of tremendous civil unrest that culminated in the fall of the Somoza regime and the Sandinista takeover. During the first years of the Sandinista government, the newly installed government opted for maintaining a fixed exchange rate regime *vis-à-vis* the U.S. dollar. As discussed below, this policy decision, together with rising domestic inflation, led to a tremendous appreciation of the real exchange rate that had to be reversed sooner or later. During the second part of the 1980s, there were repeated unsuccessful attempts to restore stability in the foreign exchange market. Nominal devaluations of the domestic currency, the cordoba, were attempted, and two new currency denomina-

---

1. For a more complete description of the exchange rate history of Central America see Bulmer-Thomas (1987) and Gaba (1990). See also Chapter 9 in this volume. Edwards (1995) analyzes some properties of the fixed exchange rate regimes of Costa Rica, El Salvador, Guatemala, and Honduras. Edwards and Losada (1994) analyze the long run implications of the Purchasing Power Parity theory for Guatemala and Honduras. These authors also have an appendix describing the history of the exchange rate regimes in these two countries. Gibson (1993) offers a detailed account of the exchange rate policy in Nicaragua during the Sandinista regime.

tions were also put in place: a new cordoba and a gold cordoba. It was not until 1991 that stability in the foreign exchange market was achieved.

Finally, within the region, Costa Rica had the least stable parity against the U.S. dollar during the pre–debt crisis period. In fact, Costa Rica had to adjust the value of its currency as early as 1961, when the Costa Rican colon was devalued from 5.64 to 6.64 units per dollar. The new exchange rate was kept unchanged until 1974, when another devaluation set the exchange rate at 8.57 colones per dollar. In January 1981, the fixed exchange rate system was finally abandoned.[2]

Figure 10-1 also provides insight into the exchange rate regimes that came immediately after the collapse of the fixed parities in Central America. On the one hand, both Costa Rica and Honduras steadily moved towards more flexible exchange rate arrangements. Costa Rica, after repeated unsuccessful attempts to stabilize its currency (none of which lasted more than a few months), began to target its real exchange rate in mid-1985 with relative success (see Figure 10-2). Honduras, after almost two years of attempting to restore the stability of its currency at 5.4 lempiras per U.S. dollar, decided to implement a more flexible exchange rate policy in late 1992. Since then, the Honduran currency has fluctuated relatively freely.

On the other hand, El Salvador, Guatemala and Nicaragua attempted to confront the collapse of their currencies with a new fixed parity against the U.S. dollar. The shortest-lived of these experiments was in Guatemala, where the attempt to establish a fixed parity of 2.5 quetzales per dollar in 1986 (up from a one-to-one parity) was abruptly abandoned two years later. In El Salvador and Nicaragua, the new pegs lasted longer. In 1986, El Salvador devalued its currency from 2.5 to 5 colones per dollar. The new parity lasted for approximately four years until it collapsed again in May 1990. Since 1993, the currency of El Salvador has remained fixed against the dollar, this time at a rate of 8.76 colones per dollar. On the other hand, following the devaluation of 1979, the recently installed Sandinista government of Nicaragua chose to keep its exchange rate fixed against the dollar. The parity was sustained until 1985, when the accumulated domestic inflation and the external conditions made adjustment of the exchange rate inevitable.[3] Since 1992, Nicaragua has implemented a managed float, with pre-announced daily changes of the exchange rate.

---

2. Edwards (1994) argues that the fact that Costa Rica abandoned the fixed exchange rate system relatively early, partially explains why that country recovered much faster from the debt crisis than did its Central American neighbors.

3. For a detailed account of the exchange rate experience of Nicaragua see Ocampo (1991) and Gibson (1993).

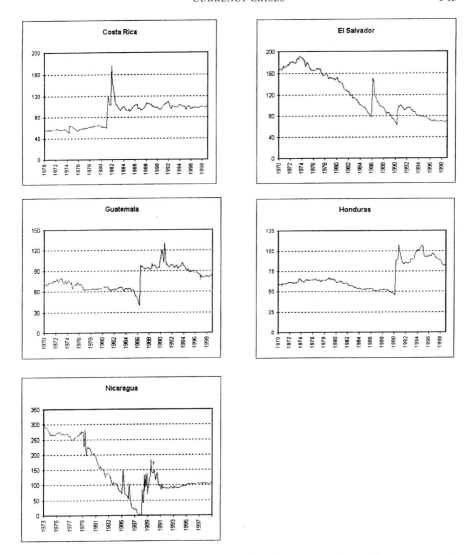

Figure 10-2.   Central America: Monthly Real Exchange Rates (December 1990 = 100)
Source: Authors' calculations based on IMF and UNCTAD data.
Note: Multilateral real exchange rates. Estimates are trade-weighted.

Real Exchange Rates

Figure 10-2 shows the monthly multilateral real exchange rates of the five Central American countries for the period 1970 to 1998.[4] The real exchange

---

4. The exception is Nicaragua, for which we have information from 1973 onwards.

rate indexes are trade-weighted and they are depicted using December 1990=100. A rise in the exchange rate represents a real depreciation.

An interesting fact that emerges from Figure 10-2 is that the endings of the fixed exchange rate parities in Central America are easily identifiable by the pronounced peaks that we observe in their real exchange rates. Figure 10-2 also shows that the collapse of the fixed parities in El Salvador, Guatemala, and Honduras was preceded by a substantial appreciation of their real exchange rates. In Costa Rica, this phenomenon was also present in the devaluation of 1974, but it was less evident during the months that preceded the devaluation of 1981. The case of Nicaragua is so extreme as to deserve a fuller discussion.

As mentioned above, the Sandinista government that took power in 1979 decided to maintain fixed exchange rate parity against the U.S. dollar. In the years that followed, however, inflation accumulated rapidly as a result of inconsistent macroeconomic policies and enormous increases in both defense (to fight the Contra war) and social government expenditures (Ocampo 1991). One of the immediate consequences of these events was a very pronounced appreciation in the Nicaraguan real exchange rate. By 1983, it was already clear that the nominal exchange rate was unsustainable. According to some calculations, the exchange rate black-market premium in that year was already above 1,000 percent.[5] In spite of the evidence, the Sandinista government was reluctant to devalue the Nicaraguan currency.[6] The resolution of the problem was then postponed until 1985, when a devaluation of the Nicaraguan cordoba took place (the nominal exchange rate went from 10 to 28 cordobas per dollar).[7]

The nominal devaluation of February 1985, however, turned out to be insufficient to restore equilibrium in the foreign exchange market. In 1986 another devaluation occurred. The attempt to restore stability failed again miserably. To make matters worse, the inflation-devaluation-inflation vicious circle had already kicked-in, and the real exchange rate continued its downward trend. By 1987, the foreign exchange black-market premium was above 17,000 percent (see Ocampo 1992). According to Figure 10-2, by mid-1987 the real exchange rate had attained incredibly low levels. In fact, the 1986–87 period has been defined by some authors as one of the "most impressive cases

---

5. See Gibson (1993) and Ocampo (1991).

6. Gibson (1993) suggests that reluctance of the Sandinista government to devalue was due to their unwillingness to "face the political consequences of an open assault on real wages and in so doing they crippled the export market."

7. Gibson (1985), using a computable general equilibrium model, argues that the devaluation should have occurred much earlier, in 1983.

of overvaluation in the economic history of Latin America, or indeed the world."[8]

By 1988, an orthodox economic-policy reform was necessary and the Nicaraguan President, Daniel Ortega, announced a major economic plan early in that year. In February 1988, the cordoba suffered a major devaluation: it went from 70 to 10,000 units per dollar.[9] Other depreciations of the currency were attempted in June of that year, in February 1989, and then again in May 1990. All these programs and measures helped somewhat to bring the real exchange rate to a more reasonable level. However, high inflation prevented full stabilization of the exchange rate. In March 1991, a new economic program was implemented ("The plan Lacayo"). This program unified the currencies and converted the old cordoba to the new gold cordoba at a rate of 5 million to 1. The exchange rate was then fixed again, but this time inflation almost miraculously stopped (Gibson 1993). As expected, this event turned out to be a crucial element in the stabilization of the real exchange rate (see Figure 10-2).

A second interesting aspect that emerges from Figure 10-2 is the clearly differentiated pattern followed by the real exchange rates of the Central American countries in the post–crisis period. On the one hand, Costa Rica, Honduras and, to a lesser extent, Guatemala, all ended with a substantially depreciated real exchange rate relative to the level they had during the 1980s. On the other hand, El Salvador and Nicaragua ended with an appreciated real exchange rate. In both cases, their real exchange rate in 1998 was slightly above one-third of the rate at the beginning of the 1970s. It is not unlikely that the Salvadoran case is somehow related to the large remittances from abroad that El Salvador receives form the large number of expatriates who live and work in the United States (Segovia 1996). The case of Nicaragua, however, has not obvious explanation and further research is needed to understand this phenomenon.

THEORETICAL MODELS OF CRISES

First-Generation Models

The first formal model of balance-of-payments crises was put forward by Krugman (1979), based on the work of Salant and Henderson (1978). Krugman argued that crises occur when a continuous deterioration in the

---

8. Taylor et al. (1989) cited in Gibson (1993).

9. In 1988 a new currency, the *new cordoba*, was introduced. The new currency was trading at a 10-to-1 parity with respect to the dollar, and each *new cordoba* was worth 1,000 *old cordobas*.

economic fundamentals becomes inconsistent with an attempt to fix the exchange rate. The original source of problems, according to Krugman's model, is the excessive creation of domestic credit to either finance fiscal deficits or to provide assistance to a weak banking system. More specifically, the model assumes that the government has no access to capital markets, and is therefore forced to monetize its expenditures. In this context, an interest-rate-parity condition induces capital outflows and a gradual loss of foreign exchange reserves. Further down the road, the economy eventually becomes the victim of a speculative attack on its foreign exchange reserves, which triggers the collapse of the fixed exchange rate system. A critical level in the amount of reserves determines the timing of the attack in Krugman's model. Once reserves reach such threshold level, speculators are induced to exhaust the remaining reserves in a short period of time to avoid capital losses.

Krugman's work was later extended and simplified by several authors. Flood and Garber (1984) constructed a simplified linear model, introducing a stochastic component. Connolly and Taylor (1984) analyzed a crawling-peg regime and stressed the behavior of the relative prices of traded goods preceding the collapse of the exchange rate regime. In their analysis, the real exchange rate appreciates and the current account deteriorates prior to the collapse. In related contexts, Edwards (1989) has also stressed the patterns of currency overvaluation and current account deterioration that tend to precede devaluations, while Calvo (1987) analyzes the role of overvaluation in a cash-in-advance model.

Krugman and Rotemberg (1991) have further extended Krugman's original model to the case of speculative attacks in target zones. More recently, and inspired by the Mexican crisis of 1994, Flood, Garber and Kramer (1996) have incorporated the role of an active sterilization policy into the analysis.

The Krugman model and its extensions represent what has become known as *first-generation models* of balance-of-payments crises.[10] Their main insight is that crises arise as a result of an inconsistency between an excessive public sector deficit that becomes monetized and the exchange rate system. In this sense, a crisis is both unavoidable and predictable in an economy with a constant deterioration of its fundamentals.

Second-Generation Models

More recently, a number of authors have come up with alternative explanations of currency crises. A unifying theme of these alternative models is

---

10. For an excellent discussion of the early first-generation models of balance of payments crises see Agenor, Bhandari and Flood (1992).

their focus on the possibility of crises even in the absence of a continuous deterioration in economic fundamentals. Models built along these lines are known as *second-generation models* of balance-of-payments crises. Some papers of this kind are Calvo (1998), Cole and Kehoe (1996), Obstfeld (1994; 1996), Sachs, Tornell and Velasco (1996), and Drazen (1999).

Characteristic of many second-generation models are two assumptions: (a) the government is an active agent, maximizing an objective function, and (b) there is a circular process that may lead to multiple equilibrium.[11] Since pure expectations may lead to one or another equilibrium, many of these models implicitly or explicitly accept the possibility of *self-fulfilling crises.* This type of crises occur, for example, when the sheer pessimism of a significant group of investors provokes a capital outflow that leads to the eventual collapse of the exchange rate system, thus validating the negative expectations. In this sense, some second-generation models emphasize the reinforcing effects of the actions of economic agents in determining the movements from one equilibrium position to another. Second-generation models also underscore the role of expectations by considering the strategic complementarities of the actions of economic agents in determining the final outcome.

Although second-generation models have several features in common, they also differ in crucial aspects. Particularly important to us is the role they assign to economic fundamentals. In some models, fundamentals play a key role in determining when a crisis may occur. In particular, they identify an intermediate range for crucial variables where a crisis may or may not occur. Thus, the probability of a crisis is determined by the position of the fundamentals, and a country with relatively "good" fundamentals will not experience a currency crisis.[12] This result suggests that even though it may not be possible to predict the timing of a crisis, it is possible to infer which countries are susceptible of falling into a currency crisis. Some of these models also suggest that unexpected shocks or sudden changes in the macroeconomic environment may induce the authorities to abandon the exchange rate system (Obstfeld 1996).

In contrast, other second-generation models suggest that crises are not affected by the position of the fundamentals. Instead, crises may simply occur as a consequence of pure speculation against the currency. There are at least two types of analyses along these lines. Models of *herding behavior* stress that information costs may lead foreign investors to take decisions based on limited information and therefore to be more sensitive to rumors (Calvo and

---

11. Krugman (1997) discusses some characteristics of these models in more detail.

12. See, for example, the model in Sachs, *et al.* (1996), and the strategic exercise in Obstfeld (1994).

Mendoza 1999). A second line of thought stresses the possibility of *contagion effects*. We identify two main variants of this hypothesis. The first variant focuses on trade linkages and on loss of competitiveness associated to devaluation by a main trading partner, which in turn leaves the domestic currency more vulnerable to an attack (Gerlach and Smets 1995).[13] The second variant is related to multiple-equilibrium, and suggests that a crisis in one country may raise the odds of a crisis elsewhere by signaling that a devaluation is more likely as a result of the initial crisis. This signal may then lead to a self-fulfilling speculative attack (Masson 1998).[14]

DEFINITION OF CURRENCY CRISIS

In this part of the chapter we present our definition of currency crisis and explain the criteria we use to identify currency crises in our sample of countries.[15]

In our view, a currency crisis exists only when there is an important change in the nominal exchange rate. Thus, unlike some of the previous studies on the topic, we exclude unsuccessful speculative attacks from our definition of crisis.[16] The rationale behind this exclusion is that we consider that identifying unsuccessful speculative attacks is a very difficult and subjective task.[17]

For a nominal devaluation to qualify as a currency crisis, we use two criteria. First, the devaluation rate has to be large relative to what is considered standard in a country (we will be more precise about this later). Second, the nominal devaluation has to be meaningful, in the sense that it should affect the purchasing power of the domestic currency. Thus, a nominal depreciation that simply keeps up with inflation differentials is not considered a currency crisis even if it is fairly large. Our definition of crisis therefore excludes many of the large nominal depreciations that tend to occur during high-inflation episodes.

---

13. Recently, Masson (1998) has termed this interpretation a *spillover effect* to differentiate it from a pure *contagion effect*.

14. Yet another variant emphasizes the political nature of the devaluation decision when a policymaker is interested in enhancing a country's political integration with its neighbors. In this context, a devaluation in one of the neighboring countries may increase speculation against the domestic currency (see Drazen 1999).

15. This section draws on Esquivel and Larraín (1998). The reader is referred to that work for further details on the methodology.

16. Some of the papers that prefer to include these events in their definition of crises are Eichengreen, Rose and Wyplosz (1995), Kaminsky and Reinhart (1999), and Sachs, Tornell, and Velasco (1996).

17. See, for example, the discussion on the "speculative pressure index" in Flood and Marion (1998).

By putting these two considerations together, we conclude that a currency crisis exists only if a nominal devaluation is accompanied by an important change in the real exchange rate (at least in the short run). If we assume that the price level reacts slowly to changes in the nominal exchange rate then, in practical terms, we can detect a currency crisis simply by looking at the changes in the real exchange rate. Before doing so, however, we need to define how large the real exchange rate (RER) movement must be in order to be considered a crisis.

We consider that a currency crisis has occurred when at least one of the following conditions is met:

Condition A: The accumulated three-month real exchange rate change is 15 percent or more, or,

Condition B: The one-month change in the real exchange rate is higher than 2.54 times the country-specific standard deviation of the RER monthly growth rate, provided that it also exceeds 4 percent. That is, if:

$$\Delta\varepsilon_{it} > 2.54 \, \sigma_i^{\Delta\varepsilon} \text{ and } \Delta\varepsilon_{it} > 4\%,$$

where ε_{it} is the real exchange rate (RER) in country i in period t, $\Delta\varepsilon_{it}$ is the one-month change in the RER, and $\sigma_i^{\Delta\varepsilon}$ is the standard deviation of $\Delta\varepsilon_{it}$ in country i over the whole period.

Condition A guarantees that any large real depreciation is counted as a currency crisis. The threshold value of 15 percent is certainly somewhat arbitrary, but sensitivity analysis shows that the precise threshold is largely irrelevant for our results.[18] Condition B, on the other hand, attempts to capture changes in the RER that are sufficiently large relative to the historical country-specific monthly change of the RER.[19]

DATA AND ECONOMETRIC METHODOLOGY

Data

In Esquivel and Larraín (1998) we estimated a model on the determinants

---

18. Other authors have also used thresholds in their definition of *crisis*. Frankel and Rose (1996), for example, use a 25 percent *nominal* exchange rate change as a threshold value. Eichengreen, Rose and Wyplosz (1995), Goldfajn, and Valdés (1998), and Kaminsky, Lizondo, and Reinhart (1998) have instead used a definition closer to our condition B.

19. Assuming that changes in the RER are normally distributed, condition B is defined so as to capture changes in the RER that lie in the upper 0.5 percent of the distribution for each country.

of currency crises for a group of 30 high- and middle-income countries from 1975 through 1996.[20] In this chapter we add Costa Rica, El Salvador, Guatemala, Honduras, and Nicaragua to our original sample. The real-exchange rate measure that we use for the CA countries was described above, with the remaining variables being obtained from several international sources (IMF, Word Bank, and UNCTAD).

Since we are interested in both explaining and forecasting currency crises, most explanatory variables enter in lagged form. Thus, explanatory variables run from 1975 to 1995, whereas our dependent variable goes from 1976 to 1996. We then have a panel dataset of 21 years for 35 countries, which makes a total of 735 potential observations. Since our dependent variable is dichotomous and takes the value of 1 when there is a crisis and 0 otherwise, our fitted values may then be interpreted as the one-step-ahead probabilities of a currency crisis.

Episodes of Crises in Central America

When our two conditions are applied to the Central American countries during the period 1970 through 1998, we identify fourteen episodes of currency crisis in the region. The dates and months of these events are shown in Table 10-1. As mentioned above, the application of our two criteria to identify instances of crisis produces results that coincide very well with situations of abrupt movements in the nominal exchange rates in Central American countries.

Number of Crises in the Sample

By imposing conditions A and B to our monthly real exchange rate data set we have identified 124 episodes of crisis, of which 111 correspond to countries in our original sample and 13 to Central American countries.[21] Figure 10-3 shows the number of currency crises per country in the Latin American countries in our sample.[22] This figure confirms that, with the exception of Nicaragua, Central American countries have had much more stable currencies than the other countries in the subcontinent.

---

20. The original sample consisted of the following countries: Argentina, Australia, Belgium, Brazil, Chile, Colombia, Denmark, Ecuador, Finland, Greece, Indonesia, Ireland, Italy, Korea, Malaysia, Mexico, Morocco, New Zealand, Norway, Peru, Philippines, Portugal, Singapore, Spain, Sweden, Switzerland, Thailand, Turkey, United Kingdom, and Venezuela.

21. Note that we "lose" an episode of crisis in Central America, because the 1974 crisis in Costa Rica does not lie within our estimation period.

22. For a more detailed description of the currency crises for other countries in our sample, the reader is referred to Esquivel and Larraín (1998).

Table 10-1. *Currency Crises in Central America*

Country	Date
Costa Rica	May 1974
	January 1981
El Salvador	January 1986
	May 1990
Guatemala	June 1986
	August 1990
Honduras	March 1990
Nicaragua	March 1979
	February 1985
	February 1986
	February 1988
	March 1989
	May 1990
	March 1991

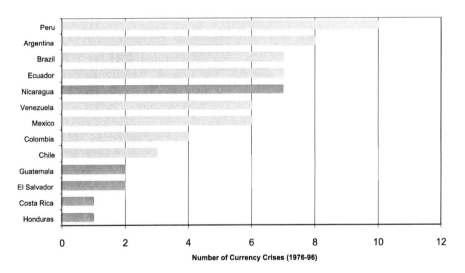

Figure 10-3. *Number of Currency Crises in Latin American Countries, 1976–96*

Estimation Methodology

We now describe our approach to estimating the determinants of currency crises. The variable to be explained (y_{it}) is dichotomous, and takes the value of 1 if a currency crisis occurred during year t and 0 otherwise. We estimate a *probit model* of the form:

$$\text{Prob (Crisis}_{it}) = \text{Prob } (y_{it}=1) = \Phi(\beta' x_{it-1})$$

where x_{it-1} is a vector of explanatory variables for country i in period t-1, β is a vector of coefficients to be estimated, and Φ is the normal cumulative distribution function.

Note that in our estimation we are implicitly assuming the existence of a an unobservable or latent variable (y_{it}^*) which is described by

$$y_{it}^* = \beta' x_{it-1} + u_{it}$$

where x_{it-1} and β are as before, u_{it} is a normally distributed error term with zero mean and unit variance, and the observed variable y_{it} behaves according to $y_{it} = 1$ if $y_{it}^* > 0$, and $y_{it} = 0$ otherwise. Please note that in this regard we depart slightly from Esquivel and Larraín (1998), since in that paper we used a probit model with random effects.[23]

Explanatory Variables

The explanatory variables that we use in this chapter are the same that we used in Esquivel and Larraín (1998). For completeness, we present a brief description of each one.[24]

Seignorage. This variable, defined as the annual change in reserve money as a percentage of GDP, attempts to capture Krugman's original insight that monetization of the government deficit is key to explaining exchange rate collapses. We expect this variable to have a positive effect on the probability of a crisis.

Real Exchange Rate Misalignment. This variable is defined as the negative of the percentage deviation of the real exchange rate from its average over the previous 60 months.[25] This definition makes our variable easily comparable across both time and countries. An increase in the RER misalignment is expected to increase the risk of a currency crisis.

---

23. In Esquivel and Larraín (1998) we showed that there are no substantial differences in the results obtained with alternative estimation methods. For this reason, and to simplify the exposition of our results, in this work we prefer to use a more standard econometric methodology.

24. For more details on the construction of these variables and for a justification of their inclusion in the empirical analysis see Esquivel and Larraín (1998).

25. Note that the RER misalignment variable is defined so that RER appreciation with respect to the previous five-year average enters with a positive sign. An *increase* in the misalignment variable then represents a larger appreciation and a higher risk of a crisis.

Current Account Balance. A deterioration of the current account balance is expected in anticipation of a currency crisis. Therefore, we expect to find a negative relationship between the current account balance and the probability of crisis. This variable enters as a percentage of GDP.

M2/Reserves. This variable is the ratio of a broad definition of money to official foreign exchange reserves. It attempts to capture the vulnerability of the central bank to possible runs against the currency. This variable is in logs and we expect to find a positive association between it and the probability of a crisis.[26]

Terms of Trade Shock. This variable is defined as the annual percentage change in the terms of trade and we expect a negative relationship between this variable and the probability of crisis.

Per Capita Income Growth. A negative per capita income growth is assumed to increase the policymaker's incentives to switch to a more expansionist policy, which can be achieved through a nominal devaluation of the currency. Our variable is dichotomous and takes the value of 1 if per capita income growth is negative in a given year and 0 otherwise. Consequently, we expect a positive coefficient associated to this variable.

Contagion Effects. It has recently been argued that crises can be transmitted across countries through many different channels (Drazen 1999). Most of the likely explanations, however, suggest that contagion effects tend to occur at the regional level.[27] This means that in order to capture the possibility of a contagion effect, we first define geographical regions. We can then specify a dichotomous variable that takes the value of 1 for countries belonging to a region where at least one other country has had an exchange rate crisis in the current year, and 0 otherwise. [28]

---

26. Other authors have suggested using the short-term Debt/Reserves ratio to capture this effect (see, for example, Radelet and Sachs 1998). However, cross-country information for this variable is available only starting in 1986. We therefore prefer the M2/Reserves variable.

27. See Glick and Rose (1998) and the models discussed in Drazen (1999).

28. We have defined the following regions: Europe, Asia, Oceania, Central America, and the rest of Latin America. See Esquivel and Larraín (1998) for an explanation of how we proceeded in the cases of Turkey and Morocco.

EMPIRICAL RESULTS

Table 10-2 shows the results when we apply the econometric methodology described above to our data. We use the individual and joint significance of the coefficients and a pseudo-R^2 measure (the so-called McFadden's R^2) to evaluate the goodness-of-fit of our model. All regressions include annual dummies and a constant,[29] and the estimated parameters have been transformed so that the reported coefficients can be interpreted as the change in probability associated with a unit change in the explanatory variables.

The numbers in parentheses in Table 10-2 are z-statistics that test the null hypothesis of no significance of the parameters associated to the explanatory variables. We use asterisks to identify the coefficients' level of significance. The next-to-the-bottom part of each table includes a chi-square statistic (and its associated p-value) which tests for the joint significance of all coefficients other than the constant and the time dummies. The bottom part of the table shows the results of a Lagrange test that is described below.

Column (1) in Table 10-2 presents the estimates when we use our original sample of 30 high- and middle-income countries. As in Esquivel and Larraín (1998), all the coefficients have the expected signs and they are statistically significant at conventional levels. Moreover, they are jointly significant at the one-percent level.

Column 2 of Table 10-2, on the other hand, shows the results when we expand our data set to include the five central American countries. There are major differences between regressions (1) and (2) in Table 10-2. Three coefficients present an important reduction in their absolute value relative to Column 1—those associated with seignorage, real exchange rate misalignment and current account variables—whereas the coefficients associated with the real exchange rate misalignment lose statistical significance when we add the Central American countries. Furthermore, when we implement a Lagrange test to evaluate whether the coefficients associated with the Central American countries are statistically different from the rest of our sample, we obtain a statistic of around 20. This result, as indicated by its low p-value, means that we strongly reject the null hypothesis that the coefficients associated with the Central American countries are no different from those of the rest of our sample.

The next step in our empirical analysis is to investigate what drives these results. Is it the case that all Central American countries are different from the

---

29. These annual dummies are intended to capture any worldwide effect that may have an impact on the likelihood of currency crises in our entire sample of countries. Thus, these variables may capture not only effects on world interest rates but they may also be reflecting any other similar worldwide phenomenon.

rest of the countries in our sample? Or, is it just that our estimates are very sensitive to the inclusion of a country, Nicaragua, whose behavior is clearly different from the rest of our sample (see Figures 10-1 and 10-2 and Table 10-1)? To investigate this question, Column (3) drops Nicaragua from the sample. The new estimates show some major changes with respect to those in Column (2). For example, now all the coefficients are statistically significant at the five-percent level. Moreover, the absolute value of all the coefficients is now much closer to those of Column (1). It is thus clear that the reduction in the absolute value and statistical significance of some of the coefficients in Column (2) was largely driven by the inclusion of Nicaragua in our sample. However, although the new empirical estimates are closer to those of our shorter sample, the Lagrange statistic that tests the null hypothesis that coefficients associated to Central America are no different is still rejected at a ten-percent level of significance.

In order to explore what may explain the different results in Central America, we now introduce some minor modifications in the definition of the contagion effect for the Central American countries. We tried two alternative specifications. The first one takes into account the possible influence of Mexico's exchange rate on the likelihood of a currency crisis in Central American countries. This effect could be important because Mexico and Central America can be seen as competitors for the U.S. market. Therefore, when Mexico devalues its currency, it also improves its competitiveness in the U.S. market vis-à-vis the Central American economies. The expected reduction in exports from Central American countries to the U.S. may therefore increase the probability of having a currency crisis in these economies, since they may be interested in restoring the pre–crisis competitiveness levels.

The modified contagion variable is introduced in Column (4). The results of this exercise are very similar to those of equation (3). In fact, when we test the null hypothesis that the countries of Central America have different coefficients relative to the rest of the sample, we still reject it at the 10 percent level of significance. Of course, this result can be partially explained by the fact that we are treating Central American countries differently from the other countries in the sample, since we are now allowing the possibility that an outsider country (Mexico) may generate a contagion effect upon them. In any event, these results suggest two possible explanations: either the determinants of currency crises in Central America are truly different from the rest of the sample, or the current specification is still inadequate to capture any likely similarities between these two groups of countries. To explore for this possibility, we once again modify our contagion variable.

Another likely explanation for the results that we have obtained so far is that our contagion variable for Central America in regression (3) still allows

Table 10-2.   Determinants of Currency Crises

Variables	Regression Coefficients (z-statistics)				
	(1)	(2)	(3)	(4)	(5)
Seigniorage (as a percent of GDP)	0.0214* (4.10)	0.0149* (3.99)	0.0191* (4.14)	0.0188* (4.03)	0.0180* (3.97)
RER Misalignment	0.0035** (2.45)	0.0017*** (1.86)	0.0033* (2.98)	0.0033* (3.02)	0.0033* (2.98)
Current Account Balance (as a percent of GDP)	-0.0103* (-2.85)	-0.0028 (-1.28)	-0.0070** (-2.24)	-0.0069** (-2.19)	-0.0076** (-2.41)
Log(M2/Reserves)	0.0411** (2.22)	0.0442* (2.68)	0.0477* (2.87)	0.0481* (2.87)	0.0495* (2.97)
Terms of Trade Shock	-0.0046*** (-1.84)	-0.0048* (-2.58)	-0.0046** (-2.25)	-0.0050** (-2.42)	-0.0048** (-2.34)
Negative Growth Dummy (1 if per capita income growth <0)	0.0810** (2.31)	0.0704** (2.26)	0.0641** (2.08)	0.0588*** (1.91)	0.0626** (2.05)
Contagion Effect (1 if at least one country in the region had a crisis)	0.0804** (2.39)	0.1029* (3.60)	0.0882* (3.08)	0.0868* (2.85)	0.1163* (3.89)

Table 10-2 (*continued*)

Number of Observations	629	734	713	713	713
Number of Countries	30	35	34	34	34
Log Likelihood	-242.2	-276.5	-264.4	-264.9	-261.1
McFadden's $\bar{R}^2$	0.17	0.17	0.17	0.17	0.18
Chi-square (Ho: Coefficients = 0)	45.92	52.85	51.66	48.06	53.83
(p-Value)	(0.00)	(0.00)	(0.00)	(0.00)	(0.00)
Lagrange Test					
Ho: Central America is no different		20.27	12.36	13.36	8.47
(p-value)		(0.005)	(0.089)	(0.064)	(0.293)

Notes: All regressions include time dummies and a constant. Asterisks indicate statistical significance at a 1 (*), 5 (**), and 10 (***) percent level.

for the possibility that Nicaragua's currency crises may affect other Central American countries. However, it is very likely that allowing for such an effect is not necessarily correct (at least for most of the period under study). It must be recalled that between 1979 and 1989, Nicaragua was ruled by the Sandinistas, who implemented non-market-oriented economic policies. As a result, the Nicaraguan cordoba became strongly appreciated in real terms (see Figure 10-2) and international trade with non-socialist countries decreased dramatically. Indeed, Brock and Melendez (1989) show that Nicaragua's foreign trade with the rest of Central America fell from 376 million to 54 million dollars between 1980 and 1986. They also show that starting in 1983, Nicaragua basically had a barter system of trade with Costa Rica, Guatemala and Honduras. These circumstances suggest that practically none of the channels that are usually called in to explain the occurrence of a crisis contagion were actually effective:[30] interregional trade was limited and likely investors were clearly able to distinguish between the policies implemented by Nicaragua and those of its Central American neighbors. The new contagion variable is defined in such a way that the contagion effect in this region can only occur among the four Central American countries included in the analysis: Costa Rica, El Salvador, Guatemala, and Honduras. That is, we rule out the possibility that a crisis in Nicaragua in this period may have had an effect on the probability of crisis in any other Central American country. The rationale for this assumption is based on the dissimilarity of policies that were implemented in Nicaragua during most of the period under analysis, as discussed above.

The results of including this modification of the regional variable for Central America are displayed in Column (5) of Table 10-2. All of the new coefficients, with the exception of the contagion effect, are very close to those obtained in equations (1) and (3), and they are all significant at the five-percent level. The new estimated coefficient of the contagion effect is much larger than in previous regressions. In the new results, if a country belongs to a region where at least one other country has recently experienced a currency crisis, its probability of also having a currency crisis increases, on average, by about 11 percentage points (up from a previous estimate of about 8 percentage points). The observed increase in the contagion effect can partially be attributed to the fact that the Central American countries tend to be more closely integrated with one another, and this in turn increases the possibility of contagion across these countries.

The most important result of Column (5), however, is that modification of the regional variable for the Central American countries now allows us to ac-

---

30. See Drazen (1999) and Glick and Rose (1998).

cept the null hypothesis that coefficients for Central America are no different from those of other countries in the sample. The Lagrange test statistic for this specification takes a value of only 8.4 and it is accepted at any significance level below 25 percent. In what follows, we use regression (5) as our benchmark. As mentioned above, coefficients are shown as marginal effects on the probability of crisis, and they are evaluated at the mean values of the explanatory variables. In consequence, the fitted values can then be interpreted as the one-step-ahead probability of a currency crisis. In the case of explanatory dummy variables, coefficients have been computed as the actual change in probability that occurs when the dummy variable switches from 0 to 1, assuming that all the other explanatory variables remain at their mean values.[31]

The first coefficient in Column (5) shows that a one-percentage-point increase in the rate of seignorage to GDP increases the probability of crisis by about 1.8 percentage points. Likewise, an RER misalignment of about 10 percent translates into an increase in the probability of a currency crisis of about 3.3 percentage points. Although this effect seems to be relatively small, it is important to keep in mind two considerations. First, this result is obtained after controlling for the current account balance (which is strongly associated with the RER misalignment variable). Second, RER misalignments as large as 30 percent often occur in our sample, which therefore represents an increase in the probability of a currency crisis of about 10 percentage points.

Column (5) in Table 10-2 also shows that a one-percentage-point increase in the current account deficit to GDP increases the probability of crisis by slightly less than 0.8 percentage points. The coefficient associated with the current account deficit is always negative and strongly significant in the five regressions in Table 10-2. As mentioned in our previous work, our current account results are of special interest because other empirical studies, summarized by Kaminsky, Lizondo, and Reinhart (1998) and Glick and Moreno (1999), have found this variable to be non-significant as a determinant of currency crises. It is also worth emphasizing the empirical relevance of this result since the current account has often been interpreted by analysts and practitioners as an indicator of an economy's vulnerability to a currency crisis. In this sense, our results can be seen as providing support to the usual interpretation given by analysts and practitioners.

Our fourth explanatory variable is the log of (M2/reserves); Column (5) shows that doubling this ratio increases the probability of crisis by around 9 percentage points. This effect reflects the widely documented result that this ratio rises very quickly during the months preceding currency crises. Column

---

31. This procedure is standard in situations with discrete explanatory variables and a qualitative dependent variable. See Greene (1996) for more details.

(5) also shows that a 10-percent terms-of-trade decline translates into a 5-percent increase in the probability of crisis. Additionally, a period of negative per capita income growth increases the probability of crisis by more than 6 percentage points. The magnitude of these two effects confirms the relevance of models that characterize the devaluation decision as the result of balancing conflicting policy objectives. In cases where the exchange rate is a policy variable, these results may be interpreted as supporting the escape-clause models developed by Obstfeld (1996) as well as other models that stress the "political" nature of some currency crises.[32]

AN IN-SAMPLE EVALUATION OF THE MODELS' PREDICTIVE POWER

In this section we present an evaluation of our model's ability to predict the presence of currency crises in our sample, with special emphasis on the fitted values for Central American countries.

In Esquivel and Larraín (1998) we assessed the overall explanatory performance of a similar empirical model by employing a standard hit-or-miss approach. By applying such an evaluation method to the benchmark regression of our previous study, we concluded that our estimated model was able to predict accurately more than 50 percent of all the crisis events in our sample. As discussed in that work, such a rate of success is much higher than previous studies have found. The application of the hit-or-miss technique to the results presented in regression (5) in Table 10-2 lead to conclusions similar to those presented in Esquivel and Larraín (1998) and therefore we will not discuss them in more detail here. Instead, in this chapter we present an alternative method to evaluate the predictive performance of our empirical model.

Testing the Predictive Performance of the Model

In this section we evaluate the predictive performance of our model based on the application of a simple non-parametric test proposed by Pesaran and Timmermann (1992). This test asks whether a set of predictions for a binary event (in this case, crisis period versus tranquil period) is statistically better than pure random guesses. Before applying the Pesaran-Timmermann test to our model, however, we need to define a prediction (or classification) rule. Following Esquivel and Larraín (1998), we have chosen the following prediction rule:[33]

---

32. See Drazen (1999) for a brief review of this literature.

33. Esquivel and Larraín (1998) discuss the relevance of choosing an appropriate threshold value.

Table 10-3. *A Test of the Model's Predictive Performance*

P*	0.20	0.25	0.30	0.35	0.40	0.45	0.50
P-T	10.02*	10.05*	10.20*	9.89*	8.90*	8.63*	8.01*

Notes: Results are obtained using regression (5) in Table 10-2. The P-T statistic is distributed as a standard normal. The null hypothesis is that predictions are no better than random guesses. An asterisk indicates that we reject the null hypothesis at the one-percent level of significance.

a) If $P_{it} > P^*$ a crisis is predicted (i.e., an alarm is issued)

b) Otherwise, a tranquil period is predicted

where P^* is a threshold value that ranges from 0.20 to 0.50.

Table 10-3 shows the result of calculating the Pesaran-Timmermann (P-T) statistic for a range of threshold values that go from 0.20 to 0.50. Since the statistic is distributed as a standard normal, results in Table 10-3 suggest that we can strongly reject the null hypothesis that our predictions are no better than random guesses. That is, our classification rule has some value from a purely predictive perspective regardless of our threshold value. Interestingly, the threshold value that maximizes the Pesaran-Timmerman statistic is $P^*=0.30$, the same value selected in Esquivel and Larraín (1998) based on an ad-hoc criterion.

Predicting Currency Crises

Yet another method to evaluate the predictive performance of our model is by comparing the average one-step-ahead probabilities of crisis in both tranquil and crisis periods. In principle, if our empirical results contain valuable information about the likely occurrence of a crisis in the near future, the average predicted probability of a crisis should be higher in periods when a crisis actually occurs in the next year than in periods when it does not occur.

Figure 10-4 and Table 10-4 show the average one-step-ahead probabilities of crisis in tranquil and crisis periods for all of the countries in our sample and for the Central American countries (both as a group and individually). The most obvious fact that emerges from Figure 10-4 is that the average predicted probability of crisis is, in all cases, higher in crisis periods than in tranquil ones. This result suggests that there is indeed some valuable information in our forecasts, since they tend to anticipate a higher probability of crisis when these events occur. Interestingly, the average predicted probabilities of a crisis in the years immediately preceding a crisis event for the cases of Guatemala, El Salvador, and Honduras were 5, 4, and 3.5 times the average predicted probabilities in tranquil periods. These results, although suggestive of a very strong predictive power of our model, are not conclusive because we

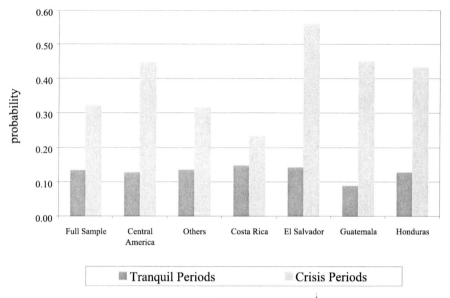

Figure 10-4.   **Average One-step-ahead Probability of a Crisis**

have only shown that average predicted probabilities are *numerically* higher in crisis periods than in tranquil ones, but we have not yet shown that these differences are *statistically significant.*

Table 10-5 shows the results of a difference-between-means test that investigates whether or not the average predicted probability of a crisis is statistically higher in years that precede the occurrence of a crisis. The test is applied separately to Central America and to the other countries in the sample. The

Table 10-4.   *Average One-step-ahead Probabilities of a Currency Crisis*

	Tranquil Periods		**Crisis Periods**	
	Probability	Observations	Probability	Observations
Full Sample	0.135	596	0.321	117
Central America	0.127	78	0.448	6
Others	0.136	518	0.315	111
Costa Rica	0.148	20	0.233	1
El Salvador	0.142	19	0.560	2
Guatemala	0.088	19	0.450	2
Honduras	0.128	20	0.433	1

results of the test strongly support the conclusion that predictions about the probability of a crisis occurring next year are statistically higher in periods when a crisis actually occurs. Therefore, this result also supports our previous conclusion that forecasts based on our empirical estimates have indeed some valuable information about the likely occurrence of a currency crisis.

Are Predictions for Central America Different?

We showed above that our empirical estimates for Central America are not different from the rest of the countries in our sample. Now, we will try to answer the following question: Are predicted probabilities different for Central American countries? In order to respond to this question we implement another difference-of-means test.

The lower part of Table 10-5 shows the results that we obtain when we test whether average predicted probabilities for the Central American countries are the same as those for the other countries in the sample during both tranquil and crisis periods. The results of Table 10-5 show that we cannot reject the null hypothesis that predictions for Central America are, on average, similar to those made for other countries in either tranquil or crisis periods.

Table 10-5. *Test of Difference between Average One-step-ahead Probabilities of Crisis*

	t	P-value
Crisis *versus* Tranquil Periods		
Central America	3.45*	0.009
Other Countries	8.70*	0.000
Central America *versus* Other Countries		
Crisis Periods	1.41	0.211
Tranquil Periods	-0.62	0.539

Note: *indicates that we reject the null hypothesis that means are equal at one-percent level of significance.

Country-by-country In-sample Forecasts

So far we have shown that the average predicted probability of currency crises for Central American countries in those years that preceded an actual crisis is higher than in other periods. Therefore, the empirical model that we have developed here has tended to correctly identify the moments of economic turbulence that have eventually led to currency crises in the region. Put another way, our model has not systematically missed forthcoming crises within the region. However, there are two types of errors when trying to predict the occurrence of an event. We can either fail to predict an event that actually takes place or we can predict an event that does not take place (that is, we may issue a false alarm). In this sense, an interesting question about our predicted probabilities arises. Does our model tend to predict a crisis when none occurs? That is, does our model tend to produce many false alarms?

In order to respond to this question, we now focus on the in-sample country-by-country forecasts that are obtained with our econometric estimates in Column 5 in Table 10-2. The fitted probabilities for each of the four Central American countries included in the estimation sample are displayed in Figure 10-5. The continuous line represents the predicted probability of a currency crisis one year ahead and the vertical lines indicate that a currency crisis actually occurred in the year ahead. A remarkable aspect of Figure 10-5 is that most crisis periods do tend to coincide with observed peaks in the forecasted probability of a crisis. This is especially true in the cases of El Salvador in 1985

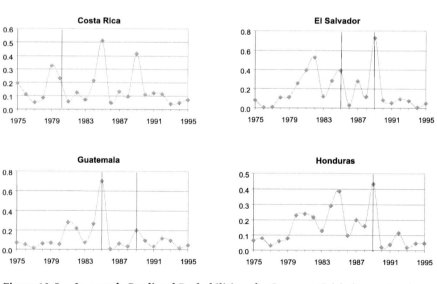

Figure 10-5. In-sample Predicted Probabilities of a Currency Crisis (percentage)

and 1989 (which "predicted" the crises of 1986 and 1990, respectively), Guatemala in 1985, and Honduras in 1989. Likewise, the Costa Rican crisis of 1981 had a relatively large anticipated probability of crisis (21 percent). In contrast, the Guatemalan crisis of 1990 was largely unpredicted.

These results, however illustrative, are only another representation of the results already described by Figure 10-4 and Table 10-4. In this section we now want to focus, instead, on the forecasts of crisis when there was actually none. To keep comparability with our previous discussion, we look at those periods when the predicted probability was greater than 30 percent. We can identify ten instances when this threshold was exceeded. The distribution by country of these episodes is as follows: Costa Rica (3), El Salvador (4), Guatemala (1) and Honduras (2). Four of these situations coincide with actual crises. Another episode actually preceded a crisis two years in advance (Costa Rica 1979). We can therefore conclude that there were only five episodes when our estimated model apparently emitted a false alarm. These occasions are the following: Costa Rica (1985 and 1989), El Salvador (1981 and 1982), and Honduras (1985).

A closer look at the periods when a false alarm was issued suggests that there is a pattern. Most of these periods can be described as years of economic turbulence and great instability in the foreign exchange market. In fact, in most of these periods there was either a modification in the exchange rate system (although not in the official exchange rate) or a large black market exchange rate premium.

For example, in August 1982 an inter-bank exchange rate system was established in El Salvador.[34] The average exchange rate in this market was 3.81 colones per dollar in 1982, whereas the official exchange rate was only at 2.5 colones per dollar (Gaba 1990). Therefore, in practice, the implementation of the new system represented a de facto devaluation of the Salvadoran currency. Moreover, the average black market exchange rate was even higher, 3.99 colones per dollar.[35] These results suggest that the relatively high probabilities of a currency crisis in El Salvador that were predicted in 1981 and 1982 were fully justified, and that they actually forecast quite well the foreign exchange market instability that ended with the de facto devaluation of August 1982.

We may find similar explanations for the other three cases in the region when a crisis was predicted and the official exchange rate remain unchanged.

---

34. On August 9 commercial banks were authorized to buy and sell foreign exchange in the parallel market under the restriction that the transactions from that market be segregated from the official market.

35. Other sources suggest even higher black market exchange rates. For example, *Pick's Currency Yearbook* suggests a 1982 average black market exchange rate between 4.6 and 5.10 colones per dollar. See Wilkie et al. (1995, p. 1037).

For instance, the average black market premium in Costa Rica in 1986 was 60 percent, and the corresponding figure for Honduras in 1985 was 36 percent. Also, on March 1985, a parallel market was established in Honduras that allowed exporters to keep foreign exchange for trade purposes. Therefore, all these pieces of evidence together seem to support the idea that high probabilities of crisis almost always were followed by periods of exchange rate instability in Central American economies. In all, they lend support to our estimated model.

Out-of-sample Forecasts

As a final test of our empirical results we implement an out-of-sample forecast of the currency crises. Recall that our model was estimated using information relative to the period that goes from 1975 to 1995, which then was used to estimate forecasted probabilities for the 1976–1996 period. In this section we compute the predicted probabilities for the Central American countries of a currency crisis in 1997, 1998 and 1999, that would have been obtained at the end of 1996, 1997, and 1998, respectively. For that purpose, we use the numerical estimates of the coefficients in Column (5) of Table 10-2, and the actual values of the explanatory variables. The out-of-sample predicted probabilities are displayed in Figure 10-6.

There are two interesting aspects in Figure 10-6. First, the predicted probabilities of a currency crisis in Central America have been relatively low in the recent years. In fact, with the exception of the 1996 forecast for Honduras, all

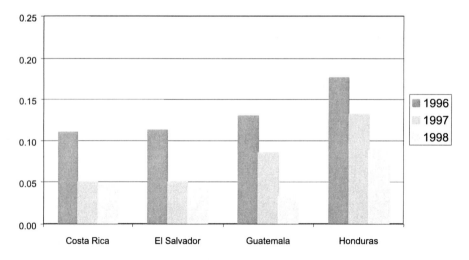

Figure 10-6. *Year-end Predicted Probability of a Currency Crisis*

the other predicted probabilities have not exceeded 14 percent. Coincidentally, as of August of 1999, the last three years had been relatively calm in the foreign exchange markets of these Central American countries. This coincidence between predicted and observed outcomes provides additional support for our results.

Finally, another interesting aspect of Figure 10-6 is that predicted probabilities follow a common declining pattern in all Central American countries during this three-year period. This trend suggests, among other things, that there may have been a regional positive shock that has reduced the vulnerability of the currencies for the whole region. An example of this is the unusually high price in 1997 of coffee, one of the main export products of the region. Another possibility is that current governments in the region have implemented sounder macroeconomic policies, and that this may be reflected in a lower risk of a currency crisis in the region.

SUMMARY AND CONCLUSIONS

In this chapter we have described and analyzed the main characteristics of currency crises in Central America since 1975. Among other results, we have shown that a small set of macroeconomic indicators are useful to explain the occurrence of exchange rate crises in the region. More specifically, we have shown that coefficients for Central American countries, once we exclude Nicaragua from both the empirical estimation and as a likely source of contagion, are no different than those of other countries in our sample. We have also shown that our estimates for two groups of countries (Central America and the other countries in our sample) provide valuable information as predictors of crises: the average one-step-ahead probabilities of crises tend to be statistically higher when a crisis actually occurs in the next period than otherwise.

Also, our average predicted probabilities for Central American countries are not significantly different from predictions made for other countries. Another important result is that our empirical model did not issued many false alarms (high probability of crisis when a crisis did not occur) in the period under study. In fact, in almost all cases when an alarm was issued, foreign exchange markets in Central America were either under stress or there was a large black market exchange rate premium.

The results of the various tests applied in this chapter support the empirical approach that attempts to explain currency crises by focusing on the behavior of a small set of macroeconomic variables. This finding is relevant because the Central American countries studied in this chapter had an exchange rate system markedly different from that of the economies that are usually analyzed in similar studies.

Finally, out-of-sample forecasts for the 1997–99 period suggest that the probabilities of a currency crisis in the region have been relatively low and that reveal a declining trend. In part, it is very likely that this trend is the result of the sounder macroeconomic policies that have recently been implemented in the region. In that sense, we believe that those variables that have been highlighted in this study as likely determinants of currency crises in the region should be watched carefully by Central American policymakers as they seek to reduce the risks of a currency crisis in all countries in the region.

REFERENCES

Agenor, P., J. Bhandari, and R. Flood. 1992. "Speculative Attacks and Models of Balance-of-Payments Crises," *International Monetary Fund Staff Papers* 39 (2): 357-94. Washington, D.C.: International Monetary Fund.

Brock Philip L., and Dennis Melendez. 1989. "Exchange Controls and the Breakdown of the Central American Trade in the 1980s." In *Latin American Debt and Adjustment*, edited by P. L. Brock, M. B. Connolly and C. Gonzalez-Vega. New York and London: Greenwood Press, Praeger.

Bulmer-Thomas, Victor. 1987. "The Balance of Payments Crises and Adjustment Programmes in Central America." In *Latin America Debt and the Adjustment Crisis*, edited by Rosemary Thorp and Laurence Whitehead. Pittsburgh, PA: University of Pittsburgh Press.

Calvo, Guillermo. 1987. "Balance of Payments Crises in a Cash-in-Advance Economy." *Journal of Money, Credit, and Banking* 19 (1): 19-32.

———.1998 "Varieties of Capital-Market Crises." In *The Debt Burden and its Consequences for Monetary Policy*, edited by G. Calvo and M. King. New York, NY: St. Martin's Press.

Calvo, Guillermo, and Enrique G. Mendoza. 1999. "Rational Contagion and the Globalization of Securities Markets." *National Bureau of Economic Research (NBER) Working Paper No. 7153*. June. Cambridge, MA: National Bureau of Economic Research.

Cole, Harold. R., and Timothy J. Kehoe. 1996."A Self-fulfilling Model of Mexico's 1994-95 Debt Crisis." *Journal of International Economics* 41: 309-30.

Connolly, Michael, and Dean Taylor. 1984. "The Exact Timing of the Collapse of an Exchange Rate Regime and Its Impact on the Relative Price of Traded Goods." *Journal of Money, Credit, and Banking* 16: 194-207.

Drazen, Allan. 1999. "Political Contagion in Currency Crises." *National Bureau of*

Economic Research (NBER) Working Paper No. 7211. July. Cambridge, MA: National Bureau of Economic Research.

Edwards, Sebastian. 1989. Real Exchange Rates, Devaluation and Adjustment: Exchange rate Policy in Developing Countries. Cambridge, MA: MIT Press.

———. 1995. "Exchange Rates, Inflation and Disinflation: Latin American Experiences." In *Capital Controls, Exchange Rates, and Monetary Policy in the World Economy,* edited by Sebastian Edwards. New York, NY: Cambridge University Press.

Edwards, Sebastian, and Fernando J. Losada. 1994. "Fixed Exchange Rates, Inflation and Macroeconomic Discipline." *National Bureau of Economic Research (NBER) Working Paper No. 4661.* February. Cambridge, MA: National Bureau of Economic Research.

Eichengreen, B., A. Rose, and C. Wyplosz. 1995. "Exchange Market Mayhem: The Antecedents and Aftermath of Speculative Attacks." *Economic Policy* (21): 249-312.

Esquivel, Gerardo, and Felipe Larraín. 1998. "Explaining Currency Crises." *Faculty Research Working Paper R98-07,* John F. Kennedy School of Government, Harvard University. (June). Also published as *HIID Development Discussion Paper 666.* Cambridge, MA: Harvard Institute for International Development.

Flood, Robert P. and Peter M. Garber (1984); "Collapsing Exchange Rate Regimes: Some Linear Examples," *Journal of International Economics* 17 (1-2): 1-13.

Flood, R., P. Garber, and C. Kramer. 1996. "Collapsing Exchange Rate Regimes: Another Linear Example." *Journal of International Economics* 41 (3-4): 223-34.

Flood, Robert, and Nancy Marion. 1998. "Perspectives on the Recent Currency Crisis Literature." *National Bureau of Economic Research (NBER) Working Paper No. 6380.* January. Cambridge, MA: National Bureau of Economic Research.

Frankel, Jeffrey, and Andrew K. Rose. 1996. "Currency Crashes in Emerging Markets: An Empirical Treatment." *Journal of International Economics* 41 (3-4): 351-66.

Gaba, Ernesto. 1990. *Criterios para Evaluar el Tipo de Cambio de las Economias Centroamericanas.* Mexico City: Centro de Estudios Latinoamericanos (CEMLA).

Gerlach, Stefan, and Frank Smets. 1995. "Contagious Speculative Attacks." *European Journal of Political Economy* 11: 45-63.

Gibson, Bill. 1985. "A Structuralist Macromodel for Post-revolutionary Nicaragua." *Cambridge Journal of Economics* 9: 347-69.

———. "Nicaragua." In *The Rocky Road to Reform,* edited by L. Taylor. Cambridge, MA.: MIT Press.

Glick, Reuven, and Andrew K. Rose. 1998. "Why Are Currency Crises Regional?" *National Bureau of Economic Research (NBER) Working Paper No. 6806.* November. Cambridge, MA: National Bureau of Economic Research.

Glick, Reuven, and Ramon Moreno. 1999. "Money and Credit, Competitiveness and Currency Crises in Latin America." *Center for Pacific Basin Monetary and Economic Studies Working Paper No. PB99-01.* San Francisco, CA: Federal Reserve Bank of San Francisco, Economic Research Department.

Goldfajn, Ilan, and Rodrigo Valdés. 1998. "Are Currency Crises Predictable?" *European Economic Review,* Papers and Proceedings 42 (3-5): 873-85.

Kaminsky, G. L., S. Lizondo, and C. M. Reinhart. 1998. "Leading Indicators of Currency Crises." *International Monetary Fund Staff Papers* 45 (1): 1-48. Washington, D.C.: International Monetary Fund.

Kaminsky, G., and C. M. Reinhart. 1999. "The Twin Crises: The Causes of Banking and Balance-of-Payments Problems." *American Economic Review* 89 (3): 473-500.

Krugman, Paul. 1979. "A Model of Balance of Payments Crises." *Journal of Money, Credit and Banking* 11: 311-25.

———. 1997. "Currency Crises." Mimeo. October. Cambridge, MA: MIT.

Krugman, Paul, and Julio Rotemberg. 1991. "Speculative Attacks on Target Zones." In *Target Zones and Currency Bands,* edited by P. Krugman and M. Miller. Oxford: Oxford University Press.

Masson, Paul R.. 1998. "Contagion: Monsoonal Effects, Spillovers and Jumps Between Multiple Equilibria." *International Monetary Fund Working Paper 98/142.* Washington, D.C.: International Monetary Fund. October.

Obstfeld, Maurice. 1994. "The Logic of Currency Crises." *National Bureau of Economic Research (NBER) Working Paper No. 4640.* September. Cambridge, MA: National Bureau of Economic Research.

———. 1996. "Models of Currency Crises with Self-fulfilling Features." *European Economic Review* 40: 1037-47.

Ocampo, Jose A. 1991. "Collapse and (Incomplete) Stabilization of the Nicaraguan Economy." In *The Macroeconomics of Populism,* edited by R. Dornbusch and S. Edwards. Chicago, IL: University of Chicago Press.

Pesaran, M. Hashem, and A. Timmermann. 1992. "A Simple Nonparametric Test of Predictive Performance." *Journal of Business & Economic Statistics* 10 (4): 561-65.

Radelet, Steve, and Jeffrey D. Sachs. 1998. "The East Asian Financial Crisis: Diagnosis, Remedies, Prospects.", *Brookings Papers on Economic Activity* (1): 1-74.

Sachs, J. D., A. Tornell, and A. Velasco (1996); "Financial Crises in Emerging Markets: The Lessons from 1995." *Brookings Papers on Economic Activity* (1): 147-215

Salant, Stephen, and D. Henderson. 1978. "Market Anticipation of Government Policy and the Price of Gold." *Journal of Political Economy* 86: 627-48.

Segovia, Alexander. 1996. "Macroeconomic Performance and Policies since 1989." In *Economic Policy for Building Peace: The Lessons of El Salvador,* edited by James K. Boyce. Boulder, CO and London: Rienner Publishers.

Taylor, L., R. Aguilar, S. de Vylder, and J. A. Ocampo. 1989. *Nicaragua: The Transi-*

tion from Economic Chaos toward Sustainable Growth. Stockholm: Swedish International Development Authority.

Wilkie, J. W., C. A. Contreras, and C. Komisaruk. 1995. *Statistical Abstract of Latin America,* vol. 31. Los Angeles, CA: Latin American Statistical Center. University of California.

INDEX